MIGRANT ANXIETIES

NEW DIRECTIONS IN NATIONAL CINEMAS
Robert Rushing, editor

MIGRANT ANXIETIES

Italian Cinema in a Transnational Frame

Áine O'Healy

INDIANA UNIVERSITY PRESS

This book is a publication of

Indiana University Press
Office of Scholarly Publishing
Herman B Wells Library 350
1320 East 10th Street
Bloomington, Indiana 47405 USA

iupress.indiana.edu

© 2019 by Áine O'Healy

All rights reserved

No part of this book may be reproduced or utilized in any form or by any means, electronic or mechanical, including photocopying and recording, or by any information storage and retrieval system, without permission in writing from the publisher. The paper used in this publication meets the minimum requirements of the American National Standard for Information Sciences—Permanence of Paper for Printed Library Materials, ANSI Z39.48-1992.

Manufactured in the United States of America

Library of Congress Cataloging-in-Publication Data

Names: O'Healy, Áine, author.
Title: Migrant anxieties : Italian cinema in a transnational frame / Áine O'Healy.
Description: Bloomington : Indiana University Press, 2019. | Series: New directions in national cinemas | Includes filmography. | Includes bibliographical references and index.
Identifiers: LCCN 2018019389 (print) | LCCN 2018021737 (ebook) | ISBN 9780253037213 (e-book) | ISBN 9780253037176 (cl : alk. paper) | ISBN 9780253037183 (pb : alk. paper)
Subjects: LCSH: Emigration and immigration in motion pictures. | Immigrants in motion pictures. | Motion pictures—Italy—History—20th century. | Motion pictures—Italy—History—21st century.
Classification: LCC PN1995.9.E44 (ebook) | LCC PN1995.9.E44 O34 2018 (print) | DDC 791.43/6552—dc23
LC record available at https://lccn.loc.gov/2018019389

1 2 3 4 5   24 23 22 21 20 19

For William Van Watson
in memoriam

Contents

IX Acknowledgments

1 Introduction

15 1. After 1989: Projecting the Balkans

51 2. Traffic from the East: Gender, Labor, and Biopolitics

78 3. African Immigration in the 1990s

108 4. Migration, Masculinity, and Italy's New Urban Geographies

136 5. Imagining an Expanded Mediterranean Borderscape

178 6. Living with Difference: From Noir to Melodrama

213 Afterword: Accented and Transnational Filmmaking in Italy

229 Filmography

233 Bibliography

249 Index

Acknowledgments

FIRST, I OWE sincere thanks to Jacqueline Reich, former editor of the New Directions in National Cinema series, who encouraged me years ago to submit my book proposal to Indiana University Press. I am equally grateful to the current series editor, Robert Rushing, and to Janice Frisch, acquisitions editor, who oversaw the publication of the manuscript. I also thank the anonymous reviewers, whose feedback has helped me to refine my ideas and sharpen my arguments.

Loyola Marymount University provided me with vital support at various stages of the book's gestation, including a semester-long research fellowship as well as three summer grants. A Fulbright award to Italy in 2010 enabled me to narrow my broader project to a manageable field of inquiry. Finally, a visiting research professorship at La Sapienza University of Rome in the spring of 2017 made it possible for me to wrap up the manuscript under the most congenial circumstances imaginable, thanks to Caterina Romeo's generous invitation and vibrant collegiality, for which I will always be thankful.

I wish to acknowledge several friends and colleagues who invited me to share portions of this project as talks at their universities or as papers at symposia they had organized; these include Guido Bonsaver (Oxford University), Rosetta Caponetto (Auburn University), Mark Chu and Silvia Ross (University College Cork), Rodica Diaconescu-Blumenfeld (Vassar College), Derek Duncan (University of Bristol), Sally Faulkner (University of Exeter), Claudio Gaetani (Università di Macerata), Terri Ginsberg (American University at Cairo), William Hope (University of Salford), Alan O'Leary (University of Leeds), Catherine Portolano (American University of Rome), Dana Renga (Ohio State University), Caterina Romeo (La Sapienza University of Rome), Sabine Schrader and Daniel Winkler (University of Innsbruck), and Marguerite Waller (University of California Riverside). I am particularly thankful to Bernadette Luciano for inviting me to present an early part of this project as a keynote talk at the Australasia Conference of

Italian Studies at the University of Auckland in 2009 and to Fulvio Orsitto for a similar keynote invitation to the Echi d'Oltremare Conference in Rome in 2011.

I also wish to thank Stefano Liberti, Andrea Segre, and Dagmawi Yimer, who offered me rich insights on many crucial issues implicated in my research. Additionally, I am grateful to Millicent Marcus for providing generous feedback on my early project proposal. To Danielle Hipkins I am grateful not only for the opportunity to exchange places for a semester in Los Angeles and Exeter but also for many helpful insights and research-related suggestions that have proved invaluable. For productive conversations with scholars engaged in similar or related research, all of which helped to move my project forward, I offer my gratitude to Rodica Diaconescu Blumenfeld, Clarissa Clò, Leonardo De Franceschi, Derek Duncan, Valerio Ferme, Shelleen Greene, Anikó Imre, Giancarlo Lombardi, Cristina Lombardi-Diop, Nicoletta Marini-Maio, Graziella Parati, Marco Purpura, Luisa Rivi, SA Smythe, and Gaoheng Zhang. A special thanks to Paola Moscarelli, my close colleague at Loyola Marymount University, whose incisive observations on contemporary Italian politics and society have enriched both my teaching and research. I also extend my thanks to Alice Bardan, film scholar, friend, and fellow cinephile, for many stimulating exchanges on film theory and on recent developments in the cinemas of Europe. To Kamil Turowski I am indebted for his expert skill in capturing and tweaking the screen shots reproduced in this book. And I thank most especially Katarzyna Marciniak, my longtime interlocutor on issues regarding migration and the transnational, without whose intellectual support, encouragement, and feedback the book might never have been finished.

I owe much gratitude to my family, especially to Ed for his enthusiasm throughout the gestation of this book and for his always useful and often challenging comments on various drafts of the manuscript. I am thankful to Lola for her vitality and creativity, which inspired me to push through with the project even when it seemed unending. I am indebted to Mairéad for her generous help with proofreading. Warm thanks also to Liz, Ann Lorraine, Ita, Seán, and Maeve for their affection and support.

Finally, I dedicate this book to the memory of Van Watson, cherished friend, gifted scholar, and exuberant traveling companion whose early death was not unconnected to systemic injustices of academic employment in the contemporary United States.

MIGRANT ANXIETIES

Introduction

THE SHIFTS AND upheavals that swept through Europe after the fall of the Berlin Wall, including the disintegration of the Soviet bloc, the outbreak of war in the Balkans, and the transformation of the European Economic Community (EEC) into the European Union (EU), were paralleled in the global South by ongoing political conflicts and economic devastation. In the early 1990s, this turbulent conjunction of circumstances prompted the simultaneous movement of large numbers of migrants from the former socialist states and the African continent toward the more affluent countries of Europe. Due to its relative prosperity and crucial location in the central Mediterranean, Italy became in a short period of time the unwitting host to growing numbers of foreigners, with tens of thousands of migrants arriving each year from various points of origin. As the country dramatically reversed its status as a predominantly emigrant nation,[1] aspiring immigrants received an ambivalent welcome, being perceived from the outset both as a potential solution to growing shortages in the labor market and a threat to the security, prosperity, and cultural traditions of Italians themselves. To add to these tensions, Italy was simultaneously being called on to conceive of itself no longer as an entirely freestanding sovereign nation but rather as a member of the supranational body of the European Union, bound by obligations formulated outside its borders.[2]

This book explores a corpus of films produced in Italy between 1990 and 2016 that reverberate to varying degrees with anxieties induced by globalization—particularly by the sharp increase in the flow of immigration from the east and the global South, the uncertainties of the neoliberal economic order, and the necessity to conform to European mandates. Encompassing both critically acclaimed dramas and popular genre films and directed almost exclusively by Italian-born filmmakers, this body of audiovisual texts offers provocative insights into Italian fears and investments vis-à-vis the globalizing world. My overarching aim is to unravel some of the complex issues interwoven in representations of the immigrant or the foreigner in these cinematic texts, representations that symptomatize the shifting identifications and oppositions that have marked Italian society since the end of the Cold War. The films explored here raise questions related to Italy's historically fragile sense of nationhood as well as its often poorly acknowledged histories of colonial conquest and emigration.

In the early 1990s, as mass immigration to Italy was in its initially intensive phase, films involving migrant characters represented a mere trickle in the total number of features released each year. In the first decade of the twenty-first century, however, the rate of output dramatically increased, reaching a high point around 2010. The increase in the number of films about immigration not only paralleled a growing concern with the issue among Italians but also reflected changes in the conditions of film production as a whole: technological developments made the creation of independent features logistically easier and enabled more flexible access to public subventions for certain types of culturally relevant film projects.[3] Indicative of the increased attention paid to immigration as a thematic focus was the fact that more than ten Italian films screened at the 2011 Venice Film Festival involved stories featuring migrants.[4] Two of these garnered important awards: Emanuele Crialese's *Terraferma* (Terra Firma) won the Special Jury Prize, the first Italian film to be so honored in several years, and Guido Lombardi's *Là-bas: Educazione criminale* (Down There: A Criminal Education) carried off the award for best feature by a first-time director. Additionally, *Io sono Li* (released in English as *Shun Li and the Poet*), the first dramatic feature by Andrea Segre, was an important critical success, while Ermanno Olmi's release *Il villaggio di cartone* (The Cardboard Village), also focusing on contemporary immigration, met with a more ambivalent response.

The encounter between Italians and those foreign-born residents seeking to make new lives in their midst has thus become a recurrent trope in Italian filmmaking, often echoing widely expressed tensions about Italy's changing demographic profile. These tensions have been exacerbated over the years by the rhetoric of specific political platforms and further intensified by the eventual criminalization of irregular immigration. In contradistinction to the rhetoric of much of mainstream media reporting, which over time has helped to fan the flames of racism and xenophobia, Italian feature films about immigration generally have attempted to provide more nuanced perspectives on this phenomenon. It must be acknowledged, however, that these films have focused for the most part on the *Italian* experience of contemporary immigration—that is, on the subjective responses of Italian citizens purportedly challenged or transformed through an encounter with alterity. The figure of the migrant in these narratives is often a fleeting, enigmatic presence inspiring pity, resentment, or distrust.

Although my study is concerned with issues of representation rather than the political economy of filmmaking, I am not proposing a literal reading of the themes and tropes found in the approximately thirty films I have selected for analysis. Rather, I am interested in the symptomaticity of cinematic representation. In other words, I explore not only the manifest content of these narratives of migration and displacement but also the elisions and inconsistencies that point to some of the unspoken fears and dilemmas underpinning Italian attitudes toward transnational mobility. Although my attention is generally focused on the study of films featuring the figure of the immigrant, in the first chapter I also examine representations of Italian mobility in southeastern Europe after the end of the Cold War. Here and at other points in my analysis, I engage with films that are implicitly concerned with the issue of Italian whiteness and its reproduction, resonating to varying degrees with the often-suppressed histories of Italian emigration, military invasion, and colonial conquest.

Clearly implicated in the construction of social identities, Italian cinema has long been perceived as playing a significant role in nation building. The capacity of films to deploy effective mechanisms of identification and disidentification with onscreen characters does not, of course, mean that cinematic fictions reflect actual social conditions, generate what Benedict Anderson has described as "imagined communities,"[5] or influence social behavior in any simple, straightforward way. Poststructuralist theorists have insisted on the instability and fluidity of the signifying process and have argued that representations generally offer a space for resistance at the point of their reception.[6] It is important to take into account, however, that despite the openness of the reception process, films often reproduce hegemonic assumptions about social hierarchies, with the potential for far-reaching reverberations.

Ella Shohat and Robert Stam have critiqued the illusory authority of Western cinematic realism in its construction of ethnic and racial others. While acknowledging the poststructuralist insistence that "we live and dwell within language and representation, and have no direct access to the 'real,'" Shohat and Stam insist that "films which represent marginalized cultures in a realistic mode . . . still implicitly make factual claims."[7] In other words, since the conventions of realism mask the illusionist strategies of the filmic enunciation, "realistic" fictions about unfamiliar communities or populations may be understood by audiences to reflect actual conditions of existence, thus giving rise to prejudicial effects. As many of the films discussed in my study deploy a realist register in their depictions of non-Italian characters, communities, or societies, I take this cautionary insight fully into account.

The films discussed in this study, though almost exclusively created by Italian filmmakers for Italian audiences, have an undeniably transnational aspect, not only in their recurring tropes of displacement, border crossing, and cultural hybridity but also in their casting practices and their unprecedented use of languages other than Italian. In many respects, they resemble films produced in other European countries facing similar political shifts and social dilemmas in the global present. The broader issue underpinning my research is, in fact, how Italian films resonate with transnational concerns and influences.

Use of the transnational as a methodological lens, which originated in the social sciences as an alternative or supplement to the concept of globalization, gradually gained ground in Anglophone literary and cultural studies toward the end of the 1990s.[8] The term "transnational" has connotations of cross-border movement, flexibility, porosity, and hybridity that distinguish it from the notion of the global. As Paul Jay has observed, literary scholars embracing a transnational perspective began to explore the capacity of literature to reveal "a multiplicity of differences grounded in personal, cultural, and political identities across locations where the boundary lines between cultures, races, genders, classes, and sexualities are much more porous than were heretofore acknowledged."[9] Almost simultaneously, the term began to be applied to the literary production of diasporic, postcolonial, or migrant writers, whose work was of particular interest to scholars adopting this interpretive lens.[10]

Emerging on the critical horizon around 2000, the rubric of transnational cinema has rapidly invigorated film studies in the English-speaking world, drawing attention to diasporic, "accented," or transcultural filmmaking and facilitating new perspectives on film and media production in various postcolonial, neocolonial, and migrant contexts.[11] The burgeoning of a transnational approach in film studies, as in other fields, parallels a wider critical questioning of the relevance of national frameworks in a globalized landscape. Nonetheless, in discussions developing among film scholars on the vast archive of transcultural and transborder films from around the world, there is a growing conviction that, although the category of the national can be limiting, discourses of nation are still a necessary component of any discussion of the transnational.

In light of the claims made by some film and media scholars that the category of national cinema has been superseded by different formulations and approaches that seem more appropriate to the global present,[12] one might ask if it is still useful to insist on the uniqueness of *Italian* films and the importance of their relation to a specific national formation. Would it not be more judicious to critically examine contemporary films made in Italy against a wider field of geopolitical and geocultural considerations, whether we wish to engage in analyses of production, distribution, and exhibition practices or whether our interest lies more squarely in aesthetic, ideological, and/or cultural inquiry? Despite the diminishing status of Italian cinema in recent decades as the purported repository of the national imaginary, I argue that those films that attempt to reconfigure Italy's social landscape in light of recent geopolitical transformations constitute a particularly compelling cinematic project.

Clearly, the years that separate us from the heyday of Italian filmmaking have brought profound changes to the fabric of Italian society, and a radical shift has occurred in the making and viewing of cinema. The international success of a handful of Italian feature films in recent years—from *Gomorra* (*Gomorrah*, Matteo Garrone, 2008) to *La grande bellezza* (*The Great Beauty*, Paolo Sorrentino, 2013) and *Fuocoammare* (*Fire at Sea*, Gianfranco Rosi, 2016)—has not impressed a substantial portion of film critics and cultural commentators in Italy, who habitually criticize an imputed lack of quality and consistency in contemporary Italian cinema. Resulting from a process that began with the deregulation of the national media more than thirty years ago, television has long outstripped cinema in its power and reach, and Italian filmmakers depend heavily on television as a source of production financing and as a venue for exhibition. Thus, for many years, the national film industry has been dominated by powerful media corporations and by RAI, the state media conglomerate.

Challenges to film production and consumption are scarcely unique to Italy in the contemporary, postcinematic era, where the audiovisual landscape is pervaded by new media and a proliferation of diverse viewing platforms. In recent years, however, two developments have served in radically different ways to revitalize or transform filmmaking practices in Italy. First, the creation of regional film commissions has greatly facilitated the financing of productions shot in diverse areas of the Italian territory, lending considerable local variety to the overall output of the national cinema. Second, through the combination of talents drawn from across different media sectors, Italy has seen the rapid growth of nationally produced quality television. Building on successful cinematic releases, two of these serial productions, *Romanzo criminale: la serie* and *Gomorra: la serie*, have been hugely successful in attracting national audiences and have gained increasing popularity overseas. The *Gomorra* series premiered in the United States on SundanceTV on August 24, 2016, and was subsequently made available on Netflix. Similarly, the *Romanzo criminale* series was first offered to international viewers on iTunes and was later streamed on Hulu.

The increasing popularity of Italian quality television has not, however, dramatically enhanced the overall fortunes of contemporary film production. On the domestic front, nationally produced features still face stiff competition from the expensively produced, aggressively promoted, and skillfully dubbed Hollywood imports that dominate multiplexes across Italy and make the distribution and exhibition of more modestly budgeted Italian films ever more challenging. Among new Italian releases, only comedies show particular strength at the box office. Meanwhile, in the global marketplace, the decline in the distribution of new Italian productions, which began more than two decades ago, continues unabated despite the triumph of a handful of art house releases.

Although current global marketing practices do not favor the international distribution of Italian films for the big screen, Italian cinema is, paradoxically, more accessible than ever before to viewers living outside Italy. Apart from the burgeoning festival circuit that regularly allows international audiences to see a small selection of contemporary releases, the increase in viewing opportunities abroad is for the most part due to the growing archive of Italian titles now available on Blu-ray or DVD or via Netflix, Hulu, and other similar services. Foreign audiences can also access Italian releases through the informal circulation of pirated copies procured by enthusiasts through download and various forms of legal and illegal reproduction. These avenues of accessibility are enhanced by the availability of optional English subtitles on increasing numbers of Italian films distributed on DVD or via streaming, which has made research on Italian cinema considerably more convenient than in the past for scholars working at a distance from Italy. Such changes have undoubtedly facilitated the growing body of work in Italian screen studies in the English-speaking world. Several of the films discussed in this study, for example, are more likely to have been watched by Anglophone scholars of contemporary Italian cinema and their students than by larger audiences in Italy. This disconcerting probability raises the issue of what the term "contemporary Italian cinema" might mean for Italian viewers and problematizes the presumed impact of the films in question on national audiences. Such concerns are part of an emerging debate on the diverse meanings that might be attributed to the term "Italian cinema" in the contemporary moment. Clearly no longer reducible to a specific, highly acclaimed, but historically circumscribed contribution to international art cinema, the history, definition, and critical assessment of Italian cinema are undergoing intense reexamination.[13] My book attempts to contribute to this larger critical operation.

This project also enters into dialogue with the work of other scholars who over the past dozen years have similarly contributed to the growing archive of studies on audiovisual representations of contemporary Italian immigration. In addition to dozens of individual articles and book chapters published outside Italy (mostly, but not exclusively, in English), two substantial collections of essays dedicated to the configuration of Italian immigration in film and media have appeared in the United States and in Britain since 2010.[14] I also take into account some of the relevant research produced by Italian academics based in Italy, where, it should be noted, the audiovisual representation of migration and diasporic subjectivities has attracted considerably less scholarly attention.[15]

The year 2017 saw the publication of the first monograph in the field written in English, Vetri Nathan's *Marvelous Bodies: Italy's New Migrant Cinema*.[16]

Unlike Nathan, I do not argue for the existence of what might be described as a "migrant cinema" in Italy. Instead, I take into account the extremely heterogeneous character of Italian films involving stories of immigration—a heterogeneity that makes it difficult to call this body of work as a whole a "cinema."

I should emphasize that my focus is not limited to configurations of the foreigner—in other words, to what Nathan describes as the "marvelous bodies" that increasingly intrude on what was previously imagined as a relatively homogenous social landscape. Instead, I am equally interested in the shifting configurations of space, both material and symbolic, marked by such intrusions. In other words, I explore the ways in which films featuring migrants remap the national territory, much as neorealist films did in the immediate postwar years. In the process, I draw on contemporary work by cultural geographers and anthropologists who have argued that as migrant mobility becomes a routine element of contemporary experience in many parts of the globe, border-crossing emerges as a vital part of everyday social life and ordinary human exchange. It is witnessed not only on the edges of the nation-state but also in streets, schools, stations, shopping centers, and other public places. As migrants inflect the social landscapes of their destination countries with the religious practices, alimentary preferences, festivities, and languages of their places of origin, such instances of border-crossing repeatedly necessitate what Jeffrey Hou describes as "the negotiation of space, identities, values, and rights in [their] encounters with others." Hou argues, in effect, that the presence of migrant and diasporic subjects contributes to the very process of placemaking.[17] At the same time, audiovisual representations of such "crossings" mediate the unfolding dramas and dilemmas of transcultural cohabitation for local audiences.

An analysis of Italian films about contemporary migrations readily reveals the ways in which they resonate with similar films produced in other areas of Europe that have experienced since the 1990s comparable patterns of xenophobia, racism, exploitative labor practices, and changing migratory policies. Some of these films—such as *La Promesse* (The Promise, Jean-Pierre and Luc Dardenne, 1996), *Code Inconnu* (Code Unknown, Michael Haneke, 2000), *Dirty Pretty Things* (Stephen Frears, 2002), and *Biutiful* (Alejandro González Iñárritu, 2010)—have achieved much broader circulation than their Italian counterparts. Yet important communalities in the scenarios they envision underscore Italian filmmakers' participation in a wider European project of reimagining social space in an era of unprecedented mobility and demographic transformation.[18]

Chapter 1, "After 1989: Projecting the Balkans," examines how in the aftermath of the Cold War Italian filmmakers responded to the opening up of borders by presenting new scenarios of transnational encounter. The early 1990s witnessed not only the dramatic beginning of mass immigration to Italy but also the outbreak of war in the former Yugoslavia and the consolidation of the European

Union. The same period saw the growth of regionalist populism in Italy, expressed in the platforms of the various regional leagues of the north, which eventually consolidated under the umbrella of Lega Nord. All of these phenomena cast into question issues of belonging and exclusion, foregrounding affects and attitudes running the gamut from isolationism or parochialism to racism and xenophobic animosity. The films examined in this chapter focus on Italian characters traveling in—or heading for—Albania or parts of the former Yugoslavia in the early 1990s, gesturing with different degrees of explicitness to Italy's relationship with the political realities of southeastern Europe both past and present, including the Italian occupation of parts of the Balkan peninsula in the late 1930s and early 1940s. These configurations collectively reveal a preoccupation with whiteness, reproductivity, and the nation's future in a transnational migratory landscape. Combining the insights of postcolonial theory with the theorization of whiteness, this chapter focuses for the most part on *Lamerica* (Gianni Amelio, 1994), *Aprile* (April, Nanni Moretti, 1998), *L'italiano* (The Italian, Ennio De Dominicis, 2002), *Teatro di guerra* (Rehearsals for War, Mario Martone, 1998), and the more recent *Venuto al mondo* (Twice Born, Sergio Castellitto, 2013).

Chapter 2, "Traffic from the East: Gender, Labor, and Biopolitics," is concerned with the construction of sexuality and corporeality in the depiction of women migrants from Eastern Europe after 1989. A substantial section of that chapter examines the recurring figure of the Eastern European woman either trafficked to Italy or otherwise lured into the burgeoning sex industry. Assessing the symbolic functions imbricated in this vulnerable, ambivalently eroticized figure, it highlights the ethical dilemmas inherent in the fictional representation of transnational sex workers and sex trafficking. It also examines the relationship between prostitution and other forms of affective surrogacy, probing in particular the biopolitical implications of feminized reproductive labor. The remainder of the chapter focuses on the emerging figure of the Eastern European care worker hired to fill the affective gap in Italy's reconfigured households, whose symbolic role lies on a continuum with that of the sex worker. The critical apparatus deployed in this chapter ranges from Giorgio Agamben's writings on biopolitics to feminist theorizations of affective labor and care work, which have been further elaborated by Sandro Mezzadra and Brett Neilson. The films explored here include two features directed by Carlo Mazzacurati, *Un'altra vita* (Another Life, 1992) and *Vesna va veloce* (Vesna Runs Fast, 1996), along with Armando Manni's *Elvjs & Merilijn* (Elvis and Marilyn, 1998), Giuseppe Tornatore's *La sconosciuta* (The Unknown Woman, 2006), and Federico Bondi's *Mar Nero* (Black Sea, 2008).

Chapter 3, "African Immigration in the 1990s," analyzes articulations of race and racism in several films featuring migrant characters from the Maghreb and from sub-Saharan Africa. It explores in particular the racialized and sexualized discourses that have subtended constructions of Arabs and black Africans in Italian cinema, observing the enduring ambivalence that characterizes the representation of nonwhite bodies on screen. Using both canonical works of postcolonial theory and contemporary reformulations of the postcolonial, I engage critically in this chapter with Michele Placido's *Pummarò* (Tomato, 1990), *L'articolo 2* (Article 2, Maurizio Zaccaro, 1993), *Teste rasate* (Skinheads, Claudio Fragasso, 1993), *L'assedio* (*Besieged*, Bernardo Bertolucci, 1997), and *Sud side stori* (South Side Story, Roberta Torre, 2000).

Chapter 4, "Migration, Masculinity, and New Urban Geographies," examines three dramatic films that unfold in a variety of urban peripheries and in locations rarely depicted in earlier Italian films, in order to highlight the ways in which immigration has not only transformed the Italian filmic landscape but has also created new narratives of personal maturation in the context of transcultural encounters. As in most dramatic films made in Italy, issues of male subjectivity and transformation dominate these narratives. Two of the films, Marco Tullio Giordana's *Quando sei nato non puoi più nasconderti* (Once You're Born You Can No Longer Hide, 2005) and Francesco Munzi's *Saimir* (2004), are structurally akin to the traditional male coming-of-age narrative, though played out in a transcultural, migratory context. The third, Carmine Amoroso's *Cover boy: L'ultima rivoluzione* (Cover Boy: The Last Revolution, 2006), moves beyond conventional narrative expectations to propose a more politically astute, if elusively articulated, story of male maturation and coming to consciousness while also commenting on the affinities that link the immigrant and the dispossessed Italian citizen in the neoliberal economy. The theoretical approaches used in this chapter are mainly drawn from the formulations of hospitality theorized by Emmanuel Levinas and Jacques Derrida, as well as Derrida's concept of spectrality.

Chapter 5, "Imagining an Expanded Mediterranean Borderscape," analyzes six films made between 2002 and 2016 against a backdrop of changing migratory policies affecting Italy's border management. These films not only speak to Italians' ongoing concerns with the continuing flow of irregular migration from the global South but also offer evolving constructions of the Mediterranean borderscape. In analyzing *Tornando a casa* (Going Home, Vincenzo Marra, 2002), *Io, l'altro* (I, the Other, Mohsen Melliti, 2006), *Lettere dal Sahara* (Letters from the Sahara, Vittorio De Seta, 2004), *Billo il Gran Dakhaar* (Billo the Big Guy, Laura Muscardin, 2007), *Terraferma* (Terra Firma, Emmanuele Crialese, 2011), and *Fuocoammare* (*Fire at Sea*, Gianfranco Rosi, 2016), the chapter draws on anthropological studies on the constitution and meaning of border zones and explores how the films themselves participate in this discursive process. The chapter's concluding section acknowledges the contribution of Andrea Segre's *L'ordine delle cose* (The Order of Things, 2017) to the growing resistance among Italian activists to EU border politics.

Chapter 6, "Living with Difference: From Noir to Melodrama," examines cinematic narratives of multiethnic cohabitation in contemporary Italy, where racialized tensions can erupt in sometimes unexpected ways. Articulated through a creative admixture of genre conventions, issues of cultural hybridity, resentment, and differential inclusion infuse the four films selected for analysis here: *Gomorra* (*Gomorrah*, Matteo Garrone, 2008), *Io sono Li* (*Shun Li and the Poet*, Andrea Segre, 2013), *Good Morning Aman* (Claudio Noce, 2009), and *Alì ha gli occhi azzurri* (*Alì Blue Eyes*, Claudio Giovannesi, 2012). Observing the ways in which these films incorporate genre influences, the chapter shows how the processes of identification, misidentification, and disidentification that they elicit from their viewers are negotiated principally through noir or the melodramatic mode. The theoretical apparatus that organizes this chapter is drawn from both postcolonial theory and genre studies.

The afterword, "Accented and Transnational Filmmaking in Italy," examines a small number of feature films that reconfigure the national imaginary from the point of view of transcultural, immigrant, or transmigrant filmmakers. There is a brief discussion of the "accented" figure of Turkish-born Ferzan Özpetek, who has by now been fully incorporated into the mainstream of the Italian film industry, as well as the contribution of less prominent immigrant filmmakers such as Mohamed Zineddaine, Rachid Benhadj, and Edmond Budina. It also explores the emerging presence of second-generation filmmakers such as Laura Halilovic and Suranga Deshapriya Katugampala, whose work addresses specifically the tensions that continue to challenge the lives of Italy's foreign-born residents and native-born diasporic subjects. The afterword concludes with an analysis of Jonas Carpignano's award-winning, transnationally produced *Mediterranea* (2015), which defies categorizations and points to future possibilities for the creation, production, and circulation of hybrid films that can be seen as both "Italian" and "transnational" at the same time.

Over the ten years during which I developed this project, important changes have occurred not only in the audiovisual landscape but also in the broader geopolitical context. The current political climate in Western democracies has seen the rise of xenophobia and nationalistic populism in Europe and in the United States—powerfully exemplified by the emergence of right-wing governments in the former Eastern bloc, the Brexit vote in the British referendum of June 2016, the election of Donald Trump to the US presidency some months later, and the formation of a right-leaning coalition government in Italy in the spring of 2018 following an electoral campaign laced with vigorous anti-immigrant rhetoric. These developments make an examination of the discourses of racism, xenophobia, and social exclusion ever more necessary and compelling.

Since Italy still retains a citizenship policy based primarily on *ius sanguinis* (the right of blood), the force of anti-immigrant sentiment affects even the children born in Italy to the country's foreign residents. Although citizenship can be granted on the basis of longtime residency, the application process is fraught with challenges. In June 2017, the then center-left government's proposal to facilitate the granting of citizenship to the children of migrants born on Italian soil, or to those who received the majority of their childhood education in Italy, was finally brought before the Senate.[19] It was met with strident assertions of xenophobic resistance by members of the right-leaning constituencies, degenerating into a chaotic situation that caused discussion to be postponed. Further postponements followed later in the year, suspending all consideration of the initiative until after the elections of 2018.

My project does not aim to provide a comprehensive overview of Italy's audiovisual construction of contemporary immigration and related representations of alterity or foreignness. I have chosen instead to develop a critique of those films that address or symptomatize clusters of specific anxieties—regarding race, gender, nativity, border construction, and multiethnic cohabitation. With this aim, I have focused on the ways in which specific films articulate or reformulate identities through a process in which alterities are made to "rhyme" with traditional formations of othering, from misogyny, gender discrimination, anti-southern sentiment, xenophobia, and so on. In the interest of tightening my focus, I have had to eliminate from consideration the discussion of some prominent films featuring migrant characters that I might otherwise have included.[20]

As I have suggested, films that deploy stories of border-crossing interweave in complex ways issues of race with other axes of difference, such as ethnicity, religion, class, gender, and other hierarchies of power in the late-capitalist world system. Instead of discussing such films as merely illustrative of social issues, I explore the cultural work they perform as productive of new subjectivities and modes of being in the world. I thus aim to show how a substantial corpus of films made in Italy since the 1990s contributes to the figuration of contemporary global migrations while bringing about a shift in the symbolic reconstruction of the national landscape. What interests me is the kind of cinema that—regardless of its imputed artistic value or lack thereof—is engaged in participating (consciously or not) in the construction of an audiovisual history of the global present, traversed by transnational mobilities and fraught with growing economic inequalities.

Notes

1. Although immigration to Italy began to overtake emigration in the 1980s, immigrant numbers did not reach significant levels until the early 1990s.
2. Italy had been a founding member of the European Coal and Steel Community, created by the Treaty of London in 1951, the European Atomic Energy Community, created by

the Euratom Treaty in 1957, and the European Economic Community, created by the Treaty of Rome in 1957. The economic mandates imposed by the EEC, however, were perceived retroactively by some constituencies as less burdensome to local interests than the more rigorous and comprehensive regulations of the subsequently formed EU.

3. In addition to the funding possibilities offered by the regional Film Commissions, support became available for productions qualifying for the category *film d'interesse nazionale e culturale* (films of national and cultural interest) in the early twenty-first century. Feature films loosely aligned with the earlier filmmaking tradition known as *cinema d'impegno* (which articulated a sense of civic consciousness through the critique of Italian society) were often granted this seal of approval following the reform in legislation on audiovisual media in 2004 (Article 5.2 of the decree issued on January 22, 2004: "Riforma della disciplina in materia di attività cinematografiche"). Awarded by MiBACT (the Italian Ministry for Cultural Heritage, Activities and Tourism), the designation is sometimes, though not always, followed by a subvention. Even when the designation is not accompanied by funding, however, a film's successful bid for the label "of cultural interest" provides institutional legitimation and prestige that can be an advantage in publicizing and marketing the films in question. The label may also influence reception and inclusion in the canon. For a discussion of the way the notion of "quality" currently functions in relation to the teaching of Italian cinema in the Anglophone context, see Danielle Hipkins and Dana Renga, "A New Canon? Contemporary Italian Cinema and Television and the Role of Quality," *Communicazioni sociali* no. 3 (2016): 375–97.

4. See Ilvo Diamanti, "Quei film sugli immigrati nel Paese di Terraferma," *La Repubblica* (Sept. 12, 2011), www.repubblica.it/politica/2011/09/12/news/mappe_12_settembre-21534651/.

5. I refer to Benedict Anderson's often-cited term "imagined communities," first used in his influential study of nationalism. Anderson identifies the nation as a discursively constructed community created and sustained through the imagination of citizens who collectively believe that they are part of it. See Benedict Anderson, *Imagined Communities: Reflections on the Origin and Spread of Nationalism* (London: Verso, 1983).

6. Richard Dyer, *The Matter of Images: Essays on Representations* (New York: Routledge, 1993), 2.

7. Ella Shohat and Robert Stam, *Unthinking Eurocentrism: Multiculturalism and the Media* (New York: Routledge, 1994), 179.

8. Early studies that adopted a transnational lens in different fields of the social sciences include Rainer Bauböck, *Transnational Citizenship Membership and Rights in International Migration* (Florence: Edward Elgar, 1994); Ulf Hannerz, *Transnational Connections: Culture, People, Places* (New York: Routledge, 1996); and Partha Dasgupta, Karl-Göran Mäler, and Alessandro Vercelli, eds., *The Economics of Transnational Commons* (Oxford: Oxford University Press, 1997). An influential collection of essays from the same period also announced an emerging transnational focus in feminist studies; see Inderpal Grewal and Caren Kaplan, eds., *Scattered Hegemonies: Postmodernity and Transnational Feminist Practices* (Minneapolis: University of Minnesota Press, 1994).

9. Paul Jay, *Global Matters: The Transnational Turn in Literary Studies* (New York: Cornell University Press, 2010), 92.

10. In Italy, the transnational has not had widespread currency in the humanities, either as a critical approach or as literary category, and those transnational writers resident in Italy who have produced a growing corpus of literature in Italian are more apt to be designated as "postcolonial," "diasporic," or "immigrant" authors (terms that are also occasionally applied in English to some of those Anglophone writers alternatively described as transnational). Emma Bond builds a strong argument in favor of using the term "trans-national" in relation to this variously designated corpus of literary production while insisting on the symbolic importance

of its hyphened form. See Emma Bond, "Towards a Trans-national Turn in Italian Studies?" *Italian Studies* 69, no. 3 (2014): 415–24. At this juncture, scholarly attention paid to the corpus to which Bond refers has reached a significant momentum. For an up-to-date overview of this remarkable and varied literary phenomenon, see Caterina Romeo, "Italian Postcolonial Literature," *California Italian Studies* 7, no. 2 (2017), https://escholarship.org/uc/item/55d0f4j7.

11. For an overview of transnational approaches and categorizations in cinema studies, see Will Higbee and Song Hwee Lin, "Concepts of Transnational Cinema: Towards a Critical Transnationalism in Film Studies," *Transnational Cinemas* 1, no. 1 (2010): 7–21. Appearing in the inaugural issue of a journal devoted exclusively to transnational film studies, this article contains indispensible bibliographical references. Additional publications on the intersection of cinema and issues of the transnational include Mette Hjort's taxonomic essay, "Plurality of Cinematic Transnationalism," in *World Cinemas, Transnational Perspectives*, ed. Natasa Durovicová and Kathleen Newman (New York: Routledge, 2009), 12–33, and two edited collections: Elizabeth Ezra and Terry Rowden, eds., *Transnational Cinema: The Film Reader* (New York: Routledge, 2006) and Katarzyna Marciniak, Anikó Imre, and Áine O'Healy, eds., *Transnational Feminism in Film and Media* (New York: Palgrave Macmillan, 2007).

12. In one of the earliest interventions in the debate on the viability of the national cinema paradigm, Andrew Higson at the turn of the century already proposed the term "transnational" as a way of overcoming the binary logic implicit in the concept of national cinema; see Andrew Higson, "The Limiting Imagination of National Cinema," in *Cinema and Nation*, ed. Mette Hjort and Scott MacKenzie (New York: Routledge, 2000), 63–74. See also Jerry White, "National Belonging: Renewing the Concept of National Cinema for a Global Culture," *New Review of Film and Television Studies* 2, no. 2 (2004): 211–32.

13. See Alan O'Leary, "What Is Italian Cinema?" *California Italian Studies* 7, no. 1 (2017), https://escholarship.org/uc/item/7z9275bz.

14. The two essay collections published in English on representations of Italian immigration in film and media are Grace Bullaro, ed., *From Terrone to Extra-Comunitario: The New Manifestations of Racism in Contemporary Italian Cinema* (Leicester, UK: Troubador, 2010) and Emma Bond, Guido Bonsaver, and Federico Faloppa, eds., *Destination Italy: Representing Migration in Contemporary Media and Narrative* (Oxford: Peter Lang, 2015). Other noteworthy analyses of specific aspects of this cinematic phenomenon include Derek Duncan, "Italy's Postcolonial Cinema and Its Histories of Representation," *Italian Studies* 63, no. 2 (2008): 195–211; Derek Duncan, "'Loving Geographies': Queering Straight Migration to Italy," *New Cinemas: Journal of Contemporary Film* 6, no. 3 (Feb. 1, 2009): 167–82; Derek Duncan, "Shooting the Colonial Past in Contemporary Italian Cinema," in *Postcolonial Italy*, ed. Cristina Lombardi-Diop and Caterina Romeo (New York: Palgrave Macmillan, 2012), 115–24; and Derek Duncan, "'Il clandestino è l'ebreo di oggi': Imprints of the Shoah on Migration to Italy," *Quest: Issues in Contemporary Jewish History* 10 (2016): 60–88. See also Giovanna Falaschini Lerner, "From the Other Side of the Mediterranean: Hospitality in Italian Migration Cinema," *California Italian Studies Journal* 1, no. 1 (2010), http://escholarship.org/uc/item/45h010h5, and Norma Bouchard and Valerio Ferme, *Italy and the Mediterranean: Words, Sounds, and Images of the Post–Cold War Era* (New York: Palgrave Macmillan, 2013), 121–54. For a discussion of a specific cluster of documentary films on Italian immigration, see Michela Ardizzoni, "Narratives of Change, Images for Change: Contemporary Social Documentaries in Italy," *Journal of Italian Cinema and Media Studies* 1, no. 3 (2013): 311–26.

15. Among Italian-based studies of what is described as Italy's contemporary postcolonial or diasporic cinema, I wish to note in particular Leonardo De Franceschi, ed., *L'Africa in Italia: per una controstoria postcoloniale del cinema italiano* (Rome: Aracne, 2013). See also De Franceschi's collection of his own previously published essays, *Lo schermo e lo spettro. Sguardi*

postcoloniali su Africa e afrodiscendenti (Sesto San Giovanni: Mimesis, 2017). Other relevant works published in Italy include Sonia Cicinelli's broad-ranging survey of cinematic representations of immigration, *Senza frontiere: L'immigrazione nel cinema italiano* (Rome: Editore Kappa, 2011). Another relevant publication on the construction of migration in Italian cinema is "In & Out: Migrazioni nel/del cinema italiano," ed. Vito Zagarrio, special issue, *Quaderni del CSCI: Rivista annuale di cinema italiano* 8 (2012), containing articles by dozens of scholars working both in Italy and overseas. Though based in Barcelona, the journal is published in Italian.

16. In *Marvelous Bodies* (West Lafayette, IN: Purdue University Press, 2017), Vetri Nathan examines fifteen films that include some of those selected for consideration in my own study, adopting an analytic lens that is guided principally by the insights and terminology of postcolonial theorist Homi Bhabha. Although I also use postcolonial theory in some of the chapters that follow, my approach is more eclectic than Nathan's. Prompted by specific questions evoked in the films on which I focus and by the social and political context in which they were produced, I draw on a diverse range of theoretical frameworks in order to consider Italian constructions of contemporary alterities within a broader, European context.

17. Jeffrey Hou, "Your Place and/or My Place?," in *Transcultural Cities: Border-Crossing and Placemaking*, ed. Jeffrey Hou (New York: Routledge, 2013), 1–16.

18. Films that feature migrant or diasporic subjectivites in a variety of settings across contemporary Europe have already received substantial scholarly attention. See, for example, Daniela Berghahn and Claudia Sternberg, eds., *European Cinema in Motion: Migrant and Diasporic Film in Contemporary Europe* (New York: Palgrave Macmillan, 2010); Yosefa Loshitzky, *Screening Strangers: Migration and Diaspora in Contemporary European Cinema* (Bloomington: Indiana University Press, 2010); Isolina Ballestreros, *Immigration Cinema in the New Europe* (Bristol: Intellect, 2015); Ipek A. Celik, *In Permanent Crisis: Ethnicity in Contemporary European Media and Cinema* (Ann Arbor: University of Michigan Press, 2015); and Nilgun Bayraktar, *Mobility and Migration in Film and Moving Image Art* (New York: Routledge, 2016).

19. I use the term "center-left" guardedly. Il Partito Democratico (Democratic Party), Italy's largest political organization, was founded in 2007 with the merger of various left-leaning and center-left parties. Many dispute the utility of the term "left" in the current political arena, where the structures of neoliberal economics have diluted the appeal or applicability of such categories.

20. Among the most interesting films about relations between Italians and migrants that I have reluctantly omitted from discussion are *Bell'amico* (Fine Friend, Luca D'Ascanio, 2001), *La giusta distanza* (*The Right Distance*, Carlo Mazzacurati, 2007), and *Là-bas* (Down There, Guido Lombardi, 2011). Using very different formal approaches, the three films engage the viewer in compelling ways that serve to interrogate and dislodge customary constructions of migrant subjectivities. The first, a comedy, depicts the psychological and artistic one-upmanship of an Angolan filmmaker staying at the home of an indecisive and ineffectual Italian acquaintance. The second, a skillfully constructed noir, unfolds in a small town in the Po Valley, where the locals appear to have accepted their foreign-born neighbors until an Italian woman is mysteriously murdered. The third, featuring a cast of African immigrants resident in the Neapolitan hinterland, is a realistically constructed drama based on an incident that occurred in Castel Volturno in 2008 in which seven immigrants were slaughtered by members of the local Camorra.

CHAPTER 1

After 1989

PROJECTING THE BALKANS

IN THE EARLY 1990s several events took place in Italy that would profoundly mark the nation's social, political, and ideological landscapes in the years to come. Following the collapse of communism in Eastern Europe, the Italian Communist Party—a significant presence in Italian politics during the Cold War—underwent a brief period of internal turmoil that resulted in its dissolution and immediate replacement by two separate parties, Partito Democratico della Sinistra (Democratic Party of the Left) and the much smaller Rifondazione Comunista (Communist Refoundation). The year 1991 also saw the creation of the new regionalist party Lega Nord (Northern League), which consolidated several smaller "leagues" in the regions of the North. The Lega's rhetoric of northern superiority, anti-immigrant sentiment, and secession from the rest of Italy was to become increasingly strident in the years that followed. Moreover, between 1992 and 1993, the country witnessed an explosive corruption scandal involving major business leaders and politicians (a phenomenon often described as *Tangentopoli*) that led to intense political upheaval and the collapse of the so-called First Republic.[1]

In the vacuum created by the elimination of two of the most powerful parties in Italy, the Christian Democrats and the Socialist Party, media mogul Silvio Berlusconi quickly established Forza Italia ("Go, Italy!"), a new center-right party named after the national soccer cheer. With sweeping success, Forza Italia drew members previously linked to a wide range of positions on the political spectrum and soon became the most powerful force in the country. Though the party experienced a setback in the elections of 1995, it would repeatedly return to power in the coming years, building strength by entering into coalitions with other parties. In addition to these new elements in parliamentary politics, a modernized right-wing party, Alleanza Nazionale, also rose to prominence. Founded by Gianfranco Fini in 1995, it replaced the Movimento Sociale Italiano and sought to gain national respectability by explicitly renouncing the Fascist ideology of its earlier incarnation. In this rapidly changing panorama, where the voice of the Left no longer constituted a significant oppositional force and where media and political interests were closely enmeshed, Italy's espousal of neoliberal policies—already underway in the 1980s—became increasingly entrenched.

Pressures exerted by factors originating outside Italy also held considerable sway over the nation's affairs due to the demands imposed by European integration and the challenges of unprecedented immigration. In November 1990, the Italian government became a signatory of the Schengen Convention, which aimed at dissolving the borders between the member states of the European Economic Community (soon to become the European Union) to facilitate greater freedom of movement of persons, goods, and capital than already achieved by the Treaty of Rome in 1957. The reality of this supranational entity, however, was far from borderless as several of Europe's western nations soon began to implement efforts to halt the growing waves of migration arriving from North Africa via the Mediterranean as well as from Eastern Europe, from which significant numbers had begun to flow after the collapse of state socialism in 1989. Italy passed its first legislation on immigration, popularly known as the Martelli Law, only in 1990.

The experience of migration from Eastern Europe hit Italy with striking force in the early spring and late summer of 1991, when tens of thousands of Albanians arrived unexpectedly in the harbors of the southeastern region of Puglia aboard dinghies, trawlers, and cargo ships. Although the country admitted over twenty thousand Albanians in the first wave of arrivals in the early months of the year, a subsequent contingent of almost twenty thousand people arriving from Albania in August received a hostile reception, resulting in mass repatriation. The outbreak of war accompanying the dissolution of Yugoslavia a short time thereafter intensified Italian anxieties about the prospect of a further onslaught of mass migration from across the Adriatic. Based on these fears, the Italian government admitted fewer refugees fleeing conflicts in the Balkans than were accepted by other European countries. Yet arrivals from Eastern Europe did not cease; a steady flow of migrants from the former socialist states continued to find ways to enter Italy and make their homes there throughout the 1990s and beyond.

Immigration was not entirely new to Italy in 1991, as smaller numbers of migrants, for the most part from the African continent, had begun to appear in both Italian cities and the agricultural landscapes of the South in the late 1970s. It was becoming clear, however, that the country's shift from emigrant nation to the receiver of growing numbers of immigrants would not be an entirely smooth transition. Periodic reports of racially motivated conflicts or xenophobic incidents indicated that many Italians resented the unaccustomed presence of foreigners in their midst. But the second surge in Albanian arrivals that occurred in August 1991 unleashed an unprecedented wave of anti-immigrant sentiment, clearly evidenced in the language of press and television reports from the era.[2]

In the decade that saw the consolidation of the European Union and the implementation of the Schengen Convention, Italians experienced new pressures to embrace a broader sense of citizenship and a European sense of self. Along with these pressures, however, there was a lingering awareness among them that Italy was still perceived by many other Europeans not so much as part of the main stage of European life but rather as a provincial, Mediterranean culture.

In this chapter, I explore how Italian responses to immigration from the east, or, more specifically, to immigration from southeastern Europe, find resonance in a small number of films concerned with the events that occurred in the Balkan Peninsula after the end of the Cold War. These films reveal anxieties about the meaning of Italian identity in the post–Cold War years as well as a subliminal concern about the future of Italian whiteness in the face of the new transnational mobilities. I aim to explore how, through processes of audiovisual enunciation, including narrative occlusions and aporias, the production of (white) alterity in such films enables the modernity of Italian citizens to be foregrounded and reasserted. First, however, I must explore the ways in which Italian whiteness has been historically constructed vis-à-vis the nation's own internal others (specifically southerners), its emigrants, and its neighboring populations, all of whom—at least to outsiders—may appear to resemble each other to a striking degree.

Concerns regarding the racial status of Italians were deeply imbricated in processes of nation building in the post-Unification period. Several recent studies argue that racist discourses in Italy, which today are directed against immigrants, are not a new phenomenon as racialization was a crucial element in the formation of the nation-state from the beginning.[3] Indeed, the project of "making Italians"—or of unifying the country's various regional populations tied to traditions and dialects that were often incomprehensible to their co-nationals—mobilized discourses of race. The concept of Italian identity was ultimately refined and consolidated around three contentious issues: the so-called southern question, emigration, and colonization.

Despite the popular claims that racism is extraneous to the Italian character and that the racist policies of the Fascist regime were an aberrant imposition, scholars have begun to identify the seeds of contemporary Italian racism not in Fascism but in an earlier moment in the country's history, pointing to circumstances that developed in the early years of the new nation-state. Immediately after national unification, a group of northern Italian politicians, bureaucrats, and intellectuals traveled to the South to begin the process of integrating its regions into the new state. This effort to explore and integrate the South—poorer than the regions of the North thanks to a history of semi-feudal government in the southern regions—has been conceptualized since the time of Antonio Gramsci as a process of both exploration and colonization.[4] Aligning Italian southerners with Africans soon became the dominant metaphor through which northerners began to perceive residents of the South. Anthropologist Alfredo Niceforo posited, for example, that there were two races in Italy, an "Aryan" and "Caucasian" race in the North and a "Negroid" race in the South.[5] The influence of this and similar classifications ultimately led US immigration officials to question the whiteness of many migrants arriving from Italy in the early twentieth century at the height of Jim Crow segregation in the United States.[6]

In the new nation-state that emerged in the final phase of Italian unification, poverty was widespread, even in parts of the North. Thus, in the late nineteenth century and the early decades of the new century, millions of Italian citizens—not only from the South but also from other impoverished pockets of the peninsula— were driven by destitution to emigrate across the Atlantic. Upon arrival in the United States, they were initially considered inferior to those originating from northern Europe, and, subsequently, some Italian immigrants were subjected to treatment similar to that experienced by African Americans in the American south, including acts of racially motivated brutality and lynching.[7]

Italy's creation of colonies in Libya and in the Horn of Africa was conceptualized in part as a way of redeeming the racial standing of Italians as a whole, which trans-Atlantic emigration had problematized. In the colonies, the discourse on race was formed on a binary axis that posited the superiority of all Italians—as "white" Europeans—over the purported degeneracy of the native occupants of the conquered territories. These historical circumstances contributed, in turn, to Italian understandings of racial hierarchies that endure up to the present. As Anna Curcio and Miguel Mellino have argued, emigration, colonialism, and the "Southern question" collectively constitute the archaeology of racial discourse in contemporary Italy.[8] In the broader global context, however, Italian racism is profoundly linked to discourses of race at work in other settings. As Curcio and Mellino contend, "The modern notion of race, like the different historical forms of racism to which it has contributed, represents a disciplinary apparatus constitutive of all modern capitalist formations."[9] They also point out that "the discourse of race cannot be treated as mere representation or manipulation; it is not a simple fiction: it is the material result of different regimes of practices and policies that have their roots in the very makeup of modern colonial capitalism."[10]

Albanian Fantasies

Several prominent politicians, including representatives of Lega Nord and the constituencies of the right, contributed to the spread of xenophobia in the 1990s by appealing to Italian citizens' concerns about the impact of immigration on their safety, economic well-being, and cultural traditions. The racializing rhetoric adopted by these groups echoed in uncanny fashion traditional northern Italian prejudices toward Italians of the South. In the 1990s, Umberto Bossi, then leader of Lega Nord, argued that the values of northern Italy (labeled Padania by Lega members, in reference to the territories surrounding the Po River) were characteristic of "European culture," a category that implies integrity, efficiency, and hard work. In contrast to the "Europeanness" of these regions, the south of Italy was cast as closer to a Mediterranean culture of questionable honesty and parasitic dependency, with which many of Italy's new arrivals were implicitly associated.[11] In this way, as Jaro Stacul has noted, Lega Nord reinvigorated the long-standing prejudice that "northern Italian culture" was being undermined by the presence of racialized southerners in the North. Simultaneously, it encouraged similar fears about the arrival of new migrants from non-EU countries. As Stacul argues, a (northern) Italian understanding of what it means to be European entails "[not only] emphasizing the distinction between West and East, Christianity and Islam [but also] contesting the inner 'cultural' boundaries of Europe by casting southerners as the 'other.'"[12] This process of othering, based on perceived cultural differences rather than verifiable somatic distinctions, builds a framework that casts southerners *and* immigrants as less than fully white.[13]

More than a handful of Italian films representing contemporary mobilities between Italy and the countries of southeastern Europe directly engage the issues of cultural boundaries and differences. They also implicitly raise the question of Italy's historical links to its immediate neighbors to the east, including the invasion and occupation of significant areas of the Balkan Peninsula between 1939 and 1944. The Italian military presence in these territories and in the Dodecanese Islands had, in fact, been largely ignored by Italian filmmakers throughout the Cold War, only to emerge in somewhat sanitized fashion in the Oscar-winning *Mediterraneo* (Gabriele Salvatores, 1991). Notably, the dialogue in this film also mobilizes the popular adage "Same face, same race," which is uttered, not without irony, on two distinct occasions in the film to draw attention to the somatic similarity between and among the Greek, Italian, and Turkish characters who show up on the Aegean island where the film's wartime story is set. Indeed, one of the tropes that emerges in several cinematic constructions of migration to Italy from the Balkans—and in some representations of migration from North Africa as well—is the racial ambivalence prompted by corporeal similarities between characters from different parts of the Mediterranean shore. These films collectively ask how one can distinguish between the national subject and the immigrant if they resemble each other to a striking degree, especially in those instances when foreigners and autochthonous Italians share a common claim to whiteness. Italian filmmakers have grappled with this concern for almost twenty-five years, beginning with Gianni Amelio's *Lamerica* in 1994.

Lamerica, whose narrative unfolds against the backdrop of the Albanian exodus to Italy in 1991, is not the first film to foreground the issue of Italian immigration. Interweaving different histories and geographies, it is nonetheless the first film featuring migrant characters to evoke the three discourses imbricated in the archaeology of Italian racism: Italian emigration of the past, the southern question, and the nation's colonizing adventures. Moreover, the manner in which this film juxtaposes two adjacent populations, Italians and Albanians, implicitly raises the question of racialized whiteness and the meaning of whiteness in contemporary postcolonial Europe.

In 1991, Italian households watched the unfolding of contemporary history on their television screens as the crowded migrant ships from postcommunist Albania arrived in the harbors of Puglia.[14] Images of Italy's coastal waters plied by ships, fishing boats, and smaller, flimsier vessels bringing migrants from various points to the south or east have appeared with insistent regularity in the Italian media since that time, serving as a stark reminder of the vulnerability of the country's Mediterranean boundaries. Although significant numbers of migrants continue to disembark on Italian shores each year facilitated by organized networks of people smugglers and traffickers, most of Italy's irregular migrants[15] do not arrive by sea but enter the country as tourists by land or air, subsequently overstaying the limited period allowed to visitors.[16] Images of Italy's "boat people" nonetheless attained prominence in the national imaginary in two distinct phases—initially as the result of dramatic television coverage of the large-scale Albanian arrivals of 1991 and 1997 and more recently thanks to intensive television coverage of irregular migration from the global South routed through Libya or Tunisia to Italy's southernmost islands.

Lamerica opened at the Venice Film Festival in 1994, where Amelio won the Osella d'oro prize for best direction.[17] Shot entirely in Albania in 1993, it is the first large-scale production to question self-consciously how cinema should engage with immigration in representational terms. Indeed, few films since that time have so poignantly questioned cinema's relationship to the nation's past as well as to the pressures of the global present.

Before shooting *Lamerica*, Amelio had already gained recognition as one of Italy's most accomplished contemporary directors with the release of the acclaimed *Il ladro di bambini* (*Stolen Children*, 1992), which offers a harsh indictment of contemporary Italian society. Although set entirely in Albania, *Lamerica* expands on the criticism of contemporary Italy undertaken in Amelio's earlier film while inviting reflection on Italians' apparent forgetfulness of their country's history of invasion and conquest, emigration, and poverty. It also observes the pervasive reach of contemporary Italian television as a form of neocolonial conquest symptomatic of late capitalism more generally, and it draws attention to the contingency of all identities in the face of global migrations.[18]

Figure 1.1. Screen capture. The crowded migrant ship. *Lamerica* (1994)

Amelio's inspiration for *Lamerica* had its source in the Italian news reports documenting the arrival of thousands of Albanians in the port of Bari in August 1991. Watching images of the seemingly destitute men and women who had undertaken the voyage across the Adriatic aboard the spectacularly overcrowded ship *Vlora*, the director was reminded of the desperation that drove his own father and uncle, along with other Italians, to emigrate to North and South America decades earlier. In the autumn of 1991, Amelio traveled to Albania to explore ideas for a new film. He later claimed that this journey was fueled by a desire not to investigate the specific conditions of postcommunist Albania but rather to explore elements of a long-vanished Italy, a country so poor that vast numbers of its inhabitants were obliged to seek new lives elsewhere and whose history had been forgotten by contemporary Italians, complacent in their newfound wealth.[19] Indirectly invoking the memory of these forgotten forebears, the title of the film is a strategic misspelling of "L'America" (the correct term for America in standard Italian), imitating the orthographic errors found in the correspondence of semiliterate Italian emigrants many years earlier.[20]

The images of contemporary migration offered by *Lamerica* had a poignant impact at the time of its release, just three years after the initial arrival of the crowded migrant vessels in the harbors of Puglia. Indeed nothing had prepared Italians for the massive exodus from Albania, an impoverished country that been more isolated than any other European nation during the communist era. Amelio's film is set in Albania over a short span of time in the summer of 1991 in the period immediately preceding the journey of the real-life Albanians who disembarked in Bari in August and were subsequently repatriated. Significantly, the film ends on a rusty ship packed with aspiring migrants still sailing toward Italy, whose ultimate fate remains unknown.

The film's powerful interweaving of fictional narrative and recent events of broad historical resonance, its on-location shooting, and its supporting cast of nonprofessional actors prompted several reviewers to describe it as a tribute to neorealism. *Lamerica* undoubtedly depicts circumstances that are intended to recall scenes and settings from postwar cinema—towns swarming with ragged children, the scarcity of food, and the theft of shoes and tires. Although these images explicitly resonate with the bleak social landscape visualized in the neorealist canon, the film is not simply a tribute to the aesthetics of neorealism. Unlike the postwar directors, Amelio had at his disposal a large production budget, and he chose to shoot the film in widescreen format, creating panoramic vistas more reminiscent of the American films he had admired as a youth than of those made by the neorealist filmmakers. Some of the film's commentators, including Guido Aristarco, a prominent critic of the historical Left, denounced the "spectacular" implications of this artistic decision, which was deemed inappropriate for the subject matter.[21] The director has explained his choice of the anamorphic format, however, as a self-conscious attempt to announce his distance from a firsthand experience of contemporary Albanian realities.[22] A similar attitude of self-reflexivity informs other instances of intertextual commentary within the film, engaging dialogically not only with neorealism but also with Fascist documentary filmmaking, contemporary Italian television, and global mass culture.

Lamerica's opening credit sequence pointedly incorporates a direct citation from Fascist cinema. As the credits roll on the right side of the screen, an Italian newsreel from 1939 is projected on the left, reporting the invasion of Albania by Italy's armed forces. Produced by LUCE, the documentary wing of the state-controlled cinema founded with the aim of bringing Fascist propaganda to the masses, the selected footage presents the arrival of the Italians as a civilizing intervention warmly welcomed by cheering Albanian crowds. The screening of the newsreel as a preface to the opening scene of *Lamerica*—which presents two Italian businessmen arriving in Albania in 1991 to a similarly enthusiastic though more informal welcome—suggests a parallel between the exploitative motives underlying the Italian invasion of 1939 and the self-interested ambition of the Italian entrepreneurs currently traveling to Albania. At another level, the use of this footage provides an immediate demonstration of cinema's capacity to manipulate and mythologize, thus indirectly calling into question the reliability of *Lamerica*'s own enunciative strategies.

Set in Durrës, the harbor serving Albania's capital, Tirana, the film's opening scene introduces the viewer to circumstances prevailing in Albania in the summer of 1991. Here, after almost fifty years of isolation, the country has opened its doors to investors from abroad. As the two Italian businessmen disembark from the incoming ferry, dozens of young men have gathered near the port in the hope of boarding a vessel bound for Italy. Rushing past the police officers attempting to block their access, they begin to cheer, "Italy, you are the world!" in a scene that clearly resonates with the earlier newsreel images of Albanians cheering the arrival of Mussolini's armed forces.

Lamerica's protagonist is Gino Cutrari (Enrico Lo Verso), the younger of these two businessmen, who drives a smart new SUV and has all the trappings of well-to-do Italian masculinity. He arrives in Albania in the company of his senior business partner, Fiore (Michele Placido), with the purported aim of creating a shoe factory. Gino and Fiore are motivated by the prospect of obtaining start-up funds offered by government agencies for the creation of businesses in post-communist Albania and have no real intention of manufacturing shoes. Their immediate concern is to fulfill the requirement of selecting an Albanian citizen as the titular president of their company in order to access the available cash. Searching for a submissive figurehead among the survivors of a recently liberated labor camp, they select a mute, senile ex-prisoner named Spiro Tojai (Carmelo Di Mazzarelli) and, after cleaning him up, prepare to present him to the Albanian officials. Reacting to the cruel treatment he has received from Gino, however, the deranged ex-prisoner soon disappears. After Gino finally catches up with him in another city, he discovers that the old man is not a genuine Albanian but rather a Sicilian war veteran named Michele, who arrived in Albania as a conscripted soldier during the Italian occupation and then deserted the army, only to find himself trapped in the country after the withdrawal of Italian troops. Despite the revelation of the old man's Italian identity, Gino proceeds back toward Tirana with him, still planning to present him as the titular Albanian president of the fake manufacturing company. Their return to the capital, however, is delayed by a series of obstacles that progressively challenge Gino's access to mobility and privilege.

A major turning point in the protagonist's trajectory occurs when he learns that his scam has been exposed, his business partner, Fiore, has abandoned him, and he must find a way to return to Italy immediately. After parting ways with Michele, Gino is arrested on charges of fraud and imprisoned in a sinister jail. He manages to secure his release only by surrendering his passport to a police commissioner, who advises him to leave Albania without delay. Deprived of all possessions—car, sunglasses, luggage, money, decent clothing, and passport—Gino finally reaches the harbor, indistinguishable from the Albanian migrants who have gathered there. In the final sequence he boards an overcrowded ship, where he is reunited by chance with Michele, and both of them sail toward Italy in the company of impoverished, passport-less Albanian travelers.

The narrative trajectory of *Lamerica* is thus organized around the visible transformation of the arrogant and historically ignorant protagonist. Though Sicilian by birth like the older Michele, Gino seems unaware of the poverty and humiliation endured by his forebears just two generations earlier, at a time when

Figure 1.2. Screen capture. Gino and Michele. *Lamerica* (1994)

parts of Italy, and particularly the South, were as destitute as today's Albania. Complacent in his identity as a well-to-do Italian, Gino views the destitution of the Albanians with contempt, following the example of his senior partner. Fiore reveals, in fact, that he and Gino's father had profited from concocting a similar scam in Nigeria two years earlier. The Italians are thus positioned by the film as belonging to the entrepreneurial class that participated in the widespread culture of scams and kickbacks culminating in the *Tangentopoli* crisis in the early 1990s.

The presence of the aged Sicilian functions as a ghostly reminder of Italy's past, particularly the poverty of the rural South that drove so many to emigrate to the Americas. Gino and Michele thus present contrasting embodiments of the southern Italian subject across a generational divide. The viewer observes on the one hand the unscrupulous young businessman with his fashionable sports clothes and expensive SUV and, on the other, the ragged old man who, despite his impaired mental state, is willing to earn the bread he eats with hard work and to share his scant resources with those around him. With these contrasting figures, the film juxtaposes the imagined integrity of a vanished peasant culture with the depravity of a new generation whose emergence in the age of neoliberal consumerism has erased historical memory and with it the capacity for accountability, solidarity, and compassion.

Two recurring images in *Lamerica* are shoes and bread, indicators of a minimal standard of subsistence in the West. While Gino and Fiore cynically promise to make shoes "for all Albanians," barefoot children roam the streets of a provincial town and almost kill Michele in an effort to steal his new shoes. In one instance in the film, the absence of shoes is linked visually to hunger, denoting the direst form of poverty. When an Albanian migrant dies, apparently of dehydration or starvation, while traveling with others on a crowded truck toward the harbor, there is a close-up of his bare feet after his body is placed on the flatbed. Accidentally brushing against the feet of the dead man, Gino recoils as if fearing contamination through contact with the Albanian's misfortune. Michele, however, responds differently. Dismayed by the youth's collapse, he produces a crust of bread in a vain attempt to revive him. This deranged intervention is depicted as an act of profound compassion.

Though materially impoverished, the Albanians constructed by the film have already been marked by their initial contact with consumer capitalism through access to Italian television, which was available in those parts of Albania closest to Italy during the final decades of communism. *Lamerica*'s critique of Italian television is repeatedly underscored. The youths encountered by Gino as they make their way to the harbor are avid viewers of Italian programming and have, as a result, learned to speak Italian. In a striking scene in a provincial tavern, Gino observes a group of men gathered to watch the Italian version of the American game show "The Price Is Right," broadcast on Italia I, one of the private television channels owned by Berlusconi. Emerging from the deprivations of communist-era austerity, the viewers are entranced by the alluring images transmitted from Italy, which they seem unable to decode with critical distance. The aspiring emigrants that Gino encounters on the road have been similarly fascinated by the seductive promises of television. For these men, Italy is a land of great abundance. They speak of the huge salaries commanded by soccer players, imagining that such wealth might also be within their grasp. Gino's attempt to disabuse them by telling them that the best they can hope for is to work as dishwashers provokes the inevitable response: "It's better to be a dishwasher in Italy than to starve in Albania."

Implicit in the film's commentary on the influence of Italian television in Albania is a critique of Italy's own infiltration by American mass culture. The forms of mass entertainment shown on Italian commercial channels were at the time mostly imitations of transatlantic television programming. Thus, just as Albanians are increasingly alienated from their own cultural realities through the appeal of Italian mass media, Italians have already succumbed to cultural models imported from the United States, which they now relay to Albanians. At the heart of these parallels and connections lies the film's pessimistic view of the effects of cultural globalization.

Lamerica suggests that Italy's capitulation to consumerism and global mass culture is accompanied by a crushing ignorance. Gino has no knowledge of history, is insensitive to cultural difference, and has no ambition other than to acquire wealth. In his many encounters with Albanians, he aggressively announces his Italian identity, expecting immediate deference. Though he admits to Michele that he comes from Sicily, he shows no awareness of the poverty that historically distinguished the island—and the South more generally—in the broader national landscape. Even as he begins to lose the external trappings that distinguish him from the Albanians around him, he continues to invoke the superiority supposedly guaranteed by his Italianness. Yet, when finally deprived of his passport, the only remaining object that proves his Italian difference, he makes no further claims of entitlement and, in fact, ceases to speak.

While Gino tries to resist becoming Albanian, *Lamerica*'s Albanians are eager to become Italian, or at least to pass as Italian. The film thus astutely demonstrates the paradoxes and contingencies of identity claims. Making their way toward the harbor in a crowded truck, the Albanian youths sing Toto Cotugno's popular hit song, "L'italiano," learned from Italian television, cheerfully asserting its refrain: "I am an Italian, a real Italian." One of these aspiring emigrants, a youth named Ismail, announces to Gino that when he settles in Italy, he will find an Italian wife and will speak to his children only in Italian so that his Albanian identity will finally be forgotten. The powerful desire of this young man to become Italian, to erase every trace of an Albanian self, suggests that the ideological influence exerted by the Italian media may have had an even more powerful symbolic impact than the Fascist occupation of Albania half a century earlier.

The exchange between Gino and Ismail also raises issues relating to Italian reproductivity and futurity.[23] The viewer is prompted to ask if Ismail will succeed in passing as Italian. Will he manage to erase his accent? Will his own child accept him as Italian? What would the consequences of such mimicry be for the wider host community? Although these questions do not become explicit, they inform other films featuring Italians and southeastern European migrants or refugees and suggest specific anxieties about the future of Italian identity in a decade that saw not only a major incursion of foreigners but also a drop in Italian birthrates.[24]

Lamerica demonstrates remarkable economy of affect for most of its duration. This restraint serves to heighten the emotional impact of the film's conclusion, which stages the unexpected reunion of Gino and Michele on board ship. The musical score by Franco Piersanti, used sparingly until now, dominates the scene, reinforcing the elegiac mood suggested by the narrative events. The instrumental theme that emerges here is a melancholy adaptation of a sequence from the popular wartime polka "Rosamunda," associated in previous scenes with Michele's fragmented retrieval of a youthful Italian identity.[25] In the final sequence, however, the melody emerges plaintively, in a slower tempo, investing the images of poverty on the visual track with a melancholic solemnity.

The scene begins as a large, rusty ship moves out toward the open sea. The image of this crowded vessel is reminiscent of news footage of the even more overcrowded Vlora, whose arrival in Bari in 1991 was relayed live to television audiences around Italy. Silhouetted against the sky, the ship is crammed beyond all reasonable limits with human cargo as passengers cling to the rails, mast, and rigging. In a closer shot of the deck, Gino emerges from the crowd—sullen and filthy. In contrast to the admiration he inspired in earlier scenes, he elicits no interest from his fellow passengers at this juncture since his once proudly asserted Italianness is no longer visibly inscribed on his person.

The reunion of Gino and Michele is a poignant reversal of their initial encounter in the labor camp, where the old man, his face blackened with soot, was intimidated and mute in the face of the imperious behavior of Gino and his partner. Now, by contrast, Gino is speechless and dirty, his face darkened by exposure to the sun, while Michele addresses him warmly, offering him bread. The general effect of the two men's appearance as they sit together on the deck, dressed in shabby, out-of-date clothing, is more evocative of the 1940s than the 1990s, suggesting that Gino has been forced to take a symbolic journey back in time to experience the destitution of his ancestors. Despite this dramatic leveling of circumstances, the film does not construct a facile rapprochement between the two men, nor does it suggest any redemptive gesture on Gino's part. The younger man remains mute to the end, offering little acknowledgment of the old man's kindness. In addition, despite his benevolence, Michele is still deranged. Believing that he is still twenty years old, he imagines that the ship is sailing not to Italy but to America. Yet the old man has intuitively understood that, for his fellow passengers, Italy has become what America once was for young Italians of an earlier generation.

As Michele gazes at a family on the deck nearby, the camera pans across the faces and bodies of parents and children, suturing the viewer into his empathetic gaze. Following the old man's glance, Gino also glances at the Albanians, perhaps seeing them anew. The shots that follow are close-ups of young people and children, looking away at first and then facing the camera. After a cut to two aerial shots of the deck with its undifferentiated mass of human cargo and a profile shot of Gino with Michele slumped against his shoulder, there are several additional close-ups of Albanian passengers—men, women, and children—looking straight at the lens until the final shot of a young Albanian, on whose radiant smile the screen fades to white.

As Constantin Parvulescu has pointed out, *Lamerica*'s dominant gaze shifts at strategic moments in the narration. Initially, the gaze belongs to Fiore, the imperious outsider, through whose perspective the shabby conditions of post–Cold War Albania are revealed.[26] When Gino takes leave of Fiore to search for the runaway Albanian Spiro (later identified as Michele), the gaze becomes his and remains his throughout the narration up to the film's concluding minutes. In scenes on board the migrant ship, the perspective is finally transferred to Michele's compassionate gaze. The visual perspective of the film thus remains tethered almost entirely to three subjective gazes—all of them Italian. Yet in the film's final moments, there is an unexpected shift, where the Albanians on board ship appear to gaze at the viewers directly, without the mediation of an onscreen character. It is tempting to read this concluding tableau as a positive assertion of Albanian subjectivity. Yet as Parvulescu points out, the migrants' faces are blank screens. Viewers may indeed choose to project their own fantasies onto these apparently hopeful gazes, but the scene reveals nothing of the specificity of these Albanian lives. At best, the scene can be construed as a generic call for compassion and humanitarian witnessing.

Apart from referencing the relatively recent events of 1991, the crowded ship at the conclusion of *Lamerica* clearly functions as the spectral double of the emigrant ships that carried millions of impoverished Italians to American shores generations earlier. Indeed the film's most compellingly affective impact develops through the emergence of Michele as a ghostly reminder of the cherished values of Italy's impoverished rural past. The identifications encouraged by the film are focused most intensely on this relic of peasant culture from the Italian South, with whom the young upstart Gino is negatively compared. *Lamerica* thus reveals a profound nostalgia for a vanished world whose humanity stands in stark contrast to the values of the globalized present. In this way, the film is ultimately less concerned with Albanian migrations than with the memory of Italy's past, exemplified in the figure of the aged Sicilian.

The appeal of the *Lamerica*'s humanitarian message is thus limited since its call for compassion and empathy is embedded in the implicit idealization of an archaic southern subjectivity, nostalgically evoked through the figure of Michele. In spite of these shortcomings, the film's representation of human encounters, temporal contrasts, and economic juxtapositions unsettles in a general way received notions of culture and identity, problematizing the terms "Italian" and "Albanian" as slippery, contingent categories rather than fixed attributes.

Although *Lamerica* was widely acclaimed by Italian and international critics and audiences at the time of its release, its ideological blind spots have become more apparent over the intervening years. The film's deployment of Albania as the setting for what is principally a meditation on contemporary Italy is essentially a gesture of symbolic appropriation.[27] Amelio readily admitted that his decision to set the film in Albania was not based on a specific concern for the country's predicament in the postcommunist era; rather—he claimed—it offered itself as a useful terrain on which to enact a symbolic juxtaposition of two Italies, that of the 1930s and that of the 1990s.[28] Within this scenario, the Albanian characters have a merely supportive function in what is a uniquely Italian story and the appropriation of Albanian landscapes and bodies to this end is an unintended replay of attitudes that subtended the Italian invasion of that country more than fifty years earlier.

Among the most noteworthy criticisms of *Lamerica* was the response of the distinguished Albanian novelist Ismail Kadaré, a longtime resident of France, who objected to what he perceived as a distortion of historical events, apparently referencing the statement made by an Albanian physician in the film about the imputed violence committed against Italian veterans left behind in Albania after the withdrawal of the Italian armed forces. Some Albanian viewers also objected to the film's portrayal of their compatriots as crude and uneducated and as infantile consumers of Italian television duped by impressions of Italy as a land of unparalleled wealth and opportunity.

Concerns about the images of Albanians propagated by *Lamerica* may have been justified to some extent. In fact, the film's representation of ragged men moving in packs through the countryside along with its iconic depiction of the battered ship packed with shabbily dressed migrants became part of a growing repertoire of representational tropes that found echo in a certain strain of Italian news reporting far from sympathetic to the presence of Albanians in Italy. Thus, despite the film's considerable aesthetic achievements, its representation of Albanian poverty and desperation unwittingly participated in a broader discursive process that served to freeze the image of the Albanian migrant into a figure of abjection. This shadowy figure gradually became a scapegoat upon which blame could be projected for the rise in crime in Italian cities. Indeed the image of an unstoppable tide of *extracomunitari* (as migrants from outside the European Economic Community were described) threatening to invade Italian territory played an important role in restructuring the national imaginary in the 1990s.

Drawing on Julia Kristeva's concept of abjection, Imogen Tyler has described how a rhetoric of abjection is repeatedly deployed to construct the image of the asylum seeker in contemporary Britain.[29] This rhetoric fulfills a precise function in the consolidation and definition of citizenship: "While we have become accustomed to thinking about the abject as that thing that disrupts or transgresses cultural values, abjection is primarily the means through which 'reality' ('way of life') is safeguarded (against the real) and reproduced. In other words, abjection describes the psychosocial processes through which hegemonic cultural values are reaffirmed."[30]

Citing Kristeva's axiom "the abject and abjection are my safeguards... primers of my culture," Tyler suggests how the discursive construction of the asylum seeker as an abject threat serves to shore up for the citizen a more secure sense of national belonging. In short, "as the abject thing, the asylum-seeker operates as something akin to a 'security blanket' for the citizen."[31] A similar construction of irregular migrants and asylum seekers can be discerned in Italian popular discourse and journalism in the early 1990s.

In *Non-persone*, an influential critique of Italian hostility toward immigrants first published in 1999, Alessandro Dal Lago argues that the surge in migration to Italy in the 1990s had provoked a process of anxious self-questioning in the host society. Although he does not invoke the term "abjection," he describes a phenomenon according to which the immigrants are discursively deprived of personhood and placed in symbolic opposition with the purported humanity of the citizen. Drawing on Dal Lago's analysis of the construction of immigration in Italian journalism, Derek Duncan has explored the configuration of Albanians in Italian cinema, arguing that the migrant's "perceived alterity . . . serves as a pole against which a singular national identity can be asserted." In other words, "the xenophobic representation of Albanians in the press is nation-building."[32] Although I agree with the general argument put forward by Dal Lago and Duncan, my point in this chapter is that the processes of polarization and "nervous self-questioning" that find expression in films about immigration from the 1990s onward often obtain their most complex articulation in representations of migrants and other foreigners who physically resemble Italians to a large extent.

Visions of the Migrant Ship: from *Aprile* to *L'italiano*

The Italian media's construction of the imputed "invasion" of abject Albanian migrants in 1991 has been recycled for various purposes in the years following the release of Amelio's film, particularly through the rescreening or reframing of news footage of the crowded cargo vessels that inspired *Lamerica*'s concluding sequence. The image of an overloaded migrant ship appears, for example, at the conclusion of the so-called Albanian episode in Nanni Moretti's self-ironizing state-of-the-nation documentary *Aprile* (1997), where it serves to comment on the filmmaker's own inability to articulate meaningful speech. This episode unfolds in the aftermath of a tragedy that occurred in March 1997, when an Italian patrol vessel collided with an Albanian boat heading for the coast of Puglia with more than a hundred irregular migrants on board. Although the precise number of victims is disputed, it is generally reported that eighty-one Albanians lost their lives, and thirty-four survived. Romano Prodi, Prime Minister of Italy during the center-left's brief term in power, had authorized the pushback mission just days earlier to prevent a new wave of migration resulting from the collapse of several major pyramid schemes in Albania.

Aprile does not concern itself directly with the tragedy. In fact, the episode appears to have been prompted by the filmmaker's anger at members of Prodi's government for failing to show up on the shores of Puglia to admit Italian responsibility for the disaster. The articulation of Moretti's protest, delivered in his typical, ironically self-deprecating style, deserves some scrutiny as it sharply avoids the broadly humanitarian call for compassion underpinning Amelio's portrayal of the earlier Albanian exodus. Nonetheless, in *Aprile* too, the Albanian characters—recently arrived migrants apparently playing themselves—serve merely as the foil against which the filmmaker articulates a message that is more intent on denouncing the shortcomings of contemporary Italian politics

Figure 1.3. Screen capture. Waiting for the Albanians. *Aprile* (1997)

and society than interested in exploring the experiences of Italy's new immigrants and asylum seekers.

The episode is divided into three short scenes. In the first of these, Nanni—the onscreen persona of the filmmaker himself—emerges with a small camera crew onto a windswept beach in Puglia and braces himself for the arrival of the next contingent of Albanians (which appears never to materialize). The scene is devoted entirely to his rant against Prodi's center-left parliamentary colleagues for their failure to show up at the scene. This performance of outraged protest resonates to some extent with the critique of the fractured state of the Italian Communist Party in Moretti's 1989 film *Palombella rossa*.

In the subsequent scene, shot indoors at a migrant reception center, the filmmaker (as Nanni) interviews a small group of Albanians and asks them which type of Italian government would be best suited to their needs, specifically inviting their opinion on the value of a left-leaning administration. Given their limited command of Italian and lack of familiarity with the Italian political scene, the Albanians struggle to answer, and their interviewer continues to interrupt their efforts to communicate by adding further comments or asking new questions. This brief encounter, laced with comic absurdity, highlights Nanni's insensitivity to the migrants' efforts to answer his questions and his lack of genuine interest in anything they might wish to communicate.

The narcissistic implications of Nanni's manic, self-defeating wordiness in his encounter with the Albanian migrants are counterbalanced by the somber articulation of the next and final scene of the episode. As the image cuts to an archival news clip showing a large migrant ship approaching an Italian harbor, the filmmaker's persona vanishes from sight. The astonishingly overcrowded vessel, with its undifferentiated mass of passengers, then slowly glides into port. Without prompting by voice-over narration, the spectator is invited to contemplate this extraordinary apparition for several seconds before the image is interrupted by a cut. The wordless, aporetic conclusion to the three-part "Albanian episode" seems to offer an acknowledgment of the filmmakers' own inability to confront the experience of the migrants while simultaneously refusing to elicit the viewer's empathy or identification.

More extensive use of archival material appears in Ennio De Dominicis's melodrama *L'italiano*, which begins with authentic RAI1 footage on the arrival of the Vlora in the harbor of Bari in August 1991 and ends with an excerpt from a Fascist newsreel from 1939, similar to the material deployed in the initial moments of *Lamerica*. In *L'italiano*, the report on the Vlora's arrival in Bari has a diegetic function as the event is being watched on a black-and-white television screen in an Albanian home by the family of the film's protagonist, Giorgio (the "Italian" of the film's title), known to be a passenger on the crowded ship. This domestic scene is intercut with images of Giorgio being captured by the police in Bari and dragged to the local stadium, presumably for detention with other Albanian migrants.

Despite its uneven mixture of genre conventions and implausible plot twists, *L'italiano* offers an intriguing sequel to Amelio's film, reintroducing the memory of the Italian occupation of Albania as the backstory for Giorgio's voyage to Italy. Believing himself to be the grandson of an Italian soldier who participated in the Fascist occupation, the young Albanian travels to Italy purportedly to track down his grandfather in a remote mountain village in Abruzzo. Like *Lamerica*, to which it refers intertextually, *L'italiano* weaves parallels between past and present, Italy and Albania, but its focus on the experience of the Albanian protagonist Giorgio and his doomed involvement in a romantic relationship with an Italian woman brings a very different affective dimension to this story of trans-Adriatic mobility and displacement. The film conjures up a rather familiar plot in which the mostly sympathetic migrant, played by Turkish actor Mehmet Günsür, emerges as both victim and criminal, suggesting that his descent into a life of crime, specifically sex trafficking, is prompted by the desperation of his pariah status as an irregular immigrant.[33]

Significantly, the film experiments with the fantasy voiced by an aspiring migrant in *Lamerica* that once he arrives in Italy, he will manage to blend into Italian society by entering into a relationship with an Italian woman, producing an Italian child with her, and burying all traces of his previous self. Although Giorgio claims to be Italian from the start, when he arrives at his ancestral village in Abruzzo, he finds that his putative grandfather has died. With no way to

Figure 1.4. Screen capture. Giorgio, the Italian Albanian. *L'italiano* (2002)

prove his lineage, his claims to Italianness make little sense to those he meets along the way.

Giorgio's outsider status, however, presents no real obstacle to his presence in Italy at first as he proves to be a hard worker and thus blends easily into the economy of the mountain village. His real troubles begin when he attracts the sexual interest of a local woman who is already being courted unsuccessfully by one of Giorgio's friends in the village, a young man named Silvestro (Luca Lionello). Their brief but passionate love affair—which the viewer later learns has led to a pregnancy—provokes the jealous rage of the Italian Silvestro and, in a fight between the two men, Giorgio accidentally stabs his rival to death. For this he is imprisoned and eventually deported.

Giorgio's ensuing criminal record blocks his access to legal employment in Italy and prompts his participation in a transnational network of organized crime, which, in turn, leads to his death years later at the hands of a Russian gangster. Although the film takes pains to suggest that Giorgio's initial act of violence was triggered by a spontaneous attempt at self-defense and that his subsequent participation in the world of crime was motivated by the needs of economic survival, the narrative simultaneously punishes him for proving to be superior to his Italian rival in attractiveness and sexual potency. Reunited by chance with his lost love in Rome years after their forced separation, Giorgio learns that she had conceived his child but subsequently suffered a miscarriage. The films ends with a note of melodramatic retribution that seems to strike a cautionary note vis-à-vis transnational romance: shortly after Giorgio succeeds in rekindling his relationship with this woman, he is hunted down and killed by his criminal associates for an unpaid debt and she becomes a helpless witness to his violent death. With the Albanian protagonist positioned at the center of an affecting tale of loss that elicits the viewer's sympathy, the trope of "too lateness" typical of melodrama is clearly being played out. Yet the film also suggests that the migrant's terrible destiny was set in motion by his own unruly attempt to assimilate into Italian society through sexual relations and reproduction with an Italian woman.

Derek Duncan has argued that cinematic stories of male immigration to Italy over a period spanning about fifteen years are "emphatically unreproductive" insofar as the sexual relations attempted between migrant men and Italian women are bound to fail and do not produce offspring.[34] Although Duncan does not discuss the central relationship in *L'italiano* in detail, it appears to conform to this pattern but in a more complex way than other films. In fact, Giorgio's romance holds out the very possibility that other migrant stories disavow as his Italian partner actually conceives a child. The promise of reproduction is overturned, however, with the intervention of a miscarriage. In this way, the narrative punishes both the Italian woman who loved the Albanian and the Albanian himself, who dared to manifest superior sexual potency vis-à-vis his Italian male counterpart.

The image of the Albanian migrant congealed in Italian public discourses of the 1990s into the iconic figure of the untrustworthy, outlawed *clandestino*, whose irregular status became constitutive of a racialized identity and signaled exclusion from the Italian national community. Such identities are constructed on the repeated insistence on a particular form of bodily presence. Indeed, the visual construction of the figure of the socially marginalized body of the Albanian male, both in *Lamerica* and in media reports in the 1990s, resonates with Giorgio Agamben's notion of "bare life," as various commentators on Amelio's film have already noted.[35]

In *Homo Sacer*, the Italian philosopher based his formulation of bare life on the ancient Roman figure of the *homo sacer* (sacred man), an outlaw banished from the polis, in order to expand on Foucault's theory of biopower. Drawing a distinction between "bios" (politicized agency) and "zoe" (unpoliticized existence), Agamben shows how the processes of excluding particular groups of people from political entitlement facilitate the construction of a governable form of life. As a figure of bare life, however, the "homo sacer" is not simply forever banished or cast out. Rather, bare life is perpetually constructed in relation to the norm, for it is through the exclusion of depoliticized forms of life that the politicized norm—exemplified in the category of the citizen—can exist. In other words, when set against the figure of the outcast, the figure of the citizen with his rights and privileges can come into view.

In this way, the citizen can be seen as belonging to the category of the sovereign and the migrant to that of the banished, oppressed, or defeated.[36] As Agamben elaborates in *Means without End*, one form of life (that of the People) prevails over other forms of life (people). Identified as belonging to the People, the citizen's access to the rights of the nation-state is thus forged at the implicit expense of others. For Agamben, "the concept of people always already contains within itself the fundamental biopolitical fracture. It is what cannot be included in the whole of which it is a part as well as what cannot belong to the whole in which it is always already included."[37] Indeed, in films about immigration in the immediate post–Cold War period, it is through the audiovisual construction of "other" (non-Italian) abject white bodies from the Balkans that perceptions of the "fundamental biopolitical fracture"—the creation of exclusive inclusion—on Italian soil are symbolically held in abeyance.

Italy and the Balkan Wars

Several films and miniseries produced in Italy since the late 1990s are set against a backdrop of the conflicts that accompanied the breakup of the former Yugoslavia. Most of these unfold in Bosnia-Herzegovina, two take place in Kosovo, and all were produced years after the conflicts to which they refer. They frame the Yugoslav wars of secession in a decisively Italian way as all of them feature an Italian protagonist through whose point of view the narrative unfolds. Maurizio Zaccaro's *Il carniere* (The Game Bag, 1997), Ferdinando Vicentini Orgnani's *Mare largo* (Open Sea, 1997), Rolando Colla's *Oltre il confine* (Beyond the Border, 2002), Giancarlo Bocchi's *Nema problema* (No Problem, 2002), Alessandro Valori's *Radio West* (2002), Vincenzo Marra's *Vento di terra* (Wind from the Land, 2004), and Sergio Castellitto's *Venuto al mondo* (*Twice Born*, 2011) are, in fact, structured around the experiences of an Italian character or group of characters venturing into the territories of the former Yugoslavia in wartime. Focusing on the traumatic encounters that ensue, these narratives do not attempt to explore the political complexity of the conflict itself but remain focused on the Italian characters and their reactions to the surrounding scene. In this way, they exemplify Italian cinema's reworking of popular projections about the Balkans in the symbolic process of national redefinition through the production of white alterity.

All of these films prompt questions about the appropriation of the conflicts in southeastern Europe for the articulation of distinctively Italian stories, wherein the traumatic setting usually serves as a dramatic pretext for action adventure stories. I am especially interested in examining the discourses of gender, whiteness, and nation that underpin these narratives and will ask which (Italian) investments might be served by projecting these preoccupations onto a "Balkan" setting. The escalation of violence in Yugoslavia in the early 1990s first registered in the Italian media as a cluster of divergent concerns, featuring most notably an anxiety about an increasing flow of immigrants and refugees from the war-torn territories across the Adriatic. Furthermore, as tensions mounted in Bosnia, the barrage of Italian media coverage on the violent conflict taking place there did little to attenuate deeply ingrained attitudes toward the Balkans as a locus of endemic violence and incomprehensible ethnic strife.

Since the 1990s many scholars have drawn attention to the overdetermined character of representations of southeastern Europe in literature, political discourse, and media reports, noting that the stereotypes that characterize these constructions do not emerge from any "truths" inherent in the historical experience of the population of that region. Instead, like Orientalism—the discursive phenomenon theorized by Edward Said—they are phantasmatic projections that have their source elsewhere. In her groundbreaking analysis of Balkanist discourse, *Imagining the Balkans*, Maria Todorova has observed that the imaginary construct of "the Balkans" has absorbed several ideological and cultural tensions that stem from contradictions experienced in other parts of Europe and, more generally, the West.[38] For Todorova, southeastern Europe has long served as a liminal space that contains a repository of negative characteristics against which a positive image of the "European" and the "West" can be built. Yet, unlike Orientalism, to which it is in many ways comparable, Balkanism is a phenomenon of imputed ambiguity rather than imputed difference.[39] Pointing to the liminal character of southeastern Europe, Todorova suggests that it is precisely this in-between-ness that prevents the rest of Europe from imagining the Balkans as purely other to itself.

Along similar lines, Slavoj Žižek has criticized the phantasmatic constructions of the former Yugoslavia that proliferated in mainstream political discourse in the post–Cold War era and particularly in representations of the conflicts that accompanied the breakup of Yugoslavia. In 1993, he argued that contemporary characterizations of the Balkans as the locus of irrational ethnic struggles served mainly to disavow the West's historical collusion in the very circumstances it purported to abhor.[40] Roundly refuting stereotypes of tribal barbarism, Žižek argued that despite the Western media's construction of the Balkans as a "madhouse of thriving nationalisms where rational rules of behavior are suspended," the motives driving all political agents in the former Yugoslavia, however reprehensible they might be, were in fact fully rational in light of the goals each of them sought to achieve.[41] The only irrational factor in the picture, he claimed, was the perspective (or "gaze") of the West itself, which persisted in "babbling on about archaic ethnic passions."[42]

The violence visualized in Italian films set against a backdrop of the Yugoslav wars of secession is never explained in these narratives. Instead the films rely on the viewers' extratextual capacity to apprehend the events unfolding in the background as the inevitable outcome of "ethnic passions." Thus the different ethnic factions participating in the conflict are almost never designated by name. *Il carniere* (Maurizio Zaccaro, 1997), for example, is an action adventure film about three Italians who travel to the forests of Bosnia on a hunting expedition in the autumn of 1991, only to find themselves caught in crossfire when armed conflict inexplicably breaks out in the surrounding countryside. Perceived through the perspective of these uncomprehending outsiders, who cannot grasp the logic of the events taking place around them and whose driving motive is to escape alive, *Il carniere* is essentially a tale of danger and survival focused entirely on the Italian characters. A similar pattern emerges in *Mare largo*, also an action-adventure film, set in 1993, in which a former naval officer from the north of Italy accepts an assignment to smuggle cargo to the former Yugoslavia. The shipment entrusted to him turns out to contain weapons, and he becomes unwittingly embroiled in the war upon his arrival in the Balkan territories. Diverging from the narrative trajectory of *Il carniere*, in which there are no heroes, this film calls for the heroic death of the Italian protagonist as he attempts to save a distressed local woman from the militia intent on killing her. No effort is made to enlighten the film's viewers on the complexities of the conflict in which the Italian becomes embroiled. We are encouraged instead to appreciate his moral growth as he progresses from a state of existential confusion to a full embrace of heroism, with a beleaguered Slavic woman providing the ground on which his heroic actions are enabled.

Colla's *Oltre il confine*, an Italian-Swiss coproduction, takes a different turn. Presenting itself as the story of a professional middle-aged Italian woman named Agnese (Anna Galiena) who ventures into the war-ravaged territories of the former Yugoslavia in 1993 to rescue a Bosnian child, the film is part road movie and part melodrama. Agnese's journey of rescue is propelled at least in part by a desire to make sense of her difficult relationship with her recently deceased father, an Italian veteran of World War II who lost his sanity and was permanently hospitalized after his return from a Russian prison camp. Her journey is thus construed as an attempt to understand the effects of war on the human psyche. Before she departs, however, she begins an affair with the child's father, Reuf (Senad Bašić), a Bosnian refugee who befriended her own father during his final days alive. The film subsequently pursues two different narrative threads— Agnese's difficult journey into Bosnian territory and Reuf's fruitless escape to Switzerland to avoid deportation by the Italian authorities.

Oltre il confine is one of the few Italian films to acknowledge the circumstances of contemporary refugees whose access to safety can be thwarted by bureaucratic obstacles and police brutality that conspire to send them back to the horrors they have barely managed to escape. Indeed Reuf receives little sympathy from either the Italian or the Swiss authorities, and the scenes of his arrest and mistreatment at the hands of the Swiss police offer a compelling mise-en-scene of the dilemmas confronting refugees and asylum seekers caught in liminal legal status. Yet the film provides this character with minimal narrative development. Although there is a brief flashback to his earlier incarceration in a Bosnian concentration camp and there are indications of a betrayal by his wife, he emerges as an enigmatic and not entirely sympathetic figure. *Oltre il confine* is effectively an Italian story, more concerned with the existential trajectory of the Italian Agnese than with the difficulties experienced by those she meets along the way. In this scenario, her interactions with the non-Italian characters—including the rescued child and, at a different moment, the child's father—are merely stepping stones on her path toward self-understanding and self-acceptance. Yet despite the film's uneven character development and occasionally overwrought dialogue, it successfully communicates the effects of wartime violence, torture, and clandestine detention, weaving parallels between the experiences of survivors of different wars in different historical contexts.

The implicit acceptance on the part of Italian filmmakers of the discourse of "incomprehensible" Balkan barbarism has a distinctive irony, given Italy's own military actions across a swath of the Balkan Peninsula during the 1940s. Memories of the Italian invasion, occupation, or annexation of a substantial part of southeastern Europe during World War II were largely repressed during the Cold War era. Recent studies have nonetheless begun to unsettle this collective amnesia. Foremost among these is Davide Rodogno's extensive research on the scope and severity of Italian military actions in Slovenia, Croatia, Dalmatia, Montenegro, Kosovo, Western Macedonia, parts of Bosnia and Herzegovina, much of mainland Greece, and several Greek islands between 1941 and 1944.[43] Describing Mussolini's efforts to subordinate the conquered regions, Rodogno provides abundant details of the economic exploitation and forced "Italianization" of the annexed lands.[44] In light of the repressed history of Italian abuses committed on Balkan territories by Italian soldiers in the 1940s, one might characterize the "Balkanist" discourses in the Italian representations of the conflicts in the former Yugoslavia as a gesture of unconscious displacement. In other words, it is the spectral power of the unspeakable Fascist past that gives particular troubling force to these images of contemporary, "incomprehensible" Balkan violence.

In sharp contrast to the films discussed above, Mario Martone's *Teatro di guerra* (1998) foregrounds the contingency of all national, regional, or local identities while drawing parallels between the city of Sarajevo under siege and the city of Naples in a time of purported peace. Set in 1994 at the height of the Sarajevo siege, the action takes place entirely in Naples, where the members of a small experimental theater group are rehearsing a production of Aeschylus's tragedy *Seven against Thebes,* which they intend to bring to Sarajevo as a gesture of solidarity with the people of the besieged city. Although the troupe completes preparations for the play against considerable odds, circumstances in Bosnia ultimately make their journey to Sarajevo impossible.

Shifting back and forth between the story world of *Seven against Thebes* and the contemporary Neapolitan location where the play is being rehearsed, *Teatro di guerra* draws on a range of performative registers to invite identification with the suffering citizens of Sarajevo. Shot mainly in the Quartieri Spagnoli, one of the most violent neighborhoods in the center of Naples, the film also draws attention to the perilous enterprise of mounting an independent theatrical production in a run-down urban setting without the support of subsidies routinely available to the state-sponsored theater. Within the film's complex signifying system, then, the battle presented in the text of the Greek playwright evokes not only the bloodshed occurring in Sarajevo but also the struggle of the Neapolitan troupe attempting to rehearse the play while caught in the crossfire of gangland violence. In a more general sense, the "theater of war" applies to the entire city of Naples, the scene of endemic crime and internecine violence.

Martone's decision not to visualize the war in Bosnia-Herzegovina has, in fact, a specific civic and ethical dimension, outlined in a diary-essay published after the film's production.[45] Dismayed at the passivity of western governments in the face of the bloodshed in Sarajevo, and particularly struck by the indifference of Italians located a short distance from the region, he created the film as an effort to reflect upon the cataclysmic upheavals that had accompanied the dissolution of Yugoslavia. Realizing at the same time that Western television audiences had been regularly assaulted, throughout the siege, with a relentless procession of violent images, he decided not to present Sarajevo in direct visual terms. Indeed the only concrete element of the besieged city that is visualized in the mise-en-scene of *Teatro di guerra* is a small piece of rubble from the destroyed Library of Sarajevo, sent to the film's main character by a Bosnian friend, who in turn presents it to a Bosnian librarian living in Naples. This element, too, draws a subtle connection between the two cities: while both Naples and Sarajevo are known at present (that is, in the present tense of the film's diegesis) as sites of chaos and destruction, these cities also have a less widely acknowledged dimension as sites of cultural production and consumption, that is, as centers of learning, literature, and the performing arts.

Far from peaceful even in peacetime, Naples stands in for Sarajevo in Martone's film, just as the ancient city evoked in the performances of Aeschylus's tragedy stands in both for Sarajevo and Naples itself. Enacting the legend of the seven heroes who warred with Eteocles over his refusal to share the Theban throne with his brother Polynices after the exile of their father, Oedipus, *Seven against Thebes* has clear symbolic resonances with the situation in the former Yugoslavia decades after the death of the "father," Marshal Josip Broz Tito.

Figure 1.5. Screen capture. A gift of rubble from the Sarajevo Library. *Teatro di guerra* (1998)

Similarly, its narrative of internecine struggle is shown to have specific meaning for the inhabitants of Naples today, a population caught between warring Camorra clans and their struggle for territorial dominance. Working through allegory and symbol, however, *Teatro di guerra* appeals more to mythology than to history, risking the erasure of all differences between and among the cities it evokes and attenuating the parallels between the effects of Balkanist discourse and those of anti-southern prejudice in Italy.

In sharp contrast with *Teatro di guerra* is Sergio Castellitto's 2012 dramatic feature *Venuto al mondo*, a comfortably budgeted, skillfully shot film coproduced by Italy, Spain, and Croatia that foregrounds the star performances of its two internationally known leads—Penelope Cruz and Emile Hirsch. Adapting a novel of the same title by Margaret Mazzantini, wife of the director, Castellitto and Mazzantini wrote the screenplay together.[46] With no trace of the representational restraint and self-reflexivity of Martone's film, several scenes in *Venuto al mondo* graphically re-envision the devastation of the Sarajevo siege. The Bosnian conflict provides the backdrop for much of the personal drama of the Italian protagonist, Gemma (Cruz), who remains in Sarajevo as the violence escalates in order to be close to her young husband, an American photographer named Diego (Hirsch). The film begins, however, in Rome in the present as Gemma, the mother of sixteen-year old Pietro (Pietro Castellitto), decides to travel back to Sarajevo with her son to attend an exhibition of siege-era photographs that include images by the long-dead Diego, Pietro's assumed father. It is their first visit to the Bosnian capital since the boy's birth in the city during the first year of the historic siege. As Gemma's memories of her experiences during that period are activated through the voyage of return, a series of flashbacks enables the viewer to unravel parts of her complex story.

The flashbacks in *Venuto al mondo* are not presented in chronological order, nor are they focalized from a single subjective point of view. Instead, they disclose the events of the past in selective fashion, withholding the most crucial revelation until the final minutes of the film. In other words, the overall narrative structure and delayed revelation bring this project closer to the conventions of popular melodrama than to those of art cinema.

Venuto al mondo is part wartime romance, part maternal melodrama, and part paternity mystery. It nonetheless aspires to that mode of filmmaking that Rosalind Galt calls the "popular art film," which, as Galt shows, "draw[s] from popular genres but circulate[s] nationally and internationally as prestige productions linked to the institutions of art cinema."[47] The negotiation of commercial and art-cinematic forms that characterizes popular art films gives them unique access to the international market. What makes this type of production distinct from middlebrow films, however, is the fact that it is "at once more *debased* in its melodramatic pleasures and more closely aligned to the international circuits of contemporary art cinema than the solidly national middlebrow."[48]

Venuto al mondo, which was first screened at the Toronto Film Festival in 2012 and then released internationally, is the most widely distributed film in the cluster of Italian dramatic features about the Balkan conflicts. Initial responses by reviewers in North America upon its release show that it was perceived to have overstepped the mark of good taste. *Variety* characterized it as a "luridly plotted melodrama" and *Hollywood Reporter* as "preposterously overwrought and overlong."[49] While various comparisons were made with other, high-profile romances set against the background of war and devastation, including *Sophie's Choice* (Alan J. Pakula, 1982) and *The English Patient* (Anthony Minghella, 1996), the ultimate critical view was that *Venuto al mondo* was as pointless as it was emotionally excessive. Discussing the film in *The Village Voice*, Zachary Wigon argues that it "irresponsibly appropriates the horrific siege of Sarajevo to serve as aesthetic backdrop for a story that exhibits no real interest in the conflict."[50]

Wigon's dismissal provides a useful point of entry as it appears to ignore one of the core elements of the narrative, found not in the story of Gemma's romance with the apparently irrepressible man-child Diego but rather in that of a secondary character, a Bosnian woman named Aska (Saadet Aksoy). This character provides not only the third term in the fateful triangle constructed by Gemma and her young American husband but also the key to the film's discourse on biopolitics. In its articulation of the story of Aska, who has relatively little screen time, *Venuto al mondo* does in fact engage with the meanings and effects of war and with the hidden legacies that war bequeaths to survivors and the generations

Figure 1.6. Screen capture. Destruction in Sarajevo. *Venuto al mondo* (2012)

that follow. It achieves this through its intermittent focus on discourses of the body, or on human bodies as bare life.

Agamben's formulation of bare life refers to a state of being when a body's social legibility is disrupted, divested of its human characteristics by the domain of power and apprehended as purely organic existence.[51] It is clear, however, that not all bodies are constituted as "bare" in equal measure. Bodies may in fact be manipulated and/or cast out to greater or lesser degrees by agencies of power.

In an astute study of the cinematic representation of the post–Cold War emergence of Eastern European women in various labor markets in Western Europe—from childcare to elder care, from sex work to coerced sex trafficking, from gestational surrogacy to mail order marriages—Anca Parvulescu claims that Eastern European women's liminal status as white but not quite white enough enables them to be consumed in specific ways as commodities of exchange.[52] Drawing on the work of Levi Strauss, Foucault, Agamben, and second-wave feminists, she describes as the "traffic in women's work" those forms of labor falling on a continuum of affective or reproductive work that, during the 1990s, were predominantly performed by migrant women without adequate working permits, and most often by Eastern European migrants, in Western Europe. What these women present, according to Parvulescu, is the biopolitical potential of bare life.

In *Venuto al mondo*, Aska's biopolitical functionality and disposability become evident in two different situations. In the first instance her body, as that of an apparently "white" Eastern European woman, is mobilized contractually for the task of conceiving a child with Diego. Organized by Diego's infertile Italian wife, Gemma, this arrangement includes a plan to register the baby at birth as Gemma's child, thus erasing the reality of Aska's participation in the process once her body has yielded the desired result. Before the planned conception can take place, however, Aska's body, now apprehended as that of a Bosnian Muslim

Figure 1.7. Screen capture. Gemma observes Aska's scar. *Venuto al mondo* (2012)

woman, is brutally raped and scarred by members of the Bosnian-Serb militia, bent on a genocidal project. After the delivery of the child conceived from this rape, Aska allows Gemma to take the infant without revealing the truth of its conception. Having witnessed the rape firsthand, Diego is fully aware of the child's genetic origins but chooses to allow his wife to believe that this is, in fact, his own son. When the infant is registered by the Bosnian doctor as the child of Diego and Gemma, he becomes Italian and first shows up in *Venuto al mondo* as the innocuous sixteen-year old Pietro, dragged unwillingly to Sarajevo to attend an exhibition of photographs by the long-deceased Diego.

The film's biopolitical subtext is encoded in an early scene that unfolds at the photographic exhibition following the arrival of Gemma and Pietro in Sarajevo in the present tense of the narrative. Visiting the photo exhibition, mother and son encounter an enigmatic image attributed to Diego, which the viewer perceives as that of a crudely designed flower inscribed on an oddly textured surface. It is only in the film's final sequence, in the course of an extended flashback, that the meaning of this image becomes legible to Gemma and to the viewer when it is confirmed that the background texture captured in the photograph is human skin. More precisely, the photograph shows the nape of Aska's neck, scarred by her rapist's lighted cigarette and subsequently embellished with a tattoo. Despite its violent connotations, the image is at the moment of its apprehension associated with endurance, care, and survival. The film ultimately reveals, in fact, that Aska recovered from the trauma she had experienced thanks to the careful ministrations of Diego, who purchased her release from a Bosnian-Serb prison (presumably the notorious concentration camp at Omarska) and later inscribed a tattoo around her scar, turning a wound into a flower. Like the film itself, the tattoo is an instrument that alternately reveals and conceals knowledge, the knowledge of genetic origins.

The revelation of the scar and its meaning occurs in *Venuto al mondo*'s final sequence, where Gemma is reintroduced to Aska and finally learns the facts of Pietro's conception, which had been concealed from her by her long-deceased husband. The film implicitly suggests that Diego's decision to claim the child as his own may have been motivated by a sense of shame for his powerlessness at the scene of Aska's rape, resulting in a desire to alleviate her from the responsibility of raising the child conceived through violent assault. The circumstances surrounding his decision are revealed in a flashback occurring in the final moments of the film, which shows the interruption by Bosnian-Serb militia of the sexual encounter between Aska and Diego arranged for the express purpose of procreating the child ardently desired by the infertile Gemma. The scene also visualizes Diego's covert witnessing of the gang rape and his subsequently successful effort to purchase her freedom.

However preoccupied with Gemma's romantic obsession with Diego, *Venuto al mondo* is ultimately about the capacity of the body's surface to hide the genetic history that lies beneath it. The boy who believes himself to be the son of an Italian woman and a deceased American is in reality the offspring of a Bosnian Muslim woman and a Bosnian-Serb militiaman who participated in a gang rape. Pietro's innocuous teenage body thus serves in the film as a nexus for the articulation of intersecting discourses on public and private history, identity and embodiment, and national belonging and foreignness.

The drama of recognition in traditional melodrama, as Carla Marcantonio describes the genre in her recent study on contemporary global melodrama, is imbricated in tropes of virtue occluded, persecuted, but finally revealed and acknowledged by the story's end.[53] *Venuto al mondo*, like many other recent melodramas that Marcantonio examines in her groundbreaking volume, does not entirely uphold such binary resolutions. Although the discovery of Diego's self-sacrificing generosity to Aska does in fact redeem his character posthumously in the eyes of the viewer, this knowledge serves no one within the diegesis except Gemma. Despite the revelation to Gemma of the sinister circumstances of Pietro's conception and his secret genetic history, the information is withheld from the boy himself so that there is no moment of recognition or discovery on his part.

The film obliquely raises important questions that it does not fully address, gesturing toward the possibilities of imagining family and community on a more inclusive or ecumenical scale than national and genetic identifications customarily allow, of embracing identities that span the confines of the nation-state and ethno-religious divisions, and of transcending historical wounds. These unvoiced questions are the most interesting and provocative issues implicit in this stylistically uneven film, particularly at the time when a generation of children conceived through genocidally motivated rapes committed during the years of ethnic cleansing are coming of age in the real world, with or without the knowledge of their genetic origins.

Gemma's apparent decision not to tell her son about his genetic history could perhaps be read as a positive assertion of the irrelevance of such histories to issues of national or familial belonging. In fact, throughout the film, Pietro shows little interest in the long-dead American photographer purported to be his father, having cemented a filial relationship with Gemma's Italian husband (Sergio Castellitto), who has cared for him almost since birth.[54] His occluded access to the truth about his genetic lineage is not construed by the film as a deprivation. In fact, it appears that Gemma will also continue to conceal from her son that she herself is not his biological mother, even after he comes face to face with Aska, the woman who brought him into the world.

Venuto al mondo's central paternity mystery, resolved for the viewer at the film's end, is of course linked to the fraught issue of Italian identity, raising a question that haunts many recent films about migration to Italy: namely, who is Italian, and who is not? While bereft of any genetic ties to the Italian parents who raised him, Pietro nonetheless "passes," both for his diegetic interlocutors and the film's viewers, as a typical Roman teenager, marked by the external trappings of his social class. With or without the knowledge of his biological origins, he will continue to pass as Italian, mostly because he shares with other Italians the attributes of urban, middle-class *Italian* whiteness, whose construction is secured by the sartorial choices of his generational cohort. Indeed whiteness, as this and other recent Italian films set in the Balkans suggest, is a more elusive and malleable characteristic than its seemingly easy legibility might suggest.

Conclusion

All of the films discussed in this chapter refer more or less explicitly to Italy's affinities or shared histories—of military occupation, violent conflicts, mobility, or migration—with populations to the east and to the uncanny corporeal similarities that link people across national boundaries. Although only three of the films address contemporary immigration directly (Amelio's *Lamerica*, De Dominicis's *L'italiano*, and Moretti's *Aprile*), the questions central to all of them point to the anxieties provoked by the onset of mass migration from the Eastern bloc at the end of the Cold War. These anxieties were prompted by the necessity for Italians to accommodate newcomers who, though experienced as foreign, were not, on the level of appearance, substantially different from themselves, often triggering reactions that tapped into racialized perceptions of southern Italians in earlier times. The tensions associated with the need to accommodate Albanian and other Eastern European migrants after the end of the Cold War find particular resonance in films that offer configurations of Italian encounters with the landscapes and populations of the Balkans. The history of Italian military conquest and occupation of areas of southeastern Europe during the Fascist period is raised directly in two of these films, *Lamerica* and *L'italiano*, which point in different ways to Italy's contemporary postcolonial status and to a collective failure to acknowledge the country's colonial-era entanglement with its European neighbors.

Linked to the depiction of trans-Adriatic mobilities in most films discussed here are traces of the discourses of national or regional superiority that were first mobilized in Italy in the post-Unification period and continue to find expression today as Italian whiteness is anxiously interrogated or reasserted. The binary oppositions of white/nonwhite and Italian/non-Italian also intersect in this body of films with other axes of difference such as gender, sexuality, and social class. Although they differ substantially from each other in terms of artistic ambition, thematic emphases, and production history, the films share a preoccupation with issues of national belonging, gender construction, biopolitics, and the reproduction of whiteness. In examining the articulation of identities in this corpus, I have also indicated a persistent anxiety vis-à-vis the future of the national subject in an age of global migrations, which emerges in a small number of these films through the themes of compromised paternity and precarious fertility.

Notes

1. The scandal known as *Tangentopoli* (roughly translated as "Kickback City") began in February 1992 with the arrest of Mario Chiesa, a politician affiliated with the Italian Socialist Party, on charges of bribery. When Chiesa decided to become a whistleblower, a vast system of corruption was exposed across a broad swath of the political spectrum. The events that unfolded from Chiesa's actions are usually described as *Mani pulite* (Operation Clean Hands), though this term is often conflated with *Tangentopoli*. The "First Republic" is the term adopted retrospectively to describe the period between Italy's inauguration as a constitutional republic in 1946 and the reconfiguration of political power that occurred when two of the major parties that had dominated Italian politics throughout the Cold War collapsed in the early 1990s.

2. For an early analysis of Italian reporting on Albanian immigration, see Adrian Vehbiu and Rando Devole, *La scoperta dell'Albania. Gli albanesi secondo i mass-media* (Milan: Paoline, 1996). For a broader examination of the status of Albanian immigrants in Italian society and media, see Russell King and Nicola Mai, "Italophilia Meets Albanophobia: Paradoxes of Asymmetric Assimilation and Identity Processes among Albanian Immigrants in Italy," *Ethnic and Racial Studies* 32, no. 1 (2008): 117–38.

3. See, for example, Lucia Re, "Italians and the Invention of Race: The Poetics and Politics of Difference in the Struggle over Libya, 1890–1913," *California Italian Studies Journal* 1, no. 1 (2010): 1–58, http://escholarship.org/uc/item/96k3w5kn. Re's article examines the discursive construction of race and racism at the outset of Italy's colonial project. For a consideration of the formation of Italian racism in connection with emigration as well as discourses of the South, see Pasquale Verdicchio, *Bound by Distance: Rethinking Italian Nationalism through*

the Italian Diaspora (Cranbury: Fairleigh Dickinson University Press, 1997). For a different, biopolitical account of the racial discourses at the heart of Italy's national formation, with an emphasis on the "life enhancing" underpinnings of its construction of "stock," or race, see Rhiannon Noel Welch, *Vital Subjects: Race and Biopolitics in Italy, 1860–1920* (Liverpool: Liverpool University Press, 2016).

4. Antonio Gramsci, *The Southern Question*, trans. Pasquale Verdicchio (Toronto: Guernica Editions, 2006).

5. Alfredo Niceforo, *Italiani del nord e italiani del sud* (Turin, IT: Bocca, 1901).

6. Sandro Mezzadra, "The New European Migratory Regime and the Shifting Patterns of Contemporary Racism," in *Postcolonial Italy: Challenging National Homogeneity*, ed. Cristina Lombardi-Diop and Caterina Romeo (New York: Palgrave Macmillan, 2013), 41. Mezzadra's consideration of contemporary Italian racism and its complex inscription within the larger history of Italian emigration draws in part on Jennifer Guglielmo and Salvatore Salerno, eds., *Are Italians White?: How Race Is Made in America* (London: Routledge, 2003).

7. See Clive Webb, "The Lynching of Sicilian Immigrants in the American South, 1886 to 1910," *American Nineteenth Century History* 3, no. 1 (2002): 45–76.

8. Anna Curcio and Miguel Mellino, "La razza al lavoro. Rileggere il razzismo, ripensare l'antirazzismo in Italia," in *La razza al lavoro*, ed. Anna Curcio and Miguel Mellino (Rome: Manifestolibri, 2012), 7–36. See also Miguel Mellino, *Cittadinanze postcoloniali. Appartenenze, razza e razzismo in Europa e in Italia* (Rome: Carocci, 2012).

9. Curcio and Mellino, "La razza al lavoro," 8.

10. Curcio and Mellino, 13.

11. The early tendency among Lega sympathizers to proclaim a self-styled "Celtic" identity could be read as a performative strategy designed to inscribe northern Italy's "racial" and "cultural" distance from the Mediterranean identity attributed to both southern Italians and many of Italy's new immigrants. In subsequent years, while remaining resolutely opposed to immigration, Lega Nord sought to expand its national influence and thus strategically attenuated its anti-southern bias.

12. Jaro Stacul, "Claiming a European Ethos at the Margins of the Italian Nation State," in *Crossing European Boundaries: Beyond Conventional Geographical Categories*, ed. Jaro Stacul, Christina Moutsou, and Helen Kopnina (Oxford and New York: Berghahn, 2006), 213.

13. Whiteness in the present context must be understood specifically as "Italian whiteness." For a useful discussion of the development of a discourse of Italian whiteness as a specific "Mediterranean whiteness," see Gaia Giuliani, "Mediterraneità e bianchezza: il razzismo italiano tra fascismo e articolazioni contemporanee (1861–2015)," *Iperstoria—Testi Letterature Linguaggi* 6 (Fall 2015): 167–82, http://www.iperstoria.it/joomla/images/PDF/Numero_6/monografica_6/Giuliani_mediterraneita_e_bianchezza.pdf.

14. Parts of this section expand on elements developed in two previously published essays: Áine O'Healy, "*Lamerica*," in *The Cinema of Italy*, ed. Giorgio Bertellini (London: Wallflower, 2004), 244–53, and Áine O'Healy, "Mediterranean Passages: Belonging and Abjection in Contemporary Italian Cinema," *California Italian Studies Journal* 1, no. 1 (2011), http://escholarship.org/uc/item/2qh5d59c.

15. There are different ways of characterizing what I describe as irregular migrants. The adjectives "illegal" and "undocumented" are often used in English, both of which I generally avoid. The first is overlaid with denigrating connotations and the second, though less negatively connoted, is often inaccurate, since many migrants carry passports or even visas that the destination countries judge to be inadequate. On the other hand, people fleeing wars and other catastrophes are often forced to travel without any identifying documents. I include these also within the category of the irregular.

16. See, among others, Ferruccio Pastore, Paola Monzini, and Giuseppe Sciortino, "Schengen's Soft Underbelly? Irregular Migration and Human Smuggling across Land and Sea Borders to Italy," *International Migration* 44, no. 4 (2006): 95–119.

17. *Lamerica* is still the most frequently discussed film about Italian immigration, and it continues to prompt new scholarly explorations. Useful readings of the film published in English over the years include Rodica Diaconescu-Blumenfeld, "*Lamerica*: History in Diaspora," *Romance Languages Annual* 11 (2000): 167–73; Marcia Landy, "On the Road with *Lamerica*: Immigrants, Refugees and the Poor," in *Metaphoricity and the Politics of Mobility*, ed. Maria Margaroni and Effie Yiannopoulou (Amsterdam: Rodopi, 2006), 141–58; Derek Duncan, "The Sight and Sound of Albanian Migration in Contemporary Italian Cinema," *New Readings* 8 (2007), http://ojs.cf.ac.uk/index.php/newreadings/article/view/21/16; Veronica Pravadelli, "Identity, Masculinity, and Postcolonial Scenarios in Gianni Amelio's *Lamerica* (1994)," in *The Cinemas of Italian Migration: European and Transatlantic Narratives*, ed. Sabine Schrader and Daniel Winkler (Newcastle, UK: Cambridge Scholars Publishing, 2013), 31–40; Rhiannon Welch, "Contact, Contagion, Immunization: Gianni Amelio's *Lamerica* (1994)," in *Italian Mobilities*, ed. Ruth Ben-Ghiat and Stephanie Malia Hom (London: Routledge, 2015), 68–87; and Luca Caminati, "Gianni Amelio's *Lamerica* and the National Body Politics," in *Italian Political Cinema: Public Life, Imaginary, and Identity in Contemporary Italian Film*, ed. Giancarlo Lombardi and Christian Uva (Oxford: Peter Lang, 2016), 319–28.

18. This was a dominant reading of the film from the beginning; see, for example, Giancarlo Lombardi's insightful analysis in "Can the Price Ever Be Right? Television and Cultural Imperialism in *Lamerica*," *Romance Languages Annual* 12 (2001): 191–95; and Nicola Mai, "'Italy Is Beautiful': The Role of Italian Television in Albanian Migration to Italy," in *Media and Migration: Constructions of Mobility and Difference*, ed. Russell King and Nancy Wood (London and New York: Routledge, 2001), 95–109.

19. Gianni Amelio and Goffredo Fofi, *Amelio secondo il cinema. Conversazione con Goffredo Fofi* (Rome: Donizelli, 1994), 7.

20. Piera Detassis, ed., *Gianni Amelio. Lamerica, film e storia del film* (Turin: Einaudi, 1994), 3.

21. Domenico Scalzo, *Gianni Amelio: Un posto al cinema* (Turin: Lindau, 2001), 199.

22. Emanuela Martini, *Gianni Amelio* (Turin: Il Castoro, 2006), 147.

23. In a compelling discussion of this scene, Derek Duncan notes that the "fantasy of radical assimilation into the nation secured through heterosexual contract" is presented in *Lamerica* as a futile one and argues that "the failure of the fantasy intimates the inherent queerness of the desire that fuels it." See Duncan, "Loving Geographies," 169.

24. A decline in Italian birthrates has been observed since the early 1990s. See Margarita Delgado Perez and Massimo Livi-Bacci, "Fertility in Italy and Spain: The Lowest in the World," *Family Planning Perspectives* 24, no. 4 (1992): 162–67, 171. For statistical information on the ongoing decline in birthrates in Italy, see "Birth and Fertility among the Resident Population," ISTAT (28 November 2017). https://www.istat.it/it/files//2017/11/EN_Births_Fertility-_20-novembre-2017.pdf

25. Of Czech origin, this polka was widely popular both as an instrumental piece and as a song during World War II in countries occupied by Axis forces as well as among the Allies. Bearing a variety of titles in different languages, it continued to gain popularity in the postwar years. In Britain it was known as "Roll Out the Barrel," in the United States as "The Beer Barrel Polka," in Germany as "Rosamunde," and in Italy as "Rosamunda."

26. Constantin Parvulescu, "Inside the Beast's Cage: Gianni Amelio's *Lamerica* and the Dilemma of Post-1989 Leftist Cinema," *Italian Culture* 28, no. 1 (2010): 50–67.

27. This point is astutely addressed in Diaconescu-Blumenfeld, "*Lamerica*: History in Diaspora."

28. Jean A. Gili and Gianni Amelio, "Entretien avec Gianni Amelio: un film non sur l'Albanie d'aujourdhui, mais sur l'Italie d'après-guerre," *Positif* 406 (1994): 25–31.

29. Julia Kristeva, *Powers of Horror: An Essay on Abjection*, trans. Leon S. Roudiez (New York: Columbia University Press, 1982).

30. Imogen Tyler, "'Welcome to Britain': The Cultural Politics of Asylum," *European Journal of Cultural Studies* 9 (2006): 192. Tyler's reference is to Kristeva, *Powers of Horror*.

31. Tyler, 192.

32. Duncan, "The Sight and Sound of Albanian Migration."

33. The casting of Günsür brings an oddly disruptive element to the film's realistic register. Apart from the fact that the actor speaks Albanian with a distinctive, non-Albanian accent (as indicated by Derek Duncan in the article cited above), Günsür's pin-up status in the wake of his role as the handsome Turkish seducer of the Italian protagonist (Alessandro Gassman) in *Bagno turco* (Ferzan Özpetek, 1997) introduces extratextual associations for Italian audiences that may undercut the effectiveness of his role as a tragic social outcast. When *L'italiano* was first released on DVD, the producers took advantage of Günsür's acknowledged sex appeal by offering consumers previously unseen footage featuring explicitly erotic moments between the actor and his co-star, Sonia Aquino. Packaged in a container adorned with an image of the nude actors locked in embrace, the DVD was thus marketed under the category of *erotico*, shaping its reception in ways that were perhaps unforeseen by the screenwriter and director.

34. Duncan, "Loving Geographies," 170.

35. See, for example, Landy, "On the Road with *Lamerica*."

36. Giorgio Agamben, *Means without End: Notes on Politics*, trans. Vincenzo Binetti and Cesare Casarino (Minneapolis: University of Minnesota Press, 2000), 31.

37. Agamben, 31.

38. Maria Todorova, *Imagining the Balkans* (New York: Oxford University Press, 1997). Todorova's nuanced study is in sharp contrast with the most influential publication on southeast Europe published in the post–Cold War period written in English—Robert Kaplan's record of his journey to the region around 1990. Resounding with the myths and stereotypes critiqued by Todorova, Kaplan describes the Balkans as "a time-capsule world: a dim stage upon which people raged, spilled blood, experienced visions and ecstasies." See Robert Kaplan, *Balkan Ghosts: A Journey through History* (New York: St. Martin's Press, 1993), xxi.

39. I refer here to Edward Said's formulation of the concept of Orientalism to explain Western attitudes toward the East. See *Orientalism* (New York: Pantheon Books, 1978).

40. Slavoj Žižek, "Caught in Another's Dream in Bosnia," in *Why Bosnia? Writings on the Balkan War*, ed. Rabia Ali and Lawrence Lifschultz (Stony Creek, CT: Pamphleteer's Press, 1993), 233–40.

41. Slavoj Žižek, *The Metastases of Enjoyment: Six Essays on Women and Causality* (London: Verso, 2005), 213.

42. Slavoj Žižek, "Ethnic Dance Macabre," *Guardian*, August 28, 1992, http://zizek.uk/ethnic-dance-macabre/.

43. Davide Rodogno, *Fascism's European Empire: Italian Occupation during the Second World War*, trans. Adrian Belton (Cambridge: Cambridge University Press, 2006). See also Davide Conti, *L'occupazione italiana dei Balcani. Crimini di guerra e mito della "brava gente" (1940–1943)* (Rome: Odradek, 2008).

44. Rodogno, *Fascism's European Empire*, 127–29.

45. Mario Martone, *Teatro di guerra: un diario* (Milan: Bompiani, 1998).

46. Castellitto and Mazzantini had enjoyed blockbuster success in Italy with their previous collaboration on *Non ti muovere* (*Don't Move*, Sergio Castellitto, 2004), also adapted from a novel by Mazzantini and also starring Penelope Cruz.

47. Rosalind Galt, "The Prettiness of Italian Cinema," in *Popular Italian Cinema*, ed. Louis Bayman and Sergio Rigoletto (Basingstoke: Palgrave Macmillan, 2013), 53.

48. Galt, 54.

49. Boyd van Hoeij, "*Twice Born*," *Variety*, September 23, 2012, http://variety.com/2012/film/markets-festivals/twice-born-1117948406; David Rooney, "*Twice Born*: Toronto Review," September 18, 2012, http://www.hollywoodreporter.com/review/twice-born-movie-review-penelope-cruz-emile-hirsch-371340.

50. Zachary Wigon, "*Twice Born* Irresponsibly Appropriates the Siege of Sarajevo for a Romantic Drama," *Village Voice*, December 4, 2013, http://www.villagevoice.com/film/twice-born-irresponsibly-appropriates-the-siege-of-sarajevo-for-a-romantic-drama-6440264.

51. Giorgio Agamben, *Homo Sacer: Sovereign Power and Bare Life*, trans. Daniel Heller-Roazen (Palo Alto: Stanford University Press, 1998).

52. Anca Parvulescu, *The Traffic in Women's Work: East European Migration and the Making of Europe* (Chicago: University of Chicago Press, 2014), 79–82.

53. Carla Marcantonio, *Global Melodrama: Nation, Body, and History in Contemporary Film* (New York: Palgrave Macmillan, 2014), 44.

54. Pietro Castellitto, cast in the role of Pietro, is the son of Sergio Castellitto, the film's director as well as the actor playing Pietro's adoptive father, and of Margaret Mazzantini, coauthor of the screenplay and Castellitto's wife.

CHAPTER 2

Traffic from the East
GENDER, LABOR, AND BIOPOLITICS

FOLLOWING THE INITIAL flow of mass migration in the 1990s, migrants of diverse nationalities began to pursue economic survival with various kinds of unauthorized labor in the streets of Italian cities—as windscreen washers, unlicensed street vendors, or sex workers. Although the number of people engaged in these activities constituted a small percentage of the immigrant population as a whole, the increasing visibility of foreigners in public spaces fed into popular perceptions of the migrant as a disruptive figure perpetually engaged in intrusive or illicit activities. Reinforcing these perceptions, the Italian media began to generate sensational reports of an imputed invasion of Italy by foreign "hordes," echoing the xenophobic attitudes expressed in the pronouncements of Lega Nord and the political right.[1]

Reports on immigration were often accompanied by images of throngs of unidentified people arriving in Italian harbors or crowds of shabbily dressed men and scantily attired women, giving visual support to the claim of the country's invasion by alien masses. The widely disseminated images of the hugely overcrowded *Vlora* arriving in Bari in August 1991 were among the first photographs to function in this way, but as the years went by, the archive grew. In the meantime, particular stereotypes emerged as part of the general linguistic currency, and migrants were classified in everyday Italian speech with demeaning or negatively coded terms such as *il vu' compra'* (street vendor; literally "wanna buy?"), *il clandestino* (irregular immigrant), *lo slavo* (generic Eastern European, with sinister connotations), *il romeno* (literally Romanian, but used disparagingly to describe Roma migrants from Eastern Europe), and so on.[2] All of these terms suggested widespread Italian characterizations of newly arrived migrants as untrustworthy people with shady intentions or connections and with little right to remain in Italy.

Such derogatory terms were most often directed at men, since male immigrants bore the brunt of xenophobic resentment. Occupying a different position in the Italian social imaginary, women migrants were subjected to a different set of assumptions, as is suggested in the films I discuss in this chapter. Describing Italian perceptions of female immigration, Ester Gallo and Francesca Scrinzi have observed that, in general, "migrant women tend to be represented in Italian popular culture as subaltern victims. In line with long-standing racist representations drawing from colonial history, they are stereotyped as either reproductive laborers or sexual objects."[3] More generally, they tend to be defined "by the spatial relations of their bodies with men and children or the elderly."[4]

Although anti-immigrant discourses in Italy were offset from the beginning by more thoughtful observations by Italian journalists, writers, and intellectuals, a generalized trend toward containment, control, and exclusion of the migrant population gradually became the norm. This tendency crystallized after Italy's ratification of the Schengen Agreement and the passing of a new legislation on migration, the so-called Turco-Napolitano Law, by the center-left government led by Romano Prodi in 1998, which instituted a sharp distinction between regular and irregular immigration. A pathway toward citizenship was delineated for migrants of the former category, and procedures were formulated for the possible expulsion of the latter, including the creation of processing and holding structures, popularly referred to by the initials CPT (Centri di Permanenza Temporanea), which signaled an increasingly systematic approach to controlling the influx of arrivals in line with Schengen directives.

Rebordering has been the tacit subtext of several policies enforced by the European Union since its inception. Though officially abolishing internal borders within the Schengen Area, the Schengen Agreement ultimately rendered the continent's external borders more complex, mobile, and exclusionary than ever before, replacing the traditional, linear model of the border with new, more dynamic mechanisms of control, as many social theorists have observed. The gradual intensification of external border controls that followed the ratification of the Schengen Conventions took place largely without protest from ordinary Italians, who were undoubtedly influenced by the rhetoric of "invasion" perpetuated by the national media and by the political right.[5] Similarly, no substantial public outcry followed the creation of the CPTs.[6] In fact, television reporters seemed less interested in investigating the degrading conditions and violations of human rights associated with these prisonlike institutions than in propagating the kind of negative sensationalism already associated with the discourse on immigration in Italian society.

As I have previously suggested, during the 1990s Italian directors began to make films that offered more complex depictions of immigrants than those available in popular journalism. Despite their apparently well-meaning efforts, these films are often laced with competing subtexts, both resisting and reinforcing the biases of the mainstream media. One of the most memorable figures to emerge in the cinematic imaginary in the post–Cold War period was that of the young, female Eastern European migrant, articulated through the intersecting discourses of gender, sexuality, race, and reproduction. My aim in this chapter is to unpack the construction of this figure in several Italian films that weave stories of migration from the east and particularly from southeastern Europe. In investigating these narratives of encounter between Italians and Eastern European women, I am interested in the kinds of affective utility or disposability that such women came to represent in the social imagination from the 1990s onward.

Bodies from the East

The figure of the young, vulnerable woman from the former Eastern Europe, appearing for the first time in Italian cinema in the early 1990s, is usually bereft of legal immigration status, frequently involved in coerced sex work, and sometimes in need of assistance or rescue.[7] Her most crucial attribute is her body, alternately fetishized or made abject by the cinematic apparatus, which becomes a site of tension and contestation. Although this Eastern European woman is apprehended diegetically as a white body, her presence is usually coded in ways that make her immediately distinguishable from other (white) characters on screen through clues provided by clothing or posture, accented speech, or indeed lack of access to speech. Assigned to both prominent and marginal roles, this alien though ostensibly attractive figure has proved to be surprisingly resilient over the years, appearing in the work of prominent filmmakers such as Marco Tullio Giordana and Giuseppe Tornatore, as well as in comedies and less prestigious genre films. Though frequently presented as a sexualized body available for exchange on the sex market, the Eastern European woman is also occasionally configured as providing other forms of affective services, particularly in domestic settings, and is sometimes shown transiting from one to the other.

In examining the figure of the Eastern European woman migrant, I draw in part on the writings of Italian political theorist Sandro Mezzadra, whose analysis of the affective labor performed by women migrants in the global era builds on the writings of Anglophone feminists, and particularly on the important volume *Global Woman: Nannies, Maids, and Sex Workers in the New Economy*, edited by Barbara Ehrenreich and Arlie Russell Hochschild in 2004.[8] The element in this significant study that Mezzadra responds to and develops is referenced in its subtitle—that is, the common thread linking the functions undertaken by the titular nannies, maids, and sex workers. For Mezzadra, migrations are infused with a set of subjective behaviors, needs, desires, and fantasies that structurally exceed the supposedly objective causes determining the mobility of people across the world, and the labor performed by migrant women as domestic employees and sex workers typically meets *affective* needs. In this way, he argues that the female migrant worker is positioned along a spectrum of feminized roles in the rapidly evolving global landscape. In an essay devoted to the foreign care worker (known as the *badante* in Italy), for example, he notes that this figure embodies affective values and services comparable to those provided by a range of other female figures from prostitutes to "good wives."[9]

Mezzadra's insistence on the productivity of migrant women's labor, and particularly unregulated or "illegal" labor, draws in turn on the insights of scholars such as Nicholas De Genova, who has argued that laws on immigration, along with the fortification of borders and the refinement of apparatuses of detention, should be understood not as an attempt to eradicate immigration but rather as a system of filters and dams that effectively produces illegality.[10] Illegality serves capital insofar as the "illegal" migrant labor force can be intimidated, abused, and exploited under conditions profitable to employers. Faced with the possibility of discovery and expulsion, irregular migrants become productive as vulnerable subjects deprived of rights. This mechanism creates a system described by Mezzadra and Brett Neilson as "differential inclusion," where irregularity ("illegality") emerges as a produced condition as well as a stake in the politics of mobility.[11]

Both the figure of the sex worker and that of the care worker (whether involved in legal or undocumented employment) are engaged in what feminist sociologists and neo-Marxist theorists, such as Mezzadra, describe as "affective labor," which is increasingly in demand in the modernized West. Defining affects as those bodily reactions and sensations implicated in power relations, Encarnación Gutiérrez-Rodríguez has shown that the categories of women's labor traditionally defined as nonproductive do in fact produce value, the value associated with their affective potential. And this value is bound up with essentializing notions of the feminine, a factor that ensures that such work will always be socially devalued and undercompensated.[12]

In bringing this discussion to bear specifically on the westward migration of women from the former Eastern bloc, I must also take into account the insights of film scholar Anca Parvulescu (whose work is briefly referenced in the analysis of *Venuto al mondo* in chapter 1), which similarly build on ideas elaborated in the work of feminist theorists and social scientists. Examining the representation of Eastern European migrant women as sex workers, trafficked women, housekeepers, nannies, or providers of other kinds of affective labor in recent European films, Parvulescu suggests that these images are not only indicative of perceptions of Eastern European women in Europe's contemporary social imaginary but are also closely bound up with the stratified forms of labor that such women are permitted to pursue. She thus argues that, since European Union "*enlargement* or *integration* is a process deeply invested in East European women's bodies, sexuality and labor," the project of pluralizing contemporary Europe must take into account the extent to which Europe itself is brought together by the "traffic" in Eastern European women.[13]

Referencing Claude Levi-Strauss's concept of the exchange of women as an essential foundation of culture, and the re-elaboration of this concept by Gayle Rubin and others, Parvulescu's study adopts a broad, biopolitical notion of reproduction, perceiving the latter as "invested equally in biology and political economy."[14] As she observes, "Reproduction is today in the process of being radically reconfigured through new reproductive and regenerative technologies (through the biological side) and new, post-Fordist economic realities (on the political economy side). The two faces of reproduction have also acquired a transnational dimension in the last decades. On the biological side, we speak of globalized markets for adoption, egg donation, surrogacy, stem cell tissues, and clinical trials. On the economic side we speak of a global market for domestic work, child and elder care, and sex work."[15]

She also points out that since the 1990s many EU governments have been concerned with the problem of plunging birthrates, and conservatives have been worried about Europe's inability to adequately replace the autochthonous population with further generations of *white* Europeans. Related to this concern, she suggests, is the fact that, in contemporary Europe, "the work of reproduction—biological and social—is in the process of being displaced on non-European and East European women." Parvulescu is sharply critical of the hypocrisy that marks Western attitudes toward the flow of reproductive labor from east to west, describing it as "the phenomenon that conservative commentators deplore on the biological side (genetic reproduction) but tacitly endorse on the social side (child and elder care, domestic work) with symptomatic exceptions on the biological side (organ donation, surrogacy, adoption)."[16]

The factors observed by Parvulescu in European society at large, as well as in the conditions refracted in cinematic representations of Eastern European women, certainly resonate with circumstances in Italy. Parvulescu's analysis is perhaps most useful in its broad understanding of reproductive work and the ways in which (white) Eastern European women engage with it. Indeed the reception of Eastern European women migrants in Italy, as elsewhere, is mapped out along the continuum of the types of reproductive labor they provide. The care worker, or *badante*, enjoys special status in Italy since, in the absence of suitable state-provided care for the elderly, women from the former Eastern bloc have become the preferred choice for Italian families seeking live-in assistance for aging relatives. Indeed they have long supplanted the Cape Verdean or Eritrean domestic workers who sometimes undertook this labor in the 1970s and 1980s. In recent years, foreign-born *badanti* have been offered expedited access to residency and work permits when needed or they have benefitted from their employer's complicity in turning a blind eye to their status where it was of mutual interest not to seek regularization.[17]

Immigrant street prostitutes, who have almost entirely replaced Italian sex workers at the lowest level of the sex industry, elicit very different reactions from the Italian public. Since the 1990s, foreign sex workers have been a prominent concern in public discourse. Assuming that there will always be a demand for paid sex, some politicians have called for the reinstitution of state-controlled brothels as a way of removing the women from the streets.[18] Supporters of the initiative generally explain their motivation in terms of a humanitarian concern for the safety of vulnerable female subjects or as a public health issue.[19] Other members of the public regard these women simply as victims in need of rescue, oblivious to the fact that some choose sex work, either assertively or reluctantly, as the initial phase of a migratory project and do not wish to be rescued.[20]

Since the early 1990s, when unprecedented numbers of women from locations beyond Italy's borders first began to work the streets of the country's largest cities, the foreign-born sex worker has appeared intermittently in Italian films, where she is frequently presented as Eastern European and rather less often as African. Although the figure of the independent yet simultaneously vulnerable *Italian* street prostitute was a staple of the heyday of the national cinema, she has almost disappeared from Italian films set in the contemporary moment, just as Italian women have largely abandoned street prostitution in order to enter more lucrative echelons of sex work.[21] In her place, the foreign woman who offers sex in exchange for money on the street and in other public places, or who is coerced into sexually compromising relationships with Italians, has emerged to the cinematic forefront. She is not, however, a symbolic substitute for the earlier figure and is constructed with very different signifying strategies.

Many of the earliest films that explore in fictionalized form the encounter between Italians and their Eastern European counterparts in the post–Cold War era construct narratives involving a young, beautiful, female migrant, almost always embodied by an alluring Slavic actress.[22] Linked to this figure are questions of power and agency that find expression through images of compromised bodily integrity and ambivalent eroticism. In short, the nexus of representational strategies recurring in films such as Carlo Mazzacurati's *Un'altra vita* (Another Life, 1992) and *Vesna va veloce* (Vesna Runs Fast, 1996), Gianluca Maria Tavarelli's *Portami via* (Take Me Away, 1994), Armando Manni's *Elvjs & Merilijn* (*Elvis and Marilyn*, 1998), Corso Salani's *Occidente* (West, 1998), Giuseppe Tornatore's *La sconosciuta* (*The Unknown Woman*, 2006), and Ivano De Matteo's *La bella gente* (Fine People, 2009) serves both to eroticize and render abject the Eastern European female migrant.

In each of these films, the female protagonist has embarked on a difficult process of uprooting and displacement, and in most cases her perilous journey is enabled at least in part by an Italian citizen, whose participation proves either futile or destructive. The ostensible perspective that dominates these narratives is well intentioned, as for the most part it refers critically to the kinds of exploitation and brutality that may confront vulnerable female migrants in unfamiliar surroundings. Simultaneously, however, the films' visual strategies are ambivalent, even contradictory, as in almost all of the films the woman is configured by the logic of the gaze as both innocent victim and alluring erotic object. The thematic element that unites these narratives is violence. Though this is an entirely plausible element in scenarios of illegal migration, it is often deployed in ways that suggest the films' complicity with the sadistic logic of the diegetically placed perpetrators. There is also an implicit suggestion in many of the films that the woman herself is at least partially compliant in her victimization.

In a groundbreaking essay written in the 1980s, Teresa de Lauretis draws on narrative semiotics, Freudian psychoanalysis, and feminist film theory to show the epistemic violence that subtends the deep structure of the oedipal narrative. Invoking Laura Mulvey's claim that "sadism demands a story," she proposes its provocative reversal, namely, that "a story demands sadism." The central point of the argument made by de Lauretis is that classical narrative conventions serve to immobilize the figure of woman as image, mute object, or terrain upon which the male protagonist is enabled to achieve fulfillment in a process that effectively occludes the possibility of female subjectivity.[23]

Italian films on female migration made in the 1990s certainly fit the paradigm described by de Lauretis. At the same time, they each offer striking images of injury or debasement enacted against the woman immigrant, whose body is ambivalently sexualized by the cinematic apparatus. Yet the violence perpetuated against this figure is carefully "justified" by the pseudo-logic of verisimilitude, ostensibly appealing to the viewer as compassionate witness to her abuse.

Un'altra vita, chronologically the first of the films listed above, was made in 1992 and recounts the relationship between Saverio (Silvio Orlando), a kind but timid Roman dentist, and Alia (Adrianna Biedrzynska), the young Russian migrant who seeks his help. In the film's opening scene, Alia shows up at Saverio's dental office late one evening pleading with him to replace the front tooth she has lost in a violent confrontation. There are traces of blood on her face, and the bleeding gap in her mouth is visible when she speaks. She is, in effect, the picture of needy abjection. The good Saverio immediately sets about healing the woman's disfiguring loss, working all night to create a dental implant that will conceal the evidence of her injury. He subsequently becomes obsessed with her and pursues her with reckless insistence even after she has tried to disappear from his life.

Figure 2.1. Screen capture. Vesna counts her earnings. *Vesna va veloce* (1996)

Despite Saverio's attempt to heal all traces of her injury, she is far from healed as she is once again submitted to violence at the hands of a shady boyfriend. Saverio's efforts to rescue her from forced prostitution are doomed from the start, and the violence he seeks to protect her from is turned against him in the film's bloody concluding scene.

In *Vesna va veloce* (Vesna Runs Fast), the second of Mazzacurati's films featuring a Slavic immigrant, the protagonist is a young, educated Czech woman who arrives by bus in Trieste in northeastern Italy on a one-day excursion. At the end of the day, Vesna (Tereza Grygarová) fails to reboard the bus. Deciding to stay in Italy, she soon begins working as a street prostitute in Rimini, a popular resort on the Adriatic coast. Although she makes some money, her life is precarious. The letters she writes home are full of inventions, suggesting that she is both strong-willed and needy, independent and vulnerable. Ultimately, however, her actions remain enigmatic, inscrutable.

The real center of the film is not Vesna but Antonio (Antonio Albanese), an unemployed Italian construction worker with whom she eventually becomes involved and whose character is developed with greater consistency than Vesna's. Although she initially rejects Antonio's interest in her, she seeks out his help when assaulted and stabbed by a local pimp. Following her refusal to be treated at a hospital since she is without a passport, Antonio enlists the help of an African doctor who discreetly takes care of needy clandestine immigrants. In a crucial scene the men collaborate in treating Vesna's injury. Here, the close-up of Vesna's bleeding knife wound is framed by two pairs of hands and arms, black and white, working together to heal her. The image evokes a ritual bonding between the two men in a homosocial pact, symbolically endorsing an ideal solidarity between an Italian man and an African immigrant in a demographically altered Italy, with the woman's body functioning merely as the terrain upon which their bond is sealed.

What becomes evident in these and similar films of the same period—such as Tavarelli's *Portami via* and Corso Salani's *Occidente*—is that the relationship between the putative male rescuer and the foreign female migrant is instantiated by her woundedness, generating a dynamic ambivalence in the unfolding of the narrative events. The visualization of female injury in all of these films is surprisingly consistent, making explicit the symbolic discourse of female abjection.

These images of wounded women resonate strongly with Julia Kristeva's formulation of female abjection, which describes how disgust and desire, repulsion and attraction compete with each other in delineating the borders that give the subject identity. For Kristeva, a sense of boundaries and a sense of otherness are established in infancy at the point when the child must separate from its mother. This occurs partly through feelings of revulsion toward bodily residues, which become symbols of defilement, separate from the "pure" self. The emotion evoked by bodily residues is a deep sense of repulsion. The experience of abjection, or the reliving of abjection, is connected to the trauma of separation from the mother. Furthermore, the conflicting feelings activated by the abject are easily transferred to others during childhood and later life and—as Kristeva argues—can be linked to the misogynistic effects of culture.[24]

More than any other migrant figure in Italian cinema, the figure of the Eastern European woman in Italian films released in the 1990s and early twenty-first century—and particularly the Eastern European sex worker or trafficked woman—is imbued with signifiers of abjection. Often visibly covered with bruises or blood, she also occasionally appears gagged or tied up. In other words, the young, attractive Eastern European woman has become a particularly potent terrain for explicit depictions of misogyny, xenophobia, sexual exploitation, and other traumatic abuses. In cinematic constructions of the East European woman involved in other forms of labor, traces of the abject persist as caregivers and domestic workers are often shown performing menial tasks associated with dirt or waste. While these depictions may be intended to critique demeaning social practices, they prompt a lingering ambiguity as they often align the viewers' perspective with the sadistic logic of the onscreen perpetrators.

One of the most remarkable constructions of female abjection is found in Armando Manni's *Elvjs & Merilijn*, where it is linked to the symbolic abjection of the Balkans in the Western imaginary. Here, a young Marilyn Monroe lookalike and amateur singer, Ileana (Edyta Olszówska), competes in a talent show at a Bucharest theater and wins the opportunity to perform at a nightclub in Italy.

After an arduous journey through the desolate landscape of the former Yugoslavia in the company of Nikolai (Goran Navojec), an Elvis impersonator from Bulgaria, she discovers that the only work available for either of them in Italy is in a pornographic floorshow.

The film opens at the Bucharest theater where Nikolai and Ileana are competing in a contest organized by an Italian impresario (Giorgio Faletti). As amateur celebrity impersonators both on and off the stage, Nikolai and Ileana are living, breathing, singing, dancing simulacra, holding on for sheer life to the trappings of the invented identities that propel them forward even at the bleakest moments. In Ileana's case, this masquerade is presented as a necessity since her life in Romania is hellish in the extreme. Working in the most menial capacity at the city dump, she lives with a pathologically depressed and incontinent mother, who tells her, "You think you're different from me because you're beautiful. But you're not different; you're just the same."

Rather than contemplating her own likeness in the face of the abject Romanian mother, Ileana reconstructs herself as the glamorous Monroe, and whenever she is afraid or discouraged, she summons up an image of herself as Marilyn, gliding serenely along a white, sandy beach in a striking red ball gown. In the film's opening shots, a series of tight close-ups of Ileana's body are presented in slow motion as she sings on stage. These are intercut with traveling shots from the vantage point of a garbage truck as it moves through the filthy city streets at night. Dressed in her strapless red gown, with matching lipstick and glittering jewelry, Ileana is clearly a spectacle to be looked at, recognizable as "Marilyn" even before she is interpellated as such by the Italian host on stage (Giorgio Falletti). Throughout the sequence we see her only in isolated fragments—her full scarlet lips, blond curls, creamy shoulders, and plunging neckline—all of which are presented without diegetic sound apart from a faint echo of the clanking garbage truck outside, until Ileana's own voice filters onto the audio track in the concluding moments. Significantly, the viewer is not sutured to the spectacle of Ileana's performance through the point of view of a specific onscreen observer. The source of the gaze here must be ascribed instead to a generalized aesthetic regime internalized by Ileana herself, who submits to constant vigilance her own performance as the idealized female body—the body as a commodity constructed for others.

As neither Ileana nor Nicolai knows the other's language, they are obliged to communicate in Italian, which they have apparently picked up in the course of watching Italian television shows over the years. Here, as in Amelio's *Lamerica*, there is an implicit critique of the increasing power and reach of Italian television channels which, by the late 1990s, were available not only to Albanian audiences but also to viewers in other parts of southeastern Europe. It is clear in *Elvjs & Merilijn* that the protagonists' fascination with the popular culture of the West is entirely gleaned from television, but they are crucially unaware that their points of reference are by then completely out of date.

Refusing to be deterred by a bureaucratic hitch at Bucharest airport, where Ileana's passport is confiscated, the two aspiring performers are convinced that fame and fortune await them in Italy and decide to travel there by land and sea. They thus proceed through the challenging terrain of the former Yugoslavia, partly thanks to the help of a Roma woman who enables them to pass without difficulty though an unguarded border crossing. The scene darkens progressively as they move westward through the Balkans, devastated by recent war. Frequently, however, the film cuts to an image of Ileana as the blonde Marilyn, gliding along at the water's edge on a white beach, her face radiant and smiling—a glamour shot that could have been extracted from a television commercial or music video.

The most intense sequence in the film occurs when the two stop on their journey at an isolated garrison occupied by Serbian soldiers, during which the young woman is subjected to a traumatic encounter with a reclusive, depressed, and unstable colonel. Played by Italian actor Toni Bertorelli, the colonel is presented as a sort of Dracula figure who becomes riveted by her beauty.[25] "You are too luminous," he tells her, consolidating for the film's audience the associations with the world of the vampire, and explains, "We have no use for the sun here. Those of us who have survived are only shadows." When he shoots himself to death while alone in her presence, the soldiers decide that Ileana is responsible for the loss of their beloved leader. Taking revenge, they force her to mimic fellatio with a loaded gun in her mouth and then throw her from their truck in the middle of an isolated rural landscape.

Yet this is not the end of her suffering. When Ileana and Nikolai finally manage to arrive in Italy, just in time for their scheduled audition, they find the promised land no less bleak and garbage-strewn than the scene they have left behind. The dream that sustained their struggle is quickly crushed when their performance is pronounced unappealing and dated by the ruthless, profit-driven managers of the nightclub who underwrote their journey to Italy and who now offer them the possibility of performing in an explicitly erotic show.

In the final sequence, which unfolds on a sunless Adriatic beach, the young Romanian is overcome by a suicidal despair and collapses into Nikolai's arms when he tries to restrain her, her hands bloodied from the shards of glass with which she had tried to cut her veins. The scene is pure melodrama, in which the image of Ileana as an abject, bleeding victim at the water's edge, trapped impossibly in a no-man's land, is intercut with the image of Marilyn, her own idealized incarnation. In this scenario, the woman's attractiveness and her victimization are symbiotically linked in a way that points to a similar process at work in the posthumous construction of Ileana's putative namesake, the iconic Marilyn Monroe.

The final scene of Manni's *Elvjs & Merilijn* evokes Slavoj Žižek's criticism of dominant Western representations of southeastern Europe and his concomitant critique of the universalization of the notion of the victim that has accompanied the worldwide triumph of liberal democracy.[26] For Žižek, the image of the victim, since it is presented as existing outside of ideology, exerts on the witness an immobilizing fascination, evoking compassion while thwarting the ability to act. It is precisely this kind of immobilizing fascination that the spectacle of woman-as-victim demands in the films discussed above since each of them refuses to problematize the sexual politics of its own representational strategies, attempting instead to evoke the dutifully compassionate though ultimately complicit gaze of the passive cinema spectator.

Maternal Noir: *La sconosciuta*

The opening sequence of Giuseppe Tornatore's *La sconosciuta* (2006) presents a scene of striking visual intensity, framed as a flashback. In a disused warehouse, furnished like a stage set, several masked women exhibit themselves in their underwear for the benefit of a hidden observer who, from a peephole, surveys each of them with close attention. As the women parade before him in groups of three, a train roars by, rattling the building and scattering dust everywhere. When the observer finally indicates a preference for a particular woman, a slender blonde steps forward, sheds her scant clothing, and mechanically repeats the same routine while nude. As soon as her selection is confirmed, the woman peels off her full-face mask, revealing simultaneously that all of the women had been wearing identical, flesh-colored masks. Before the scene ends, however, there are a few rapid cuts to the present, which establish the scene itself as belonging to the past. The high-key lighting, voyeuristic set-up, and uncanny implications of the women's identical masks lend an element of the surreal to the film's opening minutes, evoking the orgy scene in Stanley Kubrick's *Eyes Wide Shut* (1997) while also mirroring the compositional aspects of the final torture scenario in Pier Paolo Pasolini's *Salò* (1975). With its allusive citations, noir effects, and diegetic disruptions, the sequence seems to pose self-consciously the question of genre.

At a press conference following the screening of *La sconosciuta* at Cannes in 2006, Tornatore vigorously denied that the film was as an expression of social critique, explicitly distancing himself from the many recent films attempting to expose or challenge abuses and injustices in contemporary Italy.[27] Although an element of social criticism can certainly be read into its narrative, *La sconosciuta* is for the most part a self-consciously *cinematic* project that aims at engaging a wide audience with the kind of popular audiovisual spectacle for which Tornatore is well known. Like much of the director's earlier work, it constitutes a well-crafted product that offers specific visual and aural pleasures through the use of

Figure 2.2. Screen capture. Irena removes her mask. *La sconosciuta* (2006)

striking cinematography, strong acting performances, and an intensely stirring, if not overwrought, musical score. What is new here with respect to Tornatore's earlier work is *La sconosciuta*'s deployment of noir aesthetics. Much of the dramatic force of the film comes, in fact, from its unusual admixture of conventions borrowed from different genres, specifically from horror and noir but with a significant infusion of melodrama.

Despite Tornatore's effort to disavow the element of social criticism that appears to be at work in *La sconosciuta*, it is clear that the opening sequence explicitly alludes to the reality of sex trafficking to Italy from the countries of the former Eastern bloc, a phenomenon controlled by international criminal networks and carried out under brutal, dehumanizing conditions. The narrative also references another contemporary phenomenon rarely dramatized in cinema—the use of young, *white* foreign women to supply newborn infants to the clandestine adoption market. *La sconosciuta* thus dramatizes some of the difficult circumstances experienced by vulnerable female migrants through the construction of a protagonist who has survived the trials of sex trafficking and coerced childbearing. At the same time, through the self-conscious deployment of mixed genre conventions, it demonstrates a degree of self-reflexive expressivity scarcely evidenced in earlier, more realistic dramas of female migration. It is significant, for example, that the film foregrounds the image of male voyeurism in its opening sequence, raising the issue of the filmmaker's own relationship to the spectacle of women's exploitation, a question that remains only implicit in earlier Italian films offering narratives of female migration and displacement.

At the center of *La sconosciuta* is a Ukrainian immigrant (Ksenia Rappaport), who is sold into prostitution in Italy and later obliged to surrender for sale the nine children she has borne over the course of twelve years of bondage to her pimp. The present tense of the narration follows her quest, three years after her escape from a life of virtual enslavement, to track down and form a bond with the youngest of these children, whom she believes to have been adopted by the well-to-do Adacher couple in an unnamed city in northern Italy. The titular "unknown woman" is interpellated by two different names in the diegesis: Giorgia, the name assigned to her by her pimp, and Irena, the name she claims as her own, presumably an approximation of the Ukrainian Irina. Nothing is known of her life prior to her experience as a trafficked woman; no memories are associated with her native land, there is no mention of family or friends from her youth, and no explanation is given for the circumstances that brought her in contact with the world of trafficking. She has recourse to her native language only once, when she sings a lullaby to her presumed daughter, Tea Adacher, in Ukrainian. In this way, she remains to a great extent an enigma, even if the history of her abuse at the hands of her pimp and the motivations for her avenging actions are slowly revealed to the viewer up to the final scenes of the film.

Cold blue color tones signal the distance between the northern city Irena inhabits in the present and the locations in the flashbacks—presumably further to the south—where she spent her earlier years in Italy, which are shot in contrastingly golden tones. Her memories of the previous years are both painful and wistful. They are dominated on the one hand by the repulsive figure of her sadistic exploiter, Muffa (Michele Placido), who held Irena and a cluster of other young women under tight control, and on the other by a young, working-class Italian with whom she had enjoyed an idyllic if fleeting romance. The film provides brief, idealized glimpses of her stolen moments with this man, who apparently fathered the child now identified as Tea and was murdered by Muffa following the discovery of their liaison.

As events in the past and present begin to cohere for the viewer into a single narrative, explicit parallels are created on the visual track by juxtaposing Irena's experiences in the present with the haunting memories they spontaneously trigger. These parallels serve to explain the extreme measures taken by the protagonist—including injury to others—as a consequence of the many cruelties previously enacted upon her. In her quest to attain proximity to Tea, Irena is thoroughly focused and without scruple. She spies on the Adacher family, sorts through their garbage to find information about their eating habits, gains illicit access to their home, searches through their private documents, severely injures their elderly maid in order to replace this woman within the household, and lethally (if not intentionally) endangers the child's adoptive mother when the vengeful Muffa returns on the scene. All of these scenes—including several in which she is almost caught in an act of bold transgression—have a high level of dramatic tension and clearly invoke the thriller.

The tones of the thriller are also emphasized on the music track, composed by Ennio Morricone, through the use of instrumental passages dominated by strings reminiscent of Bernard Herman's work for the films of Alfred Hitchcock. Also reminiscent of Hitchcock is an unsettling use of point of view, as the gaze of the camera switches the position of observer and observed, voyeur and prey, and the physical appearance of the female protagonist is radically different in the past and in the present. A second, contrasting musical motif signals the film's investment in the melodramatic mode. This passage is a sweeter, slower melody that echoes the lullaby sung by Irena to her presumed daughter in Ukrainian.

The lullaby motif is the theme that prevails on the soundtrack as the film is gradually transformed into a variant of the maternal melodrama. Irena's desperate quest to retrieve her relationship with a lost child is, in some aspects, strongly reminiscent of this subgenre of the women's films that flourished in Hollywood in the 1930s and 1940s. Films such as John Stahl's *Imitation of Life* (1934), King Vidor's *Stella Dallas* (1937), and Edmund Goulding's *The Great Lie* (1941) introduced female characters neglected or rejected by their children or separated from them for financial, social, or moral reasons. Though victims, these protagonists ultimately achieved heroic dignity within the narrative by sacrificing their own interests for the sake of their beloved children, often concealing their maternal identity or disappearing completely to allow the child access to a better life.

In a seminal essay of feminist film scholarship, Linda Williams uses feminist and psychoanalytic discourse to unpack the power dynamics in the classic maternal melodrama *Stella Dallas*. Williams notes that the ultimate triumph for the female protagonist in this and similar dramas lies in her voluntary victimization through self-sacrifice. It is in fact the woman's self-sacrifice that achieves the obligatory happy ending, where a sense of "too-lateness" is combined with an image of heroic suffering and moral fortitude.[28]

In the present tense of Tornatore's film, though Irena is prepared to perform a measure of self-sacrifice, she is never simply a victim. To complicate her situation further, the relationship she develops with the child she believes to be her daughter is overlaid with elements of cruelty. The scene in which she forcibly instructs Tea to defend herself, to fight back and protect herself from injury, has a disturbing intensity. Irena binds the child's arms to her body, repeatedly throws her onto the floor, and then forces her to struggle to her feet before throwing her back down again. The scene is intercut with images of Irena tied and bound by her pimp as she, too, is thrown helplessly to the floor, bloodied and beaten. The editing suggests that Irena, no longer a victim, has become a resourceful agent, teaching the child skills she was unable to mobilize within herself. This awareness fails to dispel the shocking effect attained by the spectacle of the small girl being subjected to repeated acts of violence she cannot comprehend. In a subsequent scene, however, it becomes obvious that, thanks to Irena's intervention, Tea has learned to defend herself successfully when attacked by her classmates in the school playground.

Figure 2.3. Screen capture. Irena delivers tough love. *La sconosciuta* (2006)

La sconosciuta could be read as a paranoid text, reflecting a generalized anxiety about fertility, childbearing, and motherhood in a country with a declining birthrate, where many professional women entrust their child or children to the daily custody of "foreign" caretakers or babysitters. Certainly, the film's melodramatic excess unsettles any definitive reading of Irena as an entirely benevolent presence, rendering her at times as a devouring mother unhinged by the hysterical need to be reunited with her offspring. Visually, she is frequently marked with the signs of abjection—stained with blood, breast milk, and dirt from the city dump, where she digs for the body of her murdered lover. But she is ultimately undecipherable, as is suggested by her mask in the film's opening scene, as well as by her startling shifts in appearance and the presence of a Janus-faced fountain in the street near her apartment.

What marks the difference between *La sconosciuta* and the classical maternal melodrama is that Irena, when presented with DNA evidence that Tea is not her daughter, abandons her dream of recreating a spectral oedipal family and instead—as is suggested in the film's epilogue—proceeds to foster a nurturing bond with the girl, which endures throughout years of her incarceration for the crimes she has committed. The wordless concluding scene, which immediately follows the scene of Irena's entry into prison without a marked temporal parenthesis, can be read either as a straightforward narrative conclusion or a fantasy sequence. The scene's visual codes, however, are realistic. Walking through the prison gate and into the sunlight, Irena is gray-haired and somber after years of detention. Pausing at a bus stop, she appears uncertain, bewildered. Then the teenage Tea emerges into view, smiling warmly. Turning in surprise, Irena smiles back in recognition as the familiar lullaby motif swells on the soundtrack, conjuring up what is indeed an implausible happy ending. The narrative implication, however, is that Irena has maintained the promise made to Tea that she would always write to her, enabling their bond to flourish despite the intervention of time and distance. In this way, the film redeems its Eastern European protagonist by exalting her capacity for affective labor, which she performed even from the solitude of her prison cell on behalf of an Italian child that she will never be able to call her own.

The Labor of Care

Over the past fifteen years, the figure of the foreign-born domestic worker or care provider has emerged with increasing frequency in Italian feature films, referencing a growing tendency among Italian families to employ immigrants to assist with the functioning of their everyday lives.[29] This phenomenon can be linked to a nexus of social and political issues that include the feminization of migration flows to Italy, the gendered and racialized hierarchies operating within Italy's contemporary workforce, the presumed emancipation of Italian women that has prompted larger numbers than before to join the formal workforce, and the corresponding material and affective gaps created within Italy's rapidly aging households. Rarely achieving prominence in the films' narrative economy, the migrant domestic worker (almost always presented as a woman) is nonetheless a crucial component of cinema's engagement with the growing presence of migrant laborers in the Italian workforce and specifically with the anxieties that have accompanied the insertion of the migrant laborer into the intimate space of Italian domestic life. Although not ostensibly driven by a commitment to political critique, such films offer complex engagements with the fraught discourses of globalization, xenophobia, and racism currently circulating in Italian society.

In his reflections on contemporary global migrations and their imbrication in the neocolonial labor market, Mezzadra notes how the figure of the migrant domestic worker or care provider is embedded in the intimate rhythms and spaces of households in the global north while she retains ties with her own family a great distance away. Enmeshed in a complicated chain of affective relations, she is subjected to competing expectations. Mezzadra argues, moreover, that the characteristics embodied in this figure are increasingly constitutive of labor more generally considered, where the boundary between labor and life, or between commodity and noncommodity, is becoming blurred.[30]

Mezzadra's observations owe much to the work of the feminist scholars already cited, including Arlie Russell Hochschild, who in 1983 proposed the term "emotional labor" to describe the work performed by service employees who are expected to facilitate a sense of emotional well-being in those they serve.[31] Developing this concept in the context of different employment sectors, Hochschild came to focus on the crucial role that emotions play in the experiences of migrant domestic workers in the globalized world. Through the labor of this growing contingent of foreign-born women, she argued, care, concern, and love are being imported from the world's poorer areas to its wealthier regions and cities, with significant consequences for the families left behind in the women's home countries (a phenomenon now know as the "care chain" or the "care drain"). During the same period, other feminist scholars, such as Jacqueline Andall, Bridget Anderson, Encarnación Gutiérrez-Rodríguez, and Rhacel Salazar Parreñas, began to explore in similar ways the transnational dimensions of migrant domestic work and to scrutinize its affective ramifications.[32] Published in 2000, Andall's monograph relates specifically to the Italian context, directly addressing the migration of African women to Italy for domestic work from the 1970s to the 1990s. Her research reveals how the intersecting constructs of race, class, and gender during those decades served to demean and marginalize these women at the very moment that also witnessed the rise of Italian feminism and its much-touted call for global sisterhood.

Examining a broader transnational context, Anderson highlights the ways in which the field of domestic work is shaped by social hierarchization and by more or less explicit forms of racism. Mezzadra points to Anderson's work on the global politics of domestic labor to extrapolate a compelling insight: it is not so much *time* that counts in evaluating the contribution of the domestic worker but rather the personality of the worker herself—in other words, her ability to produce and sell affects. Mezzadra further argues that specific forms of subjectivity are currently being forged in the field of tensions surrounding the foreign domestic worker, shot through with affects that run the gamut from expressions of care to racist sentiment. Traditional family roles such as those of wife and mother, he asserts, have undergone a profound shift in the process.

In light of these provocative insights, I will focus here on the cinematic construction of migrant women employed in contemporary Italian households in order to probe the tensions and contradictions underpinning such representations. Although migrant sex workers have featured in Italian films almost from the beginning of the period of mass migration to Italy, the figure of the foreign-born domestic or care worker has emerged much more gradually. The reasons for this discrepancy are easy to surmise. Whereas the life of the sex worker is often dangerous and violent in ways that lend themselves readily to melodramatic or sensationalistic representations—and in fact many European films about foreign women involved in forced prostitution are genre productions—capturing the drudgery performed by foreign women working in the privacy of Italian homes may constitute a more challenging representational endeavor.

Among the migrant domestic workers featuring in recent Italian films, the figure of the Eastern European *badante* (care worker) has a prominent place. In Italy, the demand for care of the elderly has surged in recent years to such a degree that special provisions were created by the government to provide employment permits for immigrants willing to undertake this form of labor.[33] Foreign-born caregivers have thus become a familiar presence in Italy's contemporary social landscape, filling a widely acknowledged social need. Eastern European women, who constitute the majority of foreign caregivers employed in Italian households, blend in visually with the family they serve, recalling the appearance of a traditionally constituted household that is supported by extended family members.[34] Although these women may approximate or mirror the whiteness of their employers, their subaltern status belies any sense of genuine equality.

Screening the *Badante*

Accorded diverse levels of prominence and agency, the East European *badante* appears in a range of Italian feature films, including *Cose dell'altro mondo* (*Things from Another World*, Francesco Patierno, 2011), *Gianni e le donne* (*Gianni and the Women*, Gianni Di Gregorio, 2011), *Io, loro e Lara* (*Me, Them, and Lara*, Carlo Verdone, 2010), and *Mar Nero* (*Black Sea*, Federico Bondi, 2008). The scenarios constructed in these films point—whether critically or with unconscious complicity—to widely held social attitudes that construct foreign women as seductive intruders, canny exploiters, or simply as easily exploitable laborers who must be incorporated into Italian households for lack of more satisfactory solutions in an altered social landscape. As I will show, however, the construction of the migrant care worker dramatizes the ways in which the issue of labor intersects with questions of gender, race, and class.

Starring the Romanian actress Dorotheea Petre and the Italian Ilaria Occhini, *Mar Nero* is the first Italian feature film to place the caregiver in a leading role, and it is therefore worthy of particular scrutiny. Based on a script written by the director Federico Bondi in collaboration with Ugo Citi, the film was ostensibly inspired by the relationship between Bondi's own grandmother and her Romanian caregiver.[35] Although articulated as an intimate domestic drama, it is not without broader political implications as it is set mostly in the winter of 2006–7, a period that witnessed Romania's accession to the European Union. This phase of EU enlargement had, in fact, prompted widespread public anxieties about the possibility of increased migration of Romanians to Italy, often expressed in discriminatory language, including the occasional collapsing of the categories of *romeni* (Romanians) and *rom* (Romani) in everyday communication.

For most of its duration, *Mar Nero* unfolds in a small apartment in the outskirts of Florence, where the young Angela (Petre) has been summoned to take care of Gemma (Occhini), an elderly Tuscan widow. Reluctant to acknowledge her own real need for help, Gemma is still deeply resentful that her son has moved to a distant city. Venting her disappointment and rage on the defenseless Romanian caregiver, she operates under the assumption that acceptance of such treatment is part of Angela's domestic duties. The film powerfully conveys the ways in which the social devaluation of domestic work is impressed on the worker's body. As Angela struggles to meet the physical demands of her job, she seeks simultaneously to cope with harsh criticism and abuse without betraying her frustration. Occupying the devalued space of racialized, feminized labor, she is initially prevented from claiming her individual identity as her employer refuses to learn her name. For the sake of convenience, Gemma interpellates her as Luda, the name of the Russian *badante* she had recently fired. Angela's eventual rejection of this name marks the beginning of a transformation in their relationship.

The film convincingly depicts the lack of respect for personal boundaries often reported in the testimony of domestic workers. Yet the affect circulating in the partnership constructed between Angela and Gemma—just as Mezzadra and others describe in their writings on this form of care work—is composed of a cluster of complex emotions ranging from frustration and resentment to homesickness and reluctant compassion, encompassing Gemma's unfinished business with her absent son, Angela's anxiety about her unresponsive husband in Romania, and her unspoken concern that she may perhaps be pregnant. *Mar Nero* further suggests that the mistreatment of the young Romanian is not limited to the confines of the apartment she shares with Gemma. In fact, Angela is repeatedly subjected to verbal abuse by another Italian woman living in the same building, who screams at her in the stairwell, calling her a *zingarona* (gypsy) and threatening to report her to the immigration authorities.

Angela also becomes the target of the woman's husband's inopportune advances. As the film implies, her very identity as an Eastern European woman already marks her as a sexually exploitable commodity according to widely held Italian perceptions. In light of these fraught experiences and encounters, the brief scene showing Angela celebrating New Year's Eve with her Romanian friends has a special poignancy. At the moment in which 2006 gives way to 2007, the revelers jubilantly exclaim, "Europeni!" (Europeans!) as though, in an era of shared Europeanness, inequalities and exploitation will dissolve.

Mar Nero's narrative arc is built on the growing bond of trust that develops between Angela and her diffident employer, who was initially obliged by her son to accept the help of a caregiver against her own wishes. For most of the film, equal attention is paid to the older woman's resentment and the younger woman's efforts to withstand the rudeness, racism, and discrimination meted out to her as a matter of course. As the women grow more trusting of each other, however, Gemma becomes more sympathetic to the viewer and eventually moves to the center of the film's narrative focus. The turning point occurs when Angela announces that she will return to Romania to locate her troubled husband, who has inexplicably gone missing. Though limited in her cultural horizons and hindered by poor physical health, the older woman spontaneously decides to

Figure 2.4. Screen capture. Angela and Gemma in Romania. *Mar Nero* (2008)

accompany Angela on her journey to Sulina in the Danube Delta. In contrast to the straightforward realism of the earlier part of the film, the concluding scenes, set in Romania, are infused with an evocative tonality.

Echoing a trope found in earlier films highlighting journeys by Italian characters to the former Eastern bloc after the fall of communism (notably Gianni Amelio's *Lamerica* and Carlo Mazzacurati's *Il toro*), the Italian protagonist appears to step back into an earlier period of Italian history as she surveys her surroundings upon arrival in Romania. At first she is struck by the sight of horse-drawn carts that remind her of her Tuscan childhood, and later she appears to relish the old-fashioned attentions of an elderly man who kisses her hand and plies her with local brandy. *Mar Nero* thus builds to a conclusion that is less concerned with Angela than Gemma, whose relationship with her Romanian caregiver has been transformed into a journey that offers a new sense of energy and possibility. Although the missing Romanian husband is duly located and reunited with Angela, who then chooses to stay in Romania to take care of him, these circumstances are only schematically indicated for the viewer. As occurs in many other films featuring Italian immigrants, *Mar Nero*'s focus remains on what the Italian character has to gain from the encounter with the foreigner. For Gemma, this involves renewed vitality and autonomy, in short, a new lease on life that will certainly comprise further travel, at least within Italy (perhaps to Umbria, as she suggests). Angela's freely chosen immobility in her last scene in the film (where she declines to leave her husband's bed upon waking) offers an uncanny contrast to Gemma's newfound mobility. It is clear, however, that the young woman's fate is no longer a driving concern of the narrative. In its ultimate focus on the Italian

Figure 2.5. Screen capture. Carlo meets his father's wife. *Io, loro e Lara* (2009)

character's potential for transformation and redemption, the film's conclusion resonates with classical narratives of Orientalist awakening.

Though articulated in a very different comedic register, Carlo Verdone's *Io, loro e Lara* bears some comparison with Bondi's film. As in *Mar nero*, the plot involves the introduction of an Eastern European woman into an Italian household, a woman who then becomes a source of revitalization for the aging Italian entrusted to her care. In Verdone's film, Olga (Olga Balan) is a middle-aged Moldovan woman, already well settled in Italy, who has been hired to take care of Alberto (Sergio Fiorentini), the widowed patriarch of a bourgeois Roman family, who soon marries her without announcing his intention to his three adult children. The comic force of the film is unleashed by their discovery of this union. While Alberto exuberantly flaunts his happiness and renewed priapic vigor, his adult sons and daughter refuse to share his joy, appalled that their inheritance will be devoured by a woman they see as a calculating interloper. Although this Eastern European woman appears to be a regular migrant, without visa problems, she is still treated with contempt—that is, as unworthy of enjoying the status of wife in the Italian home.

In a telling scene in the early part of the film, the older son, Carlo (a sympathetic missionary priest played by Verdone himself), finds himself incapable of referring to his father's new wife by her name. Instead, he repeatedly refers to her as *la badante*, as if she were forever identified with this subaltern role. While Carlo's lapsus is presented as comedy, the viewer is simultaneously prompted to consider how the term *badante* is already inflected with derogatory or xenophobic overtones. Even if the film's overall viewpoint appears to take the side of Olga against her newfound husband's self-interested offspring, the narrative ultimately makes her pay for her unexpected good fortune by having her die of a heart attack while having vigorous sex with the Viagra-fortified Alberto. She is not irreplaceable, however. In the film's final scene, the once-grieving Alberto is seen beaming with joy in the company of a new (and younger) migrant caregiver.[36]

The films I have described in this section explicitly refer to the growing reliance on migrant labor for the provision of care in Italy. Their construction of this phenomenon through the figure of the Eastern European migrant resonates to varying degrees with Pei-Chia Lan's argument—anticipated in Italian feminist writings of the early 1970s—that paid and unpaid domestic work should not be considered as two separate entities but rather as "structural continuities that characterize the feminization of domestic labor across the public and private sphere."[37] In a study of the factors implicated in the increased use of foreign caregivers in Italian households at present, Dawn Lyon has similarly noted that "the labor of migrant carers in personal services is marginalized as unproductive and is not seen as real 'work,'" just as the unpaid labor of Italian women traditionally undertaking these caretaking tasks was devalued in the past.[38] However, despite the social perception of such labor as "unproductive," the films that I have discussed strongly suggest that Eastern European women caregivers do, in fact, produce *affect* by offering the material and emotional support once provided by wives, daughters, or other family members.

By scrutinizing the unfolding of these audiovisual narratives, it is easy to discern their conservative underpinnings; their barely concealed nostalgia for the figure of the stay-at-home mother, long-lasting marriages, and extended family networks, and their perceptible ambivalence vis-à-vis the immigrants employed to make good the resulting void. At the same time, these films clearly suggest the ways in which transnational care workers operating in Italy at present are vitally imbricated in the production of cultural and social relations in the globalized arena.

Conclusion

In a range of expressive registers, the films discussed in this chapter evoke the circumstances experienced by migrant women from the former Eastern bloc who undertook the process of migration to Italy after 1989 and found themselves enmeshed in various forms of affective labor, whether forced or willingly undertaken. I do not claim that these films illuminate in a literal way the actual social conditions prevalent at the time of their production or that they present a straightforward critique of the abuses often meted out to vulnerable women who cross borders bereft of the required visas or work permits and of material and psychological support. Rather, I observe the ways in which they resonate with contemporary concerns about the reproduction of the (white) national subject. Engaging with a phenomenon that emerged in Italy after 1990, when migration from the East began to affect Italy to a substantial degree, they build scenarios around the figure of the white (yet not-quite white) Eastern European woman, a figure that embodies both ambivalence and compensatory promise.

The films' collective preoccupation with the growing presence of Eastern European women engaged in various forms of affective labor points to a larger phenomenon of female migration occurring across the European continent. This phenomenon is referenced in numerous films from other European countries, which tend, however, to be more specifically concerned with issues of trafficking than with affective labor more generally. Examples include *Lilya 4-Ever* (Lukas Moodysson, 2002), *Svetlana's Journey* (Michael Cory Davis, 2004), *Eastern Promises* (David Cronenburg, 2007), and *Taken* (Pierre Morel, 2009).[39] In the Italian films I have discussed—which, perhaps significantly, emerged in a slightly earlier period—trafficking is not the dominant trope. Despite the occasional representation of violent and abusive practices, within the narrative economy of these films, the narrative payoff of seeing justice done in a world of brutality or exploitation is almost entirely absent. Offering more ambivalent or open-ended conclusions than the productions originating elsewhere in Europe, the Italian films collectively explore the capacity of Eastern European women to reproduce whiteness in the Italian social landscape. In other words, they posit this figure as a passable ethnoracial substitute for those native women who previously occupied such subordinate roles.

Finally, although the films I have discussed here often suggest an oblique criticism of the abuses endured by vulnerable migrant women who entered Italy in the first fifteen years after the end of the Cold War, their fascination with this wounded, often self-sacrificing female figure may, in fact, bear an inverse relationship to the image—and actual presence—of more powerful and resourceful women in contemporary Italy whose lives have been profoundly altered by the legacy of the feminist movement of the 1970s. These narratives of female migration may serve an unconscious, compensatory function through which the masochistic and sadistic mechanisms of cinematic narrative can be "logically" deployed, inadvertently revealing while simultaneously allaying the anxieties of a beleaguered Italian masculinity in the global era.

Notes

1. The image of the migrant hordes is taken up ironically by journalist Gian Antonio Stella in the title of his book *L'orda: Quando gli albanesi eravamo noi* (Milan: BUR, 2003), which translates as "The horde: When *we* were the Albanians." In response to Italy's recent migratory influx and the attendant surge in xenophobia, Stella gives an account of the massive emigration of Italians across the globe in the past, describing the ways in which they were perceived and treated in foreign lands.

2. For an exploration of the meanings and usage of such terms, see Lorenzo Guadagnucci, *Parole sporche. Clandestini, nomadi, vu cumprà: Il razzismo nei media e dentro di noi* (Milan: Altreconomia, 2010).

3. Ester Gallo and Francesca Scrinzi, *Migration, Masculinities and Reproductive Labour: Men of the Home* (New York: Palgrave Macmillan, 2016), 111.

4. Manuela Coppola and Sonia Sabelli, "Not a Country for Women, nor for Blacks," in *Teaching "Race" with a Gendered Edge*, ed. Brigitte Hipfl and Kristín Loftsdóttir (Utrecht: Atgender, 2012), 147–48.

5. Lega Nord's insistence that immigrants would deprive native Italians of their employment was entirely spurious. Given the country's consistently low birthrate in recent decades, the workforce was experiencing a growing need for the infusion of laborers from abroad.

6. For a detailed denunciation of the CPT with testimonials by former detainees, see Marco Rovelli, *I lager italiani* (Rome: Biblioteca Università Rizzoli, 2006). See also Federica Sassi, *Autobiografie negate: Immigrati nei lager del presente* (Rome: Manifestolibri, 2002).

7. My initial exploration of a small portion of the films discussed in this section appears in an earlier essay. See Áine O'Healy, "Border Traffic: Reimagining the Voyage to Italy," in *Transnational Feminism in Film and Media*, ed. Katarzyna Marciniak, Anikó Imre, and Áine O'Healy (New York: Palgrave Macmillan, 2007), 59–72. The current analysis, however, opens up the earlier discussion on migrant sex work, forced prostitution, and sex trafficking to include recent theoretical developments on the subject of trafficking and migrant women's labor.

8. Sandro Mezzadra, "Taking Care: Migration and the Political Economy of Affective Labor," March 16, 2005, Caring Labor: An Archive. July 29, 2010. https://caringlabor.files.wordpress.com/2010/12/mezzadra_taking_care.pdf (accessed July 19, 2018). Mezzadra's insights on the global caregiver are revised and updated in Sandro Mezzadra and Brett Neilson, *Border as Method, or the Multiplication of Labor* (Durham, NC: Duke University Press, 2013), 95–111.

9. Mezzadra, "Taking Care,"

10. Nicholas De Genova, "Migrant 'Illegality' and Deportability in Everyday Life," *Annual Review of Anthropology* 31 (2002): 419–47.

11. Sandro Mezzadra and Brett Neilson, "Borderscapes of Differential Inclusion: Subjectivity and Struggles on the Threshold of Justice's Excess," in *The Borders of Justice*, ed. Étienne Balibar, Sandro Mezzadra, and Ranabir Samaddar (Philadelphia: Temple University Press, 2002), 181–203. See also Mezzadra and Neilson, *Border as Method*, 23 and passim.

12. Encarnación Gutiérrez-Rodríguez, "The 'Hidden' Side of the New Economy: On Transnational Migration, Domestic Work, and Unprecedented Intimacy," *Frontiers* 28, no. 3 (2007): 73.

13. Parvulescu, *Traffic in Women's Work*, 7.

14. Parvulescu, 10.

15. Parvulescu, 10.

16. Parvulescu, 11.

17. Silvana Rugolotto, Alice Larotonda, and Sjaak van der Geest, "How Migrants Keep Italian Families Italian: Badanti and the Private Care of Older People," *International Journal of Migration, Health and Social Care* 13, no. 2 (2017): 185–97, https://doi.org/10.1108/IJMHSC-08-2015-0027.

18. Among similar initiatives, in 2008 politician Daniela Santanché argued for a referendum to repeal the 1958 Merlin Law that had abolished Italy's state-sanctioned brothels.

19. For a discussion of the complex issues subtending sex work by migrant woman in Italy today, see Irene Peano, "Excesses and Double Standards: Migrant Prostitutes, Sovereignty and Exceptions in Contemporary Italy," *Modern Italy* 17, no. 4 (2012): 419–32.

20. Rutvica Andrijasevic, "The Difference Borders Make: (Il)legality, Migration and Trafficking in Italy among Eastern European Women in Prostitution," in *Uprootings/Regroundings: Questions of Home and Migration*, ed. Sara Ahmed, Claudia Castañeda, Anne-Marie Fortier, and Mimi Sheller (New York: Berg, 2003), 251–72.

21. Some of the best-known examples are found in Luigi Zampa's *La romana* (*Woman of Rome*, 1954), Antonio Pietrangeli's *Adua e le sue compagne* (*Adua and Her Friends*, 1956),

Federico Fellini's *Notti di Cabiria* (*Nights of Cabiria*, 1957), Luchino Visconti's *Rocco e i suoi fratelli* (*Rocco and His Brothers*, 1960), Pier Paolo Pasolini's *Mamma Roma* (1963), and Lina Wertmüller's *Amore e Anarchia* (*Love and Anarchy*, 1973). For a study of the representation of prostitutes in Italian cinema from the 1940s to the mid-1960s, see Danielle Hipkins, *Italy's Other Women: Gender and Prostitution in Italian Cinema, 1940–1965* (Oxford: Peter Lang, 2016). Hipkins's research reveals the astonishing frequency with which this figure appears in the corpus of films produced during the period examined.

22. In this period of Italian cinema, the nationality of the actress rarely coincides with the roles she plays. For example, we find a Polish actress playing the part of the Romanian Ileana in *Elvjs & Merilijn*, and another Polish actress is cast as the Russian Alia in *Un'altra vita*. Similarly, the role of an enigmatic Kosovar fugitive in Valori's *Radio West* is played by Kasia Smutniak, a Polish actress based in Italy, and the Ukrainian protagonist of *La sconosciuta* is played by Russian actress Ksenia Rappoport, who has in recent years worked frequently in Italy. While the dialogue is always in a language appropriate to the character and the specific narrative situation, knowledgeable viewers can recognize a "foreign accent" in the speech of the actors attempting to approximate their character's "native" pronunciation. Although the linguistic aspect of these films signals a shift away from the long-established Italian preference for dubbing over subtitling, little attention is paid to differences within the category of "the foreign."

23. Teresa de Lauretis, "Desire in Narrative," in *Alice Doesn't: Feminism, Semiotics, Cinema* (Bloomington: Indiana University Press, 1982), 132–33. The assertion that "sadism demands a story" is found in Laura Mulvey, "Visual Pleasure and Narrative Cinema," *Screen* 16, no. 3 (1975): 14.

24. Kristeva's account of abjection has had a powerful hold on an important strain of Anglophone feminist theory over the past two decades. While this model provides a convincing theorization of the origins of misogyny and related exclusionary discourses, it is nonetheless problematical insofar as it posits the positive and transgressive potentiality of encounters with the abject. As Imogen Tyler has argued, to focus on this aspect of the Kristevan paradigm risks reproducing rather than challenging discourses of violent disgust toward "abjected" bodies. Tyler boldly reorients Kristeva's theory of the abject, arguing for a social and political account of abjection rather than a purely psychoanalytical one. Specifically, Tyler's project focuses on the consequences of being abject within specific social and political contexts. See Imogen Tyler, *Revolting Subjects: Social Abjection and Resistance in Neoliberal Britain* (London: Zed Books, 2013).

25. The vampiric nuances elicited by Toni Bertolelli's performance in this film are amplified intertextually with the actor's subsequent performance as Dracula in *Zora la vampira* (Manetti Bros., 2000).

26. Slavoj Žižek, *Metastases of Enjoyment*, 212–13.

27. Claudia Morgoglione, "Il mistero della Sconosciuta--Tornatore fra cronaca e noir," *La Repubblica*, October 18, 2006, http://www.repubblica.it/2006/10/sezioni/spettacoli_e_cultura/cinema/roma/sconosciuta-tornatore/sconosciuta-tornatore/sconosciuta-tornatore.html.

28. Linda Williams, "'Something Else besides a Mother': *Stella Dallas* and the Maternal Melodrama," *Cinema Journal* 24, no. 1 (1984): 2–27.

29. In this section I draw in part on a previously published essay: Áine O'Healy, "Bound to Care: Gender, Affect, and Immigrant Labor," in *Italian Political Cinema: Public Life, Imaginary, and Identity in Contemporary Italian Film*, ed. Giancarlo Lombardi and Christian Uva (Oxford: Peter Lang, 2016), 56–67.

30. Mezzadra, "Taking Care," 1.

31. Arlie Hochschild, *The Managed Heart: Commercialization of Human Feeling* (Berkeley: California University Press, 1983).

32. Jacqueline Andall, *Migration and Domestic Service: The Politics of Black Women in Italy* (Aldershot, UK: Ashgate, 2000); Bridget Anderson, *Doing the Dirty Work? The Global Politics of Domestic Labour* (London: Zed Books, 2000); Gutiérrez-Rodríguez, "'Hidden Side' of the New Economy," 60–83; and Rhacel Salazar Parreñas, *Servants of Globalization* (Palo Alto: Stanford University Press, 2001).

33. Franca van Hooren, "When Families Need Immigrants: The Exceptional Position of Migrant Domestic Workers and Care Assistants in Italian Immigration," *Bulletin of Italian Politics* 2, no. 2 (2010): 21–38.

34. Francesca Bettio, Annamaria Simonazzi, and Paola Villa, "Change in Care Regimes and Female Migration: The 'Care Drain' in the Mediterranean," *Journal of European Social Policy* 16, no. 3 (2006): 271–85.

35. Bondi reveals this information in an interview provided with the extras in the DVD release of the film.

36. *Io, loro e Lara* has a plot twist that unwittingly points to the differential status of the sexual labor performed by white European women on the one hand and by African women on the other. In the course of the film, Olga's daughter (who was in any case born in Italy) is revealed to be working as a cam girl, coyly exposing her breasts while chatting with clients on the internet in order to meet her financial needs. At the same time, three African girls, whom Carlo had known during his missionary work in Africa, are engaged in street prostitution in Rome. At the film's end, Carlo "rescues" the Africans and sends them back to Africa, thus removing them permanently from Italian soil, whereas Olga's daughter finds a way to free herself from the necessity of selling sex for money, retrieves her young son from foster care, and assumes a central role in Carlo's father's household.

37. Pei-Chia Lan, *Global Cinderellas: Migrant Domestics and Newly Rich Employers in Taiwan* (Durham, NC: Duke University Press, 2006), 13.

38. Dawn Lyon, "The Organization of Care Work in Italy: Gender and Migrant Labor in the New Economy," *Indiana Journal of Global Legal Studies* 13, no. 1 (2006): 207–24.

39. For a survey of European films focused on themes of trafficking, see William Brown, Dina Iordanova, and Leshu Torshin, *Moving People, Moving Images: Cinema and Trafficking in the New Europe* (St. Andrews, UK: St. Andrews Film Studies, 2010).

CHAPTER 3

African Immigration in the 1990s

IMMIGRATION TO ITALY from the African continent, already underway in the 1970s, continued to grow steadily during the last decade of the twentieth century, although the rate of growth was relatively modest vis-à-vis the surge of immigration from Eastern Europe during the same period. The immigrants arriving from Africa before the 1990s had come for the most part from Morocco and Egypt and generally arrived by air or by way of Italy's land border with France. Gradually, in the 1990s, there was an increase in immigration from Tunisia, Senegal, Nigeria, and elsewhere in Africa. Citizens of Italy's former territories in the Horn of Africa also continued to migrate to Italy, but these migrants were fewer.

Despite the relatively modest number of black Africans residing in Italy up to the end of the twentieth century, incidents of racially inflected violence committed against them were reported even in the 1980s. Such hostility, considered by many to be alien to the national character, resonated with circumstances reported simultaneously in other parts of Western Europe, which were witnessing the rapid growth of anti-immigrant attitudes and the emergence of violent skinhead organizations. In 1989 the murder of South African agricultural worker and labor activist Jerry Masslo at the hands of local thugs in the province of Caserta triggered outrage among many Italians. By drawing attention to the untenable conditions experienced by migrant laborers employed informally in seasonal agricultural work in the Italian South, Masslo's death led to changes in the legislative process that were formalized with the Martelli law, Italy's first genuine legislation on immigration, which came into force in 1990. With the tightening of visa requirements, individuals traveling to Italy from African countries were less likely to enter Italy by land or air and began a pattern of irregular maritime migration across the Strait of Sicily, a pattern that endures to this day.

In 1991 Étienne Balibar predicted that the shift in boundaries precipitated by the fall of the Berlin Wall would lead to a major transformation in the symbolic demarcation between Europe and what lies beyond. Writing at a time when incidents of violence committed against people of color were on the increase in various parts of the continent, he argued that the imaginary edge of Europe was about to shift from east to south: "The future of the 'iron curtain' and the future 'wall' threaten to pass somewhere in the Mediterranean, or somewhere southeast of the Mediterranean."[1] As Balibar's prediction gradually came to fruition in the new millennium, Italy, with its extensive maritime border, would become increasingly implicated in the securitization of the Mediterranean Sea, participating fully in the EU effort to stem irregular migration from the global South.

In this chapter I explore how tensions activated by migration from the African continent resonate in Italian cinema in the 1990s through the construction of African migrants as a compromised and compromising presence in the national space. While the presence of black and brown bodies on Italian screens was not entirely new, they acquire a more consistent narrative weight from the 1990s onward. Indeed the representation of North African, Arab, and mixed-race characters in Italian cinema has a long history, beginning with the epics of the silent era, reflecting in complex ways Italy's entanglements with ideologies of race and policies of colonial conquest, and often unwittingly revealing traces of the country's own history of internal fracture, poverty, and emigration.[2] By the 1990s, however, the cinematic response to the racial diversity of Italy's new migrants has to be considered within a broader field of tensions vis-à-vis European belonging, the pressure placed on the nation as the imputed gateway to "Fortress Europe," and the burgeoning of anti-immigrant populist rhetoric in Italy and beyond.

In 1991, in anticipation of the upcoming Maastricht Treaty, Jan Nederveen Pieterse observed the upsurge of what he described, with intended irony, as a "respectable xenophobia" mushrooming throughout the continent, "pushing some of the collective dreams for 1992 to cluster around a concept of Europe which is white, racist and much more powerful than any post-war individual state." National identities, he argued, were thus being transformed into a "white Continentalism," with European unity being defined against "alien" cultures and around a self-image of European superiority.[3] Significantly, in the course of an interview recorded in 1991, Umberto Eco moved quickly from a discussion of immigration to an observation on skin color, asserting the inevitability of a racially altered Europe. Eco's association of immigration with the issue of race takes on a troubling ambiguity as he simultaneously invokes the image of the Barbarian invasion: "We are facing a migration comparable to the early

Indo-European migrations, East to West, or the invasion of the Roman Empire by the Barbarians.... The new migration will radically change the face of Europe. In one hundred years Europe could be a colored continent."[4] Adding that contemporary Europeans must be "culturally, mentally ready to accept a multiplicity, to accept inter-breeding,"[5] Eco thus envisions the demographic transformations currently taking place in Europe as a potentially enriching phenomenon comparable to the infusion of diversity brought about by the arrival of the so-called Barbarians in late antiquity. His audience, on the other hand, was unlikely to be reassured by the image of miscegenation, associated here with the highly charged image of "Barbarians." Indeed, if taken out of context, Eco's prediction of a "colored continent" seems to foreshadow the reactionary discourses of Lega Nord and Alleanza Nazionale. At a time when discourses of "Europeanness" and "Italianness" were being reaffirmed in the face of a rapidly growing immigrant population, references to skin color were often used as a signal for exclusionary or even violent practices.

An understanding of the discourses of race and racism in Italy today requires a broader consideration of its history of colonial conquest. It is often argued that Italy was a comparatively minor player in the vast enterprise of imperial expansion: it came relatively late to the colonial project, conquered fewer overseas territories than the major European powers, and withdrew from these before the end of World War II. Even today, references to Italy's contribution to infrastructural improvements in its occupied territories are frequently offered by Italians wishing to bolster the image of a uniquely benign colonial history, summed up in the popular cliché "Italiani brava gente" ("Italians, decent people"). Although there has been a marked increase in interest in Italian colonialism on the part of historians and cultural theorists over the past twenty years, this interest has not resulted in greater awareness at the popular level, where clichés and stereotypes rooted in the colonial era have been recycled in the service of anti-immigrant sentiment.

One of the distinctive aspects of Italian colonial history is that it involved the appropriation of territories both external and internal to the Italian peninsula itself. Arguing for the necessity of bringing postcolonial discourse to bear on discussions of contemporary Italy, Pasquale Verdicchio has pointed to the annexation of southern Italy to the new nation-state formed in the northern regions as essentially a colonizing project. Echoing Gramsci, Verdicchio claims that Italian identity was constructed at the outset on the purported racial alterity of southern Italians and on the representation of Italy's South as a bridge to Africa.[6]

Over the past fifteen years, the postcolonial lens has proved a useful tool in the analysis of contemporary Italian culture and society, enabling scholars working in Italy to refine their understanding of Italian constructions of race and subalternity within the larger historical picture. Along lines similar to Verdicchio's argument, Miguel Mellino claims that Italy is postcolonial not only because it once had colonies overseas but also because of what he describes as the "internal colonial fracture" instantiated by the takeover of the southern territories during Unification. The nineteenth-century conquest of the South—he asserts—was driven by the logic of colonialism and imperialism, anti-Southern racism, and the rhetoric of civilizing purpose. Promoted by the northern elites after Unification, these tactics ultimately reflected a "local translation of the Western 'civilizing mission' discourse and its constitutive colonial racism."[7]

Unlike nations such as France and the United Kingdom that experienced massive immigration from areas they had colonized or annexed in the past, Italy is inhabited by a relatively small percentage of migrants hailing from the countries that were once the major focus of its colonizing ambitions. As Cristina Lombardi-Diop and Caterina Romeo point out, the application of the term *postcolonial* to the circumstances of contemporary Italy must be adjusted in accordance with the specificity of the Italian case. They propose, in effect, that a postcolonial perspective on Italy should position itself "not in relation to the British and French histories of empire, in which the migratory fluxes were almost exclusively coming from previous colonies, but rather to the post-Cold War reconfiguration of Europe and its emerging postcolonialities."[8]

Like Europe more generally, Italy is a space that is fully implicated in the neocolonial regime of global capitalism, a system whose borders are both more ubiquitous and elusive than those of historical colonialism but whose modalities of exclusion and marginalization are no less insistent. Indeed, as Sandro Mezzarda has argued, the "metaborder" between the metropole and its respective colonies that characterized the colonial era has given way to a vastly altered geographical disposition as the mechanisms of domination and subordination inherited from colonialism are currently being reproduced within the space of Europe itself.[9] This, of course, does not mean that Italy's postcolonial status is the same as Europe's as a whole. Writing specifically about the Italian context, Mellino discerns a contemporary proliferation of "(post)colonial fractures" within the space of the national territory as Italy's social space is increasingly segmented and disturbed "by material and symbolic racist violence against postcolonial migrant subjectivities as well as by antiracist riots against institutional, popular, and cultural racism."[10] These are the tensions that I highlight in my analyses of the films selected in this chapter, but I first examine the racial discourses embedded in the conventions of visual representation at the national level over the decades preceding the advent of mass immigration.[11]

In Italian visual culture more generally, images of Africa and Africans have been circulated since the period following Unification, when Italian adventurers made their initial forays into the Horn of Africa and settled in what is now known as Eritrea. It was not until the early twentieth century, however, that configurations of black Africans became a significant element in public discourse. This process was intensified with the burgeoning of Fascist propaganda in the 1920s and 1930s, when Italy laid claim to progressively larger swaths of East Africa.

Central to the iconography of the Fascist regime, the figure of the black African served as a foil against which Italy's national identity could be consolidated. Heavily charged representations of Africanness, which oscillated between fetishizing constructions of racialized eroticism to straightforward images of debasement, were routinely circulated in Italian magazines, newspapers, advertising campaigns, domestic objects, food packaging, and films. This practice has had an enduring impact on the national imaginary, outlasting the relatively short span of Italy's colonial adventures, as several scholars writing on the visual culture of postcolonial Italy have compellingly demonstrated.[12] Yet no formal process of decolonization drew the nation's attention to the crimes Italy had committed in the occupied territories or to the discursive legacy that its imperializing ambitions had embedded in popular visual culture and everyday attitudes.

Although images of Africa and Africans continued to circulate in various forms in late twentieth-century Italy, these were not consistently associated with the memory of colonialism. Indeed, from the 1960s onward, the pejorative use of the adjective "African" was more likely to be applied to the citizens of Italy's southern regions than to populations south of the Mediterranean. While the legacy of colonial attitudes has cast a long shadow on Italian articulations of otherness, the racializing tropes deployed during the expansionist era and adapted for various uses over the intervening years constitute an archive of images and attitudes that have been naturalized over time in a culture where the historical experience of violent occupation is to a large extent disavowed.

Throughout most of the second half of the twentieth century, an awareness of Italy's geographical proximity to Africa expressed itself in popular discourse in subtle, indirect ways. Unspoken anxieties regarding the nation's relative isolation from the principal centers of European life, its simultaneous closeness to North Africa, and the occasionally disputed "whiteness" of Italians themselves were projected onto southern Italians, who were often referred to disparagingly as "Moroccans" or "Africans" by some of those born in regions farther to the North. The racialization of southerners was particularly acute during the economic boom of the 1960s, when migration from the southern regions to the industrial centers of northern Italy was in its most intense phase.[13] However, in the wake of the more recent migrations to Italy from North Africa and from the sub-Saharan region—a phenomenon that refocused the nation's attention on the proximity of Africa and on the permeability of Italy's Mediterranean boundary—these terms of disparagement could no longer be applied in quite the same way to southern Italians as Moroccans and other migrants from the African continent arrived to claim a place in the cities, towns, and villages of Italy. These generalized shifts in perception resonate implicitly in specific films made during the last decade of the twentieth century.

From *Pummarò* to *L'Articolo 2*: Expelling African Men

Around 1990, Africans from the Maghreb and sub-Saharan countries began to appear in a range of roles in Italian feature films. At first, the figure of the explicitly racialized other—the "Arab" or the "African"—was deployed principally as local color in narratives set against a backdrop of Italy's urban landscape, as occurs, for example, with the appearance of African street vendors in Federico Fellini's penultimate feature film, *Intervista* (Interview, 1988). Soon, however, characters from Africa began to inhabit more important roles in Italian films. *Pummarò* (Tomato, Michele Placido, 1990) and *L'Articolo 2* (Article 2, Maurizio Zaccaro, 1994) are the two principal films made in the early 1990s that self-consciously attempt to critique the growing xenophobia directed against African and Arab immigrants to Italy. With an immigrant from Africa occupying the lead role in each film, the events unfold from the point of view of the beleaguered foreigner, calling on the viewer to identify with his circumstances. Adopting a more or less explicit position on the need for greater intercultural understanding in Italian society, the films thus position themselves within a tradition of social critique that harks back to the *cinema d'impegno* of the 1960s and 1970s. While I acknowledge that each of them engages critically with problems of racial discrimination, violence, and negative stereotyping, I am interested in exploring the gaps and contradictions in their representational economies, observing how they stop short of questioning their own access to the perspectives they purport to recount.

Both *Pummarò* and *L'Articolo 2* were inspired in part by recent events. The first was prompted by the murder of Jerry Masslo in the Neapolitan hinterland in 1989 and the second by a news story about a North African immigrant whose attempt to reside in Italy with his two wives led to a confrontation with the legal authorities. Both films construct chilling scenes of racially motivated violence reminiscent of incidents reported in the national media and are clearly intended to draw sympathy for the circumstances of racially marked migrants attempting to settle in Italy. Their protagonists, a Ghanaian migrant in the first film and an Algerian worker and resident of Milan in the second, are immediately apprehended by their diegetic interlocutors as racially or ethnically other. This instantly perceived otherness prompts a variety of reactions from their Italian interlocutors, ranging from exploitation, resentment, and physical attack to charitable intervention, romanticizing projection, and erotic fascination.

Pummarò is the directorial debut of Michele Placido, one of Italy's most popular screen actors.[14] Placido also receives a screenwriting credit, along with

Sandro Petraglia and Stefano Rulli. The story follows the journey of Kwaku (played by nonprofessional actor Thywill A. K. Amenya), a young Ghanaian physician who enters Italy as a stowaway with the intention of tracking down his older brother Giobbe, who has been supporting his studies. The film's title, which means "tomato" in Neapolitan dialect, is the generic nickname attached to Giobbe, who, until just before Kwaku's arrival in Italy, worked as a laborer in the tomato fields of Campania, in an area where unscrupulous *camorristi* are known to exploit the immigrant workforce (the same territory where the South African migrant Masslo had been killed a short time before the film was made). Following a dispute about unjust wages, Giobbe had threatened his employers at gunpoint and fled to Rome in a hijacked truck. After working for some days in the tomato fields, Kwaku follows Giobbe's path up through the boot of Italy, first searching for him in Rome, where he meets a Kenyan prostitute who is expecting Giobbe's child. On hearing that his brother has moved to Verona, however, Kwaku resumes his northward journey. Although he fails to find Giobbe in Verona, he pauses there for some time, beginning a romantic relationship with an Italian woman, taking a job in a foundry, and eventually experiencing firsthand the brutality of Italian racism. Upon receiving news that his brother had found a job in Frankfurt, Kwaku then heads for Germany. His search comes to an end in a German morgue where, in the company of the pregnant Kenyan woman who had also loved Giobbe, he contemplates the lifeless body of his dead brother.[15]

The narrative is structured around set scenes that constitute "typical" situations experienced by impoverished African migrants living in Italy. The three labor sectors explored by the film—unregulated agricultural work in Campania, female prostitution in Rome, and nonunionized industrial labor in the north of Italy—are intended to encapsulate the circumstances experienced by many Africans working in Italy in the early 1990s. In the process, a number of grim social realities are briefly dramatized in a rather schematic fashion.

Kwaku's unscrupulous Italian employers on the tomato farm in Campania emerge as predictable characters, similar to the *mafiosi* or *camorristi* in countless popular films, while the African workers are shown for the most part as innocent victims with little recourse to justice. The sequence in the tomato fields, however, also features an eccentric local character, known to all as "the Professor," who labors alongside the Africans and earns some extra cash by obtaining forged work permits on their behalf. Though not beyond extorting money from vulnerable migrants, the so-called Professor is not averse to living with the Africans, making his bed alongside them among the tombs of a nearby cemetery. Thus the image of the exploitative Italians is counterbalanced at the outset of the film with that of an eccentric, purportedly benevolent southern Italian who seeks the companionship of immigrant laborers, even if he retains tacit dominance over them through his ability to exploit them. Sympathetic Italian characters are nonetheless rare in this film, which presents a bleak picture of pervasive prejudice, exploitation, and hostility. In fact, the "Professor" is eventually brutalized by the *camorristi* for his effort to help Kwaku, just as Kwaku's Italian girlfriend in Verona is threatened and punished for her association with him later in the film.

In an astute analysis of *Pummarò*, David Forgacs lays bare some of the flaws underpinning the film's representation of its protagonist, arguing that Kwaku is not only exoticized by the camera but is also eroticized. This process is enabled by the film's visual strategies, which present Kwaku as a figure to "be looked at [even] as he ... looks," implicating the viewer in a position akin to voyeurism.[16] As Forgacs notes, however, the fascination of the filmmaker with the exotic other is not immediately apparent but is "driven down into the film's unconscious—repressed from its impeccably anti-racist storyline, [and] returns in the ambivalent structure of looking which the film offers the spectator."[17] What the film provides, as Forgacs's description implies, is an unconscious expression of (post) colonial desire.

Pummarò is also marked by an effort to idealize the African migrant in the name of multicultural inclusiveness; its delineation of Kwaku as a kind, hardworking, intelligent, accomplished, and loyal individual is clearly overdetermined. The simple gesture of reversing the stereotypical qualities attributed to the immigrant in popular discourse is patronizing at best, implicitly shoring up the Eurocentric value system of the colonizing imagination. To make Kwaku sympathetic to Italian audiences, the film presents him as an exceptionally accomplished human being. Not only is he a hard worker, willing to earn his living by any honest means, including shoveling manure, but he is also a qualified physician, en route to Canada to pursue a specialization in surgery. Not only did he study English as a boy in Ghana, but he also played the lead in a highschool production of *Romeo and Juliet,* from which he readily quotes an excerpt to his astonished Italian girlfriend as they stand beneath the balcony associated with the star-crossed Juliet. Kwaku, moreover, is linguistically gifted. Apart from English and presumably his native language, he has managed to acquire a command of Italian even before his arrival on Italian soil. He embodies, in effect, the ingratiating characteristics of colonial mimicry described by Homi Bhabha.[18]

As Forgacs has also noted, the awkwardness of the film's evocation of Kwaku's attractiveness sometimes borders on the comical, as occurs in the scene where Eleonora is visibly aroused at the sight of him playing the drums. Even though the filmmakers' intention here is to foreground yet another of the protagonist's many accomplishments, the film does this by deploying one of the most commonplace racial stereotypes, that of the black man "with rhythm." It is in fact precisely at this moment that Kwaku's purportedly irresistible "Africanness" emerges in full seductive force. As might be expected, the following sequence culminates in a scene of intense lovemaking at Eleonora's home. Though the

Figure 3.1. Screen capture. Kwaku in Frankfurt. *Pummarò* (1990)

film's signifying strategies eroticize Kwaku through the gaze of Eleonora, one can discern a simultaneous effort to avoid presenting him purely as an object of sexual desire. Indeed much care is taken to forestall the impression of the hypersexed predator that is part of the repertoire of stereotypes attributed to African men in the popular imagination. Thus, the sex scene is preceded by manifestations of Kwaku's good manners, his reserve, and his ability to cite Shakespeare at just the right moment.

For all his Euro-friendly accomplishments, for all his colonial mimicry, the narrative ultimately rewards its African protagonist. While Kwaku is tormented by racist thugs in Verona, abandoned by his Italian girlfriend, and disappointed in his expectation of finding his brother alive, he will clearly succeed in his personal goal—to go to Canada to complete his studies, a venture that his brother Giobbe had promised to support. Indeed, it is precisely through the brother's death that Kwaku achieves this possibility, and in the final scene of the film we see him receive a check from Giobbe's employer in Germany in compensation for his death.

The renegade brother, who appears less gifted, less exceptional, more typically "African," the young man who swaggeringly hijacked a truck in broad daylight, wielded a gun, and impregnated the Kenyan prostitute, is killed off by the narrative, unwittingly reflecting Italian society's negative attitudes toward immigrants. It should be noted, however, that although the film rewards Kwaku for his exceptionality, it nonetheless ejects him from Italian territory as he never wavers in his plan to continue on his path to faraway Canada. In an interesting twist, however, the final scene shows Kwaku strolling arm in arm through a Christmas market in Frankfurt with Giobbe's pregnant Kenyan girlfriend, suggesting that a deeper relationship may develop between them in the future. This concluding scenario is entirely consistent with similarly constituted fraternal triangles in other screenplays written by Petraglia and Rulli, most notably *La meglio gioventù* (*The Best of Youth*, Marco Tullio Giordana, 2003) and *Mio fratello è figlio unico* (My Brother Is an Only Child, Daniele Luchetti, 2007). A major difference, however, is that in this case, the compensatory legacy (the gift—or "exchange"—of a woman) bequeathed by a dead brother to his surviving counterpart is pointedly allocated to a space outside Italy's borders.

Zaccaro's *L'Articolo 2* also presents a migrant from the African continent who, by the story's end, is definitively removed from Italy, a country he had lived in for many years. The film nonetheless offers a more nuanced construction of Italian responses to the presence of immigrants than *Pummarò* and raises some important questions about the difficulties inherent in building a multicultural society.[19] The fact that *L'articolo 2* was shot for the most part in Arabic and subtitled in Italian is in itself an important departure from the practices of Italian cinema, which throughout its history had tended to avoid subtitling in favor of dubbing.[20] Zaccaro's concession to linguistic realism should not be underestimated, and this aspect of the film already situates it at a different level of commitment to the cultural realities of contemporary Italy than that represented by *Pummarò*.

L'Articolo 2 begins in a remote community in the Algerian desert, where a young woman is caring for an elderly dying man. For the first twenty minutes of the film, there is frequent crosscutting between this setting and the densely populated Milan suburb where the woman's husband lives with his first wife and her children. The tranquility of the desert landscape is contrasted with the ear-splitting noise of the husband's construction job and the vulgarity of his Italian coworkers. This contrast inevitably exoticizes the North African setting. Though apparently a deeply patriarchal society rooted in Islamic custom, rural Algeria is constructed as a location inhabited principally by women, children, and old men and as a land where modernization has failed to penetrate.

The oppositions of modern and primitive, secular and religious, masculine and feminine are deployed repeatedly within the film, sometimes with more subtlety and ambivalence than might be expected. While Saïd, the protagonist (Rabia Ben Abdallah), wields uncontested authority as husband and father in his own family, for example, he is frequently humiliated or feminized in the presence of his coworkers and the Italian legal system. At one level, the film seems to valorize the stern family values of the protagonist in opposition to the promiscuity practiced (or at least claimed) by his Italian colleagues, one of whom decorates his locker with pin-ups and taunts Saïd with an anecdote about a tryst with an adolescent prostitute encountered in Morocco. At home, however, Saïd treats his wives and daughters in a manner that is alien to contemporary Western practices. Although his young son goes to school and learns to read, write, and speak Italian and to form companionships with Italian children, his adolescent daughter is kept at home to help her mother with household tasks. On a number of occasions, the film foregrounds Saïd's imperious behavior toward his wives, from whom he expects absolute obedience. Arriving in Italy sooner than expected with her three small children, the younger wife, Fatma, is greeted with a sharp slap on the face for having dared to begin her journey without her husband's prior permission. Yet the two women who submit to this regime do not express dissatisfaction, and the older wife quietly yields her place in the marriage bed as soon as the younger woman arrives in Milan. Ultimately the film constructs these long-suffering, virtually mute women as devoted to their husband and apparently content with their place in the family system.

The dramatic focus of the narrative is the cultural disruption that comes into play when the husband tells the immigration authorities that Fatma is his second wife. The rules of the Italian law are clear, however. Since a visa has been granted for one wife, the state cannot recognize the married status of the second woman or accept her application for a residence permit. The validity of this view is challenged by Saïd in court. Discovering that his trade union has provided a woman lawyer to represent him before the judge, he is astonished to the point of bitter hilarity; in fact, this is the only time he laughs in the course of the film. Saïd's demoralization increases in the courtroom as he listens to the lawyer aggressively arguing his case on the grounds of cultural pluralism. Although her assertive style of argument makes sense to the Western viewer, he grows increasingly worried as her voice is raised to shouting pitch. In short, he appears to understand nothing of her impassioned arguments or the values in which they are couched. When a court ruling finally emerges, it is unsatisfactory: Fatma will be allowed a visa provided she lives in a separate residence; yet, as the viewers already realize, this is financially impossible given the family's economic constraints. The Italian system, it is clear, cannot accommodate the social complexity of new multicultural realities.

L'Articolo 2 ultimately resorts to a deus-ex-machina intervention to provide the necessary narrative closure: in the next scene, Saïd is crushed to death in an industrial accident that occurs at a dangerous work site. The death scene is articulated in a highly melodramatic fashion, where Saïd, at the moment that he is about to expire, imagines himself as a boy digging for water in a deep hole in the desert, guided by the voice of his father, who waits for him above ground. This dreamlike vision leads into the film's brief concluding sequence, which consists of a long shot of the man's Algerian homeland as his coffin is unloaded from a van. A voice-over commentary tells us that even in death, no one paid attention to the specificity of Saïd's identity as the Italian undertakers had thoughtlessly assigned his body to a coffin embellished with a cross. Indeed, this lack of respect for his identity (as a Muslim rather than a Christian) parallels the way in which he was repeatedly referred to as Moroccan rather than Algerian by his interlocutors earlier in the film.

L'Articolo 2, unlike *Pummarò*, does not attempt to subvert the negative stereotypes associated with immigrants by constructing an idealized protagonist. Nor does it offer a completely negative picture of the Algerian family's interactions with Italians at a day-to-day level. While some of the Italian characters display hostility toward Saïd and his family, others appear to respond with ordinary decency. The central issue raised by Zaccaro's film, however, is a haunting one: namely, how are contemporary Italians going to accommodate the practices of Muslim immigrants in a modern, secular society that has been traditionally Christian? The acceptance of polygamy (which is not practiced by the vast majority of Muslim immigrants living in Italy) is just one of the challenges presented by the country's changing demographics. While the film is bold enough to broach some of dilemmas implicit in the shift to a multiethnic society, it ultimately subverts the urgency of these issues in its abruptly melodramatic conclusion. In the final scenes of the film, the thought-provoking contradictions raised earlier in the narrative are all too readily subsumed in a final rush of pathos. This pathos makes the film digestible as entertainment—complete with the conventional dream of a reunion of father and son—while letting its audiences off the hook on the more difficult issues of cultural assimilation and difference. Indeed it could be argued that the film simply dispenses with or kills off its "alien" characters as soon as its own didactic mission is achieved. And it is telling that neither of the wives is accounted for in the narrative conclusion. They seem to have been forgotten in the film's effort to wrap up and bury Saïd in a strategy that simply cuts all unresolved issues out of the picture. It is even more significant that *L'Articolo 2*, like *Pummarò*, anchors its conclusion in an appeal to the patriarchal family romance: the father calls out to his son in the vision of the dying Saïd, just as the older brother—clearly a father figure for Kwaku—reaches across the boundary of death to help his younger brother in the final scene of *Pummarò*.

Although *L'Articolo 2* attempts with greater subtlety than *Pummarò* to acknowledge the difficulties faced by foreigners in a postcolonial nation uneasy with cultural diversity, it, too, fails to make plain the blind spots in the liberal ideology that underpins the narrative's inspiration. Here as elsewhere, there is tendency to foreground the "folkloric" aspects of multiculturalism while underplaying the implications of some of the more daunting issues associated with immigration on a massive scale. Ultimately, while projecting onto the immigrant "other" the sentimental connotations of the patriarchal family romance, both narratives deftly disavow the difficulties of difference by appealing to what is assumed to be the same for all communities—the valorization of a bond that binds men to men, to the ultimate exclusion of women. One might well ask at what price to women—of all ethnicities and backgrounds—is this configuration being reinscribed in the name of multiculturalism?

Colonial Legacies and the Black Female Body

One of the most striking manifestations of the lingering power of colonial discourse in Italian films made before 2000 is the recurrent representation of the eroticized black female body. This trope emerges with varying degrees of self-reflexivity in three very different films constructing narratives of female migration from sub-Saharan Africa: *Teste rasate* (Skinheads, Claudio Fragasso, 1993), *L'assedio* (*Besieged*, Bernardo Bertolucci, 1997), and *Sud side stori* (South Side Story, Roberta Torre, 2000). Though all three of these films ostensibly place themselves in opposition to the patently xenophobic responses to immigration found in other Italian media sources, their attempts to construct narratives of cross-cultural encounter in a sympathetic manner are subverted by narrative or visual stratagems that convey contradictory impressions of the viability of the African woman's claim to a foothold in the national space. In other words, these films variously deploy, problematize, or ambivalently engage the stereotype of the Black Venus, upon which colonial configurations of the desire of a white male for a black African woman most often hinged.

In the course of Italian colonial history, the colonial encounter was imagined as a scene of desire.[21] In this scenario, the image of the alluring black woman came to stand for the populations whose willing submission would enable the realization of the colonial project. Furthermore, from the perspective of the white male colonist, the lure of African femininity was erotically charged. As Robert Young has observed, constructions of racial difference in various global contexts were linked from the outset to fantasies of "interminable, adulterating, aleatory, illicit, inter-racial sex."[22]

The figure of the black woman, which was relatively infrequent within the overall corpus of Italian cinema until the first decade of the twenty-first century, has played a significant place in the iconography of Italian political culture. Although interracial sexual relations were regarded with increasing suspicion during the Fascist period and were eventually banned outright, the sexual allure of indigenous women was abundantly documented by Italian photographers in the colonies during the 1930s and 1940s. According to Sandra Ponzanesi, "The exotic and alluring representations of the native served the purpose of inciting the virile and adventurous Italian soldiers and workers to venture into the unknown, uncharted and virgin soil of Africa. The inscriptions of the local women—as 'black Venus'—beautiful, docile and sexually available—corroborated the most important aspect of the rhetoric of empire which used the sexual metaphor as a way of fusing the public discourse with the private."[23]

In the ideological economy of Fascist propaganda, the representation of African women was thus linked alternately to the territorial allure of the distant colony and to the imagined horror of "interbreeding." In this way, hegemonic representations of the black female body oscillated between images of exotic beauty—which prevailed when young men were being recruited for Italy's expansionist projects—and those evoking repulsion. Even in the latter case, exemplified most dramatically in 1938 with the dissemination of an image of the so-called Hottentot Venus as a deterrent to interracial unions in Italian East Africa, the visualized black female body retained some of its sexual charge.[24]

Anxieties about contamination and hybridity were scarcely unique to Fascist Italy; they had been consolidated across the world through the concepts of racial difference formulated in Europe and the Americas throughout the long history of slavery and its racist consequences from the early seventeenth century to the second half of the twentieth century. As Young has argued in his analysis of nineteenth-century theories of race, this discursive process was fraught with ambivalence: "Racial theory, which ostensibly seeks to keep races forever apart, transmutes into expressions of the clandestine, furtive forms of what can be called 'colonial desire.'"[25] The legacy of nineteenth-century theories of race are indeed alive and flourishing in postcolonial Italy, where discussions of racial difference are often shot through with sexual implications.

Although the Italian colonial adventure ended with the collapse of Fascism in Italy, there has been a periodic recurrence of the figure of the Black Venus stereotype in Italian film production since the end of World War II. During the Cold War era, the figure of the African woman haunted the margins of several prominent Italian films, rarely occupying the focus of an entire scene but encroaching sporadically in silent, yet highly visible, ways on the space of the "real" agents of the narrative action—usually white, Italian males. In the 1950s and 1960s, black women tended to appear on screen for no more than the length of a dance routine or floorshow, in scenes invariably coded with elements of carnivalesque excess.[26] These eroticized projections of primitivism—where the African woman is invested with sexual connotations perceived as oppositional to the repressive atmosphere of a conservative, Catholic society—align the female African body with an animal sexuality, whose pleasures and dangers are contrasted on screen with the cool restraint of the diegetic Italian spectators.

Black women began to feature in Italian cinema as full-fledged characters only in the 1970s, in art cinema and in popular genres. In 1974, Ines Pellegrini, an Italian actress of Eritrean descent, appeared as the leading female character—a slave girl named Zumurrud—in Pier Paolo Pasolini's internationally distributed

Il fiore delle mille e una notte (*Arabian Nights*). Though she is shown nude in a sexual encounter early in the film, Pellegrini is not sexualized by the camera in the manner typical of configurations of black femininity. In fact, she spends most of her screen time dressed as a young man, a disguise adopted by her character to facilitate freedom of movement. Yet Zumurrud is scarcely devoid of representational tensions. As Giovanna Trento has pointed out, the film's construction of this character, whose main desire is to be the slave of a beautiful young man, is firmly imbricated in values and assumptions inherited from the colonial imagination.[27] In 1976, Pellegrini went on to play a much more conventionally sexualized figure in the erotic comedy *Una bella governante di colore*, directed by Luigi Russo. In this film, set in contemporary Italy, she embodies an attractive black housekeeper whose sexual appeal wreaks havoc in the dynamics of the family she is employed to serve. In this way, the beauty and menace conventionally associated with the Black Venus make an explicit return to Italian screens.

Another black actress, whose career paralleled that of Pellegrini, was the Ethiopian-born Zeudi Araya. Emerging into the spotlight in a series of erotic films in the early 1970s, she soon transitioned to celebrity status as the sexually appealing protagonist of several mainstream comedies such as Sergio Corbucci's *Il signor Robinson* (1976) and Giulio Paradisi's *Tesoromio* (1979). By the time these films were made, African women had begun to migrate to Italy in search of work, although their numbers were still small. As Marco Purpura has astutely observed, both films pinpoint Italian cultural anxieties about immigration that were emerging among Italian citizens for the first time due to the influx of African and Cape Verdean women finding employment in Italian households. Noting that the arrival of the African women on the Italian scene coincided with the first stirrings of women's liberation, Purpura observes that the tropes of racial masquerade enacted in these films locate "the black immigrant woman within adulterous romances in which Araya's exotic and submissive characters substitute for the emancipated white woman in the Italian family."[28] He argues that this doubling works both to invoke the colonial-era image of the docile Black Venus and to restore sexual potency to the ineffectual Italian male, threatened by the rise of feminism. What is crucial, as Purpura contends, is that these scenarios are framed "within a geographical dichotomy of inclusion in private spaces and exclusion from public spaces," so the black woman is either trapped within the domestic space of the Italian home or, when appearing in public, is located outside Italy's national borders.[29]

Although the sexual and racial politics underlying the representational economy of these films from the 1970s may seem problematical to many viewers today, the eroticization of the figure of the African woman, redolent of the Black Venus, has scarcely been superseded in more recent Italian cinema.[30] In what follows, I explore *Teste rasate, L'assedio,* and *Sud side stori* to analyze their configurations of African women while attempting to determine to what degree these representations are underpinned by an unwitting attachment to earlier discursive influences.

Teste rasate revolves in part around an interracial romance between a young Somali housekeeper named Zaira (Fabienne Gueye) and an unemployed, middle-class Italian youth named Marco (Gianmarco Tognazzi) who lives with his mother in the apartment building where Zaira works. Though encumbered by a flawed screenplay, uneven direction, and over-the-top performances, Fragasso's film has the merit of bringing attention to the phenomenon of anti-immigrant racism developing among Italian youth at the time, specifically among groups of young men described as *naziskin* (skinheads). The film opens, in fact, with a montage sequence set in the headquarters of such a group, where several young men, surrounded by Nazi insignia, engage in a rhythmical workout to the pounding beat of diegetic music. In this, the most carefully orchestrated scene in the film, the camera fetishizes the men's faces, movements, and muscular white bodies to an almost obsessive degree. Although the scene may be understood retrospectively as encapsulating the appeal the group will hold for the young male protagonist, it provides a puzzling introduction to the film.

Not long after meeting Zaira, Marco befriends the charismatic leader of this neo-Nazi group and falls under his spell. While concealing his relationship with Zaira from the group, and his skinhead status from Zaira herself, Marco is obliged by his newfound comrades to participate in violent attacks against foreigners sleeping in the streets. Although he continues to spend time with Zaira, there is a growing sense of danger in their association.

The film's designation of Zaira as Somali is not without significance in relation to Italy's colonial history. As Karen Pinkus observes in her study of visual culture during the Fascist era, of all the African women encountered by Italians in the colonized territory, it was generally agreed that the Somalis were the most desirable.[31] These attractive figures, whose features purportedly bore a resemblance to the physiognomy of Italians themselves, appeared in adventurers' photographs and written accounts, as well as in Fascist-era advertising, as enticing sirens, holding the promise of passionate, illicit sexuality.[32] Taking this figure back to the metropolitan hearth, however, was not the intended focus of colonial fantasy. *Teste rasate* thus undertakes an interesting narrative experiment in transplanting her to contemporary Rome.

In recent Italian cinema, African women are typically presented as sex workers or as maids. Indeed, as occurs in the case of Eastern European women, they are almost always associated with the types of labor that Italian women have abandoned in increasing numbers over the past twenty years. Though Zaira is explicitly presented as a housekeeper, the film's visual codes construct her as shifting between the dominant stereotypes, morphing from the hardworking, domestic figure seen in the initial encounter with Marco to the image of an alluring seductress and back again. The dialogue nonetheless provides her with a briefly sketched personal history by referring to her impoverished family in Mogadishu and to the money she has saved in the hope of alleviating their difficulties. These details are introduced, however, not to endow Zaira with any meaningful agency but as a pretext for the film's climactic sequence, where she inadvertently delivers a fatal stab wound to Marco while trying to prevent him from stealing her savings. Since the real focus of *Teste rasate* is Marco, once she has performed this act of violence, she literally vanishes from the scene. Like her colonial-era prototype, she is ultimately no more than an alluring image on the horizon of a masculine *Bildung*, to be summarily forgotten as soon as her symbolic function is fulfilled. Significantly, the film's final scene focuses on the pageantry of the skinheads' participation in Marco's funeral procession, which his mother witnesses in powerless anguish.

Reinventing the Black Venus: *L'assedio*

Despite the unprecedented demographic shifts that have occurred on the national scene over the past twenty years, female characters of color rarely feature in important roles in contemporary Italian cinema and in fact rarely speak. Both *L'assedio* and *Sud side stori* are exceptions to this trend in the 1990s. The films diverge from each other, however, in important ways. Distributed internationally, *L'assedio* is a dramatic feature made in English by one of Italy's most acclaimed directors, whereas *Sud side stori* is a carnivalesque musical directed by a then-emerging filmmaker that was never widely distributed, although it circulated to some acclaim on the film festival circuit. Yet, in their deployment of an interracial romance, both *L'assedio* and *Sud side stori* raise provocative issues vis-à-vis the cinematic construction of social subjects in relation to race, gender, and contemporary migration. Significantly, the female protagonists of these films are involved in the two forms of labor stereotypically associated with African women currently living in Italy: housekeeping and prostitution.

Adapted from a screenplay developed by Bertolucci's wife, Clare Peploe, *L'assedio*, which is considered a minor film in Bertolucci's overall corpus, constructs a relationship between a reclusive British musician and his young African housekeeper against a backdrop of contemporary Rome. Although the growing presence of Africans residing in Rome is referenced sporadically in the course of film's narrative unfolding, the larger question of immigration is incidental to the evolving love story. In fact, on a superficial level, *L'assedio* seems complicit with the ideological underpinnings of colonial discourse with its insistence on the extraordinary benevolence of a white man toward his African employee, a woman who eventually expresses gratitude for his chivalry by making her way to his bed.

Figure 3.2. Screen capture. Shandurai challenges Kinsky. *Besieged/L'assedio* (1997)

The film's inscription of race and class has provoked predictable resistance from critics and scholars.[33] It has, however, a greater degree of complexity than a stripped-down narrative outline suggests. Shandurai (Thandie Newton) is not only a housekeeper but is also a student of medicine, driven into exile by political circumstances, while her English employer, Kinsky (David Thewlis), though a gifted musician, seems more isolated and socially inept than she is. *L'assedio* merits a less literal reading than is generally offered since its signifying strategies—casting, camera work, art direction, editing, and sound—reveal a complex network of competing discourses that render totalizing dismissals problematical. The discursive polarities of power and vulnerability, desire and renunciation, seduction and surrender are articulated through an intricate interplay of stylistic techniques that make this one of the most complicated films in Bertolucci's body of work.

L'assedio is essentially a two-hander, a drama of seduction played out in an enclosed space between a man and a woman for whom the world outside becomes increasingly unimportant. Within this space, sounds, objects, and colors take on magnified meaning. The evolution of the central relationship is signaled by a change in spatial relations and in musical rhythms. The virtuosity of the camera movements—which alternate between handheld trolley shots and Steadycam—foregrounds the shifting balance of power between the two, and diegetic music largely replaces dialogue as the relationship intensifies. Kinsky's classical repertoire ultimately gives way to a hybrid, syncopated composition that he creates in response to the music that Shandurai loves to hear, the fusion sounds of world music, specifically in recordings by Alif Keita and Papa Wemba.

The predominance of transgressive erotic tension that underpins Bertolucci's earlier, more famous two-hander *Last Tango in Paris* is replaced in *L'assedio* by a more restrained articulation of desire, with elements that hark back to the fairytale. The familiar story of a humble working girl courted and conquered by a wealthy suitor is in fact inscribed within the tradition of High Romance, a tradition whose patriarchal underpinnings have been radically deconstructed by feminist criticism over the past thirty years.[34] The film's deployment of this age-old formula in a scenario that adds racial difference to disparities of class must, of course, be addressed.

L'assedio is loosely adapted from "The Siege," a short story by English writer James Lasdun, which in turn was inspired by a tale from Boccaccio's *Decameron*, a narrative of courtly love and self-abnegation.[35] Shandurai, the film's leading female character, has moved to Rome from an unnamed African country to study medicine following her husband's imprisonment under a military dictatorship. Employed as a part-time housekeeper by Kinsky, who has inherited an impressive if slightly dilapidated palazzo overlooking the Spanish Steps, she does not initially disclose her married status and keeps mementoes of her African past locked away in a chest.

When Kinsky, who is unaware of her history, abruptly accosts her with a declaration of love and simultaneous proposal of marriage, she recoils, blurting out that the only thing he can do to earn her love is to get her husband out of prison. Reluctantly accepting the need to continue living in Kinsky's home, she then adopts an awkward display of aloofness, while he, having apologized for his ignorance of her circumstances, appears to relinquish his romantic pursuit. As the house is gradually despoiled of its valuable contents, however, Shandurai realizes that Kinsky has sold virtually all his possessions, including his precious piano, to pay for her husband's freedom. The eventual announcement of the husband's release and imminent arrival in Rome does not bring her joy, however, but rather a sense of confusion, which culminates with her making her way upstairs to Kinsky's bedroom, where she lies down alongside her sleeping employer. The film ends as the husband arrives at the house at dawn, when Shandurai, awakened by the doorbell, slowly rises from Kinsky's bed, perhaps to open the door. The film's final image is a long shot of the husband standing in the street outside the palazzo, repeatedly pressing the doorbell.

The mise-en-scène of *L'assedio* gives prominence to two vertical figures, the elegant spiral staircase at the center of the palazzo and the dumbwaiter that moves up and down between the floors, by way of which Kinsky sends his tokens of affection to Shandurai's cramped downstairs room. These vertical figurations are contrasted with horizontal planes—the deep, gaping entrance to the Metro station, the underground tunnel from which the trains emerge, and the narrow passageway that constitutes Vicolo del Bottino, where Kinsky's home is located.

The horizontal spaces are mainly the domain of Shandurai as she moves through the city for her studies and for shopping, whereas the vertical space of the staircase marks the mobile dynamics of the couple's relationship, the shifting balance of power between them.

At the outset, Kinsky is dominant, looking down at Shandurai from an upstairs window or from the staircase within the house. She is clearly subservient to his needs, as she spends her time in the house making his bed, dusting, mopping, vacuuming, ironing, and mending his clothes. He invades her space at night with the messages sent via the dumbwaiter, which she experiences as noisy, terrifying intrusions. The sound of his piano music is also experienced as an invasion. However, unlike Kinsky, Shandurai has another, more active, self-determined existence outside the house. As a medical student for at least part of the day, she occupies an altered positionality. No longer the object of the look, she submits patients to her professional gaze, scrutinizing the bodies of physically compromised Italian subjects. In these scenes, it is clear that Shandurai has a sense of purpose, of direction toward the future, as well as an evolving relationship with the social landscape of Italy.

Though constructed through Kinsky's perspective as an aestheticized object of desire, Shandurai is also intermittently aligned with abjection. Like other configurations of African womanhood in Western cinema, Shandurai has an overdetermined relationship to the body, its functions, excretions, and exertions. At various junctures in the film, she urinates involuntarily in a state of terror, vomits publicly in a moment of panic, and drools when distressed, all of which align her with the abject. Yet, even if the script insists on Shandurai's Africanness, the casting of Thandie Newton, the well-known biracial British actress already on her way to international stardom, undercuts the construction of her character's origins. When Shandurai appears in the frame with other African characters, her visual difference immediately sets her apart from her interlocutors. One of the most startling moments in the film occurs at an outdoor market frequented by African merchants and their clients, where Shandurai looks oddly out of place. When another African woman calls out to her by name and approaches her with friendly concern, she recoils, unable to speak to her; then, suddenly and inexplicably, she steps aside to vomit.

This is undoubtedly a troubling moment. One might ask how the viewer is intended to interpret Shandurai's visceral reaction to an encounter with a woman who, like her, comes from Africa. Some clues regarding her traumatic relationship to the world she has come from are revealed in the flashbacks and dream sequences that punctuate scenes in the present tense of the narrative. Not all of these sequences are univocally associated with Shardurai's subjectivity. Instead, the majestic opening sequence—featuring an aerial shot of Lake Turkana in northern Kenya—is consistent with the epic mode of Bertolucci's international films, such as *The Last Emperor* (1987) and *The Sheltering Sky* (1990), and invokes the imperializing gaze of the colonizer. As the camera moves forward, high above the shimmering water of the lake, it takes in a vast expanse of unpopulated territory and circles the volcanic crater that emerges from the water. The scene then cuts to a grizzled bard seated under a giant tree, strumming an ancient instrument and singing a mournful ballad about Africa. Young boys appear in the branches, climbing above him. The past and the future of Africa are crystallized in this idealized scene, presented in majestic, almost operatic fashion.

The mood of timeless grandeur, however, soon gives way to images that encapsulate the suffering, political violence, and uneven modernization of Africa's present, ending with a sequence in which Shandurai witnesses the brutal arrest of her dissident husband at the country schoolhouse where he works as a teacher. At various junctures throughout the film, the scene returns to Shandurai's run-down village, marked by encroaching capitalism. On the village walls are posters advertising condoms alongside ubiquitous images of the dictator, whose face is superimposed on a map of Africa. In one of Shandurai's hallucinatory dream sequences, however, Kinsky's face unexpectedly replaces the image of the African dictator on the village posters, revealing her anxiety about the uneven configuration of power in her relationship with him.

Shandurai's body is repeatedly fetishized by Kinsky's longing but ultimately passive gaze. More troubling still is the process through which he, as her white, British employer, effectively divests himself of his dusty antiques presumably to acquire in exchange the living, breathing body of a beautiful African woman. Furthermore, by presenting Kinsky as a British recluse, confined almost perpetually to the space of the house, *L'assedio* seems to disavow the relevance of this story to the space of contemporary Italy. The colonial history implied in the film's backstory belongs to Britain, not Italy. Although Shandurai's native country is not named in the film, her husband bears the eminently resonant name of Winston, and he is heard speaking English to his African students, leading the viewer to surmise that they are citizens of a former British colony.[36]

The film provides no easy resolution to the complex emotional and political dilemmas that it constructs. Withholding clear narrative closure, *L'assedio* is not simply a contemporary cinematic variant of the Cinderella story with racial difference thrown into the mix. Far from negating the problems inherent in the desire it constructs between the reclusive Englishman and the vulnerable African woman who find themselves in the interstitial space that is Rome—midway between Africa and northern Europe, a space of fluid movement and negotiation—Bertolucci's film insists on the difficulty if not impossibility of their union, asking the viewer to consider the destructive effects both of Kinsky's renunciation (since he has by now lost the piano, apparently his only source of livelihood) and of Shandurai's final capitulation to his seductive generosity.

The Carnival of African Migration

Roberta Torre's *Sud side stori* takes a very different approach to the configuration of the African woman migrant. Unlike other films focused on interracial relationships that construct a story of impossible romance, it is devoid of pathos since it is articulated not as a realist drama but as a carnivalesque musical. Torre's only previous feature film, *Tano da morire* (1988), also a musical, offered an exuberant send-up of Mafia culture. Though blatantly unflattering to Sicilian society, the film was a huge hit with local audiences. Nonetheless, when Torre applied a similar approach to *Sud side stori*, which she shot under comparable conditions three years later with the help of Sicilian locals and actual Nigerian sex workers recruited from the city streets, her effort was met with much less enthusiasm, and the film was widely criticized.

Like the Hollywood classics that it parodies, *Sud side stori* relies significantly on solo and choral song numbers, dance routines, and a major set piece that slows down the narrative, subordinating plot to spectacle. The setting in which the story unfolds—an animated, run-down urban neighborhood re-created on the sound stage—is also reminiscent of the Hollywood tradition, suggesting in particular the 1961 hit *West Side Story* (directed by Robert Wise), to which it clearly refers. Yet, unlike the streamlined spectacle of the Hollywood model, Torre's visual style is a postmodern feast of hybrid influences, from cabaret to folk art, from trash aesthetics to religious iconography. The music track reveals a similar mishmash of sources and influences, using jazz and heavy metal, as well as the rockabilly music of the Italian Elvis, better known as Little Tony, and the African rhythms presumably brought to Italy by the new immigrants. It is nonetheless the popular Neapolitan tradition so beloved in Palermo that dominates *Sud side stori*. Thus Mario Merola, the once widely acclaimed singer of the "melodico" vein, appears in person in several scenes where he resurrects one of his cabaret acts of the 1960s. Intense colors (deliberately reminiscent of Sri Lankan cinema), bizarre lighting effects, manic camera movements, and digitally manipulated editing add to the sensory overload set in motion by the music. Furthermore, the dominant carnivalesque sequences are intercut with footage invoking contrasting generic styles, including the documentary.

Chronicling the encounter between the local people of Palermo and a large group of recently arrived Nigerian sex workers, *Sud side stori* involved bringing together two communities with little sympathy for each other in order to reenact a comic version of their mutual incomprehension. In spite of, and perhaps because of, the difficulties inherent in this project, *Sud side stori* is one of the most original films about Italian immigration to have been made to date. Grotesque comedy periodically invests both the representation of the Africans and of the local Sicilian population. The male protagonist's three aunts, the

Figure 3.3. Screen capture. Nigerian women arrive in Palermo. *Sud side stori* (2000)

Giulietto sisters, appear in one of the opening scenes, expressing racist attitudes in hyperbolic language and bodily gestures. This colorful scene is intercut, however, with a documentary video sequence of an encounter between a local client and the African women he accosts on the streets of Palermo, women whose knowledge of Italian seems limited to the most rudimentary language of commerce—the vocabulary of the body parts they are willing to rent and the fee for each service.

There are also scenes in which Torre's Nigerian performers restage, in English, their nightly interactions with their African madam and middleman as they turn in their evening's wages along with a statement of net takings and are scolded by the older woman if the amount earned does not measure up to expectations. In the scenes reconstructed within the local African community, the appalling conditions of the Nigerian women are thus sketched out—circumstances that are confirmed in contemporary sociological studies of prostitution among foreign immigrants to Italy.[37] As Torre has indicated in her interviews, the Nigerian women work in conditions of indentured servitude, conditions that endure to the present moment. After their initial journey to Italy at the expense of the middlemen, they are obliged to surrender their passports, which can be retrieved only after they have paid their handlers a huge sum of money, amounting at the time of *Sud side stori*'s production to thirty million lire. The characters in Torre's film receive an average of thirty thousand lire for each sexual transaction, suggesting that the retrieval of their passports could take years of indentured labor on the streets.

Despite its intertextual allusions to *Romeo and Juliet* (Torre's protagonists are named Romea Wacombo and Toni Giulietto) and to *West Side Story*, Torre's film is ultimately the story of an encounter between two Souths, each seething with resentment toward the other. In this regard, it is one of the very few Italian films to suggest that racism thrives in immigrant communities as well as among Italians. Much of Torre's film crosscuts from one community to the other, highlighting the unsuspected parallels between them. Prominent in each group is a stridently expressed racial prejudice. Appalled to learn of Romea's affection for the Sicilian street singer Toni, the African women warn her away from him, telling her that he is a *mangiasalsiccia* (sausage eater), that white men stink of cheese, that their music is unbearable, and that their women grow absurdly fat. Toni, in the meantime, is treated to similar warnings from his shrewish aunts, who do everything in their power to alienate him from his beloved Romea and lead him back toward his heavyset Sicilian girlfriend. Also present in both communities is a reliance on magic and superstitious practices. While a black witch is enlisted by Romea's colleagues to resolve the problem of the young woman's fatal attraction, Toni's aunts consult a white witch, played by a real-life Sicilian *maga*. Finally, music is central to the experience of both communities, though the film gives more prominence to Toni's musical tastes, especially to his alcohol-induced hallucinations featuring Mario Merola and Little Tony, than to the African rhythms of his Nigerian counterparts. As the film progresses, Torre's attempt to construct a tale of two Souths becomes overburdened with visions of parallel exotica. Indeed, one might question to what degree this film, made by a northern Italian filmmaker, perpetuates the stereotypical, racialized perception of southern Italy as Italy's "Africa."

The uneven results achieved by *Sud side stori*, despite its striking visual design and conceptual daring, are due at least in part to the director's strained relationship with the African women employed to participate in the film. Torre reports, in fact, that the Nigerians were unwilling to invest themselves too wholeheartedly in the performance of their own "identities." While the local Sicilian performers were able to enter at will the liminal state of being and yet not quite being themselves, the Nigerians were not entirely convinced of a qualitative difference between their performance on the set and the work they performed for clients solicited on the street.[38] Once again, Gayatri Spivak's provocative and frequently cited query, "Can the subaltern speak?" seems apt in this context. The Nigerian women, while revealing their relative lack of access to speech, are at the same time exhibiting some reluctance to being spoken for, even by the sympathetic Torre and her crew. Their performance also calls into question the presumed effectiveness of send-up as social critique. In fact, Torre's gentle mockery of Sicily's contemporary human landscape simultaneously destabilizes and reinscribes the dominant ideology. Her images are transgressive to the extent that they invite fresh perspectives on troubling contemporary issues. Yet, like other films that refer in a contrastingly realist vein to the difficult circumstances of many immigrants in Italy at present, they scarcely constitute a genuinely subversive threat to endemic racism, established gender arrangements, or the implacable demands of global capital.

Mediterranean Affinities

Although racism and xenophobia were on the rise in Italy in the early 1990s, there were also some public expressions of solidarity with Italy's new immigrants, as a youthful, antiracist subculture developed around the country and particularly in the South. This subculture gave birth to a vibrant musical movement that found expression through the proliferation of self-managing, self-producing bands that blended aspects of US rap and African, Caribbean, and Middle Eastern musical traditions with Italian folk elements to create hybrid sounds and rhythms. Inspired by a principle of contamination, these musicians undoubtedly played an important role in articulating a contemporary awareness of Italy's heterogeneous ethnic identity and history of transnational affinities. Their lyrics are often explicitly antiracist, sometimes alluding to links between Italians and the people of North Africa and evoking a sense of solidarity with Italy's new migrants.[39]

In 1993 the Neapolitan hip-hop group Almamegretta recorded a song titled "Figli di Annibale" (Children of Hannibal), inviting Italians—and particularly southern Italians—to acknowledge their ancestral ties to the Maghreb. To the accompaniment of a reggae organ, the lead rapper, Raiz, summarizes the story of Hannibal's invasion of Italy with tens of thousands of North African soldiers during the Punic Wars and suggests that the dark complexion of many of his compatriots is a sign of the interbreeding that occurred in the course of this historical event. In explicit defiance of the racist rhetoric simultaneously gaining currency in the national media, the song concludes with the provocative assertion: "If you know your history, you know where you come from. Hannibal's children, blood of Africa."

The possibility of fraternal affinities between people from different Mediterranean shores expressed in the music of the *posse* groups that began to emerge in the late 1980s was slower to find expression in Italian cinema. One of the only echoes of these countercultural discourses in films of that period is the use of Almamegretta's "Figli di Annibale" on the soundtrack of Davide Ferrario's 1998 feature film of the same title. This comic tale follows the antics of two inept Italians on the run from the law, pursuing a path of escape that brings them from North to South. In the final scene, while sailing from Italy's Adriatic shore toward Egypt to start a new life, they intersect with a boatload of irregular migrants traveling in the opposite direction. The scene is a lighthearted acknowledgment of the fact that while the influx of migrants toward Italy is on the increase, the movement of Italians to places beyond national borders continues unabated, even if in smaller numbers than in earlier times.

Ferrario explains his decision to use the Almamegretta song both as the film's title and on the soundtrack as follows: "Like Hannibal, the two lead characters go North first and then return to the South. They are two of Hannibal's sons, black on the inside, economically precarious, Mediterranean."[40] Ferrario's suggestion that his characters are "black on the inside . . . Mediterranean" nonetheless rings hollow, appropriating too rapidly a claim to blackness on their behalf. Unlike the Almamagretta song, which directly challenges its listeners' assumptions about their ancestral lineage and claim to whiteness, the film of the same title conjures up a superficial sense of multicultural inclusiveness, where the Italian characters' imputed affinity with blackness is intended to invest them with a special aura of vitality in the absence of any actual encounters with people from the global South. The symbolic attribution of blackness to Italians performed by this film functions as "spice," participating in the discursive phenomenon that is astutely critiqued by bell hooks in her important deconstruction of racial tropes in dominant Western culture: "within commodity culture, *ethnicity becomes spice*, seasoning that can liven up the dull dish that is mainstream white culture."[41] In other words, the kind of diversity proposed in cultural texts like *Figli d'Annibale* is a kind of supplement that can be evoked haphazardly and superficially rather than part of a dynamic process that must be placed within a larger discursive, economic, and historical context.

Conclusion

If, in the early 1990s, Umberto Eco proposed the possibility of Europe becoming a "colored continent," this vision is not mirrored in a direct way in Italian cinema of that decade.[42] Yet the prospect of what Eco calls "interbreeding" presents itself as a subtext in a handful of films foregrounding potentially reproductive relationships between Italians and migrants from the African continent, where it is ultimately disavowed or deferred. The interracial relationships dramatized in *Pummarò*, *Teste rasate*, and *Sud side stori* appear doomed from the start, and each of them ends in violence (with death in the case of the last two and with physical attack in the first), thus symbolically deferring the imagined threat of miscegenation. Since the interracial romance at the center of *L'assedio* does not involve an Italian citizen, the risk of "interbreeding" is displaced onto two foreigners living in Italy, and its narrative thus dispenses with the trope of violent interruption. Significantly, in all the films I have examined in this chapter (again, with the exception of *L'assedio*), the principal African character is ultimately removed from Italian territory or otherwise killed off by the narrative, forestalling all further influences, interactions, or exchanges with Italian citizens.

While these films point to the growing presence of nonwhite bodies on Italian soil in an ostensibly sympathetic way, they resonate simultaneously with broader cultural concerns about the displacement of Italian whiteness as the authentic core of national identity. Such anxieties are clearly linked to ways of thinking inherited from the nation's colonial past. Since the racial ideology that underpinned Italy's historical project of colonial conquest was never systematically renounced, traces of this ideology, however subliminally deployed, can be identified to different degrees in each of the films examined in this chapter, particularly in their tendency to exoticize or eroticize African characters, to disavow the possibility of their permanent inclusion in Italian society, and to foreclose the fantasy of interracial reproduction.

Notes

1. Etienne Balibar, "'Es gibt keinen Staat in Europa': Racism and Politics in Europe Today," *New Left Review* 1, no. 186 (March–April 1991): 5–19.
2. Over the past decade there has been a sharp increase in scholarly interest in the representation of African or mixed-race subjects in Italian cinema. See, in particular, Shelleen Greene, *Equivocal Subjects: Between Italy and Africa—Constructions of Racial and National Identity in the Italian Cinema* (New York: Continuum, 2012). For a discussion of the construction of race in Fascist cinema of the imperial period, see Ruth Ben-Ghiat, *Italian Fascism's Empire Cinema* (Bloomington: Indiana University Press, 2015), 118–213.
3. Michael T. Martin, "'Fortress Europe' and Third World Immigration in the Post–Cold War Global Context," *Third World Quarterly* 20, no. 4 (1999): 832.
4. Umberto Eco and Richard Kearney, "Chaosmos: The Return of the Middle Ages," in *Debates in Continental Philosophy: Conversations with Contemporary Thinkers*, ed. Richard Kearney (New York: Fordham University Press, 2004), 228.
5. Eco and Kearney, 228.
6. Pasquale Verdicchio, "The Preclusion of Postcolonial Discourse in Southern Italy," in *Revisioning Italy: National Identity and Global Culture*," ed. Beverly Allen and Mary Russo (Minneapolis: Minnesota University Press, 1997), 191–212.
7. Miguel Mellino, "Deprovincializing Italy: Notes on Race, Racialization, and Italy's Coloniality," in *Postcolonial Italy: Challenging National Homogeneity*, ed. Cristina Lombardi-Diop and Caterina Romeo (New York: Palgrave Macmillan, 2012), 84.
8. Cristina Lombardi-Diop and Caterina Romeo, "Paradigms of Postcoloniality in Contemporary Italy," in *Postcolonial Italy: Challenging National Homogeneity*, ed. Cristina Lombardi-Diop and Caterina Romeo (New York: Palgrave Macmillan, 2012), 2.
9. Sandro Mezzadra, "Citizen and Subject: A Postcolonial Constitution for the European Union?" *Situations: Project of the Radical Imagination* 1, no. 2 (2006), https://ojs.gc.cuny.edu/index.php/situations/article/view/22/31.
10. Mellino, "Deprovincializing Italy," 84.
11. Lombardi-Diop and Romeo, "Paradigms of Postcoloniality," 2.

12. See, for example, Gaia Giuliani and Cristina Lombardi-Diop, *Bianco e nero: Storia dell'identità razziale degli italiani* (Milan: LeMonnier Università, 2013).

13. For a discussion of the ambiguous racial classification of Italians in the United States in the early part of the twentieth century, see Guglielmo and Salerno, *Are Italians White?* For a brief reflection on the shifting "racial" perceptions of Italians—and particularly of southern Italians—by Italians themselves, see Verdicchio, who writes, "The expression 'Italy ends at Rome. Naples, Calabria, Sicily, and all the rest are part of Africa,' spoken perhaps by a respectable nineteenth-century Grand Tour traveler, is still heard today in Italy, and it encapsulates the whole question of what might constitute the nation." Verdicchio, "Preclusion of Postcolonial Discourse," 193.

14. Placido attained universal popularity as the result of his leading role in the hugely successful television series *La piovra* (*The Octopus*), which was screened in the 1980s in several countries around the world, from Australia to the USSR.

15. There is some similarity between the plot line of *Pummarò* and *La promessa di Hamadi*, a narrative published the same year by an African immigrant, Saidou Moussa Ba, in conjunction with an Italian collaborator, Alessandro Micheletti. It is not clear, however, if Placido and his co-screenwriters were aware of this work. See Saidou Moussa Ba and Alessandro Micheletti, *La promessa di Hamadi* (Novara: De Agostini, 1991).

16. David Forgacs, "African Immigration on Film: *Pummarò* and the Limits of Vicarious Representation," in *Media and Migration: Constructions of Mobility and Difference*, ed. Russell King and Nancy Wood (London: Routledge, 2001), 87.

17. Forgacs, 90.

18. Homi Bhabha, *The Location of Culture* (New York: Routledge, 1994), 85–92.

19. The film's title refers to Article 2 of the Universal Declaration of Human Rights, which states, "Everyone is entitled to all the rights and freedoms set forth in this Declaration, without distinction of any kind, such as race, color, sex, language, religion, political or other opinion, national or social origin, property, birth or other status." The full text of the Universal Declaration of Human Rights (1948) is available on the United Nations website, http://www.un.org/en/universal-declaration-human-rights/ (accessed July 15, 2018). Some commentators have suggested, however, that the film's title invokes Article 2 of the Italian Constitution: "The Republic recognizes and guarantees the inviolable rights of the person, both as an individual and in the social groups where human personality is expressed. The Republic expects that the fundamental duties of political, economic and social solidarity be fulfilled." "Constitution of the Italian Republic," 1947, Senato della Repubblica, https://www.senato.it/documenti/repository/istituzione/costituzione_inglese.pdf (accessed July 15, 2018).

20. This practice would soon change when, around the mid-1990s, there was a general shift toward synchronous sound recording.

21. According to Gabriella Campassi and Maria Teresa Sega, "The black woman becomes the symbol of Africa . . . and the white man/black woman relationship is symbolic of the relationship between the nation and the imperial colony: the man, for his part, supplies a fertile and life-giving virility, and the woman receives from this a sense of enrichment and self-fulfillment through her complementary role in the expansion of the male ego." See Gabriella Campassi and Maria Teresa Sega, "Uomo bianco, donna nera: l'immagine della donna nella fotografia coloniale," *Rivista di Storia e critica della fotografia* 4, no. 5 (1983): 55.

22. Robert Young, *Colonial Desire: Hybridity in Theory, Culture and Race* (New York: Routledge, 1995), 181.

23. Sandra Ponzanesi, "Beyond the Black Venus: Colonial Sexual Politics and Contemporary Visual Practices," in *Italian Colonialism: Legacy and Memory*, ed. Jacqueline Andall and Derek Duncan (Oxford: Peter Lang, 2005), 173.

24. This early nineteenth-century drawing of the South African woman Sara Baartman, who was exhibited as an anatomical curiosity in Britain and France, was published in the Fascist propaganda organ *La difesa della razza* in 1938. See Barbara Sòrgoni, "'Defending the Race': The Italian Reinvention of the Hottentot Venus during Fascism," *Journal of Modern Italian Studies* 8, no. 3 (2003): 411–24.

25. Young, *Colonial Desire*, 8.

26. One of the most memorable examples is a sequence in Fellini's *Le notti di Cabiria* (*The Nights of Cabiria*, 1957), which features a dance routine by two seductively attired African women. The dancers are each equipped with a long, hairy tail, and their routine, accompanied by African drumbeats, culminates in a series of frenzied rhythmic vibrations. Similarly, Michelangelo Antonioni's *La notte* (Night, 1961) includes a nightclub sequence where a black woman performs an acrobatic dance routine, in the course of which her thighs, buttocks, and groin are repeatedly scrutinized in close-up, to the virtual exclusion of her face.

27. The troubling semiotic complexity of this figure is deconstructed by Giovanna Trento as follows: "In *Arabian Nights* the slave Zumurrud is an icon of subalternity. She is a black African female slave located somewhere in Pasolini's 'Pan-South.' She is assertive and has some agency, being blessed with the joy and the 'reality' that only belong to subaltern classes and are constitutive of the 'popular body.' At the very end of the film, though, in order to retain her essentialized subaltern condition, Zumurrud is happy to return to the slave-master-lover dynamics, without wishing to escape her enslaved condition." See Giovanna Trento, "Pier Paolo Pasolini in Eritrea: Subalternity, Grace, and the 'Rediscovery' of Italian Colonization in the Horn of Africa," in *Postcolonial Italy: Challenging National Homogeneity*, ed. Cristina Lombardi-Diop and Caterina Romeo (New York: Palgrave Macmillan, 2012), 144.

28. Marco Purpura, "Racial Masquerade Italian Style? Whiteface and Blackface in Zeudi Araya's 1970s Comedies," *Italian Studies* 69, no. 3 (2014): 394.

29. Purpura, 394.

30. In what follows, I draw on and develop material first published in Áine O'Healy, "'[Non] è una somala': Deconstructing African Femininity in Italian Film," *Italianist* 34, no. 2 (2014): 175–98.

31. Karen Pinkus, *Bodily Regimes: Italian Advertising under Fascism* (Minneapolis: University of Minnesota Press, 1995), 54.

32. Pinkus, 54.

33. Invoking nuances of the Black Venus stereotype, J. Hoberman comments on *L'assedio* as follows: "Shandurai may speak three or four languages and be a medical student but, dazzled by the white man's voodoo, she's a tongue-tied, barefoot child of nature at heart," see J. Hoberman, "Artists in Love," *Village Voice* 44, no. 21 (June 1, 1999): 119. Another reviewer described the film's central premise as the story of "a slave's capitulation to a master." See Bruce Sklarew and Bernardo Bertolucci, "Returning to My Low-Budget Roots," *Cineaste* 24, no. 4 (1999): 16–20.

34. See, for example, de Lauretis, "Desire in Narrative," *Alice Doesn't*, 103–57.

35. The tale of Dianora and Ansaldo—sometimes referred to as "The Winter Garden" in reference to the "impossible" gift demanded of the unwelcome suitor—is the fifth story of the tenth day.

36. Clare Peploe—Bertolucci's wife and the film's principal screenwriter—grew up in Rhodesia (now Zimbabwe) as the daughter of British settlers, and a keen nostalgia for her African childhood can be sensed in the voice-over commentary she contributed to the English-language release of the DVD.

37. See, for example, Luca Trappolin, "Gender Victims and Cultural Borders: The Globalization of Prostitution in Italy," *Dialectical Anthropology* 29 (2005): 335–48.

38. Personal communication with Roberta Torre, Palermo, July 2001.

39. For a detailed analysis of this phenomenon, see Michela Ardizzoni, "*Posse*'s Music of Occupation and Practices of Social Justice," in *Matrix Activism: Global Practices of Resistance* (New York: Routledge, 2017), 113–36. See also Tom Behan, "Putting Spanners in the Works: The Politics of the 99 Posse," *Popular Music* 26 (2002): 497–504; Ashley Dawson and Patrizia Palumbo, "Hannibal's Children: Immigration and Antiracist Youth Subcultures in Contemporary Italy," *Cultural Critique Journal* 59 (2005): 165–86; and Joseph Sciorra, "Hip Hop from Italy and the Diaspora: A Report from the 41st Parallel," *Altreitalie* 24 (Jan–June 2002), http://www.altreitalie.it/ UPLiew OAD/ALL/00026.pdf.

40. Davide Ferrario, *Figli di Annibale* (excerpted interview), *La Repubblica* (January 29, 1998), cited in *Enciclopedia del Cinema in Piemonte*, http://www.torinocittadelcinema.it/schedafilm.php?film_id=1386&stile=large.

41. bell hooks, *Black Looks* (Boston: South End, 1992), 21.

42. Eco and Kearney, "Chaosmos," 128.

CHAPTER 4

Migration, Masculinity, and Italy's New Urban Geographies

BY THE TURN of the twenty-first century, the number of foreigners living legally in Italy had exceeded one million and was growing steadily. After the victory of Berlusconi's rightwing coalition Casa della Libertà (House of Freedom) in the election of 2001, immigration control became a central priority of the new government. The following year saw the passing of the so-called Bossi-Fini law—named after the leaders of Lega Nord and Alleanza Nazionale, respectively—which introduced the most repressive measures to date, including the criminalization of failure to comply with expulsion orders.[1] It was followed, however, by an amnesty decree facilitating the regularization of undocumented foreigners already resident in the country. Yet irregular arrivals from the former Eastern bloc, the African continent, and other locations in the global South continued, with the flow of newcomers accelerating or decelerating at different points in the years that followed.

Thanks to the substantial growth of the immigrant population, both regular and irregular, the demographic makeup of Italy's cities had undergone a visible transformation ten years after the initial, unprecedented influx of migrants experienced during the immediate post–Cold War period. New spaces, structures, and institutions were emerging in urban centers and peripheries that reflected, on the one hand, the agency and vitality of Italy's new residents and, on the other, Italian attempts to contain or expel them. All of the country's urban centers presented visible signs of transnational flows and connections, evidenced, for example, in the proliferation of international call centers and money-transfer offices, the emergence of ethnic markets, restaurants and new places of worship, and the presence of advertising aimed at migrants. These shifts in the visual landscape find expression in several Italian films produced from the early twenty-first century onward, where they sometimes feature prominently in the mise-en-scène and at other times function merely to convey a sense of contemporary urban life.

In this chapter, I examine three films made between 2004 and 2006 that unfold against urban and peripheral locations where the presence of new migrants was vividly perceptible by the turn of the twenty-first century. Highlighting the dilemmas and challenges of interethnic habitation, as well as the often conflicting needs of migrants and Italian residents, each film unfolds from the perspective of a young male character. The youth's growing awareness of the complex realities of Italy's migratory landscape and his own position within it prompts an ethical crisis in each narrative, leading him to take decisive action and embrace a sort of self-willed maturity. Invested in tropes of exclusion and belonging, the three films offer a reflection on male maturation in the global era while introducing viewers to situations, institutions, and settings previously unseen (or rarely seen) in Italian cinema.

Quando sei nato non puoi più nasconderti: Coming of Age in Multiethnic Italy

Marco Tullio Giordana is generally considered one of the heirs of the tradition of politically motivated filmmaking that flourished in Italy in the 1960s and 1970s, as exemplified by the work of Francesco Rosi, Elio Petri, Gillo Pontecorvo, and the brothers Paolo and Vittorio Taviani. Generally, however, his films are set in the past, scrutinizing well-known and often controversial episodes of Italy's relatively recent history. His first film set in contemporary Italy, *Quando sei nato non puoi più nasconderti* (Once You're Born You Can No Longer Hide), presents a story centered on contemporary migration, a topic he deemed too pressing to ignore. When presented at the Cannes Film Festival in 2005, however, it was received with rather less enthusiasm than his earlier, critically acclaimed features, *I cento passi* (*The Hundred Steps*, 2000) and *La meglio gioventù* (*The Best of Youth*, 2003). Produced by the major production company Cattleya in collaboration with Rai Cinema, *Quando sei nato* attracted solid audience attendance in Italy and traveled abroad to several festivals. It won both the Prix François Chalais and a Nastro d'Argento for Best Producer.

Significantly, *Quando sei nato* is one of the first Italian features to visualize the distinctive locations traversed or inhabited by migrants entering Italy and attempting to make their lives there. Among the spaces shown in the film are the small factories of northern Italy staffed almost exclusively by immigrant labor (also glimpsed briefly in *Pummarò*), the precarious vessels transporting people to Italy from various parts of the Mediterranean, the overcrowded processing and holding centers (Centri di Permanenza Temporanea e Assistenza or CPT) for irregular arrivals, and the derelict urban structures appropriated for habitation by immigrants lacking access to legitimate employment and housing. Indeed the film makes a sustained effort to communicate the abject conditions of the physical spaces frequented by irregular migrants attempting to make a new life in Italy.

Scripted by Giordana in collaboration with Stefano Rulli and Sandro Petraglia, the film is at one level an adventure story, loosely inspired by the central premise of Rudyard Kipling's late nineteenth-century novel *Captains Courageous*, which tells the tale of a wealthy adolescent rescued at sea by a group of fishermen in an accident of fate that allows him to develop in ways that transcend the narrow perspectives of his privileged background.[2] Giordana's film takes its title, however, from a volume of investigative journalism by the Italian reporter Maria Pace Ottieri, which offers a compelling account of the experiences of recent immigrants who dwell in squatted spaces in Italy's urban centers and whose lives are marked by hardship as well as courage and resilience.[3]

Although Giordana's narrative is entirely a work of fiction, it shares with Ottieri's project a declared interest in the *popolo sommerso*, the "submerged" population whose unrecognized faces and unintelligible voices are routinely screened out, both literally and metaphorically, by the nation's dominant population. Believing that immigration was one of the most crucial social issues currently facing the country, the filmmaker chose to weave into the film's narrative several emblematic aspects of contemporary global mobilities, including the phenomenon of cross-border people smuggling, the trafficking of women and girls, the perilous conditions of irregular sea crossings, the detention of irregular migrants in crowded facilities, the establishing of deportation criteria through recourse to biometrics, and the divergent responses of Italian citizens to the demands placed on their society by rapid change. Rather than attempting to recount these circumstances through the perspective of an immigrant, however, Giordana chose to have his Italian protagonist, the well-to-do twelve-year-old named Sandro (Matteo Gadola), become an accidental witness to some of the devastating circumstances of irregular migration.

As occurs traditionally in Italian cinema, the male child is implicitly positioned as the future of the nation, and "sons" are automatically envisioned in a certain relation to the legacy of the past and to what the nation will bequeath to future generations. The figure of the child or adolescent as witness or moral conscience, which emerged in pronounced fashion in Italian films of the 1940s, has reappeared in a wide range of Italian films over the past twenty years.[4] It is therefore unsurprising that the events of *Quando sei nato* are experienced for the most part from the boy's perspective. A native of Brescia, a prosperous city in northern Italy, Giordana's protagonist is very different from the children of neorealist cinema insofar as he is a wealthy, even worldly adolescent. As the only son of Bruno (Alessio Boni), a self-made man who built his wealth through the acquisition of a small manufacturing plant almost entirely staffed by migrant labor, Sandro enjoys a life of privilege. Yet the boy is not entirely comfortable with his privileged status, wincing in embarrassment when his father boasts jovially about buying a new Porsche in the presence of his immigrant employees.

The beginning of Sandro's journey toward maturity coincides with his attempt to decipher a phrase spoken by a stranger in an unknown language in the film's opening minutes, a phrase that is eventually translated for him and for the cinema audience much later in the narrative with the words of the film's title, "Once you're born you can no longer hide." In Giordana's decision to appropriate the title of Ottieri's book, we can discern a desire to intervene in the broader discussion about immigration and integration that had emerged among journalists, politicians, and intellectuals. Although the director's films are known to engage with political issues, *Quando sei nato* seems inspired by more broadly humanitarian concerns. Philosophically, the questions posed by the film resonate with the concept of hospitality or openness to the other theorized by Emmanuel Levinas and subsequently by Jacques Derrida.[5] Throughout most of *Quando sei nato*, the issue of openness to the other is the primary factor driving the young protagonist's journey toward maturity.

For Levinas, a Jewish Lithuanian exile writing in France in the postwar period, ethics precedes ontology, and the "I" is always already responsible for the other. Throughout his work, Levinas insists on the primordial importance of the other, identifying the other's being and claim on the self as constitutive of human subjecthood. He asserts, moreover, that the obligation to attend to the needs of the other by offering hospitality precedes any judgment or knowledge of the other's identity. Hospitality, therefore, is not a courtesy or a gift but simply an ethical duty demanding respect for the other's absolute alterity. Levinas describes this openness to the other as "an incessant alienation of the ego . . . by the guest entrusted to it . . . being torn from oneself for another in giving to the other the bread from one's mouth."[6] In other words, it is a form of hospitality that shatters the ego, does not demand reciprocity, and withholds nothing. Derrida, in turn, draws on Levinas's writings to assert that ethics is coextensive with hospitality, with the unconditional invitation infinitely open to anyone.[7] For Derrida, as for Levinas, despite the difficulty or impossibility of pure hospitality, the subject's openness to the needs of the other, of all others, should remain without limits or conditions.

Resonating with the question of ethical responsibility to the stranger, *Quando sei nato* asks, What does it mean to encounter the other? Or, what is the ethical way to relate to the needs of those who exist outside one's own sphere of interest or sense of relatedness? That this film is about the encounter of the citizen with the abject other is made plain in an early scene where Sandro experiences a shattering of indifference of the kind described by Levinas in his unexpected encounter with the demands of an alien other.

In the film's opening moments, Sandro gets off a bus in the center of the city of Brescia in northern Italy. An African woman alights at the same time, signaling that this Italian city is already a multiethnic space. Stopping to admire a scooter on display in a store window, Sandro hears an agitated voice shouting a phrase in an unknown language and turns around to discover that a distressed African migrant is pounding on a public telephone. The boy approaches the stranger to tell him that the phone is out of order. As the African turns toward him, however, he continues to repeat his exasperated utterance, beating his chest in demented fashion and tearing off his clothes until he is interrupted by the arrival of two policemen who quickly put an end to the drama by carrying him away. Visibly troubled, Sandro memorizes the man's utterance—"Soki obotami okoki komibomba lisusu te"—and later tries unsuccessfully to have it translated into Italian by his African acquaintances. The persistence with which he pursues the task—and the mere fact that he has managed to memorize this complicated sequence of sounds—suggests that he has been profoundly troubled by his encounter with the stranger. When the meaning of the puzzling utterance is revealed to him as "once you're born you can no long hide," it seems to encapsulate the dilemma of the irregular migrant as an abject figure of bare life—that is, as an individual who has no discernible place in the structures of the nation-state but whose irreducible physical presence cannot be concealed or negated by a simple act of will.

The first ten minutes of the film establish the outlines of Sandro's everyday world, revealing that he is already accustomed to living in a multiethnic society and that his family (or at least his father) is keeping an eye on his evolving masculinity. One of his close friends at school is a black adolescent named Samuele who speaks Italian as fluently as Sandro. Samuele, however, is stronger, faster, and more motivated than Sandro at the swimming lessons the boys attend together, a point that the coach makes to Sandro's mother. The viewer also learns that Bruno, Sandro's father, is concerned about his son's apparent lack of drive and competitiveness. The boy's developing masculinity is thus flagged as a source of concern for the grown men in his life; his father, and later his father's friend Popi, continue to goad him about his presumed interest in girls, as though hoping to accelerate his maturation.

In another early scene that presages events to come, Sandro and his mother (Michela Cescon) are stopped at a traffic light, where he observes an Eastern European sex worker standing close by their car. Signaling discomfort, he asks his mother to close the car window as though to banish the woman from sight. As

Figure 4.1. Screen capture. Radu, Sandro, and Alina at sea. *Quando sei nato non puoi più nasconderti* (2005)

the window goes up, however, the viewer sees the young woman's face reflected in the glass as she stares at the boy. Sandro is mature enough to understand the woman's circumstances at least to some extent since he later asks his father if he has ever had sex with prostitutes. The exchange between the pair is played as comedy, with the father vigorously denying that he—a handsome man—might ever have had the need to seek out the company of women since he was always besieged by excessive female interest. The scene establishes both the easy intimacy of the father-son relationship—a relationship that will be threatened as the boy begins to assert his own path—and Sandro's attempt to understand issues of sexuality, power, and gender relations, which will also become part of his coming to consciousness.

When Sandro falls overboard during a yachting trip off the coast of Greece a short time afterward, he is eventually rescued by a Romanian youth traveling on a crowded fishing trawler along with other migrants heading for Italy. The boy's protracted struggle in the sea and his gradual surrender to the possibility of drowning are accompanied by a musical passage composed by Michael Nyman previously heard in the scene of near drowning in Jane Campion's *The Piano* (1997), an intertextual clue signaling a threshold point that will lead to a process of personal transformation. Pulled aboard the migrant vessel while unconscious, Sandro awakens to find himself surrounded by people of multiple ethnicities speaking different languages. Like those huddled around him, he is now entirely at the mercy of the two unscrupulous southern Italian people smugglers at the helm. Savvy enough to fear extortion, he is reluctant to reveal to the men transporting the migrants that he is the son of a wealthy Italian industrialist. Thus, when questioned about his identity, he refuses to speak Italian, responding instead with the words pronounced by the deranged African in the streets of

Brescia, the meaning of which still eludes him. When pressed for further information, he accepts the prompting of his Romanian rescuer and claims a Kurdish identity. Here, as in several other films about migration, the trope of passing is crucially linked to the issue of survival.

The sequence on the migrant vessel signals an obvious intertextual link with Amelio's *Lamerica*. In both films, the Italian protagonist has been stripped of his possessions, passport, and clothing and finds himself sailing on a crowded boat toward Italy in the company of a large number of aspiring immigrants. In each case, the Italian is not somatically distinguishable from at least some of his traveling companions (in *Quando sei nato* the other travelers are both Eastern European and African, whereas in *Lamerica* they are exclusively Albanian), confounding any easy attribution of national belonging. Indeed in both cases the ability of the Italian to blend into the throng of dispossessed people facilitates his passage to some degree. *Lamerica*, however, comes to an end with the sea voyage. For Sandro, by contrast, the journey marks a new and important stage of his development.

When the foundering fishing trawler, long abandoned by the two Italian ferrymen, is finally intercepted by the Italian Coast Guard, Sandro chooses to reclaim his Italian identity. Responding to the officer who asks if anyone on board speaks Italian, Sandro replies, "Sono italiano" (I am Italian). This admission of identity, however, has none of the assertive swagger attached to Gino's multiple assertions of Italian belonging in *Lamerica*. Furthermore, it comes with a price as it will automatically separate Sandro from his newfound friends, Radu (Vlad Alexandru Toma), his rescuer, and the adolescent Alina (Ester Hazan), when they reach dry land.

Sandro's friendship with the two Romanians is cemented early in the voyage aboard the fishing trawler, during which Radu acts like a protective older brother, offering him comfort, advice, and assistance. But from the start, Sandro lacks the maturity to discern the deeper motivations of Radu's behavior or to comprehend the relationship between the pair, who claim to be siblings. The short scene depicting the sexual exploitation of the adolescent Alina by one of the two Italian ferrymen on board the trawler allows the viewers to grasp the elements that lie beyond Sandro's understanding.

Shot with day-for-night lighting effects suggestive of the horror genre, the scene unfolds in the engine room at night, where the skipper obliges the girl—who, unknown to Sandro, is being transported to Italy for sex work—to submit to sexual contact in exchange for water. Focalized through the boy's gaze as he unexpectedly disrupts the encounter, it evokes the Freudian primal scene, where the child witnesses a sexual encounter between adults and interprets it as an act of aggression. The hallucinatory quality of the sequence may suggest at first that Sandro—a northern Italian adolescent who is perhaps immune to the subtle racism transmitted by adults in his environment—is displacing his fears about the potential violence of his own father, a self-made entrepreneur and employer of immigrant labor, onto that age-old scapegoat, the southern Italian male, traditionally characterized as violent, instinctive, or degenerate. His horrified reaction to the scene, however, is enough to discourage the skipper, who then angrily dismisses both adolescents. Even when Alina chides Sandro for interrupting the encounter and thus depriving the three of them of drinking water, the boy fails to realize that the exchange with the skipper had been anticipated by Alina and carried out at Radu's behest.

By the time Sandro disembarks in Italy, the bond he has established with the Romanians exerts a powerful hold, and the prospect of being separated from them fills him with anxiety. When the migrants emerge from the processing procedure (visualized in a striking montage sequence where each arriving migrant is photographed, fingerprinted, and identified by name, age, and national origin), he begs the Italian authorities to allow him to stay with his friends at the holding center. His request is partially granted by the gruff but apparently kindhearted priest who oversees the institution and allows Sandro—now identified as the Italian boy presumed dead at sea—to accompany his friends into the compound before insisting that the boy sleep alone in a separate space.

The fundamental ambivalence of *Quando sei nato* vis-à-vis the issue of irregular migration begins to surface in the scenes at the migrant holding center as it becomes clear that no one believes Radu when he claims to be seventeen years old (a circumstance that would allow him to remain legally in Italy as an unaccompanied minor). It is precisely at this juncture that the Romanian's behavior becomes volatile, contradictory, and difficult to read. The film's uncertainties about irregular migration, increasingly evident in the ongoing figuration of Radu, might indeed be understood as an unintended projection of the attitudes toward alterity that are manifest on a wider social level, often characterized by an outward display of acceptance that is undercut by a persistent distrust. This generalized attitude is implicit in the scenes where Sandro urges his parents to adopt the two Romanians he has befriended, while the lawyer interviewing the family, resistant to this request, attempts to justify the teenagers' ongoing detention in humanitarian terms, failing to address the actual conditions of their incarceration. Moreover, while the film attempts to demonstrate the harshness of the biopolitical apparatuses that serve to process and classify the aspiring immigrants, it also suggests the effectiveness of these same mechanisms as instruments of justice, for it is indirectly due to his enforced submission to a bone scan and other investigative procedures that Radu, Sandro's rescuer and presumed friend, is exposed as a liar and a criminal.

Although *Quando sei nato* appears at first to offer a sympathetic depiction of irregular migrants of different nationalities and ethnicities who are ferried across the Mediterranean, apprehended by government patrols on Italy's southern coast, and detained indefinitely in overcrowded facilities, it subsequently undermines this initial impression. The Romanian youth who saved Sandro's life at sea and pledged his undying friendship eventually shows up at the family home in Brescia, only to plunder the house and run off into the night with Alina. Reacting to this event—which mirrors stereotypical fears about irregular immigrants—Bruno prohibits his son from engaging in further communication with the pair, an injunction that Sandro ultimately finds impossible to obey. It is, however, only in the film's final sequence that the boy realizes that Radu is not Alina's brother but rather her pimp, responsible for transporting her to Italy with the aim of producing pornographic videos. Indeed Sandro's final challenge in the narrative is not to help both of his young friends avoid deportation, as viewers might have expected, but rather to rescue the adolescent girl from the clutches of her devious Romanian companion.

The scene of Alina's rescue is set in a large, disused factory on the Milanese periphery to which Sandro has been summoned in a phone call from the frantic, needy girl. He travels there alone from Brescia, unknown to his parents, manages to find the building on the city's outskirts, scales the high fence intended to keep intruders at bay (in the film's only allusion to contemporary politics, the fence is covered with election posters promoting Berlusconi), and enters the compound. The entire building has been appropriated as living space by dozens, if not hundreds, of immigrants. Squatted spaces of this sort have, in fact, mushroomed in various locations around Italy since the late 1990s, providing temporary or long-term shelter to otherwise homeless individuals, as is described in the investigative project by Ottieri that gives its title to Giordana's film.

Sandro's entry into the structure is shot in sinister tones. Clearly intimidated, he observes people huddled around a makeshift fire or staring at him in an unsettling way. As he proceeds through the dimly lit space—following a trajectory reminiscent of a sequence in Rossellini's *Germania anno zero* (*Germany Year Zero*, 1948)—he hears the faint sounds of Alina's favorite pop song, the achingly sentimental "Un'emozione per sempre," by Eros Ramazzotti, and is guided acoustically to her room below ground. Coming face-to-face with the girl—barely recognizable in heavy makeup, cheap jewelry, and a precocious outfit—and observing a video camera in the corner of the room, he finally understands why she has called for his help, and he begins to weep for the first time in the film. Curiously, it is the girl he has come to rescue who then comforts him, presumably giving him the strength and resolve to remove her from her sordid surroundings and accompany her into the open, anonymous space of the city streets.

Despite the ambivalence toward irregular immigration that emerges in the course of the film, the final sequence reaffirms the kind of unconditional hospitality described in the writings of Levinas and Derrida. It is here, in fact, that

Migration, Masculinity, and New Urban Geographies | 117

Figure 4.2. Screen capture. The scene of Alina's rescue. *Quando sei nato non puoi più nasconderti* (2005)

Sandro fully embraces the ethical necessity of responding to the call of the other, regardless of the consequences for the self. While *Quando sei nato* makes clear that the undocumented migrant, the destitute, and the homeless, though undeniably victims, are not always innocent, it also suggests that this does not diminish the subject's responsibility to recognize their human needs.

Yet it is also significant that in this otherwise conventional *Bildung*, ultimate mastery is denied to its Italian bourgeois protagonist. In contrast to the tidier narrative conclusion constructed in the screenplay, which involved Alina's self-defensive killing of Radu, the final version of *Quando sei nato* ends instead with a sense of indeterminacy.[8] After rescuing Alina from the scene of her exploitation, Sandro takes her to a busy intersection, where they sit for a moment in the middle of a construction site. Darkness has already enveloped the city. The concluding shot frames the pair sitting side by side in this anonymous urban space, sharing a sandwich. When the camera finally pulls away from the figures and the image decomposes to a blur, the viewer realizes that they have no clear destination. Aware of his father's disapproval of any further attempt on his part to aid his migrant friends, Sandro has already refused to answer his mother's phone call. He has also denied his identity to a sandwich vendor who recognized him from televised reports about his dramatic adventure at sea. By ignoring his father's injunction, and effectively disavowing his father's name, he becomes—at least for the moment—a fugitive. His last gesture in the film, the sharing of bread in an anonymous urban space, has a radical simplicity, suggesting his intention to remain alongside the defenseless, fugitive girl while acknowledging his inability to incorporate her into the structures of Italian bourgeois life.

The most crucial element in the film's narrative development is clearly Sandro's coming to manhood—not in terms of physical endurance or heteronormative sexual development as prescribed by the adult men in his life but rather through a series of moral choices and his ongoing embrace of the principle of openness to the other. His final act of rescue is the ultimate confirmation that this maturity has been achieved. Yet, in the scheme of the overarching narrative trajectory, the Romanian teenagers, like the two southern Italian ferrymen, function merely as a foil for the northern Italian boy's quest for self-determination. Alina's usefulness to the narrative lies in direct relation to the opportunity she offers Sandro to make his own ethical choices in defiance of his father. Yet Sandro's act of rescue, while signaling his moral courage and self-determination, will not save Alina in a meaningful way as there is apparently no place for her to go. *Quando sei nato* thus offers a particularly compelling example of the contradictory mechanisms through which Italian cinema attempts to conjure up a sympathetic response to the needs of Italy's new migrants, while at the same time falling prey to the processes of discursive abjection that separate the nationally desirable subject—white, middle-class, and properly European—from the outsiders, those not-quite-white-enough foreigners who cannot yet be absorbed into the social body of the European Union.

Saimir: Liminal Subjectivity

Saimir (Francesco Munzi, 2004) offers a compelling counterpoint to Giordana's *Quando sei nato*. At the narrative level they have several commonalities: both films configure crucial encounters between Italian citizens and immigrants who live at the margins of society and include a scene in which young Eastern European immigrants violate and plunder the domestic space of ordinary Italian citizens. Additionally, each of them features a decisive scenario in which the young male protagonist comes to the rescue of a distressed migrant girl in explicit defiance of his father, thus marking his passage to self-determined maturity. However, unlike the affluent Italian adolescent at the center of *Quando sei nato*, Saimir, the eponymous protagonist of Munzi's film, is an economically deprived Albanian teenager living with his father in a coastal suburb near Rome, whose contact with autochthonous Italians is sporadic at best. Thus, while both Giordana's and Munzi's characters defy a paternal injunction in order to aid a vulnerable migrant girl, they do so from contrasting positionalities, and their activities occur in radically different social contexts. Stylistically, the films also stand in sharp contrast to each other. *Quando sei nato* is an expensively made, stylishly photographed production, directed by an acclaimed filmmaker and featuring well-known Italian actors in the adult roles; *Saimir*, by contrast, is a low-budget film made by a then-unknown filmmaker that deploys a naturalistic, almost ethnographic approach and uses nonprofessional or little-known actors who speak their own languages more often than Italian.

Munzi's film charts the coming of age of the sixteen-year-old Albanian Saimir (Mishel Manoku), who assists his father, Edmond (Xhevet Feri), in transporting irregular migrants from a secluded landing point on the Adriatic coast to various destinations across the Italian peninsula. Since Saimir appears in almost every scene, the viewer is invited to identify closely with his point of view. The broader hermeneutic question that underpins the film is how Italy is experienced by those who are marked as outsiders by virtue of their poverty and limited proficiency in Italian and must attempt to survive without the benefit of legal residency, adequately remunerated work, or protection from violence and exploitation. While *Quando sei nato* introduced the viewer to locations seldom visualized previously in Italian cinema, *Saimir* also provides glimpses of rarely explored sites indicative of Italy's evolving social landscape, including a sizable Romani encampment, Rome's coastal neighborhoods populated by immigrants, and, more fleetingly, the small rural enterprises whose survival depends on undocumented migrant labor. *Saimir*'s Albanian protagonist, unlike the Italian Sandro in *Quando sei nato*, is depicted as part of this unfamiliar, morally ambivalent, and often squalid environment.

Immersing the viewer in Saimir's daily routine of assisting his father in his work, the opening sequence of the film has a subtly disorienting effect. As the two characters set out by truck across a wintry, mountainous terrain, it is clear that the teenager is accompanying his father on a prearranged assignment, but it is difficult to determine their location. The music on the car radio has a southeastern European or Turkish sound, raising the possibility that they are traveling through Albania or elsewhere in the Balkans. The subsequent sequence, however, reveals that Saimir and his father have arranged to meet a group of irregular migrants whom they will accompany to an inland destination. The enigma of the film's geographical setting is finally resolved for the viewer when one of the recently arrived migrants, a small boy from Kosovo, asks the protagonist in Albanian if Italy is still far off and is told, with mild amusement, that he has already arrived.

The geographical disorientation generated in this opening sequence thus serves a clear purpose. Defamiliarizing the Apennine landscape through the acoustic overlay of Albanian dialogue and music coded as exotic, the film introduces the viewer to the land of Italy entirely through the eyes of two non-Italians who are attempting to make this territory their home. When the Kosovar boy proceeds to ask Saimir, "What is Italy like?" his question is met with a telling silence, as if the teenager is hesitant to alarm the child with an account of his own experience. But the boy's curiosity encapsulates the question that the film itself will seek to answer as it explores what Italy might look like through an outsider's eyes. The protagonist's immersion in a marginalized world of poverty and petty crime effectively prompts the viewer to identify with the sense of alienation and frustration that can challenge the efforts of irregular migrants to improve the quality of their lives. Though Saimir eventually finds a way to achieve what might appear to be a solution—the ability to stay legally in Italy—he does so at a painful price.

Unhappy with his father's resigned acceptance of his grueling job in the service of Albanian smugglers and with his decision to marry an Italian woman in order to regularize his immigrant status, Saimir fitfully attempts to carve out a social space of his own. Shortly after being initiated into sexual activity at a lurid nightclub managed by an Albanian cousin—a location similar to the environment frequented by the Albanian protagonist of *L'italiano*—he begins a romance with Michela, an Italian schoolgirl his own age. This brief idyll—which begins on the socially fluid, open space of the beach—finally brings him some happiness but abruptly comes to an end when he reveals to her the spoils of his adventures as a petty thief. Startled by his ignorance of the implications of these activities, Michela abruptly walks out of his life. In a subsequent scene, Saimir shows up at her school unannounced, bursting into the classroom to ask her loudly if she considers him inferior to her simply on the basis of his immigrant identity. Saimir's affect, appearance, and behavior are visibly out of line with the protocols of the school, and he is forcefully removed from the building. Eliciting empathy for the perplexed immigrant who cannot comprehend the Italian girl's rejection, the film conveys his growing frustration with his seemingly insurmountable marginalization.

The dramatic crux of the narrative occurs when Saimir discovers that a fifteen-year-old Russian girl—whom he helped to smuggle from the coast of Puglia to the suburbs of Rome—has been sequestered, brutalized, and raped by his father's employers. At great risk, he takes decisive action by reporting her whereabouts to the police, provoking the arrest of his own father in the process. The film ends as Saimir is led away from his home by uniformed *carabinieri* after a devastating encounter with his detained father. Although Saimir's fate is not explicitly explained in the diegesis, Italian audiences understand that, as an unaccompanied minor, he will remain a ward of the Italian state until he reaches the age of eighteen, at which point he may be conceded the possibility of staying in the country permanently.

Saimir, which is Munzi's first feature film, has a rigorous visual austerity. Though partly the result of budgetary limitations, this aesthetic is well suited to the harsh circumstances foregrounded in the diegesis, the shabby settings frequented by the characters, and the emotional isolation of the film's protagonist. The fact that Munzi came to feature films following some experience in documentary filmmaking is evident in his skillful deployment of locations, including the scene shot at a Romani campsite, and the casting of somatically diverse, non-Italian, nonprofessional actors who perform their roles in their own language.

Figure 4.3. Screen capture. Trafficked Russian teenager rescued by Saimir. *Saimir* (2004)

For the most part Albanian is the dominant language in *Saimir*, but minor characters are also heard speaking Romani and Russian, respectively. Most of the film was shot in winter on the coastal strip west of Rome, which, though a popular destination for city beachgoers in the summer, is inhabited in the offseason almost exclusively by residents of diverse national and ethnic origins.

One of the most striking sequences in the film shows Saimir's participation in a burglary at the villa of a wealthy Italian family. His companions are a handful of Romani teenagers with whom he has established a routine complicity. Far from depicting the event as a reprehensible crime, the film foregrounds the vitality and curiosity of the Romani boys, their sense of wonderment in the discovery of new surroundings, in contrast to Saimir's morose detachment. The mood of the entire sequence combines elements of lyricism and pathos with a pronounced note of comedy.

Saimir's companions initially approach the task of burglary with focused attention, tying up the Filipina maid in businesslike fashion and swiftly selecting objects they deem to have value as they move through the house. Their focus dissolves, however, when the temptation to play takes the upper hand. The delinquents are then suddenly transformed into children. One boy struts about in a fur coat, and another approaches the piano and plays haphazardly on the keyboard, while a third, captivated by the sight of the swimming pool, pulls off his clothes and dives in to enjoy an impromptu swim. Cutting back and forth among the various characters, the scene is presented as an interval of pure *jouissance*, highlighted on the soundtrack by the *Allegro non molto* movement from Vivaldi's "Summer" Concerto.[9] Only Saimir remains detached from the dominant mood of uninhibited play as he continues to gather up valuable objects with an expression of mournful perplexity. Finally, opening the door to a bedroom, he catches sight of an emaciated old man lying in bed attached to a feeding tube. Though the audience's sympathies are now aligned with Saimir, the image of the terrified, speechless Italian, lying helplessly on his back, seems momentarily to dramatize Italians' worst fears about the dangers presented by immigration. But the Albanian stops short in his path. In a brief tableau where the citizen symbolically occupies the space of the disenfranchised other, Saimir stares mournfully at the old man and then quietly retreats. Though entirely wordless, this fleeting encounter signals Saimir's growing awareness of the consequences of his actions on others and prepares us for the film's dramatic resolution.

The peripheral locations in which the film is shot, the lawless, outsider status of its principal characters, and the choral effect achieved by the ragtag group of male adolescents befriended by the protagonist who have no hope of attaining the privileges enjoyed by the mainstream are reminiscent of the early films of Pier Paolo Pasolini, particularly *Accattone* (1961) and *Mamma Roma* (1962). Yet a different sensibility emerges in Munzi's work, along with a more ambivalent engagement with issues of belonging and exclusion. Clearly, the social context to which these films refer—the economically marginalized communities of the Roman periphery—has changed considerably since the 1960s as the representatives of Italy's underclass now seem to hail not from the South or the hinterland but from beyond the nation's borders. Unlike the idealization of the outsider witnessed in Pasolini's films, a more conservative ethos underpins *Saimir*, which narrates the dilemma of a teenager actively seeking to escape his father's influence and with it the material constraints and moral compromises of his marginalized existence. The film is ultimately less reminiscent of Pasolini's work than of *La Promesse* (1996), directed by the Belgian filmmaking duo Luc and Jean-Pierre Dardenne, which recounts the ethical transformation of a working-class youth who initially collaborates with his father in exploiting irregular immigrants, only to repudiate these activities by the film's end. In fact, recurring shots of Saimir riding his moped through the streets of the urban periphery establish a striking intertextual link with the protagonist of *La Promesse*.

Saimir is one of a small number of Italian films to feature a male Eastern European migrant as protagonist. Munzi was well aware of the challenges posed by his decision to construct the film around the viewpoint of an irregular Albanian migrant, and he aimed self-consciously to avoid simplification, stereotypes, and facile binarisms.[10] The ethical problem of constructing the other, of speaking for the other, has indeed been the focus of theoretical discussion for several years, especially in feminist and postcolonial scholarship.[11] The challenge for artists representing those who are ethnically, racially, or economically "other" is marked by the need to observe, respect, and "translate" the other's differences while avoiding the pitfalls of erasure, disavowal, or phantasmatic distortions. The major risk to be avoided—and one that is witnessed throughout the history of representational practices—lies in the mechanism of constructing the other simply in terms of the self: as the opposite of the self, a process that conflates the other with the self-same.

Munzi reports in the commentary that accompanies the DVD version of *Saimir* that his initial version of the screenplay was flawed by a surfeit of *buonismo* (a well-meaning but ultimately self-indulgent attitude of sympathy), noting that while the protagonist was constructed in a uniquely positive way, other characters had no redeeming features. The final version, which the filmmaker wrote in collaboration with Serena Brugnolo and Dino Gentili, avoids this binary model, particularly in its delicate portrayal of the tensions between father and son. The film's leading character is certainly far from idealized. He can be sympathetic, even admirable, but he is also often a rude, recalcitrant teenager. His father, Edmond, is similarly nuanced. Despite his moral cowardice, blinkered resignation to a life of illegal employment, and occasional bouts of anger, he clearly cares for his son. Munzi has attributed the balance achieved in the final version of the script to his experience, in the months intervening between the drafts, of preparing a documentary on a family living in a Romani encampment in the Roman suburbs. Living in close contact with this community for an extended period of time allowed him the opportunity to observe the complexities of a way of life very different from anything he had previously known. Although the documentary was never completed, Munzi includes a brief scene in a similar encampment in *Saimir*, where a Romani mother chides her wayward children (who, the viewers realize, have just burglarized the villa of a wealthy Italian family) for their bad behavior. In effect, the film's delineation of all non-Italian characters, including the Albanians and the Roma, demonstrates a degree of sensitivity to the complexity and ambivalence that imbue immigrant lives.

Saimir does not aim at offering a broad picture of the Albanian immigrant experience. The contours of the narrative certainly lack the broad historical resonances of Amelio's *Lamerica*. By focusing the dramatic weight of the film on the conflict between father and son, the filmmaker gives *Saimir* an intimate, familiar scope, calculated to appeal to a wide audience. In effect, the viewer is called on to identify with a young man engaged in the timeless struggle to shake off the yoke of paternal authority. Sympathy for this character is achieved at least in part through the deployment of a conventional oedipal narrative, where the youthful protagonist engages in an ultimately successful struggle to overturn the oppressive rule of the older man.

Saimir's ultimate triumph, however, is laced with ambiguity. The boy is not definitively rewarded for his conscientious action, for his attempt to shake off the taint of his problematical "Albanianness," despite the fact that his ability to

Figure 4.4. Screen capture. Saimir meets Michela. *Saimir* (2004)

remain in Italy at least for the moment seems assured. His access to the opportunity of legitimate residency has been achieved, in effect, by betraying his own father and his associates to the police. Furthermore, having alienated himself through this betrayal from his other relatives in the expatriate community who are similarly involved in the criminal underworld, he is implicitly exposed to the risk of reprisal. And even as he progresses toward the possibility of legitimate status on Italian soil, he has learned enough from his former Italian girlfriend, Michela, to grasp the unlikelihood of his being welcomed into the mainstream of Italian social life. In this way, the film dramatizes in a compelling fashion the sense of liminality, uncertainty, and risk shared by many irregular migrants living in Italy at present.

Despite the film's sympathetic construction of the Albanian teenager and its nuanced rendering of the boy's father as a victim of economic pressure and the threat of deportation, on a literal level, the narrative seems to confirm the commonplace equation of "Albanian" with "criminal," suggesting that it is in part thanks to the harsh lesson provided by his Italian girlfriend that the protagonist begins to question behavior that he might otherwise have taken for granted. In this scenario, the Italian girl functions as a catalyst to set in motion the oedipal dimension of Saimir's trajectory—that is, to defeat his father's power over him and pursue a path of his own making. In an even more spectacular way, the brutalized Russian girl he succeeds in rescuing from coerced prostitution becomes a vital instrument in his journey to maturity.

Though the protagonists of *Quando sei nato* and *Saimir* are from contrasting locations within Italy's contemporary social landscape, the narrative trajectories of the privileged Italian adolescent and the marginalized Albanian migrant have some striking similarities. In each case, the passage to ethical responsibility and masculine maturity is marked by the boy's decision to rescue a young Eastern European girl from the scene of forced sex work. Little is revealed in either film about the motivations or experience of the trafficked girl as her subjectivity is overshadowed by the subjective focus on the young male hero. Ultimately, what we find in both narratives is variation on the classical oedipal paradigm critiqued by de Lauretis, who has shown how, in the traditional narrative structure, the girl or woman is merely of secondary interest to the hero's progress.[12] Thus in *Saimir* the Russian teenager's captivity ultimately functions as the ground on which the young protagonist must take action to defy his father's authority, becoming, in the process, a man in his own right.

Amoroso's *Cover Boy*: Shifting Margins

Cover boy: L'ultima rivoluzione (Cover Boy: The Last Revolution, Carmine Amoroso, 2006) differs from the two films discussed earlier in this chapter insofar as its protagonist is a young man rather than an adolescent or teenager. Yet this, too, is a story of male maturation and transnational encounter that unfolds in Italy's migratory landscape. As in *Saimir*, the leading character in *Cover boy* is from southeastern Europe, but in this case the imputed abjection of the southeastern European subject is radically called into question rather than implicitly confirmed.[13]

Directed by Carmine Amoroso, the film is clearly an ambitious project, though budgetary constraints resulted in a radical modification of the narrative originally envisioned in the screenplay. Layering different histories and geographies, it unfolds for the most part in contemporary Rome and Milan, with a substantial prologue set in Bucharest during the events leading to the overthrow of Romanian dictator Nicolae Ceaușescu. Opening with a montage of highlights from the history of the Cold War, the film introduces its protagonist, Ioan, as a six-year-old boy during the uprising that convulsed Bucharest and killed his father in December 1989. The main body of the film unfolds in Italy, however, beginning at the moment when the twenty-two-year-old Romanian Ioan (Eduard Gabia) arrives alone at Termini Station in Rome, after Bogdan, his Romanian friend and fellow traveler, was detained by the police during a passport check. The film thus establishes itself as Ioan's story, though some subsequent scenes unfold through the perspective of an Italian named Michele, whom Ioan befriends upon arrival in Rome. The mise-en-scène of Ioan's arrival at Termini Station—itself an iconic location in Italian cinema since the 1940s—is emblematic. In a long shot he is seen standing, perplexed and unkempt, in the middle of the station's crowded atrium, dwarfed by the large-scale advertisements for Emporio Armani displayed on the wall above him. As fashion images become an important trope later in the film, their visibility at this moment of arrival and their contrast with the abject figure of the penniless migrant are not accidental.

Ioan soon meets Michele (Luca Lionello), a forty-year-old Italian who is working temporarily as a janitor at the station. Hostile at first, Michele eventually offers to share his apartment with Ioan for a modest sum. Though he makes clear that he feels superior to the Romanian by virtue of his status as an Italian, he tells Ioan that he originally came to Rome as a student from the Abruzzo region. Hence he, too, is a migrant and is marked as a southerner in the capital. Precariously employed, he struggles desperately to achieve a level of economic security that is perpetually beyond his grasp. Describing himself as *uno straniero in patria* (a foreigner in his own land), Michele is scarcely less marginalized or lacking in resources than his migrant friend. A closeted gay man, he is drawn to Ioan sexually but struggles to hide his feelings. Although the Romanian does not show any awareness of this attraction, the film continues to suggest the erotic potential of their relationship, often showing them in close proximity with each other and, in the film's happiest moment, frolicking together naked in the sea.

After Michele is suddenly dismissed from his job as a janitor, he searches for casual employment alongside Ioan. In a scene marked by elements of farce, the Italian poses as Romanian in order to get a job washing cars with Ioan. This venture proves to be a failure as Michele is unable to withstand the abuse meted out to him by Italian clients who presume he is an immigrant. Soon afterward, Ioan happens to meet his old friend Bogdan, who has just arrived in Rome and offers him the possibility of making easy money in an undisclosed line of work. Accompanying Bogdan to his presumed workplace, Ioan discovers, to his apparent horror, that his friend makes a living providing sexual services to wealthy male clients. Finally understanding that the lucrative work he was promised before his departure from Romania was in fact male prostitution, he rejects Bogdan's proposal and returns to the streets to try washing windshields for money.

Ioan has now realized that he and Michele share a similar status of economic precariousness. Their common circumstances are highlighted in the tag line with which the film was initially advertised: "Love and Rage of a Precarious Generation." A tentative solidarity evolves between the immigrant without a work permit (significantly, the film is set just before the accession of Romania to the European Union) and the sporadically employed Michele, thanks to the shared fragility of their material existence. In the course of a conversation between Michele and a clerk at an employment agency, the film reveals that the Italian has always had to make a living through temporary work, facing intermittent periods of unemployment.[14]

Cover boy diverges from almost all other Italian films featuring immigrant characters by showing that despite the xenophobia and racism directed at migrants, many Italians share with them a sense of economic precariousness and a desire to secure a better life. Amoroso's film neither idealizes the status of the outsider nor asserts the importance of the center. Rather, it subverts conventional beliefs about how citizens and migrants are fundamentally different from each other. Struggling perpetually to pay the rent, Ioan and Michele live in a shabby apartment on the outskirts of Rome, in the area once frequented by the ragtag characters of Pasolini's early films. Their landlady (Luciana Littizzetto) is an out-of-work actress who, though struggling to make ends meet, is contemptuous of her impoverished tenants. The film thus suggests that marginalized people create their own borders, distancing themselves from those they perceive to occupy lower rungs of the social ladder. As Étienne Balibar has argued, borders "are no longer entirely situated at the outer limit of territories; they are dispersed a little everywhere."[15]

Writing about contemporary European cinemas, Temenuga Trifonova observes that recent films about migration and diaspora no longer focus solely on the most visible conflicts between center and periphery, between foreigners and nationals, but have instead begun to depict conflicts at the periphery itself. She argues that migration films "deterritorialize nationality by deterritorializing the notion of the border, not by opening up borders but by redrawing them along transnational, social, class, gender, political and generational lines."[16] On a number of occasions, *Cover boy* dramatizes the deterritorialization of the borders within the European city. For example, shortly after his arrival in Rome, Ioan is obliged to relinquish his sleeping space along the external wall of Termini Station because other homeless individuals have created their own boundaries by laying claim to the public space he attempts to occupy.

Similarly, when he tries to sleep on the grass near the Coliseum, a man dressed as a Roman gladiator (presumably involved in precarious work at the margins of the tourist industry) wakes him up, telling him that he is not allowed to sleep there—that is, in the public space over which the Italian feels he has jurisdiction. In another scene, Ioan's efforts to make money by washing windshields at a busy intersection are thwarted by a Romani youth, also a migrant. Claiming the intersection as his own working area, the young man expels Ioan from of the territory he has appropriated. In this way, Amoroso's film reveals the perpetually shifting configurations of public space in the contemporary metropolis.

In addition to illuminating these shifting territorial configurations, *Cover boy* also refers to issues of racial boundaries and racial passing. It suggests, in effect, that racial distinctions in the contemporary Italian setting are not organized around a simple opposition between white and nonwhite. In one scene, Michele worries whether he will be able to pass as a Romanian migrant in order to keep a job at a car-washing service, the sort of poorly paid labor generally available to migrants. Although he has previously worked as a janitor, he is unused to the kind of humiliating manual labor that he is now desperately obliged to seek. The implication is that although Michele has a visibly darker complexion and hair than Ioan, he perceives himself ideologically as whiter, and he is now afraid that his whiteness will be recognized, curtailing his chances of being hired.

Although Michele is destined to remain trapped in the cycle of unemployment and poverty, an important shift occurs in Ioan's fortunes when he encounters Laura, a fashion photographer who is apparently captivated by his innocent, unspoiled look when she spots him in the streets of Rome and begins spontaneously to photograph him. She then takes him to Milan, transforms him into a fashion model, regularizes his immigration status, and eventually becomes his lover. Ioan's life thus changes dramatically overnight. He becomes a survivor, successfully rescued as if he were a character in a fairytale.

Ioan appears at first to be rather passive, immature, and out of touch. When he is first reunited by chance with Bogdan in Rome's Piazza della Repubblica, his friend tells him to wake up and come to terms with the fact that, as an impoverished immigrant, he will always be considered a worthless piece of meat. He reminds Ioan that only money counts in Italy. Without it, he claims, an immigrant is considered the equivalent of a floor cloth. Unlike Bogdan, who has learned to smile and hone his social skills to survive, Ioan remains relatively sullen throughout the film, refusing to make any special effort to promote himself or to please those around him.

Despite Bogdan's explicit warning about the particularly abject status of foreigners, at several moments *Cover boy* blurs or overturns the conventionally imagined roles of the (foreign) victim and the (native) victimizer. In the relationship between Michele and Ioan, it is the immigrant Ioan who remains calm and decisive in the face of difficulties, while Michele is more vulnerable, constantly on the verge of rage or tears. In a reversal of the usual scenario, the Italian begins to dream of going abroad to Romania in the hope of remaking himself as a businessman in a foreign land and in this way escaping destitution in Italy.

Problematizing the conventionally depicted trajectory in which Eastern Europeans go West looking for employment, Amoroso shows the less frequently explored path of Westerners traveling to the former Eastern Europe to exploit its resources in the shifting global economy. As already suggested, *Cover boy* deterritorializes the simple notion of border crossing. Although Eastern Europeans in Italian cinema are usually coded as trapped in a space from which they wish to escape, Amoroso's film shows that Italians can experience a similar sense of entrapment and a similar desire to leave for a better place. In this case, however, the desired place is no longer empirically better; it is instead a fantasy space, an abstraction. The yearning expressed by Ioan and Michele to move to the Danube Delta is not based on the tangible qualities of this location since neither of them has actually seen it. Rather, they long to move there because Ioan reports that his own father had said just before his death that it was "the most beautiful place on earth."

When *Cover boy* rescues Ioan from destitution through Laura's intervention, his departure proves devastating for Michele. Unable to secure further work as a janitor and now bereft of the only friendship that holds any meaning for him, he becomes increasingly desperate. A striking image of his outstretched hand attempting to sell religious medals to tourists visiting the Vatican from the global South underscores his desperation and humiliation. This is but one instance in which the film places Michele in the same position as the hapless foreigner, a trope that clearly sets it apart from other films structured around stories of Italian immigration.

The contrast between Michele's previously assumed superiority as an Italian and the realization that he is powerless and without prospects eventually provokes him to hang himself. The catalyst occurs as he listens to the televised speech given by Berlusconi at a conference hosted by Confindustria (the umbrella organization representing Italy's manufacturing and service companies) in March 2006. Sharply denying evidence of financial mismanagement, Prime Minister Berlusconi is heard accusing the Left of falsely promoting a discourse of economic crisis.

The scenes charting Michele's final days alive are crosscut with scenes in which Ioan pursues new opportunities in Milan, becoming immersed in Laura's glamorous world while seeming to forget his friendship with Michele. Spectacle and image manipulation are the tropes mobilized in the Milan scenes, which take place against the backdrop of the global fashion industry. Though Laura assumes that Ioan has no memory of the violence that briefly convulsed his city during his childhood, there are hints in the film that reminders of the past can surface at any moment, triggered by unexpected cues.

The most emblematic image in *Cover boy* is a large-scale black-and-white photograph that appears at a crucial point near the end of the Milan sequence. Created through Laura's editing skills, the photograph is presented as a large publicity poster for Exile (presumably a clothing line), which Ioan observes as he enters a bar with Laura at the conclusion of a fashion show. Inscribed with the words "Wear the Revolution," the scene depicted in the photograph ostensibly invokes the events that unfolded in Bucharest in December 1989, showing a soldier in the uniform of the Romanian Army pointing his weapon at a naked youth, whose arms are raised in surrender as he faces the viewer. The nude figure in the picture is Ioan, originally photographed by Laura as he stretched his arms above his head on rising one morning from her bed. Unbeknownst to him, she has superimposed his image onto a documentary photograph glimpsed in an earlier scene, showing the same Romanian soldier pointing his gun at a defenseless civilian.

Figure 4.5. Screen capture. Ioan's manipulated image on a fashion poster. *Cover boy* (2006)

Though Laura assumes that her young lover does not remember the events of the Romanian uprising, she is mistaken. The manipulated photograph functions as a site of uncanny spectrality, which allows for a juxtaposition of Ioan's traumatic experience of history in the Romanian context and the effects of memory in the present. Upon viewing the digitally altered photograph for the first time and recognizing his own body within it, the young man experiences a dramatic revisiting of the moment in which he witnessed the shooting of his own father in December 1989. As he remembers this, the event itself, which was partially revealed in the film's prologue, unfolds in full in an extended flashback. It then becomes clear that Ioan experiences the image depicted on the poster as a violent betrayal by the woman who had become his mentor and lover, only to exploit his body in a way that he did not foresee. His reaction is not unlike his earlier rejection of the opportunity to make money through sex work; once again he refuses to be commodified and consumed as an attractive, white, foreign body. Turning toward Laura in anger, he utters, "Shame on you!" and walks out of her life for good, abandoning the life of privilege she had offered him. The moment marks his decisive coming to maturity.

The complex imagery of the poster placed in the mise-en-scène of *Cover boy* invites multiple visual associations. It appears to reference the controversial advertising campaign created by photographer Oliviero Toscani for United Colors of Benetton, which was distributed around the world in the late 1980s and 1990s. The Toscani posters often depicted shocking scenes of human suffering or hardship (showing, for example, a dying AIDs patient in one case and, in another, the Vlora packed with Albanians at the moment of arrival in Italy) or offered provocative juxtapositions of diverse human types. Voided of historicity, detached from their social context, and clearly unrelated to the product they were supposedly advertising, these images functioned as free-floating signifiers.

In the large-scale photograph placed in the mise-en-scène of *Cover boy*, the gestural dimension of the young man's raised arms has a stark visual effect that transcends commercial associations, rendering the nude body at the center of the image not as an erotic object but as an uncanny spectral presence. The most obvious association that emerges from the poster's figural composition is the iconic image of the anonymous child usually referred to as "the Warsaw Boy," which was taken in the Warsaw Ghetto as Jewish families were being rounded up by the Gestapo. In fact, two key figures are central to both images: a defenseless young male, his upraised arms indicating surrender, and an armed soldier pointing a gun in his direction. The film thus communicates the complex significance of its title and subtitle, which point to the tendency of the contemporary image industries to appropriate images of human bodies, private experiences, and traumatic histories for purely commercial purposes.

Ioan's discovery of Laura's appropriation of his image becomes the trigger that enables him to remember his connection with Michele and to abandon Milan for good. Within the moral order constructed by the narrative, Michele now represents a more appealing point of reference for him than the illusory world of spectacle in which he had become embroiled. After failing to reach his friend by telephone, Ioan begins the long drive to Rome in a mood of happy anticipation. His nighttime journey is intercut with the scene of the landlady's discovery of Michele's body in his Rome apartment, an event that is represented in such oblique terms that the viewer might miss its significance upon the first viewing. In the scene that follows, Ioan is still at the wheel of his car but now appears to be driving through the Romanian countryside in daylight. In a subsequent cut, Michele is seated next to him, chatting about their plans for the restaurant in the Danube Delta. The reappearance of the Italian thus serves to reassure the viewer that Ioan's friend is alive and well and that they are happily on their way to the Danube. A subsequent shot confirms this as both men are seen standing on a wharf, looking out over a broad expanse of the river. When, in the final shot, it becomes clear that Ioan is in fact alone, the viewer understands the spectral status of the entire sequence. Michele is indeed deceased but refuses to be fully dead and insists on coming back.

These final images link *Cover boy* to a growing body of European films that disrupt the conventional chronology of realist fiction by withholding the markers that usually designate diegetic shifts. What this entails for the spectators is a provisional suspension of the ability to distinguish between what is supposedly real and what is merely imagined or to tell the difference between past, present, and future. Thomas Elsaesser has described such films as "post-mortem" since they convey a sense of haunting and raise issues of memory, history, and identity through a nonrealistic configuration of temporality.[17]

By definition, films that employ the trope of haunting have an ambivalent, asynchronous temporality. In contemporary post-mortem films, time seems to freeze, making it unclear whether it is the past that haunts the present or the future that haunts the past. The shifts in temporality remain unmarked, and the continuity editing characteristic of realist narratives is fractured, posing hermeneutic challenges to the spectator and character alike. As Elsaesser points out, post-mortem films fail to register the difference between actual characters and imagined ones, between those who know about their post-mortem status and those who do not. Thus, in *Cover boy*'s final scenes, the usual techniques such as flashback, fade-in, or superimposition, which typically designate transitions from the supposedly real to the imagined, are absent.

Elsaesser's reflection on how cinema can address the problematics of living together in a new Europe resonates with Derrida's reflections on temporal disjunctures in his volume *Specters of Marx*, a text inspired by the question of how to live in a rapidly changing world.[18] Written after the fall of the Berlin Wall, the imputed reunification of Europe, and the founding of the European Union, it attempts to articulate a social critique adequate to an altered political landscape. In an era that Derrida considers to be bereft of ethics or politics, he outlines a critique of the globalizing world while calling for a fundamental break with the present.

In the face of widespread claims that Marx and Marxism are defunct, *Specters of Marx* argues against the triumphal claims of neoliberalism and asserts that an adequate critique of late capitalism must appropriate Marx while simultaneously criticizing him. Rejecting as inadequate the predominantly political and economic considerations that tend to characterize critical approaches to globalization, Derrida builds his critique from the standpoint of a politics based on the nonpresentist temporality of spectrality, a standpoint that rejects any understanding of the present as presence.

For Derrida, the question of learning to live entails coming to terms with death—that is, with the spectral. He sees the specter, the revenant, in terms of untimeliness and anachronism. In his reading of Marx's reflections on Shakespeare, he observes that learning to live requires transcending Hamlet's opposition of being and not being, of life and death.[19] As an entity that both is and is not, the specter represents temporalities that cannot be grasped in terms of present time. Such temporalities include a past that has not ended and a future that breaks with the present. Spectrality thus expresses that which does not exist solely in the "chain of presents."[20]

Derrida's critique of the present as presence is undertaken from the standpoint of a politics based on the nonidentical, nonpresentist temporality of spectrality. He characterizes this politics as one of responsibility to the past, to the dead—victims of war, violence, and oppression—and to the future, those not yet born.[21] Derrida coins the French word *hantologie* (hauntology) as a substitute for its near-homonym, *ontologie* (ontology), thus replacing the priority of being and presence with the figure of the ghost—a figure that is neither presence nor absence, neither dead nor alive.[22] To learn to live, he argues, an individual must acknowledge death because it is only through the other and by death that individuals come into configuration as themselves. People must learn how to live with ghosts, in their company, and above all to learn how to talk to them and enable them in turn to speak again.

Despite its uneven development, due largely to production problems, *Cover boy* offers a more complex commentary on Italy's human and economic landscape than the films discussed previously in this chapter. It is perhaps unique in the overall panorama of Italian films about migration insofar as it self-consciously rejects the simple binary of victim and abuser/exploiter mapped onto the figures of migrant and citizen. Most importantly, through its deployment of the trope of spectrality, this film also suggests that violence and oppression are not limited to the present but should be considered in terms of broader temporalities, paying attention to the weight of history and to the ghosts of those whose lives are truncated by abuses of power.

Conclusion

Quando sei nato non puoi più nasconderti, Saimir, and *Cover boy: L'ultima rivoluzione* bear a discernible relation to Italy's tradition of *cinema d'impegno* and seem committed, at least on the surface, to probing the tensions and dilemmas presented by the phenomenon of Italian immigration. Though they offer a familiar *Bildung* of male maturation, the circumstances prompting their protagonists' transformation are distinctive to Italy's global present. Notably, all three films narrate the deployment of a young, white, Eastern European body as a fetishized commodity in Italy's migratory landscape.

Quando sei nato and *Saimir* are structured in linear fashion in the style of traditional coming-of-age narratives, and in each film the young protagonist's assumption of masculine maturity is triggered by the encounter with an underage Eastern European girl transported to Italy for sexual exploitation. Yet, whereas the adolescent in *Quando sei nato* is an Italian citizen, the young protagonist of *Saimir* is himself an immigrant, making this the first coming-of-age film centered on a migrant character to emerge in Italian cinema. *Cover boy* is similarly focused on a migrant youth. Although he is no longer a teenager, he, too, undergoes a process of maturation upon observing the sexual or visual exploitation of migrant bodies in the Italian context. Finally, however, he rescues himself from such exploitation, proving to be more adept at survival than his Italian counterpart, who is unable to overcome his economic misfortunes. The three films thus articulate male maturation in diverse ways, presenting Italians and foreigners, insiders and outsiders in varying configurations, yet always through the prism of a distinctively masculine subjectivity.

Linking these three narratives is the messiness—and the potential fruitfulness—of transcultural encounters in Italy's changing urban geographies and migratory trajectories, which present new challenges for ethical discernment. These landscapes become the ground for their respective protagonists' attainment of maturity, thanks to their growing consciousness of migrant exploitation. While each of the films articulates either an explicit or implicit critique of the exploitation of the Eastern European body for sexual pleasure, in each case the protagonist's stark rejection of this practice becomes the catalyst in his final gesture of self-determination. Crucially, *Cover boy* extends its interest in the exploitation of migrant bodies to embrace the discourse of precarious lives more generally understood, including the disenfranchised of the host society.

Notes

1. Among the most important changes were immigrant quotas, mandatory employment contracts, and sterner deportation measures.

2. Victor Fleming directed an adaptation of *Captains Courageous* in 1939, which is perhaps more widely known than Kipling's 1899 novel.

3. Maria Pace Ottieri, *Quando sei nato non puoi più nasconderti: Viaggio nel popolo sommerso* (Milan: Mondadori, 2004). In the film's credits the book is inaccurately described as a novel.

4. In this group I include several films directed by Francesca Archibugi as well as Carlo Carlei's *La corsa dell'innocente* (*The Flight of the Innocent*, 1993), Gabriele Salvatores's *Non ho paura* (*I'm Not Scared*, 2002), and Kim Rossi Stuart's *Anche libero va bene* (*Along the Ridge*, 2006).

5. Relevant works by Levinas include *Otherwise than Being, or, Beyond Essence*, trans. Alphonso Lingis (Pittsburgh: Duquesne University Press, 1981); *Totality and Infinity: An Essay on Exteriority*, trans. Alphonso Lingis (Pittsburgh: Duquesne University Press, 1969); and *Entre Nous: On Thinking of the Other*, trans. Michael B. Smith and Barbara Harshav (New York: Columbia University Press, 2000). I have previously elaborated on the significance of the work of Levinas and Derrida for an analysis of *Quando sei nato* in Áine O'Healy, "Hospitality, Humanity and the Detention Camp," *International Journal of the Humanities* 4, no. 3 (2006): 68–77.

6. Levinas, *Otherwise than Being*, 79.

7. Jacques Derrida, *Of Hospitality: Anne Dufourmantelle Invites Jacques Derrida to Respond*, trans. Rachel Bowlby (Stanford: Stanford University Press, 2000). See also Jacques Derrida, "Hospitality, Justice, and Responsibility: A Dialogue with Jacques Derrida," in *Questioning Ethics: Contemporary Debates in Philosophy*, ed. Richard Kearney and Mark Dooley (New York: Routledge, 1999), 65–83.

8. The published version of the screenplay reflects the conclusion originally planned by the screenwriters, which indicates that Alina shoots Radu to death. See Marco T. Giordana, Sandro Petraglia, and Stefano Rulli, *Quando sei nato non puoi più nasconderti* (Venice: Marsilio, 2006).

9. The use of classical music as background for this scene of youthful delinquency is reminiscent of Pasolini's use of classical music in both *Accattone* (1961) and *Mamma Roma* (1962).

10. This information is found in an interview with Munzi in the extras included in the DVD version of *Saimir*.

11. See, for example, E. Ann Kaplan, *Looking for the Other: Feminism, Film and the Imperial Gaze* (New York: Routledge, 1997); Nancy N. Chen and Trinh Minh-ha, "'Speaking Nearby': A Conversation with Trinh T. Minh-ha," *Visual Anthropology Review* 8, no.1 (1992): 82–91; Gayatri Chakravorty Spivak, "Can the Subaltern Speak?" in *Marxism and the Interpretation of Culture*, ed. Cary Nelson and Lawrence Grossberg (Urbana: University of Illinois Press, 1988), 271–313.

12. De Lauretis, "Desire in Narrative," *Alice Doesn't*, 103–57.

13. This section develops a portion of a previously published article: Alice Bardan and Áine O'Healy, "Transnational Mobility and Precarious Labor in Post–Cold War Europe: The Spectral Disruptions of Carmine Amoroso's Cover Boy," in Schrader and Winkler, *Cinemas of Italian Migration*, 69–90. I am grateful to my coauthor, Alice Bardan, for permission to incorporate some of this work into the present project. Published with the permission of Cambridge Scholars Publishing.

14. *Cover boy* is one of many relatively recent films produced in Italy, and in Europe more generally, that offer an implicit critique of precarious employment practices characteristic of the neoliberal economy. For an astute analysis of this phenomenon, see Alice Bardan, "The New European Cinema of Precarity: A Transnational Perspective," in *Work in Cinema: Labor and the Human Condition*, ed. Ewa Mazierska (New York: Palgrave Macmillan, 2013), 69–90.

15. Étienne Balibar, *We, the People of Europe? Reflections on Transnational Citizenship* (Princeton: Princeton University Press, 2004).

16. Temenuga Trifanova, "*Code Unknown*: European Identity in Cinema," *Scope* 8 (2007): 4–5, http://www.nottingham.ac.uk/scope/documents/2007/may-2007/trifonova.pdf.

17. Thomas Elsaesser, "Real Location, Fantasy Space, Performative Place: Double Occupancy and Mutual Interference in European Cinema," in *European Film Theory*, ed. Temenuga Trifanova (New York: Routledge, 2009), 58. For Elsaesser, such films include *Abre los ojos* (*Open Your Eyes*, Alejandro Amenábar, 1997), *The Others* (Alejandro Amenábar, 2001), and *Gegen die Wand* (*Head On*, Fatih Akın, 2004). To his list one could add several Italian titles, including *Non ti muovere* (*Don't Move*, Sergio Castellitto, 2004), *La doppia ora* (*The Double Hour*, Giuseppe Capotondi, 2009), *Good Morning Aman* (Claudio Noce, 2009), and the previously discussed *La sconosciuta* (Giuseppe Tornatore, 2006).

18. Jacques Derrida, *Specters of Marx, the State of the Debt, the Work of Mourning, and the New International*, trans. Peggy Kamuf (New York: Routledge, 1994).

19. Derrida, 2–20.

20. Derrida, 3.

21. Derrida, xviii–xix.

22. Derrida, 5–10.

CHAPTER 5

Imagining an Expanded Mediterranean Borderscape

DURING THE 1990S most irregular seaborne arrivals occurred in the region of Puglia on Italy's southeastern coastline. This pattern shifted dramatically in the early years of the twenty-first century, when there was a significant surge in the number of migrants heading for Italy from the African continent across the Strait of Sicily—the narrowest stretch of the Mediterranean between Italian territory and the North African coast.[1] As the visibility of Arabs and black Africans increased in Italy, so did the circulation of racist discourses and widespread demands for stricter border controls with particular focus on the Mediterranean, perceived not only as the border between the north and global South but also between Christianity and Islam, modernity and backwardness. Italy's Mediterranean border, like other stretches of sea around the world, has thus become a focus in the symbolic definition, reinforcement, and defense of the white, Western self.[2] Italian media discourses emerging over the first decade of the twenty-first century conjure growing concerns regarding the porousness of the nation's southern frontier and fears of imputed invasion by migrants from the global South.

Several events occurred in the early years of the new century that drew attention to Italy's contested Mediterranean frontier, all of which provide context for the films I have selected for analysis in this chapter. Following the attacks of

September 11, 2001, in the United States and the subsequent outbreak of war in the Middle East, a general concern with securitization became manifest not only in Italy but also throughout the European Union. Prime Minister Berlusconi's attempt to obstruct irregular arrivals from the southern shore of the Mediterranean involved soliciting the collaboration of Muammar Gaddafi, a move that resulted in the creation of extraterritorial detention centers in Libya. Funded largely by Italy, these structures were intended to stem the northward flow of migrants from sub-Saharan Africa. At the same time, Italy increased its surveillance of international waters, aided by the European Union. In 2004 the EU founded the European Border and Coast Guard Agency, generally known as Frontex. Headquartered in Warsaw and working in coordination with the Coast Guard fleets of EU member states, this organization became responsible for controlling the borders of the Schengen Area. Thus, since the beginning of the twenty-first century, military vessels from different EU nations have periodically patrolled the Strait of Sicily alongside Italian patrols. Both Tunisian and Libyan vessels, at Italy's behest, have also collaborated in policing this stretch of the Mediterranean. The variety of nations participating in the surveillance of Italian maritime borders is surpassed, however, by the diversity of origins represented by the migrants attempting to cross the Mediterranean from African shores and the variety of destinations toward which they ultimately aspire. In effect, the numerous nationalities and geographical trajectories that characterize the constituencies patrolling, crossing, or drowning in the Strait of Sicily in recent years lend a particular dynamism to this border zone, linking together multiple locations across a geographical territory that reaches from sub-Saharan Africa and the Middle East to several nations of the European Union.

In this chapter, I examine a handful of films that speak in specific ways to the influx of seaborne mobility from the African continent since 2001. As in the films on African migration produced in the 1990s, discussed in chapter 3, issues of racial and religious difference provide a central node of concern in many of these more recent productions. Yet there is now a more intense focus on the border zone itself, on the territories traversed between "here" and "there," and on the challenges, opportunities, and perils of migrant mobility. Furthermore, these films demonstrate in powerful though often oblique ways how various boundaries—political, geographical, religious, and racial—are being symbolically negotiated and reproduced across the North–South axis, thus actively engaging in the process of reimagining the Mediterranean border.

Since the films I focus on in this chapter conjure up a vast swath of territory corresponding to diverse trajectories of their migrant characters, the configuration of mobilities and transit spaces visualized within them effectively participates in the imaginary construction of an expanded borderscape. I borrow the term "borderscape" from theorists in the field of critical border studies, whose initial focus on the border as a marker of territorial divisions and political institutions has given way to a consideration of borders not only as political boundaries but also as social and discursive processes.³ Given the flexibilization and multiplication of border construction that has occurred in the policing of contemporary global migrations, there is an implicit acknowledgment among scholars who envision the possibility of a trans-Mediterranean *communitas* that the notion of the border needs to be understood as both a symbolic and material construction. The term *borderscape*—first used by Chicano artist Guillermo Gómez-Peña in the title of his 1998 performance piece, *Borderscape2000*—has been retooled by cultural theorists to account for the complexity of border construction and to highlight how narratives and images of the border are constitutive of its meanings and effects.⁴

Writing about border control in Australia in 2007, Suvendrini Perera first proposed the use of "borderscape" to theorize the spatial and conceptual complexity of the contemporary border, envisioned no longer as a fixed boundary but rather as a mobile and changing entity perpetually traversed and modified by persons, discourses, practices, and relationships. This processual understanding of the border unsettles distinctions between inside and outside, citizens and denizens, and challenges traditional understandings of national, regional, racial, and ethnic separations. Offering a compelling description of the multiplicity of crossings and recrossings, resistances and counterclaims involved in border construction, Perera notes how "allegiances and loyalties are remade, identities consolidated and challenged, as border spaces are reconfigured by discourses and technologies of securitization and the assertion of heterogeneous sovereignties."⁵ Rejecting the conventional, static representation of the border on the modern map, though acknowledging the continued power of nation-states and other, supranational agencies to define their territorial limits, the most recent work in critical geography continues to demonstrate how the border is constructed not only on the ground but also in the imagination, that is, through different forms of representation.⁶ The films I examine in this chapter specifically involve narratives of Mediterranean crossings and thus contribute in various ways to a reimagining of the Italy-Africa borderscape.

Trans-Mediterranean Affinities: From *Tornando a casa* to *Io, l'altro*

Vincenzo Marra's *Tornando a casa* (Going Home, 2001) and Mohsen Melliti's *Io, l'altro* (I, the Other, 2006) take the idea of Mediterranean migrations in a different direction from most other films about Italian immigration by foregrounding the sea itself, not only as the locus of contemporary migratory flows but also as a common ancestral home traversed daily by fishermen from opposite shores. Both films feature characters from Italy and the Maghreb who make a meager living working side by side in the waters of the Strait of Sicily. This narrative device implicitly draws attention to the proximity of Italy to North Africa, while also foregrounding the everyday human connections that bridge the maritime border. By giving visibility to interactions between people originating from different Mediterranean coasts, the films echo one of the dominant tropes that emerge in the rich array of recent work on the Mediterranean by historians, sociologists, and critical geographers.[7]

Tornando a casa is the first feature film by Vincenzo Marra, a young Neapolitan filmmaker who has subsequently built a reputation as an accomplished director of both features and documentaries. Stylistically and thematically reminiscent of the model of socially conscious filmmaking that has its origins in neorealism, the film offers a realistic depiction of a specific social environment, highlighting the difficult day-to-day routine of four fishermen based in the province of Naples. Due to the hostility of local *Camorristi*, who control local markets, the fishermen are frequently obliged to sail far from home to cast their nets, venturing illegally into Tunisian waters in the hope of obtaining a substantial catch. Played by an ensemble of nonprofessional actors, three of the men are Neapolitan, and the fourth is an immigrant from the Maghreb. All of them, including the immigrant, communicate for the most part in Neapolitan dialect rather than standard Italian. This linguistic dimension infuses the narrative with a heightened sense of realism, with effects similar to those sought by Luchino Visconti in his neorealist epic *La terra trema* (*The Earth Trembles*, 1948) while at the same time complicating the film's appeal to mainstream audiences.

Visually, *Tornando a casa* dwells on the harsh physical labor carried out by the fishermen aboard the trawler, the dangers they endure at sea, and the kinds of surveillance to which they are subjected—by maritime patrols on the one hand and by the Camorra on the other. The narrative also sketches out an evolving friendship between the two youngest members of the crew, Franco (Aniello Scotto D'Antuono), who is considering emigrating to America, and Samir (Azouz Abdelaziz), the immigrant. It thus establishes a degree of mutuality between these men, each of them prompted by financial necessity to confront the possibility of leaving home. Franco's plan to emigrate to the United States, however, evaporates after the sudden death of his wife (due to a stray bullet fired by a child in an environment where lethal violence is the order of the day), and he sinks into suicidal despondency. In the course of a regular fishing expedition to the Strait of Sicily, he notices a shipwrecked migrant struggling to stay afloat and, unobserved by the other fishermen, dives into the water vainly hoping to save the man. Upon being rescued by a patrol vessel, Franco is assumed to be of North African origin. Instead of insisting on his Italianness, he spontaneously accepts this error as an opportunity for change and destroys his identity card. He thus allows himself to be transported to the coast of Africa along with other apprehended men, to whom he offers the Arabic salutation he has learned from his friend Samir: "Salaam aleichum." Abandoning his birthplace in the province of Naples, Franco is, paradoxically, "returning home" to a different Mediterranean shore while traveling in the opposite direction from those pursing a new life in Italy.

On a symbolic level, the film problematizes images of contemporary Italy as an affluent, progressive nation with a standard language spoken by all and the shared aspiration of European belonging. It builds a counter-narrative focusing on economically marginalized, southern characters who speak a local dialect not readily comprehensible to a mainstream audience and who inhabit a location where the rule of the Camorra rivals the power of the state.[8] *Tornando a casa* thus gestures toward a broadly conceived Mediterranean *communitas* as an alternative point of identification for disenfranchised Italians disillusioned with the hollow promises of neoliberal capitalism. The film's conclusion must be read metaphorically, however, as the narrative does not indicate what kind of future Franco envisions for himself as he travels toward the shore of North Africa, bereft of material resources, identification papers, or the ability to speak more than two words of Arabic.[9]

Though less stylistically coherent than *Tornando a casa*, Melliti's *Io, l'altro* has been more widely screened and reviewed, thanks at least in part to the strong support of Raoul Bova, one of Italy's most popular actors, who plays the leading role.[10] Known primarily as a creative writer, Melliti was born in Tunisia in 1967 and arrived in Italy in 1989 as a political exile. Coming to filmmaking relatively late in his creative career, this is his first and only feature to date, and he is credited as both its screenwriter and director. Like *Tornando a casa*, Melliti's film envisions the possibility of a trans-Mediterranean *communitas* but suggests that this vision has been radically compromised by contemporary ideological pressures and the sensationalism of media broadcasting.

Reminiscent to some extent of the friendship between Franco and Samir in *Tornando a casa, Io, l'altro* constructs a close, quasi-fraternal relationship between two fishermen originating from opposite Mediterranean shores. In Melliti's film, however, the relationship between the Tunisian migrant and the Italian is seriously undermined by tensions resulting from the growing xenophobia that followed the terrorist attacks in the West in the early years of the new millennium. Reminding viewers of these events and their complex ramifications, the film is explicitly dedicated to "the victims of the war on terror."

Unfolding almost entirely on a fishing trawler in the Strait of Sicily, *Io, l'altro* is structured as a two-hander, foregrounding the interactions between Giuseppe (Bova), a Sicilian native, and his Tunisian fishing partner, Yousef (Giovanni Martorana), over the course of a single day and night. It is noteworthy that Melliti agreed to cast a Sicilian rather than an actor of North African origin in the role

Imagining an Expanded Mediterranean Borderscape | 141

Figure 5.1. Screen capture. Yousef and Giuseppe at sea. *Io, l'altro* (2006)

of Yousef, a choice purportedly motivated by the lack of alternative options.¹¹ Martorana had in fact been previously cast as a Maghrebi migrant in Marco Tullio Giordana's widely screened *La meglio gioventù*, in which he played a Moroccan suspect unjustly beaten while in police custody. The somatic adaptability of the actor to both Italian and North African roles underscores the physical similarities frequently observed between Mediterranean populations from different shores.¹²

At a socially realistic level, the presence of a Tunisian fisherman on a Sicilian fishing vessel is consistent with the long-time presence of Tunisian immigrants in Sicily, where they have formed a sizable immigrant community since the 1970s, most notably in the town of Mazara del Vallo near Trapani.¹³ In *Io, l'altro*, however, Yousef does not intend to stay in Italy. On the contrary, he repeatedly urges his Sicilian counterpart to move to Tunisia, where they will be able to conduct their business far from the watchful eye of the small-time *mafioso* boss who controls the local fishing trade, perpetually threatening their economic survival. Giuseppe, moreover, appears receptive to this possibility. In these plot details— the precarious employment conditions of fishermen working off the Italian coast due to pressures exerted by local *mafiosi*, as well as the fantasy of migrating to the southern Mediterranean shore—the film resonates with elements already present in *Tornando a casa* and suggests a similar line of continuity between the northern and southern Mediterranean.

Although the action takes place almost entirely in the present, *Io, l'altro*'s brief prologue—which has the oneiric quality of a scene vaguely remembered— belongs to the past, centering on the figure of a small Arab boy playing on a rocky beach. As the child contemplates his own reflection in a mirror found among the stones, his mother calls out his name, "Yousef!" The narrative then cuts to the present, introducing the two principal characters as adults. It is significant that the men are named Giuseppe and Yousef, the Italian and Arabic versions of a widely used name of Semitic origin rendered in English as Joseph. This naming strategy resonates with the motif of specularity contained in the prologue and highlights the juxtaposition of identity and alterity already suggested in the title.

The crisis driving the narrative occurs at sea when Giuseppe hears on the ship's radio that, in the aftermath of a terrorist explosion in Spain, the police are searching for a Tunisian fugitive named Yousef, known to reside in Sicily. Although Giuseppe initially dismisses the possibility that his friend is the Tunisian in question, his attitude shifts to suspicion after receiving a call from an associate who has been following the news and suggests that Yousef is the terrorist sought by the police. The tension that develops between the two men on board the trawler is thus fueled by the media and quickly undermines their longtime friendship. In paranoid fashion, Giuseppe begins to misinterpret various visual clues. To convey his state of mind and justify his rapid descent into a kind of insanity, these hallucinatory misperceptions are conjured up with strategies borrowed from horror, sharply disrupting the film's dominant stylistic register. When Yousef realizes that Giuseppe has telephoned the Coast Guard, appealing for help, he severs the line, immobilizes his friend, and accelerates the engine so forcefully that it gives out, leaving them adrift.

Though Yousef eventually succeeds in assuaging his friend's suspicions, another confrontation flares up when the corpse of a fully clothed woman is caught in a fishing net and pulled aboard. Giuseppe is determined to keep the body on deck, with the expectation that, on his return to dry land, he will be able to contact the bereaved family. Yousef, however, disagrees with this option for fear that the body's presence on board will incriminate him if the vessel is intercepted by police. In the quarrel that erupts about disposing of the woman's remains, Giuseppe stabs his friend to death. In the film's final moments, the tearful Giuseppe addresses Yousef as though he were still alive, speaking of their shared dreams for a future as business partners in Tunisia, while ignoring the fact that the boat's engine is dead, the vessel is adrift, and telephone contact with dry land has been severed. Just as he ceases to speak, a voice on the ship's radio announces that the real terrorist, Yousef ben Ali, has been arrested in Tunisia, and the image fades to black.

The undoing of the close bond between the Tunisian and the Sicilian is thus at the heart of the film's affective trajectory. Nonetheless, though constructed by the script as a tragic event linked to forces more powerful than either of the characters, the killing of Yousef and the subsequent scene of the distraught Giuseppe addressing his dead friend fail to achieve the resonance of tragedy. In the film's final moments, the Italian fisherman's soulful iteration of his vanquished hopes and dreams is infused with heightened sentimentality. In fact, the foregrounding of Giuseppe's tears as he articulates his attachment to his dead friend serves to align the scene with male melodrama, a subgenre currently enjoying favor among Italian filmmakers, which often involves scenarios of intense male bonding or homosocial romance.[14] What is attenuated in the process is the film's impact as a politically inflected morality tale about the fragility of trans-Mediterranean affinities in the age of global terror.

Although the presence of the Arab child in the prologue suggests that the film is Yousef's story, it is Giuseppe who dominates the scene almost throughout, and the visual track gives vivid emphasis to his subjective experiences. The viewer is offered frequent close-ups of Bova's handsome features and deep blue eyes as the camera lingers on his brooding expressions, suggesting a sense of inner torment. In contrast with Bova, Martorana, playing Yousef, is physically a much less imposing figure. With his irregular facial features and dark, unruly curls, he provides a marked contrast to the attractive star who plays opposite him. More significantly, his mannered approximation of an "Arab" accent and lilting intonation complicate the plausibility of his performance and hence the tragedy of his character's death.

Despite its underlying didacticism and uneven stylistic merits, *Io, l'altro* is remarkable in several respects, including the manner in which it updates cinematic figurations of the contemporary borderscape. By 2006, the Strait of Sicily had already attained notoriety as the watery grave of untold numbers of migrants who had lost their lives while attempting to reach Italian shores. It was nonetheless still frequented by fishermen of different nationalities who plied its waters daily, as their ancestors had done for thousands of years. Melliti's film was one of the first to reference the disturbing fact that bodies and body parts have regularly been entangled in fishermen's nets in the Strait since irregular maritime crossings began to surge in the early twenty-first century.

In addition to functioning as a reminder of the perils experienced by desperate migrants attempting to reach Europe, the sequence featuring the recuperation of the drowned migrant's body in *Io, l'altro* invites a particular, postcolonial reading. Upon seeing the woman's corpse, Yousef immediately identifies her as a Somali migrant (in other words, as one who hails from a former Italian colony in East Africa), and he speculates that she was thrown overboard by smugglers during a difficult crossing. There is, however, an uncanny element in the confidence with which he identifies her origins, and it is in this implicit postcolonial dimension that the sequence has its richest resonance.

What is especially disturbing about the presence of the corpse in this scene is its status as subject/nonsubject. The inexplicably untouched state of the woman's body and clothing suggests she is an apparition or ghostly revenant rather than a literal victim of drowning. As I have briefly discussed in chapter 4, Jacques Derrida famously used the term *revenant* to describe the spectral quality of similarly uncanny visitations in literature, theorizing their function as symptoms of hitherto suppressed historical memory.[15] The notion of spectrality additionally resonates with a particular emphasis in postcolonial theory. Following Homi Bhabha, postcolonial theorists have focused on tropes of haunting as a clue to hidden colonial histories in order to revise conceptions of the contemporary nation and its cultural relations.[16] Identifying the "time-lag" that marks the emergence in the contemporary moment of the ghostly figures of the colonial era, Bhabha speaks of the "furious emergence of the projective past."[17]

The Somali woman dredged from the sea in *Io, l'altro* is not literally a reminder of colonial history, a history that is often ignored by contemporary Italians. Rather, her irruption into the mise-en-scène suggests the impossibility of keeping the past securely buried, of preventing it from haunting the present in disquieting ways. What the scene of this irruption accomplishes most powerfully is to bring that past into implicit alignment with contemporary migrations from south to north. It not only invites us to consider the colonial effects of the neoliberal economy that drive migrations from Africa but also prompts us to contemplate Italy's specific, colonial-era relationship with both Libya and Tunisia, the two Mediterranean countries from which migrants most often embark on their maritime journeys to Italy.

In Libya, Italy's colonization was direct, and the suppression of local populations was violent and pitiless. Reminding Berlusconi of that fact in the early twenty-first century, Ghaddafi succeeded in extracting considerable reparations from Italy for its past atrocities and pledged, in exchange, to participate in the extraterritorial control of northbound migration. In Tunisia, by contrast, Italy's hegemony was exercised indirectly in the colonial era. While the country remained a French protectorate throughout the colonial period, it was inhabited by a large community of Italian settlers who vastly outnumbered its French residents, who, in turn, considered themselves superior to the Italians. As Mark Choate puts it, "Italians [in Tunisia] remained both colonizers and colonized."[18]

Though none of these historical circumstances are indexed directly in *Io, l'altro*, the Tunisian fisherman's interpellation of the dead Somali woman as his "sister," which may certainly be interpreted simply as a reference to their shared Islamic faith, simultaneously invites the viewer to consider the complexity of Italy's multiple colonial entanglements. Even if the legacy of these entanglements is routinely disavowed by many contemporary Italians, the experience of territorial invasion, oppression, or conquest, as well as the institutional commitment to a system of racial discrimination that accompanied it, has undoubtedly contributed to the embedding of a racialized consciousness in Italian culture more generally. This has facilitated a structure of feeling that inflects contemporary

Italian attitudes toward immigrants from the global South. Though stylistically and tonally flawed, Melliti's *Io, l'altro* thus participates in the contemporary representation of Italian immigration in a way that serves to underscore the nation's contemporary postcolonial condition. More specifically, it not only suggests that age-old affinities between populations of different Mediterranean shores have been challenged by current political shifts but also points to the ways in which the anti-Arab, anti-Muslim discourses perpetuated in the West after 2001 can reactivate the toxic legacy of colonial-era racism.

From Senegal to Italy and Back in *Lettere dal Sahara* and *Billo il Gran Dakhaar*

Lettere dal Sahara (Letters from the Sahara, Vittorio De Seta, 2006) and *Billo il Gran Dakhaar* (Billo the Big Guy, Laura Muscardin, 2007) contribute to configurations of the North-South borderscape in novel ways, revealing a multilayered space across which the movement of migrants prompts heterogeneous affiliations, existential dilemmas, and contested religious or cultural loyalties.[19] Produced almost simultaneously, both films present a strong Senegalese protagonist who makes his way to Italy by land and sea and eventually returns to Senegal, if only temporarily. In the course of these travels, issues of faith and secularism, tradition and modernity, come into conflict with each other as the young Muslim migrant confronts unfamiliar values and undergoes a personal crisis. The Wolof language is used extensively in both films, with subtitles provided for Italian audiences. Furthermore, a significant part of each film unfolds on location in Senegal, showing the landscape and cultural practices that the migrants have left behind before undertaking their long northward journey. Such efforts to achieve a fuller representation of the migrant experience distinguish these films from the majority of cinematic constructions of immigration to Italy.[20] What is more remarkable, however, is that both films benefited from the creative input of their Senegalese performers and other Senegalese contributors with the aim of making the dialogue, narrative development, and mise-en-scène as authentic as possible. Thus, although the films are directed by Italians and addressed to Italian audiences, the transnational, transcultural collaboration that underpins their creation offers a distinctive, if sometimes uneven, texture to the results achieved.

In spite of their similarities, the two films contrast sharply with each other in tone and affect. While *Billo il Gran Dakhaar* is for the most part a picaresque comedy, *Lettere dal Sahara* is a dramatic film that deploys ethnographic elements, with aesthetic effects reminiscent of the director's own earlier work. De Seta, whose critically acclaimed career stretches back to his influential documentaries of the 1950s, interrupted his retirement to make this film, believing that immigration from the global South was the most important issue of the moment. Shot in high-resolution digital format, *Lettere dal Sahara* self-consciously announces its concerns at the outset with a montage of thirteen iconic images of migrant journeys and clandestine arrivals, images which by now have a generic recognizability for Italian film and television audiences. This montage of still shots, presumably borrowed from standard electronic journalism, constructs an epic vision of migrants making their arduous journey to Italy by land and sea and delivers a calculated affective charge. Some of the images presented, such as that of a crowded Albanian ship, hark back to the large-scale Adriatic migrations of the 1990s. Others show the smaller vessels typically associated with clandestine migration from Africa at the time of the film's production. One aerial photograph suggests the accidental sinking of a boat from which passengers are thrown into the churning waves. Another image, in medium shot, depicts exhausted African migrants being escorted to dry land by a uniformed Italian official. The overall vision offered by De Seta's montage is one of widespread desperation and life-threatening danger. The sequence concludes, however, with images in medium range or close-up that suggest private moments of weariness or bewilderment and is followed by a statement appearing on screen in the subsequent shot: "To escape famine, calamity, war, and hunger, millions of people of different languages, religions, and cultures are emigrating from poor countries to rich countries. All of this gives rise to hardship, uprooting, and discrimination, but sometimes to dialogue and hope as well."

Although *Lettere dal Sahara*'s striking introductory montage gives visual prominence to the Mediterranean and the irregular aspect of immigration to Italy, these elements were, at the time, much less dominant in the overall scheme of Italian immigration patterns than had been the case some years earlier. Nonetheless, the director's deployment of archival news photographs gestures to the kind of truth claims associated with the tradition of neorealist cinema. Similarly, the casting of nonprofessional Senegalese actors in major and minor roles, some of whom are migrants themselves, the use of authentic locations and techniques reminiscent of television reporting (such as the digital "scrambling" of the faces of African sex workers appearing in street scenes to protect the women's identities), and the deployment of a quasi-ethnographic style of filmmaking in the long concluding sequence, set in Senegal, clearly aim at a heightened sense of realism. Yet, rather than suggesting an up-to-date, realistic account of the conditions of contemporary migration to Italy, the film functions as a generic call for compassion in the face of the massive uprootings and displacements of late modernity.

The composition and intensity of the film's opening montage sequence gesture toward a wide-ranging and diversified vision of contemporary trans-Mediterranean migrations. Nonetheless, *Lettere dal Sahara* is focused almost entirely on the odyssey of a single individual. Assane (played by nonprofessional actor Djibril Kébé) is a young Senegalese migrant who, just before reaching what is understood to be the coast of Lampedusa, is thrown into the sea by his smugglers. After witnessing, to his horror, the drowning of a friend and fellow traveler, he is rescued by Italian border guards and submitted to biometric processing at a nearby reception facility. Eventually escaping police custody, he embarks on a difficult journey up through the boot of Italy. His experience of racially motivated brutality in Turin ultimately prompts him to return to Africa. In the film's thirty-nine-minute concluding section, he is back in Senegal, where he tells his former teacher of his daunting experiences in Italy and passes along a word of caution to his younger compatriots who might contemplate undertaking a similarly challenging voyage.

The northbound journey through the boot of Italy has been a classical trope in Italian cinema since the release of Roberto Rossellini's *Paisà* (1946) and serves to link *Lettere dal Sahara* to the socially committed strain of the neorealist legacy. It also largely replicates the trajectory of the African protagonist of *Pummarò* (Michele Placido, 1990), showing similar patterns of discrimination, resentment, accommodation, or hospitality among the Italian characters encountered along the way. Although more than fifteen years separate these productions, little appears to have changed in the everyday circumstances of migrants on Italian territory, with the obvious exception of sterner border controls and technologically enhanced screening processes.

Relying on a strategy adopted in his earlier feature films, De Seta used his nonprofessional actors and extras as ethnographic informants, to remarkable effect. Assane's first stop on his journey northward is a crowded, ramshackle house in the countryside of Campania inhabited by immigrant day laborers, where he locates his cousin Makhtar. The building's occupants are played by actual immigrants, and the conditions in which they live reflect the ongoing destitution of many undocumented agricultural workers in the south of Italy.

Assane's stay in Campania is brief. Repelled by the discovery of illegal activity among the migrants and by the violence with which their dwelling is attacked by local thugs, he moves on with a decisiveness that already establishes him as different from the compatriots he meets along the way. As he travels up the peninsula, he remains unwavering in his loyalty to his Islamic faith and code of conduct. This is observed most forcefully in the scene where he repudiates his cousin Salimata, currently living in Tuscany, for her abandonment of Muslim tradition. Soon after their reunion, the dialogue establishes that the young woman, who works as a fashion model, is not fully Senegalese as her mother is French. For Assane, this seems to suggest that she is inherently less likely to adhere to the precepts of Islam, including the mandate to cover her hair. Furthermore, despite her efforts to provide hospitality to Assane and to make some allowances for his expectations, he is ultimately repulsed by her compromises—particularly by her extramarital cohabitation with an Italian lover—and abandons her home

Figure 5.2. Screen capture. Assane visits his mentor in Senegal. *Lettere dal Sahara* (2006)

without delay. The severity he displays in this sequence challenges the sympathies of the viewer, even as the script adheres to the promptings of De Seta's ethnic informants.

Once Assane arrives in Turin, he begins to achieve the elements of a livable life thanks to his encounter with Caterina, a kindhearted Italian teacher who offers him a job as caregiver to her disturbed adolescent brother, and thus the opportunity to apply for legal resident status. As his relationship with the boy progresses fruitfully, he also develops a potentially romantic bond with Caterina, who makes no demands on him that challenge his Islamic beliefs. His migrant trajectory thus moves in the direction of happy resolution as he begins to enjoy the material benefits of Western modernity without being asked to relinquish his principles. After being observed in the streets in the company of Caterina, however, he is accosted by a group of racist thugs who severely injure him, prompting him to relinquish his ambition to remain in Italy, and to return to his native land.

Unlike Zaccaro's *L'Articolo 2*, which resolves the impasse of cultural incommensurability by killing off the protagonist in an industrial accident, *Lettere dal Sahara* suggests that Assane voluntarily renounces his migratory project to return to Senegal, removing himself from the Italian scene to recover a sense of personal dignity. His experience of migration has reduced him to a state of existential crisis. After arriving in Senegal, he seeks out Thiam, his former teacher and mentor, confessing, "I don't know to whom I belong anymore. I feel as if I have lost my roots, my culture . . . I feel as if I have drifted loose from my moorings."

The film's concluding scenes, which focus on Assane's journey to a remote hamlet to visit Thiam, conjure up a tranquil, premodern community in a tropical landscape that stands in sharp contrast with the film's Italian locations. Here the ethnographic aspect of the De Seta's project prevails, as he did not provide the local actors with a script, allowing them to proceed freely with dialogue in Wolof. In the extras included in the DVD version of the film, the director admits that he did not understand the words heard in these scenes until the sequence was translated for him in the postproduction process.

The film's final sequence is dominated by Thiam, Assane's mentor, who has retired to the village of his birth, devoting himself to helping local farmers and craftsmen. There is a strong didactic element in the older man's pronouncements to those who have assembled in the village. Most remarkably, however, Thiam does not disavow the necessity of emigration for his listeners, nor does he imagine that Assane himself will remain in his native country. Assuming that all of them will be obliged to leave for Europe for economic reasons, he offers a stern account of the various historical abuses committed by Europeans against Africans and adds a cautionary comment: "You should never feel that you are better than whites. This must never occur. Stay humble." When Assane has the opportunity to address the group, he, too, warns the men to be prepared for the difficulties and affronts they are likely to confront as migrants.

In her extended critical analysis of these scenes, Giovanna Falaschini Lerner writes:

> The African sequences of the film show a very different Africa from the one that the European viewer is used to seeing in newscasts and documentary films. In these scenes, we do not see a land torn apart by ethnic conflicts, destroyed by famine, and riddled by poverty and disease. On the contrary, De Seta focuses his camera on farmers, fishermen, artisans, men and women engaged in productive activities that do not require "help from the whites." While the spectacle of violence and death to which the Western public is accustomed reinforces the racist notion of qualitatively different human groups, De Seta's visual choices cause his audience to question those representations of the African continent.[21]

In my view, the film's depiction of Senegalese rural life—described above by Lerner—is an idealization, the input of De Seta's native informants notwithstanding. Despite the visual appeal of the sequence, which is set in a lush rural landscape, the vision of happy villagers engaged in age-old skills, listening attentively to the teacher's exemplary lesson on race relations, and finally performing a lively collective dance seems formulaic. Western audiences may well be prompted to ask, for example, why women's voices remain unheard throughout almost all of the Senegalese sequence. In effect, the film's depiction of rural Senegal conjures up a deeply patriarchal world. Remaining true to his ethnographic impulse, the filmmaker does not seek to problematize this aspect of his protagonist's native culture, just as he does not judge the self-righteous determination with which Assane spurns his cousin Salimata in the earlier scene.

De Seta's image of the aspiring immigrant as a principled, idealized figure at odds with the corruption and violence of Western modernity provides a sharp contrast to *Billo il Grand Dakhaar* (Laura Muscardin, 2007). Relying on hybrid formal strategies as well as the input of several African artists and performers, this film provides a more complicated articulation of Senegalese migration to Italy than *Lettere dal Sahara*, ultimately envisioning the possibility of interracial marriage and reproduction within a panorama of transnational, polygamous relationships. Yet, as in De Seta's film, at the center of the plot lies the conflict between the values of the protagonist's Muslim upbringing and the permissiveness of contemporary Italian society.

Laura Muscardin was invited to direct this independently produced collaborative project after previously directing just one feature film, *Giorni* (*Days*, 2001). The original idea for *Billo il Grand Dakhaar* came from actor and producer Marco Bonini, who decided to create a film based on the life of Thierno Thiam, a Senegalese migrant living in Italy who had achieved some success as an entertainer. To finance the project, Bonini requested the direct investment of the director and film crew, inviting each of them to become a co-producer. Intrigued by his encounter with Thiam, who first came to Italy as an undocumented sixteen-year-old, Bonini cast him in the lead, inviting him to play a fictionally enhanced version of his earlier self. While writing the script, Bonini also enlisted the collaboration of fiction writer Mbacke Gadji, a Senegalese migrant who had lived in Italy since 1994.[22] Another important contribution was provided by the well-known Senegalese recording artist Youssou N'Dour, who composed the film's score and whose involvement in the production assured the director's access to locations and shooting facilities in Senegal.[23]

Though *Billo: Il Gran Dakhaar* opens with a Muslim prayer performed by a migrant on a desolate shore, the protagonist, Billo (Thierno's nickname both in the film and real life), is a flawed, picaresque figure, and the film is peppered with comic incidents. His story proceeds in a complex temporal sequence that crosscuts scenes from his past in Senegal into scenes of his life as an immigrant while highlighting his efforts to reconcile the conflicts between and among his traditions, desires, and ambitions. As in *Lettere dal Sahara*, the scenes shot in Senegal differ visually from those shot in Rome. There is a striking contrast, for example, between the grayness of the Roman winter and the warm tones that characterize the scenes that unfold in coastal Senegal and in Billo's native village. This contrast serves for the most part to highlight the subjective development of the protagonist himself as he struggles with a sense of disorientation and homesickness after his arrival in Italy.

Figure 5.3. Screen capture. Remembering a Senegalese childhood. *Billo il Gran Dakhaar* (2007)

Despite its comedic moments, the film underscores some of the intolerance and incomprehension at play in Italy's increasingly multiethnic, multiracial society. Billo's trajectory is scarcely smooth. He begins his new life in Italy selling bootleg tapes at a flea market and sleeping in a wrecked car. He is later dismissed from a job at an upholstery shop on the false accusation of sexual assault, and he is briefly incarcerated due to mistaken identity. In the overall scheme of contemporary migration narratives, however, this is not a story of exceptional hardship. Despite his irregular status, Billo seems to cross borders without significant challenges, and he eventually finds acceptable housing, hospitable Italian roommates, success as a clothing designer, and a relationship with an attractive Italian woman who does not share the limited worldview and racialized perspectives of her own working-class parents.

The most painful difficulties faced by Billo arise from his effort to negotiate the contrasting imperatives of his native culture and Italian custom, particularly through his relationship with Laura, the Italian woman with whom he becomes romantically involved. Soon after their relationship begins, Laura reveals to Billo that she is pregnant. Panic-stricken by the prospect of this commitment, he leaves for Senegal, where he marries his childhood sweetheart and impregnates her on their wedding night. Returning to Rome, and still unaware of his new wife's pregnancy, he eventually agrees to marry the pregnant Laura as well. Although initially devastated to learn of her lover's marriage in Senegal, Laura decides to go through with the wedding. What enables her to enter this polygamous arrangement is the awareness of her own father's extramarital affairs. Realizing that sexual fidelity is not a behavioral standard practiced by all Italian men, she decides she would rather be with a partner who acknowledges his multiple conjugal commitments than with a man like her father, whose extramarital relationships are hidden under a veil of hypocrisy. Laura's insight functions within the film as a call for a more open-minded attitude toward unfamiliar cultural practices.

The film's final scene, presenting the marriage of Billo and Laura, gestures toward the possibility of a more diverse and accommodating future for Italians and the new residents in their midst. Set outside the municipal building in Piazza del Campidoglio, an iconic location overlooking the ancient Roman Forum, the wedding brings together not only the bride and groom but also Laura's family—including her reluctant father—and Billo's Senegalese compatriot, who acts as groomsman. The two gay men who are present at the ceremony, Laura's brother and his partner, express the hope that they too will one day be able to formalize their relationship, thus proposing an understanding of marriage as a less narrowly conceived union than the bond constituted by the traditional, Western, heterosexual couple.[24] In the same scene, Laura's heavily pregnant body signals the fact that she will soon deliver a biracial Italian child. Although such children have been present in Italy in growing numbers since the 1990s, *Billo il Gran Dakhaar* offers the first explicit acknowledgment of the possibility of interracial reproduction between Italians and African immigrants in recent Italian cinema. As I have observed previously, the heterosexual romances between Italians and foreigners represented by contemporary Italian filmmakers generally preclude the possibility of reproduction.[25] In this sense, *Billo* makes a landmark contribution to the Italian cinematic imaginary.

Highlighting issues of racial and religious difference, *Lettere dal Sahara* and *Billo il Gran Dakhaar* propose the potential richness of embracing transcultural encounters in a traditionally white, and nominally Christian, postcolonial society. In different ways, the films enliven the cinematic representation of the transit zone between West Africa and urban Italy, showing how the moving bodies of migrants create a fluid, interconnected space characterized by different landscapes, histories, languages, and religious practices. With the input of Senegalese collaborators, they also open up the vista of West African landscapes for Italian viewers, who, until this point, had rarely been invited to contemplate cinematically the territories from which Italy's new immigrants arrive. In this way, they provide an antidote to the general tendency of the Italian media to give prominence primarily to details of the migrants' arrival rather than the context of their larger journey and thus reduce a complex experience to a single phase of its unfolding. As Marco Bruno puts it in his pointed critique of the shortcomings of mainstream representations, "Landing often becomes a true media icon for the entire migration phenomenon."[26]

The Border of Lampedusa: From *Terraferma* to *Fuocoammare*

Since 2009, there has been a marked shift in Italy's implementation of migratory controls as well as an overall increase in the numbers attempting to cross the Mediterranean to Italy, which grew to tens of thousands of migrants each year. Scarcely known to the international public twenty years ago, the island of Lampedusa has attained a degree of hypervisibility in the international media as it has become inextricably linked to irregular migration from the global South and with the intertwined discourses of securitization and militarization. The power of the signifier "Lampedusa" lies in its ability to shape national news about migration as it has become the dominant site for the increasing spectacularization of irregular migration to Italy."[27]

Among those who have attempted to draw attention to the humanitarian implications of the events occurring on and around the island is Jorge Bergoglio (Pope Francis), who, after his election to the papacy in 2013, decided that his first journey outside Rome would be to Lampedusa. As others had done before him, he spread dozens of white roses onto the sea where thousands of African immigrants had drowned while trying to reach Europe. Recalling the primordial fratricide of the Hebrew Bible and Cain's attempt to avoid responsibility for killing his brother, Abel, Bergoglio denounced "the globalization of indifference" toward migrants.

Shot on Linosa and Lampedusa, respectively, the feature film *Terraferma* (Emanuele Crialese, 2011) and the documentary *Fuocoammare* (Gianfranco Rosi, 2016) point to the escalating militarization of Italy's migration regime and its effects not only on the migrants but also on the inhabitants of Italy's southernmost communities in the second decade of the twenty-first century. These neighboring islands, which form a single municipal entity, are located at a point in the Strait of Sicily closer to Africa than to Sicily itself and have seen the arrival of tens of thousands of migrants crossing from African shores.[28]

Although reflecting a steep, overall increase, the density of the flow of mobility to Lamepdusa-Linosa has oscillated over the past decade due to a variety of factors, including a temporary reduction in numbers for a period between 2009 and 2010 following Italy's implementation of the pact with Muammar Gaddafi to push back to Libya all irregular migrants crossing the Mediterranean.[29] The number of arrivals has also shifted in response to political events in North Africa, most dramatically during the so-called Arab Spring of 2011, which triggered arrivals of unprecedented intensity and prompted the Italian government to declare a state of emergency in February of that year. The landings increased tensions among the different agents involved in migratory policy at the European level and implicitly called into question the viability of Europe's supranational border regime.[30] The use (or disuse) of Lampedusa's reception and processing centers has varied in accordance with these contingencies. Often accommodating numbers that exceeded by several factors their intended capacity, the centers have repeatedly been the focus of media attention for their mismanagement and overcrowding and for the purportedly inhumane treatment extended to detainees.[31] Images of interception, mass arrivals, dramatic rescues, inadequate reception centers, or evidence of disasters at sea thus have come together in forming contemporary perceptions of Lampedusa. Such perceptions serve a distinct political purpose. As Heidrun Friese puts it, invoking Agamben's concept of the state of exception, "Images of 'flow', 'invasion', 'crisis' or 'emergency' are an integral part of [the migration industry] as the media gaze produces and disseminates dominant views of undocumented mobility. The dominant gaze situates the mobile subject both as a victim and as a threat to national security and systems of welfare, and is part of a powerful social imaginaire of catastrophes and thus legitimizes policies by which the emergency, the exception, becomes the rule."[32]

Simultaneously, however, Lampedusa and Linosa have been since the 1990s sought-after tourist destinations for discerning travelers attracted by the appeal of the islands' far-flung setting and unspoiled beaches. Nonetheless, tourist revenues have declined periodically in response to events surrounding the island, as occurred in the summer of 2014, following the catastrophic shipwrecks of the previous autumn. Drawing on Michel Foucault's concept of "crisis heterotopias," which describes spaces that simultaneously accommodate disjunctive accounts and experiences, Joseph Pugliese has pointed to the "disorienting problematics of space" that characterize Lampedusa, an island that not only provides hotels for tourists and detention facilities for migrants but also belongs historically to a "carceral archipelago" to which political dissenters were banished in Italy's post-Unification period.[33] As Michael Ebner observes, like a handful of Italy's other outlying islands, Lampedusa has served as a site of imprisonment or forced exile for thousands of years.[34] Although this little-known history was unlikely to deter tourism in the twenty-first century, the ongoing existence of detention and processing facilities for irregular migrants was for many years almost impossible to ignore.

Until the sharp increase in naval operations in the Strait of Sicily since late 2013, keeping the flow of vacationers and the flow of migrants hidden from each other in such a small territory was perceived as a challenge. Although tourism and migration management are significant sources of revenue for the Italian state and for other agents in the region, the mutual visibility of such contrasting forms of mobility posed an image problem. While the recurring association made by national and international news between Lampedusa and the continuing flux of irregular migration boosts official justification for police and military reinforcement and for the funding of related facilities on the island, this association is perceived by some as a threat to the island's reputation as an attractive tourist destination and by others as a distraction from the ongoing neglect and marginalization experienced by the islanders themselves at the hands of the Italian government. Since 2013, however, the realities of the Lampedusa border zone have been widely known, and ever-present military patrols are visible to all. Furthermore, migrants are now intercepted by the navy or Coast Guard long before reaching Lampedusa, and, upon arrival, they are taken rapidly to the processing center in a secluded part of the island so that no interactions with locals or tourists can occur.

Shot on Linosa in 2010 (that is, before the massive militarization of the area that occurred later), *Terraferma* is the first full-length feature film to engage with the effects of irregular arrivals in Italy's southernmost islands and the first to dramatize the heterotopian aspects of this prominent border zone.[35] Though it received mixed reviews upon its release, Crialese's film became Italy's (ultimately unsuccessful) entry for consideration in the Academy Awards of 2012 and was widely reviewed and discussed both at home and abroad. Its approach to the issue of immigration is problematical, however, both in its almost exclusive focus on Italian characters and in the specific articulation of its humanitarian message.

Crucial to the director's inspiration for the film was a major amendment to immigration law introduced by the center-right government in July 2009, which criminalized irregular entry into Italy.[36] The film reflects the widespread perception that this legislation automatically turns those who attempt to rescue or assist clandestine immigrants into criminal accomplices. The most socially concerned of Crialese's projects to date, it articulates a rejection of the legal framework that imposes constraints on the basic human impulse to assist those in dire need, exploring the issues that come into play when the inhabitants of Italy's southernmost islands are called upon to shelter helpless migrants whose very presence on Italian soil has been labeled by the penal code as criminal. Self-reflexively evoking the earnestness of the neorealist era, the literal meaning of its title (*terra firma*, or firm ground) cleverly suggests a reversal of the title of Visconti's well-known 1948 drama set among Sicilian fishermen, *La terra trema* (*The Earth Trembles*).[37]

Like all of Crialese's earlier work, *Terraferma* is a formally accomplished film. Fabio Cianchetti's impressive cinematography, which highlights the stark beauty of Linosa, is accompanied by a stirring musical score by Franco Piersanti, who also wrote the music for Amelio's *Lamerica*. The director's casting strategy serves to reinforce a sense of geographical specificity as the four members of the local family at the center of the story are played by Sicilian performers, only two of whom (Donatella Finocchiaro and Giuseppe Fiorello) are professional screen actors. For the role of the Ethiopian migrant needing shelter, Crialese also selected a performer without professional training, Timnit T., a young woman from Eritrea whose own journey to Europe via Lampedusa was among the most harrowing imaginable.[38] Despite the film's formal merits, the thematic oppositions that underpin the director's inspiration lend a didactic edge to the delineation of the characters and the conflicts they embody.

One of the novelties of *Terraferma* lies in its construction of the competing forms of human mobility and immobility that characterize contemporary life on the islands, affecting islanders, tourists, and irregular migrants. Several images in the film link the migrants to the tourists in visually arresting ways, most dramatically in the early scenes that juxtapose the sight of a distressed migrant raft—with passengers jumping into the water to swim toward safety—with the vision of a pleasure boat pulsating with happy tourists who jive to loud music and then dive in unison into the sea. The film also contrasts the carefree northern Italian tourists with the islanders themselves—disadvantaged southerners whose awareness of their own economic, social, and educational limitations is all too evident. It thus sets up an interesting dynamic between and among the three groups, implying that although the islanders share the tourists' nationality, they simultaneously share the migrants' sense of precariousness, entrapment, and desire to pursue a better life in a place that seems frustratingly out of reach.

Terraferma is structured as an ensemble piece, highlighting the contrasting reactions of the members of a single family to a group of irregular migrants who arrive on the island at a time when a new Italian law prohibits Italian citizens from assisting them. The soul of the film is Ernesto (Mimmo Cuticchio), an elderly fisherman who clings to the traditional values of the island despite encroaching modernization. His son, Nino (Giuseppe Fiorello), by contrast, has abandoned fishing and turned to tourism as the only way to earn a living in a changing economy, a choice that mirrors the dominant social reality in Lampedusa and Linosa at present. Ernesto's grandson, the twenty-year-old Filippo (Filippo Pucillo) helps his grandfather on the family's aging fishing trawler but is unsure of where his future lies. Daunted by poverty, Filippo's widowed mother, Giulietta (Donatella Finocchiaro), believes that the island holds no promise for her son and decides to convert their modest dwelling into a guesthouse for summer visitors in order to fund their move to a more auspicious location, presumably on the mainland. These plans are thrown into question when a heavily pregnant Ethiopian migrant shows up at Giulietta's home with her young son, begging for refuge. Assisted by Giulietta, the woman soon gives birth to another child, while the police comb the island looking for the migrants who have eluded their grasp.

If the principal ethical question posed by the film is how to welcome the irregular migrant in the face of daunting obstacles, Filippo's shifting reactions to the needs of the foreigners he encounters are central to its narrative arc. At the outset, the twenty-year-old islander is torn between the influence of his uncle, a small-time entrepreneur anxious to maintain his grasp on the tourist trade, and that of his grandfather, whose loyalty to what is described as the "law of the sea" impels him to rescue any person in danger, regardless of the prevailing laws of the state. Though Filippo does not systematically embrace the rigorous altruism modeled by his grandfather, his actions at the film's conclusion suggest that he has finally accepted the old man's example.

The conflict between the unwritten law of the sea and the written law of the state is thus at the heart of the film's inspiration, juxtaposing the life-affirming values of the elderly Ernesto with those of a heartless government intent on stemming the flow of migration. Within the narrative economy of the film, the authority of the state is embodied in the rather crudely drawn figure of the customs and border policeman, a nameless *finanziere* from the Italian mainland who confiscates Ernesto's boat—the source of his livelihood—as a rebuke for his suspected complicity in assisting the missing migrants. The justification he offers for confiscating the vessel is that Filippo has attempted to use it as a pleasure boat for tourists without first obtaining a license. Yet this is clearly a pretext; the family is being punished not only for having rescued the migrants at sea but also for having enabled them to escape apprehension and almost certain deportation.

Although the opposition between the life-affirming principles enshrined in the law of the sea and the merciless logic of official legislation is clearly delineated in *Terraferma*, this opposition does not entirely dominate the conflicts played out among the characters. When, at different moments, Giulietta and Filippo falter in their willingness to assist the migrants, their hesitation springs not from a refusal to break the law but from a concern that the presence of the migrants might jeopardize their relationship with tourists who would not wish to have their enjoyment compromised by the proximity of human desperation. Since, for Giulietta, the decision to accommodate paying guests at her home constitutes a crucial step in financing her move away from the island, she does not wish take the risks associated with hiding the Ethiopian fugitives in an adjoining space. Yet, despite her initial attempt to refuse shelter to the migrant family, she finally relents in the face of their overwhelming need. Her concession is framed as a gesture of maternal solidarity, springing from a tacit understanding of the need of another mother to care for her young.

Filippo's change of heart is more complex and dramatic. In the film's early rescue sequence, he eagerly helps his grandfather in taking aboard the distressed migrants, which suggests that he has unquestioningly accepted the law of the sea. Later, he assists Giulietta in delivering the Ethiopian woman's child and keeping the migrant family safe from discovery. It is only when his personal happiness seems threatened that his behavior suddenly shifts. Attracted to one of the tourists, he invites her to join him for a midnight boat trip around the island. In the course of this adventure, they are suddenly confronted with the sight of several black bodies approaching the boat like alien creatures arising from the deep. The scene has a shocking impact, recalling the effects of horror, and prompting a sense of spectrality even more powerful than the apparition of the Somali

Figure 5.4. Screen capture. Giulietta, accidental host to a migrant family. *Terraferma* (2011)

woman in the crucial episode of *Io, l'altro* described above. Whereas the dead woman hoisted from the sea in Melliti's film is a victim and clearly presents no physical threat to the Italian fisherman, Filippo's panic in the face of the rapidly approaching group of strong black men unwittingly evokes colonial-era fears of the potency of African men and the imputed need to protect white women against them.

Clinging to the boat, the desperate migrants attempt to climb aboard. Rather than offering assistance, Filippo assaults them violently with an oar to drive them back into the water. The force of his blows may in fact have killed the most tenacious among them, though this is never clarified. Instead, the film focuses on Filippo's ethical coming to consciousness as he witnesses the exhausted but still living bodies of several migrants being dragged ashore the following morning. The scene is rendered in slow motion to emphasize its subjective impact on the young Italian. But the rescued migrant men, now clearly depicted as victims rather than powerful invaders, remain distanced and nameless. It is with Filippo's subsequent, impulsively conceived effort to smuggle the Ethiopian family to the mainland aboard the family's dilapidated fishing boat that the film ends, a gesture that seems as generous as it is perilous.

The culmination of *Terraferma*'s narrative is thus Filippo's change of heart, prompted, presumably, by a desire to make amends for his earlier violence. The possibility that the solution he adopts will endanger the lives of his passengers is not explored by the film, nor is it clear that they would have consented to the risk had they been consulted. This narrative blind spot is linked to a significant problem in the film's conceptualization: in a project that appears to be concerned with the lives of migrants, the migrant characters are mostly denied the kind of agency and subjectivity accorded to the natives.

Among the migrants seen in *Terraferma*, only the Ethiopian woman is accorded any significant onscreen time. In her early scenes she is virtually speechless, and it is only after she has spent some time at Giulietta's home that she briefly recounts her journey. The details of her story are sparse but plausible, recalling circumstances reported in the testimony of many migrants who entered Italy through Libya over the past ten years. As the survivor of a two-year trek from sub-Saharan Africa to the Mediterranean, she has experienced imprisonment in Libyan holding centers, has been repeatedly raped by guards, and has become pregnant as the result of one of these assaults, resulting in the birth of an infant girl shortly after her arrival at Giulietta's home. In another, shorter scene, she speaks quietly to her son in her own language, reassuring him that his father will not reject the child conceived during her Libyan imprisonment. Apart from these brief statements, entirely focused on the most dramatic aspects of her journey, she has little to say.

Describing Crialese's choice of perspective in *Terraferma*, Norma Bouchard and Valerio Ferme argue as follows:

> In *Terraferma* the perspectives that emerge are Ernesto's and his family's ... they grant dignity to the clandestine mother and her children, even as they develop the complex gamut of reactions by the island's inhabitants. By choosing this perspective, Crialese presents a specific kind of discourse from the South that makes its inhabitants the subjects and connects their responses to the foreign other to a millenary tradition of hospitable humanity that contrasts with the one embodied by the hedonistic tourists whose every whim the islanders must meet, and the one represented by the authorities who, responding to the central authority of Rome and its policies, apply the law indiscriminately.[39]

Acknowledging that a work of fiction demands the selection of a particular perspective or point of view, I argue nonetheless that in exalting the "millenary [southern Italian] tradition of hospitable humanity," the film does not "grant dignity" to the clandestine mother and her children, as Bouchard and Ferme claim. Rather, it reduces them to two-dimensional figures whose identities are at one with their victimhood. Furthermore, within the film's diegesis, the migrants are nameless. Although Sara is the name attributed in the credits to the character played by Timnit T., it is absent from the dialogue. In fact, the very presence of this anonymous figure in the diegetic economy of *Terraferma* seems to be necessitated only by the ennobling effects she will elicit in the Italian family. In this way, the film's narrative trajectory reflects a paradigm common to many recent films on immigration to Italy, in which the migrant characters ultimately function as a catalyst in the transformation of the Italian protagonists.

Terraferma's main focus thus remains on how the locals respond to the ethical challenges that confront them. The other characters—migrants, tourists, and police—are thinly constructed, bordering on stereotype. The villain of the film is, of course, the police officer, an outsider from the North (or at least from somewhere other than the South), who attempts to impose the punitive law of the state on an honest, hardworking community, exemplified above all by the aging patriarch Ernesto, whose first loyalty is to the principle of life itself. And it is in Filippo's final daring act of intervention that the values transmitted by his grandfather appear to bear fruit. All other voices in the film, including the more cautious counsel of Filippo's mother, prove ineffectual in the end. In privileging the wisdom of Ernesto, *Terraferma* is reminiscent of Amelio's *Lamerica*, which identifies in an elderly Sicilian veteran of Mussolini's Albanian campaign the remnants of an ancient peasant culture of the South, a culture whose generosity and compassion shine through in the heartless modern world. Ultimately the film is less concerned with the experience of contemporary migrants than fascinated with the imagined values of an idealized Italian past.

In its construction of the interactions between and among islanders, migrants and police, *Terraferma* also unwittingly taps into some of the problems inherent in contemporary media representations of immigration from the African continent and the Middle East. As Friese has argued, whereas most media representations of female migration from the global South at present conjure up notions of care, victimhood, or needy motherhood, the arrival of male migrants—purportedly motivated by a sharper sense of agency—"is usually correlated with invasion, aggression, danger and threat." In effect, the media's continuous replay of images of boats packed with dark-skinned men reinforces "prevailing images of the 'assault,' the racialized male migrant as aggression and menace, the catastrophe or the biblical 'flood' that has to be contained."[40] As I have shown, *Terraferma* evokes at least temporarily the vision of vigorous male migrants endowed with threatening agency (although this vision is clearly attributed to the limited perspective of the Sicilian protagonist Filippo). The Ethiopian mother played by Timnit T., by contrast, is not depicted as a threat but rather as a needy, traumatized victim in a way that resonates with Friese's observation about dominant perceptions of migrant women: "The entanglement of signifying processes of the social imagination brings forth the figure of mobile women as traumatized victim and/or as caring mother."[41] In the real-life border regime of the global present, these contrastingly gendered figures—the male migrant-as-threat versus the female migrant-as-victim—are being mobilized by multiple constituencies in the service of two apparently very different responses, securitization and humanitarian intervention.

In *Terraferma* individual humanitarian activity is envisioned as the just response to the needs of migrants, and it is presented in direct opposition to the security-driven priorities of an unfeeling, inhospitable government. No larger political or moral questions cloud the final sequence, which remains focused on the imputed courage and decisiveness of its young Italian protagonist. In the film's concluding moments, the fishing trawler carrying Filippo and the small Ethiopian family away from the island connotes, on the one hand, the young man's escape from the limited, insular life his mother had hoped he would abandon and, on the other, the possibility that this voyage will allow his passengers to elude the grasp of the state authorities and move on toward a better life, on firmer ground. Nonetheless, moving rapidly skyward to reveal the small vessel tossed about in the vast expanse of sea, the camera's perspective in the closing shot depicts a scenario of extreme vulnerability and isolation. The "firm ground" evoked by film's title may lie forever out of reach, and Filippo's brave humanitarian gesture may be as hopeless as it is well-intentioned.

Terraferma was first screened at the Venice Film Festival in September 2011 to much acclaim as well as controversy and was subsequently screened in several countries around the world, bringing its particular vision of the Lampedusa-Linosa borderscape to the attention of international audiences. In the meantime, circumstances in the Strait of Sicily were rapidly changing. The sharp increase in the numbers of migrants arriving on the islands during the Arab Spring of 2011, first from Tunisia and later from Libya, had led the Italian government to declare an emergency and to seek a major intervention from the European Union.[42] From then onward, the surveillance of the Mediterranean began to evolve with increasing intensity. Yet the flow of migrants did not cease, despite the increased risks involved in crossing. On October 3, 2013, one of the most tragic shipwrecks in the history of Mediterranean migrations occurred at a short distance from the coast of Lampedusa, claiming the lives of 366 people. This disaster prompted the Italian government to initiate large and effective search-and-rescue operation known as Mare Nostrum that patrolled an expansive stretch of sea between Italy and North Africa.[43] Providing surveillance as well as rescue, this costly initiative was funded almost completely by Italy and was perceived by many both in Italy and Europe more generally as creating a pull factor for migrants. It was thus discontinued after a year. In November 2014, Mare Nostrum was replaced by Triton, an EU-funded operation led by Frontex involving the participation of maritime forces from the various EU member states. Limiting its area of operation to a more circumscribed expanse of water than its predecessor, Triton has been criticized by activist and human rights groups for being mainly dedicated to blocking migration.⁴⁴ Although its activities included taking aboard and processing people intercepted while crossing the Strait of Sicily, its primary aim was not to rescue those in need but simply to police and enforce Europe's southern border.

Shaken by the tragedy of October 3, 2013 (which was followed a week later by another similar tragedy in the Strait of Sicily in which hundreds of people died), Gianfranco Rosi began to prepare the ground for a documentary project on Lampedusa. Fresh from the success of *Sacro GRA*, which had earned him the Golden Lion at the Venice Film Festival of 2013 (the first documentary ever to do so), he had been approached by LUCE to make a short film about the island, and traveled there late in the same year to explore it. It soon became clear to him, however, that he would undertake a full feature-length documentary, and he announced at the outset that it would pay primary attention to the residents of Lampedusa.⁴⁵

Several documentaries had, in fact, already been made about Lampedusa that did not always pay much attention to the islanders.⁴⁶ Though varying widely in quality, thematic focus, and mode of address, these projects collectively offer an intriguing portrait of life on the island that is currently at the forefront of Europe's border regime, pointing to the alternating visibility and audibility of the many constituencies that inhabit or pass through this unique borderscape, from migrants to police, military personnel or NGOs, from tourists to residents, and from journalists to filmmakers. While mainstream television reporting has largely provided sensationalizing images of Lampedusa-Linosa as a site of crisis, focusing on drownings and dramatic rescues, mass arrivals and overcrowded reception facilities, the documentary projects have provided, with varying degrees of commitment and integrity, a more textured account of Lampedusa's contemporary realities.

Fuocoammare is undoubtedly the most widely seen and critically acclaimed documentary on the defining aspects of the Lampedusa border zone. Formally rigorous, it has no superimposed narrative voice. Different voices, languages, and musical influences inform the soundtrack (where all music is anchored diegetically to local radio broadcasts). Life on the island is captured through careful observation of the routines of the twelve-year-old Samuele (Samuele Pucillo, younger brother of actor Filippo Pucillo in *Terraferma*) and his extended family, including the radio deejay, a relative of some sort. Scenes of everyday family life give contrastive force to alternating glimpses of the dramatic rescue operations performed on the high seas south of the island. Although the two worlds exist in proximity to each other, there is no communication between them. Only the local doctor Pietro Bartolo has a foot in each of these realities, providing medical care to both the imperiled refugees and the local population.

The film opens and closes with the figure of Samuele, whose evolution toward manhood becomes one of its principal preoccupations. Happiest when shooting at birds with his slingshot, Samuele is not entirely reconciled to the idea that he will become a fisherman like his father. His tendency to become seasick bothers him, and he fails to overcome it. His flawed eyesight is another concern, but by carefully retraining his "lazy eye," he improves his ability to see. Although Samuele's world is circumscribed, he moves independently around the seemingly unpopulated, hardscrabble territory beyond the town. At home, he learns of his family's seafaring legacy and some of the island's history through stories told by his grandmother and father. Yet there is no evidence that he has any direct knowledge of the life-shattering events unfolding in and around Lampedusa at present. His aunt's response to a radio news flash announcing the latest drowning disaster off shore is simply to utter, "Poveri cristiani (Poor souls)!" One can assume that at best the boy is learning the rhetoric of distanced compassion, couched in classical Christian empathy.

Samuele's juvenile restlessness provides a contrast to the quietly authoritative figure of Bartolo, the island doctor whose reflections on his participation in multiple acts of rescue—and failed rescue—are undeniably moving. The film's visual focus on bodies both living and dead, healthy and wounded, is a consistent element in the mise-en-scène across the contrasting story lines. In one scene, Bartolo displays for Rosi's camera an image of an adolescent immigrant whose body is covered with permanent burns caused by contact with the fuel oil that routinely floods the crowed holds of migrant ships. The doctor describes the boy's injured body with obvious distress, and with similar pain he describes the necessary task of violating the bodies of the dead in order to preserve samples for eventual identification.

The wounded migrant seen in the image on Bartolo's screen is apparently not much older than Samuele, who, in a subsequent scene, appears stripped to the waist at the same doctor's office. Complaining of breathlessness and a vague sense of unwellness, the causes of which cannot be perceived on his healthy torso and limbs, the boy hopes in vain that the doctor can find an explanation for his symptoms. The film's oblique comparison of the two adolescent bodies has a sharp poignancy, one so cruelly disfigured by burns and the other so apparently healthy and whole, despite the boy's own inexplicable anxiety.

Fuocoammare's most provocative scene, lasting just under thirty seconds, is composed of three static shots of the tangled corpses of people asphyxiated in the crowded hold of a migrant vessel. Neither music nor verbal commentary explicates the disturbing scene. Despite the presumed pedagogical function of these images and their implicit plea for compassion, they raise ethical questions regarding the symbolic violation of the dignity of the dead for the purpose of provoking spectatorial involvement. Although such questions certainly apply to many other situations in the history of documentary filmmaking, in the scene I describe here, the graphic images of the dead unwittingly participate in

164 | Migrant Anxieties

Figure 5.5. Screen capture. Rescued migrants aboard an Italian vessel. *Fuocoammare* (2016)

a problematical tendency usually characterized as the spectacularization of the Mediterranean border. As Friese has argued, the repeated call for spectatorial involvement made by various media outlets has become an instrument of governmentality in the contemporary border zone: "The media hype, the pathos of the event society and the 'economy of attention' make the tragic border regime work. Lampedusa has become a prominent part of the popular media spectacle, a constant backdrop of 'tragic' and 'catastrophic' events."[47]

Fuocoammare's most poignantly dramatic moment, however, occurs during a sequence shot at Lampedusa's processing center. It is here that a Nigerian migrant offers a powerful call-and-response performance detailing the dramatic journey that took him and his fellow travelers from their native land by way of the Sahara and Libya to where they now find themselves, with many of their companions already dead. Surrounded by other migrants who respond to his narration with rhythmic affirmation, he conjures up a searing testimony of the horrors endured by those who survive the trans-Sahara/trans-Mediterranean borderscape.[48]

While *Fuocoammare* strives to give visibility, agency, and voice to subjects muted in dominant representations, most of the film is occupied with the islanders and the mundane details of their daily lives. Apart from the doctor, who has an important role in mediating the encounters with the migrants, the islanders appearing on screen belong mostly to Samuele's extended family. Rosi's depiction of these individuals suggests the pull of deeply rooted customs in a society where men and women know their places and are content to stay there. Only two island women appear in the film, Samuele's aunt, Zia Maria, and his grandmother, both of whom feature exclusively in indoor scenes while engaged in domestic tasks. While the male adolescents adopt forms of play that are thousands of years old, contemporary electronic devices are absent from the domestic scene. Rosi's film thus offers his viewers a world that seems remarkably behind the times. Women's apparent invisibility in public spaces is all the more striking given Italian viewers' extratextual awareness that the most important public figure in the island at the time of the film's production, Giusi Nicolini, the mayor of Lampedusa and Linosa, was a woman. Rosi has been criticized for limiting his focus to a single family of islanders, for the apparent anachronism of his perspective on the islanders, for aestheticizing the military apparatus that patrols the island and its waters, and for failing to present other, more complex experiences and realities that currently prevail in Lampedusa.[49]

Fuocoammare, however, does not aim at inclusive or conventionally realistic representation. Instead, it proceeds by indirection, implication, and synecdoche. The viewer is thus obliquely invited to read Samuele's restricted vision as indicative of the islanders' inability to see—through no fault of their own—the ongoing multitude of northbound travelers intercepted at sea, transported to their island, and brought to the processing facility just a few kilometers from their homes. Whereas years earlier, islanders and the migrants passing through the island were often visible to each other—and on some occasions interacted with each other—the increasing militarization of the borderscape means that this is no longer the case.[50] The boy's anxiety and breathlessness seem inexplicable even to him, but his efforts at mimic-warfare—shooting birds with his slingshot, maiming cactus plants that he has cut to resemble humans, and aiming his imaginary rifle skyward—signal a perhaps unconscious response to the intense military apparatus that patrols the island night and day. As Rosi himself has noted, the presence of military personnel in and around Lampedusa has brought a sense of anxiety to the island that is palpable to outsiders.[51]

Unlike *Terraferma*, *Fuocoammare* was shot at a time when the mechanisms of securitization had increased to such an extent that irregular migrants could no longer access Lampedusa by sea of their own accord; they arrive there now only after being intercepted by the Coast Guard or by military vessels. Yet the film does not draw an explicit distinction between the exercise of securitization on the one hand and the provision of rescue and care on the other. The interceptions are envisioned, at least at first, simply as acts of rescue, carried out in response to the voices of imperiled migrants begging for help on their cell phones.

When the migrants are brought aboard the Italian naval vessels, however, they are processed by Italian crewmembers wearing full-body protection suits, their faces barely visible under their white hoods, conjuring up Italian fears of potential contamination by the new arrivals. Registered by number rather than

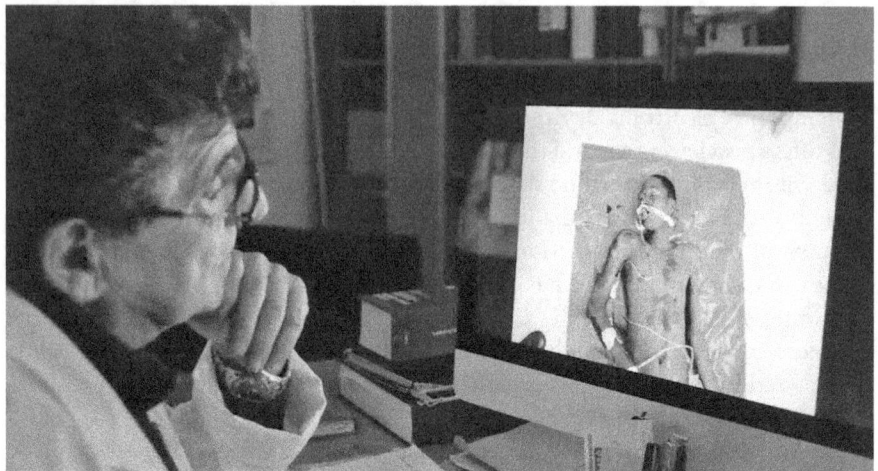

Figure 5.6. Screen capture. Dr. Bartolo contemplates the wounds of a migrant youth. *Fuocoammare* (2016)

by name, the newly arrived migrants are obliged to expose their full faces for the photographer associated with the processing procedure, even in the case of a Muslim woman clearly unwilling to show even a trace of her hair. These images resonate to some degree with the scenes of human processing present in films set in wartime concentration camps. Although *Fuocoammare* does not refer to the protocols that enforce a sharp distinction between refugees and economic migrants, between those who will be deemed worthy of staying in Europe and those who will be expelled, this scene evokes the expectation of sorting and channeling. The tensions that emerge in these representations are alleviated only by the presence of the good doctor Bartolo, who is seen performing a prenatal ultrasound on a heavily pregnant migrant woman. But this scene, too, has a certain ambivalence, as the nameless woman lies supine and silent, her face in the shadows and her bare abdomen exposed to the viewer's gaze, while the doctor passes his electronic wand over her flesh, projecting onto the nearby screen a sonar image of her uterus and the two young lives stirring within it.

The political debate that emerged around the Mare Nostrum initiative was focused on the rescue politics performed by the Italian Navy charged with a humanitarian mandate, that is, the rescue of people at sea. People fleeing conflicts are—in the absence of available visas—obliged to make the dangerous maritime crossing to Europe, thus becoming what Martina Tazzioli calls "lives to rescue."[52] Rescue, in turn, requires the deployment of military vessels and monitoring equipment. Furthermore, as Tazzioli astutely argues, the politics of rescue "indicates the implicit and unquestioned consideration of migrants as shipwrecked lives,"[53] a description that clearly resonates with the representation of migrant people as bare life in *Fuocoammare*.

The official discourse of rescue informing dominant representations of military operations in the Strait of Sicily has elided what Tazzioli calls "the particular politics of life that underpins military-humanitarian operations."[54] Since migrants and refugees must become "lives to rescue" in order to reach Europe, their freedom is undermined from the outset. Tazzioli observes that the politics of life at stake in the management of migration function to determine who is considered worthy of rescue and who is not. Such politics also work through "a more radical operation that consists in presenting migrants at sea as shipwrecked persons—and not as subjects in need of protection."[55] Paradoxically, the repeated configuration of bodies drowning or floating in the Mediterranean, waiting to be rescued on a crowded ship or asphyxiated in the hold, may feed into an iconography of the migrant as a faceless figure *homo sacer*, a figure that serves rhetorically to reinforce support for rescue operations while forestalling questions about the enmeshment of humanitarian and securitarian goals. As Tazzioli puts it, "humanitarian measures hold a specific political technology over migrant lives by rescuing, sorting and channelling migrants, one in which people escaping wars can seek asylum only by first becoming shipwrecked persons to rescue."[56]

Similar insights can be deduced from clues in *Fuocoammare*, though they are never made explicit. The film's initial presentation of the intercepted migrants as nameless people exemplifying bare life appears deliberate since the apparatus of rescue and securitization has already positioned them in this way. Nonetheless, Rosi's camera continues—often intrusively—to probe their faces, bodies, gestures, and expressions. Denied the opportunity of interviews, the filmmaker was able to fully humanize the migrants only during his final encounter with them in Lampedusa's processing center. Even here, however, he does not meet them face-to-face, but simply observes them, filming them as they play football, perform their ritual prayer, and participate in the riveting call-and-response performance.

Shortly after *Fuocoammare* was released, Askavusa—a group of activists on Lampedusa—launched a sharp criticism of the film, characterizing it as a purely lyrical exercise that is ultimately indifferent to the implacable complexities of the border regime and its destructive consequences for migrants and islanders alike.[57] Even in the absence of any explicit political critique, however, Rosi appears to be at least partially aware of the film's entanglement in these complexities, obliquely acknowledging the difficulty of showing without spectacularizing the theater of human suffering in the Mediterranean and the practices of interception, rescue, sorting, and containment that surround it.

Conclusion

Collectively, the six films discussed above contribute in important ways to an evolving social imaginary at a time when Italian attitudes toward migration from Africa and the Middle East were rapidly changing. In contrast to the concerns often voiced in mainstream media regarding the increase in irregular migration from North Africa and the sub-Saharan region (sometimes linked to a specific cultural anxiety about the growing presence of Muslim migrants), the first four films offer depictions of sympathetic, hardworking men who happen to be Muslim and who pose no real threat to the body politic, even when they enter Italian territory by irregular means (as occurs in *Lettere dal Sahara* and *Billo il Grand Dakhaar*). The films' overall configuration of migrant bodies and subjectivities, however, reveal other, more troubling discursive operations at work.

Economic migrants who enter Italy irregularly, in contrast to mobile people who can be classified as refugees, are often demonized in public discourses as an active threat to the availability of Italian jobs and benefits. This denigrating construction of irregular migrants is not present in any of the six films. Instead, the sense of agency popularly attributed to male economic migrants (which is often perceived as part of the threat they present) is valorized in the first four. In the same films, female economic migration is referred to just once, and only fleetingly, in the representation of Assane's biracial cousin in *Lettere dal Sahara*.[58] Although women migrants are featured in both *Terraferma* and *Fuocammare*, they are passive figures with little agency. These configurations unwittingly reinforce mainstream patterns of gendered representation.

Both *Terraferma* and *Fuocoammare* were produced against a backdrop of increasing surveillance and militarization in the Strait of Sicily, a phenomenon that is nonetheless more visible in the second film than in the first, given its more recent setting. These films evoke a very different world from the one represented in *Lettere dal Sahara* and *Billo il Grand Dakhaar*, whose protagonists, though entering Italy without papers, manage eventually to move through Italy's national territory and envision making a life there. Since 2010, the attention of the Italian media has been sharply focused on the Lampedusa-Linosa border zone—perceived as "remote" from everyday Italian life—as though it encapsulates the entire phenomenon of contemporary Italian immigration. *Terraferma* and *Fuocoammare*, made during this period, serve to reinforce this impression while also referencing (albeit in contrasting ways) the processes of securitization as well as the gestures of humanitarian rescue that then prevailed in popular perceptions of the Mediterranean border zone.

The acts of humanitarian care offered both in the fictional world of *Terraferma* and the "real-life" world of Rosi's documentary may have a consolatory power for Italian audiences. They bolster a self-image of solidarity with people experiencing genuine need (it is no coincidence that both films feature scenes of heavily pregnant migrants being cared for by Italian citizens). In the background of these humanitarian actions, however, there is the presence of a securitizing apparatus that threatens to collapse the distinction between needy mobile bodies and those that might be perceived as threatening or dangerous.

In contrast with the films discussed above, Andrea Segre's recently released *L'ordine delle cose* (*The Order of Things*, 2017) is the only feature film produced to date that provides an unambiguous critique of Italian border politics, starkly suggesting that Italy's border is no longer aligned with its Mediterranean shore but has been pushed southward to Libya as part of Italian (and European) efforts to block Mediterranean crossings.[59] Reprising issues explored in three of Segre's earlier documentaries—all of which are critical of Italy's attempts to delegate migration management to Libya during the Gaddafi regime—the new film points to the disconcerting events unfolding in Libya as Italy enters into new agreements with both government agents and Libyan militia leaders to stem the northward mobility of irregular migrants, despite the lack of verifiable guarantees for the protection of the migrants themselves.[60]

The protagonist of the film is Corrado Rinaldi (Paolo Pierobon), a rigorously self-disciplined and largely sympathetic police commissioner working on behalf of the Italian Ministry of Internal Affairs who is sent to Libya to negotiate the expansion of migrant detention centers in Libyan territory as well as to secure the cooperation of the local Coast Guard in pushing back migrant vessels while still in Libyan waters. Dedicated to safeguarding the "order of things," Rinaldi never questions the ethical consequences of his efforts to stem the flow of irregular migrants to Italian shores. He appears more irritated by the supposedly exorbitant financial demands of the Libyans for their cooperation in migration management than perturbed by the violations of human rights he witnesses in the detention centers he visits on Libya's western coast.

The self-confidence underpinning the protagonist's professional commitment and existential outlook is threatened, however, when he briefly engages with a young Somali woman detained in a Libyan detention center and accepts her request to contact a relative in Italy who will secure her passage across the Mediterranean. Although he is already aware that migration management in Libya is deeply corrupt and flawed, Rinaldi continues with his mission to secure the arrangements desired by the Italian Ministry while privately considering the possibility of helping the Somali woman obtain a transfer to Finland, where her husband resides. At this point in the film, the narrative appears to be taking a recognizable turn: an Italian citizen (like Sandro in *Quando sei nato* or Filippo in *Terraferma*, for example), when confronted with the dangers and injustices of the migrant's circumstances, is called upon to step outside his familiar points of reference by taking unprecedented risks to secure her safety and well-being.

The originality of Segre's film, however, lies in the fact that it ultimately denies its audience the consolatory assurance that this Italian everyman is principled enough to meet the humanitarian challenge. Thus, upon his return to his wife and family in their elegantly appointed home in Padua, Rinaldi abandons the temptation to intervene in the rescue of the Somali woman. The film's concluding tableau, a long shot of the Italian family united around the dinner table, leaves the viewers to speculate on the fate of the other, absent family—that of the detained Somali woman and her faraway husband, who may never share a meal again. Rinaldi's final decision, though shocking to viewers expecting a different outcome, is coherent with his worldview, with the affective aloofness required by his job, and with the hypocrisy of a government unable to resolve the contradiction between its declared humanitarian values and its abdication of responsibility for the circumstances of those migrants who remain trapped in Libya, a country that has yet to establish a reliable record of safeguarding of human rights.

L'ordine delle cose was hailed as prophetic by some reviewers since the kinds of arrangements sought by its protagonist were just beginning to unfold in real life as the film opened in Italy.[61] As a consequence of the widespread internal strife in Libya that followed the assassination of Gaddafi, Italy had been struggling for years to establish a binding collaboration with Libyan authorities on migration management. Thus, until the summer of 2017, the numbers of migrants crossing the Strait of Sicily from Libyan harbors continued to grow, reaching an estimated 180,000 in 2016. In early July 2017, John Daluisen, director of Amnesty International Europe, wrote that 2017 "looks set to become the deadliest year for the deadliest migration route in the world."[62] Contrary to his prediction, however, in the month that followed, the number of migrants crossing the Strait dropped by 86 percent with respect to the same period in 2016. This dramatic decrease in migrant arrivals was interpreted by most Italian media outlets as the consequence of recent agreements between the Italian government and various constituencies within the notoriously fractured territory of post-Gaddafi Libya. Marco Minniti, Italy's Minister of Internal Affairs at the time, is reported to have brokered a series of deals with representatives of the Libyan government, tribal leaders, and militia to fund the creation of additional detention centers on Libyan soil and to support the Libyan Coast Guard in pushback operations carried out in Libyan waters. Segre had been openly critical of Minniti's policy, insisting on the hidden human cost of reducing the flow of migrants to Italy's shores.[63]

While the films analyzed in the main body of this chapter elicit sympathetic responses vis-à-vis their migrant characters (including the real migrants foregrounded in Rosi's documentary) through their configuration of the hardships of the migratory experience, *L'ordine delle cose* articulates its affective impact in a more complex and challenging way. The film initially draws viewers into the subjective experience of an Italian official committed to reducing the migratory flow from Libyan harbors. It builds sympathy for his predicament as he starts to consider intervening on behalf of the incarcerated Somali woman but finally confronts the audience with his unexpected, yet fully credible, refusal to compromise his professional mandate and his comfortable familial routines. Segre's objective in making the film was neither simply to evoke sympathy for the circumstances of migrants nor to offer reassurance that ordinary Italians are likely to summon up the courage to take the necessary (and entirely feasible) action when confronted with a migrant's urgent call for help. Rather, the film offers its audience a bracing representation of the cowardice of an Italian citizen faced with the inhumane treatment of large numbers of migrants imprisoned in structures financed by the Italian government in collusion with its offshore counterparts.

Evoking concern for the migrants' circumstances is nonetheless an important component of the film's spectatorial address, particularly in the two sequences that visualize for the first time in an Italian feature film the appalling conditions prevailing in the Libyan detention camps, conditions that are routinely ignored or denied by Italian policymakers. Focalized through the perspective of Rinaldi, however, these scenes have a restrained emotional charge. With a preponderance of long shots and an almost complete absence of close ups, the mise-en-scène conveys the professional detachment of the Italian official, who for the most part maintains an emotional aloofness vis-à-vis the scenario of human suffering that surrounds him.

It is precisely the protagonist's aloofness that *L'ordine delle cose* ultimately asks its viewers to examine, an aloofness that points to Italy's general abdication of responsibility for the far-reaching effects of its migratory politics. As the film implies, it is scarcely a moral victory for Italians that fewer people are currently crossing the Strait of Sicily than at an earlier moment if the migrants are instead languishing in horrific circumstances in Libya, trapped in detention centers financed at least in part by the Italian state. Seeking to make a specific political intervention, the film can thus be understood as an integral part of a larger project currently gaining ground among Italian activists who aim to change the prevailing order of things through resistance, solidarity, and the eventual undoing of Italy's migration policies.

Following the release of *L'ordine delle cose*, Segre spearheaded a new initiative known as "Forum per cambiare l'ordine delle cose" (Forum to Change the Order of Things). With the support of ZaLab, Amnesty International, Doctors without Borders (Italy), Banca Etica, and other humanitarian organizations, its participants held a public meeting in Rome on December 3, 2017, with the purpose of exploring "ideas and proposals from everywhere in Italy to change the politics on migration and to construct a more open and concerned society."[64] Following this event, which was attended by more than five hundred people, similar gatherings were held elsewhere in Italy and abroad, including a screening and discussion of *L'ordine delle cose* at the European Parliament in January 2018.[65] On February 28, 2018, just four days before Italy's national elections, members of the forum held another meeting in Rome to which they invited electoral candidates with the purpose of informing them of their goals and objectives vis-à-vis the reform of migration policies.[66] Yet in light of the subsequent creation of the new government, which saw the coming to power of individuals such as Deputy Prime Minister Matteo Salvini, known for his xenophobic, anti-immigrant rhetoric, the task of attaining the goals articulated in the manifesto created by Segre and his colleagues faces ever more daunting challenges.

Notes

1. The African nations bordered by the Strait of Sicily are Tunisia and Libya. At its closest point, the Tunisian coast lies seventy miles from Lampedusa. In 1999 the total number of irregular landings in Sicily, including its outlying islands, was 1,973, compared with 49,999 for Italy as a whole. By 2003 these numbers had changed to 18,225 for Sicily and 23,719 for Italy as a whole. By then Lampedusa, a Sicilian island that is closer to North Africa than to Sicily itself, had emerged as the principal focus of all maritime arrivals, a pattern that has remained in place since then, with the exception of 2010, when the policy of maritime pushbacks temporarily reduced landings in Italy. These numbers are taken from Paolo Cuttitta, "'Borderizing' the Island: Setting and Narratives of the Lampedusa 'Border Play,'" *ACME: An International E-Journal for Critical Geographies* 13, no. 2 (2014): 202.

2. See, for example, the discussion of Australia's extraterritorial enforcement of measures to stem irregular maritime immigration in Suvendrini Perera, "A Pacific Zone? (In)Security, Sovereignty, and Stories of the Pacific Borderscape," in *Borderscapes: Hidden Geographies and Politics at Territory's Edge*, ed. Prem Kumar Rajaram and Carl Grundy-Warr (University of Minnesota Press: Minneapolis, 2007), 201–27.

3. Chiara Brambilla, "Exploring the Critical Potential of the Borderscapes Concept," *Geopolitics* no. 20 (2015): 15.

4. Gomez's use of "-scape" is inspired by Arjun Appadurai's influential work on the cultural dimensions of globalization, which identifies five different "-scapes" characterizing the contemporary moment: ethnoscapes, mediascapes, technoscapes, financescapes, and ideoscapes. See Arjun Appadurai, *Modernity at Large: Cultural Dimensions of Globalization* (Minneapolis: University of Minnesota Press, 1996).

5. Perera, "Pacific Zone," 206.

6. See, for example, Elena Dell'Agnese and Anne-Laure Amilhat Szary, "Introduction—Borderscapes: From Border Landscapes to Border Aesthetics," *Geopolitics* 20 (2015): 4–13.

7. Several of these works highlight the millennial interactions between populations from different parts of the Mediterranean coast, along with the shifts in geography and trade, power and sovereignty that alternately connected and divided them. This multidisciplinary corpus includes David Abulafia, *The Great Sea: A Human History of the Mediterranean* (New York: Oxford University Press, 2012); Iain Chambers, *Mediterranean Crossings: The Politics of an Interrupted Mobility* (Durham, NC: Duke University Press, 2008); and Peregrine Horden and Nicholas Purcell, *The Corrupting Sea: A Study of Mediterranean History* (Oxford: Blackwell, 2000). Among contributions by Italian scholars, the most influential is Franco Cassano,

Southern Thought and Other Essays on the Mediterranean, trans. Norma Bouchard and Valerio Ferme (New York: Fordham University Press, 2012).

8. Given the limited comprehensibility of local speech patterns for wider audiences, the film was subtitled in standard Italian for national distribution. See "Tornando a casa," Cinema Italiano, http://cinemaitaliano.info/tornandoacasa (accessed July 15, 2018).

9. For an extensive analysis of *Tornando a casa* in light of its "emigration/immigration parallels," see Teresa Fiore, *Pre-Occupied Spaces: Remapping Italy's Transnational Migrations and Colonial Legacies* (New York: Fordham University Press, 2017), 50.

10. Bova received a Globo d'oro (Golden Globe) award in 2007 for his performance in this film. (The annual Globo d'oro awards are juried by the Rome Foreign Press Association.) The film itself won in the category of Best First Film, and Maurizio Calvesi was awarded the Globo d'oro for cinematography.

11. According to Melliti, "The choice of Martorana [for the role] was due to the unavailability of North African actors in Italy." See Guido Bonsaver, "Accented Voices in Contemporary Italian Cinema," in Bond, Bonsaver, and Falloppa, *Destination Italy*, 353.

12. The actor has reported, in fact, that he is often mistaken for an Arab immigrant. See the interview with the director and cast of this film in "Raoul Bova in barca contro il pregiudizio," Movie Player, May 14, 2007, http ://movieplayer.it/articoli/raoul-bova-in-barca-contro-il-pregiudizio_3515/ (accessed July 20, 2018).

13. The film's representation of the Tunisian and the Sicilian fishermen as equal partners and aspiring co-owners of a small fishing vessel seemed nonetheless implausible to various online reviewers and commentators at the time of the film's release, suggesting that this kind of arrangement is far from likely in an insular society where xenophobia still exerts a powerful hold.

14. See Catherine O'Rawe, *Stars and Masculinities in Contemporary Italian Cinema* (New York: Palgrave, 2014), 69–93.

15. See Derrida, *Specters of Marx*. Although Derrida's example is the ghost in Shakespeare's *Hamlet*, the concept of the revenant can be used as a general analytic tool.

16. See Michael F. O'Riley, "Postcolonial Haunting: Anxiety, Affect, and the Situated Encounter," *Postcolonial Text* 3, no. 4 (2007), http://postcolonial.org/index.php/pct/article/view/728/0.

17. Homi Bhabha, *The Location of Culture* (New York: Routledge, 1994), 254.

18. Mark I. Choate, "Tunisia Contested: Italian Nationalism, French Imperial Rule, and Migration in the Mediterranean Basin," *California Italian Studies Journal* 1, no. 1 (2010), http://escholarship.org/uc/item/8k97g1nc.

19. I offer a tentative translation of "il gran Dakhaar" as "the big guy," based on personal communication with director Laura Muscardin in Rome in April 2010.

20. An obvious exception is Maurizio Zaccaro's *L'Articolo 2*, discussed in chapter 5.

21. Lerner, "From the Other Side of the Mediterranean."

22. For information on the film's production history summarized here, see Bonsaver, "Accented Voices," 356–57.

23. Personal communication with Laura Muscardin, Rome, April 2010.

24. At the time the film was made, Italy had not yet recognized same-sex civil unions, which were finally permitted in June 2016.

25. See Duncan, "Loving Geographies."

26. Marco Bruno, "The Journalistic Construction of 'Emergenza Lampedusa': The 'Arab Spring' and the 'Landings' Issue in Media Representations on Migration," in Bond, Bonsaver, and Falloppa, *Destination Italy*, 69.

27. Nicholas De Genova has created the term "border spectacle" to denote "a spectacle of enforcement at 'the' border, whereby migrant 'illegality' is rendered spectacularly visible." See Nicholas De Genova, "Spectacles of Migrant 'Illegality': The Scene of Exclusion, the Obscene of Inclusion," *Ethnic and Racial Studies* 36, no. 7 (2013): 1181.

28. Smaller than Lampedusa, Linosa is situated slightly farther from the African coast and has witnessed the arrival of fewer irregular migrants from North Africa. Although Pantelleria—another of Sicily's southernmost islands—is closer to the Tunisian coastline than either Linosa or Lampedusa (it is located to the west and north of both) and has also experienced an influx of migrants, it is considered a less convenient transit point for migrants traveling from the sub-Saharan region through Libya toward Europe.

29. The collaboration between Italy and Libya began in 2003, when the Italian government entered into an agreement with Muammar Gaddafi, promising ships, helicopters, and arms to Libya and providing funds for the construction of detention centers for northbound migrants apprehended there. This move was intended to stem the flow of sub-Saharan migration into Europe. The terms of the agreement became public on the occasion of the Treaty on Friendship, Cooperation and Partnership, signed in August 2008. A system of joint patrols by Italian-Libyan forces was established in 2009 to push migrant vessels back to Libya, resulting in a radical drop in the numbers arriving in Italy. The pushbacks were widely criticized by the international community as Libya had never ratified the Geneva Convention on refugees, and no guarantees were offered for the safety of the migrants upon their return to Libya. The pushbacks were subsequently suspended as new practices of border control were devised. The treatment of sub-Saharan migrants in Libya, even after the change of regime, continued to give rise to humanitarian concerns. In 2017 an arrangement was put in place between Italy's government (led by the Partito Democratico) and Libya, similar to that devised between Berlusconi and Gaddafi to stop departures from Libyan harbors. After the Italian elections of March 2018, and the formation of a new populist government led by a coalition of the antiestablishment Five Star Movement (M5S) and the hard-right Northern League, co-operation with Libya continued to intensify, and official hostility toward irregular arrivals reached unprecedented heights with the closing of Italian harbors to all NGO rescue ships and migrant vessels in June 2018.

30. Giuseppe Campesi, "The Arab Spring and the Crisis of the European Border Regime: Manufacturing Emergency in the Lampedusa Crisis" (working paper 59, European University Institute, Robert Schuman Centre of Advanced Studies Working Papers, 2011): 1, http://cadmus.eui.eu/handle/1814/19375.

31. The first widely disseminated report on the deplorable conditions experienced in the Lampedusa reception center appears in Fabrizio Gatti's "Io clandestino a Lampedusa," *L'espresso*, October 7, 2005, http://espresso.repubblica.it/palazzo/2005/10/07/news/io-clandestino-a-lampedusa-1.594 (accessed July 15, 2018). To gain entry to the facility, Gatti, adopting the name of Bilal, pretended to be a shipwrecked Kurdish migrant who swam ashore at Lampedusa.

32. Heidrun Friese, "Border Economies: Lampedusa and the Nascent Migration Industry," *Shima: The International Journal of Research into Island Cultures* 6, no. 2 (2012): 67.

33. Joseph Pugliese, "Crisis Heterotopias and Border Zones of the Dead," *Continuum: Journal of Media and Cultural Studies* 23, no. 5 (2009): 664.

34. See Michael R. Ebner, *Ordinary Violence in Fascist Italy* (New York: Cambridge University Press, 2011): 1. During the Fascist era Lampedusa became one of the remote locations to which political dissenters were banished in accordance with the system of internal exile known as the *confino*.

35. Part of the analysis of *Terraferma* in this section draws on a previously published essay: Áine O'Healy, "Imagining Lampedusa," in Ben-Ghiat and Hom, *Italian Mobilities*, 152–74.

36. The new legislation, generally described as the Security Package, tightened the restrictions of the Bossi-Fini law and effectively criminalized irregular migration as well as all efforts to assist irregular migrants. See Giorgio Tintori, "Italian Mobilities and the *Demos*," in Ben-Ghiat and Hom, *Italian Mobilities*, 111–25.

37. The allusion to Visconti's film was noted even by reviewers outside Italy. See, for example, Nicolas Rapold, "On a Sicilian Island, Boat People Who Can't Be Ignored: Emanuele Crialese Tackles Migration in 'Terraferma,'" *New York Times*, July 23, 2013, http://www.nytimes.com/2013/07/24/movies/emanuele-crialese-tackles-migration-in-terraferma.html.

38. Timnit T. left Tripoli on August 20, 2009, along with seventy-seven other immigrants from the Horn of Africa aboard a thirty-six-foot dinghy. Intercepted three weeks later near Lampedusa, she was one of only five passengers to survive the journey.

39. Bouchard and Ferme, *Italy and the Mediterranean*, 153.

40. Heidrun Friese, "Representations of Gendered Mobility and the Tragic Border Regime in the Mediterranean," *Journal of Balkan and Near Eastern Studies* 19, no. 5 (2017): 543.

41. Friese, "Representations of Gendered Mobility," 545.

42. It has been argued that the reception of these migrants was deliberately mismanaged by the Italian authorities to intensify the impression of crisis and thus elicit external intervention. See, for example, Giacomo Orsini, "Lampedusa: From a Fishing Island in the Middle of the Mediterranean to a Tourist Destination in the Middle of Europe's External Border," *Italian Studies* 70, no. 4 (2015): 528.

43. To various observers, the selection of the name Mare Nostrum ("our sea") for the Italian Navy's search-and-rescue operation was both puzzling and problematical. First used in ancient Rome to denote the Mediterranean, the term was recuperated to some extent by Italian nationalists in the post-Risorgimento period. It was not used again until appropriated by Fascist rhetoric in the 1920s. The Fascist deployment of the signifier Mare Nostrum resonated with Mussolini's attempt to present the Italian invasion and occupation of overseas territories as replicating the greatness and reach of Imperial Rome. After the fall of Fascism, the term was no longer considered politically respectable.

44. As Martina Tazzioli indicates, however, even after the inauguration of Operation Triton, the Italian Navy continued to patrol the Strait of Sicily, independently of the Triton framework. See Tazzioli, "Border Displacements: Challenging the Politics of Rescue between Mare Nostrum and Triton," *Migration Studies* 4, no. 1 (2016): 2, https://doi.org/10.1093/migration/mnv042.

45. "I will approach this project on tiptoe with the intention of telling the stories of the island and its people, avoiding the risk of treating them as mere extras or treating the island merely as a container." See Stefano Stefanutto Rosa, "La sacra Lampedusa di Rosi," Luce Cinecittà, June 5, 2014. http://www.cinecitta.com/IT/it-it/news/45/5014/la-sacra-lampedusa-di-rosi.aspx (July 15, 2018).

46. Earlier documentary projects and video essays on the Lampedusa-Linosa border zone include productions as diverse as *Sudeuropa 2005–2007* (2007), a video essay by Raphael Cuomo and Maria Ionio exhibited as part of a larger project at various venues in Africa and Europe; Giuseppe di Bernardo's *Viaggio a Lampedusa* (2010); Dagmawi Yimer's *Soltanto il mare*, made in collaboration with Fabrizio Barraco and Giulio Cederna; the French-produced *Mare Magnum* (2014), by Letizia Gullo and Ester Sparatore; Dagmawi Yimer's *Azmat* (2014), a video essay commemorating the tragedy of October 3, 2013; and the television compilation *Lampedusa, Europa*, directed by Alfredo di Giovampaolo, Paolo Poggio, and Serena Scorzoni and produced by RaiNews24 in 2014.

47. Friese, "Representations of Gendered Mobility," 544. For a further critique of the Mediterranean "spectacle" of bare life, see Nick Dines, Nicola Montagna, and Vincenzo Ruggiero,

"Thinking Lampedusa: Border Construction, the Spectacle of Bare Life and the Productivity of Migrants," *Ethnic and Racial Studies Review* 38, no. 3 (2015): 430–45.

48. The narrative is performed in English and is framed as an act of choral witnessing. The young man's account poignantly recalls the personal testimonies offered by several Ethiopian migrants in *Come un uomo sulla terra* (Like a Man on Earth), a documentary directed by Andrea Segre, Dagmawi Yimer, and Riccardo Biadene in 2008. Similarities between the Ethiopians' testimony in that film and the more recent account offered by the Nigerian in *Fuocoammare* suggest that the experience of migration through Libya has not improved since the change of government that followed the assassination of Gaddafi in 2011.

49. One of the sharpest criticisms of the film has come from Askavusa, a group of activists operating on the island since 2009 and building bridges between the islanders and migrants from various parts of the world through the organization of an annual festival and a networking facility. Not only did the authors of this critique find the depiction of Samuele's family limited and anachronistic, but they also accuse the film of representing the migrants in a superficial way, spectacularizing their suffering and aestheticizing the military apparatus present on and around the island. See "*Fuocoammare*: Considerazioni del collettivo Askavusa," *Askavusa*, February 24, 2016, https://askavusa.wordpress.com/2016/02/24/1428/ (accessed May 2, 2017).

50. During the spring of 2011, for example, given the severe shortage of accommodations for those arriving in Lampedusa from North Africa, several local residents offered food and hospitality to the migrants obliged to sleep in the open air. See Orsini, "Lampedusa."

51. "A Conversation with Gianfranco Rosi" (interview by Alberto Barbera), AFI Fest, Egyptian Theater, Los Angeles, November 17, 2016.

52. Martina Tazzioli, "The Politics of Counting and the Scene of Rescue: Border Deaths in the Mediterranean," *Radical Philosophy* 192 (July/Aug 2015), https://www.radicalphilosophy.com/commentary/the-politics-of-counting-and-the-scene-of-rescue.

53. Tazzioli.

54. Tazzioli.

55. Tazzioli, "Border Displacements," 8.

56. Tazzioli, "Politics of Counting."

57. "*Fuocoammare*: Considerazioni del collettivo Askavusa." Askavusa. February 24, 2016. https://askavusa.wordpress.com/2016/02/24/1428/ (accessed July 15, 2018).

58. As I have noted previously, in Italy, women economic migrants were until recently stereotypically associated with sex work and care work; the Senegalese protagonist of *Lettere* seems to regard his cousin's career as a model as close to the former.

59. *L'ordine delle cose* premiered at the Venice Film Festival on August 31, 2017, and was subsequently released in Italy. On September 6, 2017, it was screened at the Italian Senate, where it was introduced by Senator Luigi Manconi and subsequently discussed by a panel of speakers that included Senator Emma Bonino, Andrea Segre, writer Igiaba Scego, and two of the actors in the film.

60. The relevant documentaries are *A sud di Lampedusa* (Andrea Segre and Stefano Liberti, 2006), *Come un uomo sulla terra* (Andrea Segre, Dagmawi Yimer, and Riccardo Biadene, 2008), and *Mare chiuso* (Stefano Liberti and Andrea Segre, 2012).

61. Lucia Tedesco, "'L'ordine delle cose.' Libia, Europa e migranti nel film di Segre," *Officina dei Saperi*, September 18, 2017, http://www.officinadeisaperi.it/eventi/lordine-delle-cose-libia-europa-e-migranti-nel-film-di-segre/ (accessed September 30, 2018).

62. "Central Mediterranean: Death Toll Soars as EU Turns Its Back on Refugees and Migrants," Amnesty.org, July 6, 2017, https://www.amnesty.org/en/latest/news/2017/07/central

-mediterranean-death-toll-soars-as-eu-turns-its-back-on-refugees-and-migrants/ (accessed July 16, 2018).

63. Federico Pontiggia, "Mostra del Cinema di Venezia 2017, Segre scuote 'L'ordine delle cose' sui migranti," *Il fatto quotidiano*, September 1, 2017, http://www.ilfattoquotidiano.it/premium/articoli/segre-scuote-lordine-delle-cose-sui-migranti/.

64. "Per Cambiare l'Ordine delle Cose—Forum Nazionale Roma," Cronache di ordinario razzismo, November 9, 2017, http://www.cronachediordinariorazzismo.org/cambiare-lordine-delle-cose-forum-nazionale-roma/. (accessed July 18, 2018)

65. "Libia. Al Parlamento europeo proiezione de 'L'ordine delle cose,'" Articolo 21, January 30, 2018. https://www.articolo21.org/2018/01/libia-al-parlamento-europeo-proiezione-de-lordine-delle-cose/ (accessed July 18, 2018).

66. "Per Cambiare l'ordine delle cose: le proposte per i candidati alle prossime elezioni," Cronache di ordinario razzismo, February 21, 2018, http://www.cronachediordinariorazzismo.org/cambiare-lordine-delle-cose-le-proposte-candidati-alle-prossime-elezioni/ (accessed July 18, 2018).

CHAPTER 6

Living with Difference

FROM NOIR TO MELODRAMA

ACCORDING TO DATA released by Italy's National Institute of Statistics (ISTAT) there were just over five million immigrants living in Italy on January 1, 2017, or 8.3 percent of the total population.[1] While anti-immigrant groups routinely rehearse the rhetoric of foreign invasion, this percentage is modest in comparison to many other European nations. Italians' inflated perception of the number of foreigners residing among them may perhaps be explained by the rapid rate of increase in the immigrant population over a relatively short period of time.[2] What makes Italy's immigrant community genuinely remarkable, however, is not its size but its diversity. Representing about two hundred different nationalities, Italian immigrants constitute the most diversified constituency of nonnative residents in the countries of the European Union.

Several Italian films made since 2008 construct a diegetic world where immigration is envisioned neither as a novelty nor a pressing emergency but rather as part of everyday urban life in a society where long-settled immigrants and their offspring, as well as relatively recent arrivals from diverse corners of the globe, brush up against the daily routines of Italian citizens, triggering conflicts not easily contained. The immigrant characters populating these films represent a range of national origins, generations, and abilities to adapt to the host society. Their daily lives involve interactions not only with Italians but often with migrants of different origins. This body of films generally demonstrates greater stylistic diversity than those released in earlier years; it encompasses documentaries, blockbuster comedies, small independent features, melodrama, noir, and other categories. In this chapter, I explore some of the formal variations that have come into play in the audiovisual depiction of Italy's increasingly multiethnic society.

As the most frequently used register in the tradition of *cinema d'impegno* and the socially committed filmmaking that evolved from it, realism was until about a dozen years ago the dominant mode deployed in the narration of migrant journeys and the construction of characters of non-Italian origins.[3] This tendency has shifted as genre films now often include migrant characters in minor or major roles. Most notably, migrant characters have begun to appear with increasing frequency in popular comedies (whether "light," "grotesque," or using a mixed-genre approach), where they are implicated in scenarios that range from benign to offensive.[4]

The most widely seen example of comedy as a vehicle for the narration of encounters between native and nonnative characters is Gennaro Nunziante's blockbuster hit *Che bella giornata* (What a Beautiful Day!, 2011). Starring the hugely popular comedian Checco Zalone (whose real name is Luca Medici), the film has been seen by tens of millions more Italian viewers than any other nationally produced film foregrounding such encounters.[5] Like several other Italian comedies staging relationships between Italians and foreigners, *Che bella giornata* derives much of its humor from the deployment of stereotypes that challenge any notion of political correctness. In this case, negative stereotypes of Islam are proposed not only through the clueless utterances of the bumbling Italian protagonist but also insofar as the story revolves around a plan hatched by a small group of Arabs to place a bomb under the Maddonina statue at the top of Milan's cathedral. At a press conference, however, Zalone explicitly defended *Che bella giornata* against potential accusations of xenophobic stereotyping with a specious but predictable argument: "When, in the course of the film, I say that Arabs don't respect women, and then loudly demand that mother bring me a cup of coffee right away, I'm making fun of us, not them, and it's like that through the whole film."[6]

Despite their popularity in Italy (at least in relation to dramatic films with comparable stories), comparatively few comedy films featuring migrant characters have been shown on the festival circuit. Fewer still have achieved international distribution. In this respect, *Che bella giornata* is typical. Although scoring an unprecedented triumph at the domestic box office, it has not been exported overseas.

Noir—or more precisely neo-noir—has also become a vehicle for stories foregrounding the flux of migrants to Italy, but unlike the comedies mentioned above, these films have attained both critical attention and significant international visibility. Building on the writings of scholars such as Jennifer Fay and Justus Nieland on the use of noir in contemporary cinema from various parts of the world, Derek Duncan has identified the emergence of a corpus of Italian films on the figure of the migrant that draws on noir aesthetics.[7] Acknowledging anxiety as a defining term of noir, Duncan points out that "disruptions [of conventional] narrative structure, techniques of lighting and sound that intensify feelings of fear or suspense," though not unique to noir, serve in such films to create a "defining mood of crisis."⁸ The crisis in question—his argument implies—is triggered by the uncertainty about how to envisage the nation's future in the face of increasing immigration. In a similar vein, Paolo Russo has offered an extensive analysis of two Italian films, Giuseppe Tornatore's *La sconosciuta* (*The Unknown Woman*, 2006) and Matteo Garrone's *Gomorra* (2008), where noir conventions are deployed for specific effects in the delineation of migrant characters.⁹ For Russo, the Italian reworking of noir conventions participates in what David Desser identifies as "global noir," a transnational genre that has become a compelling vehicle for communicating the tensions and conflicts that characterize societies in the global era.¹⁰

Gomorra's Dark Shadows

Garrone's *Gomorra* is undoubtedly one of the most internationally successful Italian films of the new millennium.¹¹ Inspired by Roberto Saviano's bestselling book of the same title, which served to expose the ferocity of the Neapolitan crime syndicate known as the Camorra, it won the Grand Prix at Cannes in 2008 and was distributed globally to widespread critical acclaim.¹² Following its commercial and critical triumph, the film eventually inspired a successful television series, *Gomorra: la serie*, the first season of which was broadcast by Sky Italia in 2014. The series was subsequently distributed by Sundance for the Anglophone market with the English title *Gomorrah*.

 The biblically allusive title of both the film and the television series functions as an obvious pun on the word "Camorra." Presenting five interlacing stories centered on characters involved directly or peripherally with the violent Neapolitan mob, Garrone's film offers a striking portrait of the societal desolation generated by a closed system of organized crime. Promoted overseas as a gangster film, *Gomorra* nonetheless lacks the edgy glamour of American mafia movies. Although shot in authentic locations using dozens of dialect-speaking, nonprofessional actors residing in or near Naples, it is also devoid of the type of sober realism usually associated with the Italian social issue film. Disavowing any intention either to criticize or glamorize the world of the Camorra, Garrone has described his project as a war film, mentioning Roberto Rossellini's multi-episode neorealist classic *Paisà* (Paisan, 1946) as an inspiration.¹³ This reference has led a number of critics to pursue readings of the film as a realist, neo-neorealist, or even poetic-realist work.¹⁴ More fruitfully, others have explored Garrone's genre influences, particularly the noir elements that pervade the film's enunciation, evoking an atmosphere of anxious foreboding through the calculated deployment of specific elements of the mise-en-scène.¹⁵ As Russo astutely observes, *Gomorra*'s mannerist mise-en-scène frames and qualifies the characters' actions.¹⁶

Garrone's film does not concern itself in a focused way with issues relating to immigration, yet migrant characters appear in three of its five narrative strands. Never emerging to the forefront of the narration, these characters are configured as part of the everyday social landscape, a landscape pervaded by routine moral compromise and life-threatening danger. Although the migrants are found only in minor roles, their presence in the diegesis is quantitatively significant, as Russo has pointed out in his careful analysis of this aspect of the film.[17] Coming from diverse regions of the globe—Eastern Europe, Africa, and China—they engage in various kinds of irregular or illegal employment as drug dealers, textile workers, lap dancers, truck drivers, and handlers of toxic waste. Since they inhabit the lowest rung of the social hierarchy, they are often exposed to extreme peril—shot at, carelessly exposed to toxic chemicals, and deprived of medical assistance when injured. Although they may serve a specific function in the underground economy, they are entirely disposable and replaceable by other, similar exemplars of bare life.[18]

The narrative strand that gives most prominence to immigrant characters is the story focusing on Pasquale (Salvatore Cantalupo), a diligent, highly skilled tailor who earns a pittance laboring under the surveillance of his boss, Iavarone, a low-level associate of the Camorra. Attached to the same workshop since boyhood, Pasquale is subjected to merciless deadlines that require him to produce large quantities of high-fashion garments in short order. When approached in secret by Xian (Ronghua Zhang), a Chinese factory manager who invites him to provide couture lessons during the night at a local sweat shop in direct competition with Camorra-ruled workshops such as Iavarone's, Pasquale immediately accepts the chance to earn more money. Knowing the risks implicit in the arrangement, he agrees to travel to and from the Chinese factory hidden in the trunk of Xian's car.

In a variation of the standard scenario of the citizen-immigrant encounter, the Neapolitan Pasquale finds unexpected creative redemption in the opportunity to share his expertise with the Chinese workers. Not only does Xian remunerate him for his expertise in a way that exceeds his wildest expectations, but the factory employees, like their boss, appear to be in awe of his skills, addressing him as "Maestro" and bowing respectfully when they greet him. As he begins the first lesson, he basks visibly in this unaccustomed acknowledgment of his artistry. Over the course of repeated visits to the factory, he establishes a closer bond with Xian. But the easygoing relationship that develops between the men quickly results in disaster. As Pasquale becomes less vigilant about staying out of sight when traveling in Xian's car, he is soon spotted by Iavarone's associates. The shooting attack provoked by this discovery culminates in a crash that injures Pasquale and possibly kills Xian.

As Russo suggests, the specific mise-en-scène through which Pasquale's story is told is characterized by the repetition of long takes, depth of field, and

Figure 6.1. Screen capture. Pasquale teaches his craft to Chinese workers. *Gomorra* (2008)

same-frame composition, which serves to create alienating effects.[19] What is remarkable here is that the Chinese characters never achieve full visibility in the frame. Even when they occupy the foreground, their faces remain out of focus, are not clearly lit, or are seen only fleetingly. This visual fuzziness serves to mimic the perceptual frame through which the non-Italian characters are observed by the Italian Pasquale. Since Xian is the only non-Italian character in the film who is accorded a name and exerts any agency, it is clear that he has greater narrative importance than the other migrants. Yet—as Russo also points out—his face remains in the shadows, out of focus, or only partially visible for the duration of his association with Pasquale. Even in the last scene featuring Xian and Pasquale, where the two chat casually in the car while making their way back after a night's work at the factory, Xian's face does not emerge fully into view. Pasquale's face, by contrast, remains in focus as he sticks his head up from the baggage area at the back, where he is supposed to be hiding, in order to participate more fully in the conversation. This scene of almost comical camaraderie is interrupted by the outbreak of gunfire that causes the car to careen into a graveyard, raising a cloud of dust and dirt. Slowly, three of the four occupants of the car stagger out into the dust, like ghosts silhouetted against the funerary monuments. While the injured Pasquale is one of the survivors, Xian does not emerge from the car, and no information is provided about his status. When Iavarone subsequently reveals to Pasquale the Camorra's participation in the attack, he does not mention Xian's fate and clearly expects that his once-faithful employee will return to business as usual. Pasquale, however, decides otherwise. Abandoning the trade he had pursued with dedicated artistry, he starts a new life as a truck driver, releasing himself from the shadow of Iavarone and his Camorra connections. Pasquale's encounter with the Chinese entrepreneur is thus framed as prompting a life-changing move that though unsatisfying from a creative viewpoint, enables the Neapolitan tailor to abandon his subordination to fringe elements of the mob.

As the shadowy mise-en-scène of Pasquale's story suggests, the Chinese—along with the more elusively constructed African and Eastern European characters in the other narrative strands—function simply as minor figures in a social world that attributes little importance to them. Granted only partial visibility, they appear in the narrative only when they have a role to play in the circumstances of the more prominent Italian characters, vanishing without explanation immediately thereafter. Like the Eastern European truck driver who is burned by the toxic chemicals he is obliged to transport to a quarry for illegal disposal, Xian undergoes a trauma that may or may not have been catastrophic. The film does not dwell on such losses. Instead, in the final scene of this narrative strand, we see Pasquale glance at a television screen while taking a break at a truck stop. As he does so, he notices Scarlett Johansson attending the Venice Film Festival wearing the haute-couture gown he had created in Iavarone's workshop and on which the television commentator now lavishes praise. The identity of its creator, of course, remains unacknowledged. As Pasquale gazes at the image before turning away to resume his drive, the viewer is prompted to grieve the losses and disappointments he has sustained—the lack of adequate financial compensation and recognition for his tailoring skills, as well as the recent loss of an occupation that provided him with creative satisfaction. The scene thus provides a quietly dramatic moment in a film that is otherwise not much concerned with interiority. Clearly, no such grieving is evoked for Xian. His life and the lives of the other immigrants glimpsed in *Gomorra* are implicitly imagined as ungrievable, their disposable status reinforced by the shadows that render them virtually invisible in the mise-en-scène.

The Uses of Melodrama

As Duncan and Russo have shown, noir conventions invest at least a handful of contemporary films addressing Italy's complex transition to a multiethnic society. In many films about migrants, however, noir is mixed with other genre influences, particularly melodrama. When immigrant characters occupy the narrative foreground of Italian films, the melodramatic mode invests the expressive register of these films in various ways and to different degrees. To illustrate this phenomenon and its hermeneutic implications, I examine three relatively recent films with immigrant protagonists, *Io sono Li* (Shun Li and the Poet, Andrea Segre, 2011), *Good Morning Aman* (Claudio Noce, 2009), and *Alì ha gli occhi azzurri* (*Alì Blue Eyes*), Claudio Giovannesi, 2012), which are linked to each other on the level of affect. My aim is to explore how, in different ways, they conjure up affective resonances that can be associated with the category of transnational films defined by Carla Marcantonio as "global melodrama."[20]

Realism and melodrama have often been considered antithetical to each other. Whereas melodrama tends to be equated with excess, realism is sometimes associated with the sobriety of social critique. Italian critics on the left, from Antonio Gramsci to Giuseppe De Santis and beyond, have denounced melodrama on the basis of its purportedly inherent tendency to support the status quo. Anglophone scholars of Italian cinema, such as Marcia Landy and Maggie Günsberg, have nonetheless challenged this view.[21] Offering recuperative readings of Italian film melodramas of the prewar and postwar periods, respectively, Landy and Günsberg show how these often critically neglected works, far from wholeheartedly embracing the status quo, function to cast doubt on the dominant social order and particularly on traditional gender arrangements, if not always in a consistent way.

What has been lacking in Italian film scholarship is a sustained analysis of the productive presence of a melodramatic sensibility both in art films (*cinema d'autore*) and in other categories and genres. For many years, it was commonplace for scholars either to ignore or strategically justify the extensive use of melodramatic elements in the neorealist canon while denouncing manifestations of a melodramatic sensibility in less prestigious productions. This tendency, however, appears to be shifting. Louis Bayman, for example, offers an affirmative assessment of the deployment of melodrama even in classical neorealist film: "Neorealism uses melodrama to make more intense and more vivid the desperation of the popular masses, under subjection to material circumstance.... Melodrama helps neorealism assert that the genuine pathos of social restrictions and important moral questions are found in ordinary people's lives."[22]

A more sweeping challenge to the assumed opposition between realism and melodrama, along with a similar insistence on the possibility of a meaningful dynamic achieved through the combination of different expressive registers, can be found in Carla Marcantonio's *Global Melodrama*. The overall aim of this study is to theorize the particular role of the melodrama in cinematic representations of the contemporary transnational context.[23] With its focus on the deployment of the melodramatic mode in films featuring transitional, transnational, or interethnic settings, the project makes a particularly pertinent point of reference for my own examination of recent Italian cinema.

Among the points put forward by Marcantonio is the claim that the use of melodrama in Italian neorealism already marked a shift from melodrama's previously stark instantiation of binary oppositions. Citing Karl Schoonover's recent, provocative study *Brutal Realism*, she argues that the sheer scope of the postwar devastation at the basis of (and as the inspiration for) neorealist filmmaking necessitated a shift in the perspective through which human suffering could be understood.[24] In effect, the retooling of melodrama by neorealism, with its attention to widespread human deprivation and injury, enabled this new perceptual framework. As Marcantonio puts it, "postwar melodrama [in neorealist films] viewed the body through a new lens, one that could speak to a fundamental violence that emerged as a binding element of global interdependency."[25] This new lens—she argues—dislodged to some extent the stark Manichean oppositions of traditional melodrama, allowing for a broadly humanist contemplation of human suffering. The insight provides context for her subsequent exploration of the melodramatic mode as an explanatory frame in transnational art cinema of the global era.

Like Peter Brooks, whose seminal work on melodrama has had a significant influence in film studies, Marcantonio locates the origin of melodrama—first associated with stage productions and later with literature—in the period following the French Revolution, with the rise of nationalism.[26] For Brooks, melodrama is not simply a genre but rather a modern mode of expression, characterized by excess.[27] Pinpointing melodrama's "desire to express all," he suggests that this expressive excess is rooted in an effort to "make the world morally legible."[28]

With its conventional, often "excessive" opposition of good and evil, the melodramatic mode has been deployed on occasion in the service of nation building, consolidating myths of home and nation, and thus exercising a potentially conservative or restorative political force. Marcantonio argues, however, that after the waning of the nation-state as a uniquely compelling discourse—thanks to the emergence of global flows, the formation of supranational sovereignties, and the economic sweep of neoliberalism—cinematic melodrama is being deployed in a different way to address the complexities of the transnational moment. Through an updated prism, the category of films she calls "global melodrama" seeks to make legible the dizzying complexity of a political landscape transformed by transnational forces. Some of the issues implicated in the thematic preoccupations of these films are the startling sophistication of new biotechnologies, the simultaneous opening and hardening of borders, and the impact of changes in the urban landscape on disenfranchised people. Marcantonio acknowledges, however, that much work still needs to be done on this corpus of films "to elucidate the ways in which melodrama allows for the contested and redistributed character of sovereignty to come into view and thus to outline the new cartographies of intimate universes made possible by transformed spatiotemporal, political, and affective landscapes."[29]

Prompted by the potent possibilities of this analytical framework, I turn to the analysis of the three recent Italian films named above. My aim is to explore the ways in which a melodramatic sensibility, in combination with other formal elements, serves to highlight the tensions infusing contemporary Italian society, animating the intersections among places, spaces, bodies, and affects, and thus making visible the incommensurabilities of the nation's postcolonial and transnational status. As I have indicated at an earlier point, I do not use the term "postcolonial" to refer in the narrow sense to Italy's contemporary relationships with the countries and populations it formerly sought to dominate. Rather, I use the descriptor to speak of a society that is inhabited on the one hand by Italians who, to a greater or lesser extent, disavow the racist legacy of their country's colonial history and internal divisions, and, on the other, by immigrants or the descendants of immigrants hailing from multiple formerly colonized nations, including those that were the focus of Italy's colonial ambitions. Throughout this volume I have also argued that contemporary Italy is fully enmeshed in the neocolonial empire of global capitalism, where the mechanisms of exclusion and marginalization, domination and subordination are no less pervasive than those of historical colonialism.[30]

Constructing Chineseness on Italian Screens

Not all of Italy's immigrants are perceived as equally foreign. Instead, a tacit system of differential exclusion and inclusion has enabled the assimilation of some immigrants more readily than others.[31] In a fluid and constantly changing process, immigrant groups tend to be triangulated in Italian public opinion, with Italians themselves as the axis of comparison. Although Albanians were the specific target of xenophobic discourse in the 1990s, as I have discussed in chapter 1, in subsequent decades migrants who are perceived as somatically different from Italians have had greater difficulty in achieving acceptance. The underlying source of such differentiation is racism, but justifications for exclusionary practices are usually articulated in economic or cultural terms. An example of the process of differential inclusion/exclusion and the racializing matrix that underpins it is explored in the diegetic world of Andrea Segre's *Io sono Li* (*Shun Li and the Poet*, 2011), which tells the story of a doomed friendship between an aging fisherman from the former Yugoslavia and a more recent immigrant from China who longs to be reunited with her young son.

Although there has been a consistent Chinese presence in Milan since the 1920s, the Chinese community in Italy did not reach a substantial mass until the 1990s, when policy changes taking effect in the People's Republic began to facilitate the global mobility of its citizens. With numbers rising sporadically over the years, particularly since the turn of the millennium, it is calculated that over 280,000 people originating from mainland China now live and work legally in Italy.[32] The Chinese are currently ranked among Italy's four largest immigrant groups, after Romanians, Albanians, and Moroccans. Estimates of irregular Chinese migration, however, suggest that the total number of Chinese present in the country is much higher than official statistics suggest.

Periodically, incidents of crime or civic unrest occurring in the Chinatowns of Rome, Milan, and Prato, most notoriously the Via Sarpi riot in Milan in 2008, have registered on television, on the internet, and in print journalism, often articulated in a reporting style that is laced with racist connotations. In the meantime a burgeoning crop of stereotypes and urban legends has emerged to capture the truth of Chineseness, at least in the Italian context.[33] Despite the vividness and pervasiveness of these popular discourses, images of Chinese immigration were slow to register in Italian cinema. *Gomorra*, discussed above, was one of the first feature films to offer even a minimal acknowledgment of the Chinese presence in Italy. In the last ten years, however, there has been a small surge of films—both documentaries and commercial features—in which Chinese immigrants are accorded a greater degree of prominence.

The representation of Chinese characters in Italian feature films may appear at first to resonate with stereotypical constructions that emerged decades earlier in British and American cinema, with films as diverse as *Broken Blossoms* (D. W. Griffith, United States, 1919) and *The Mysterious Dr. Fu Manchu* (A. E. Coleby, United Kingdom, 1923). What marks the Chinese figures appearing in many contemporary Italian films such as *Mozzarella Stories* (Edoardo De Angelis, 2012), *Gorbaciof* (Gorbachev, Stefano Incerti, 2010), and *Questa notte è ancora nostra* (Tonight Is Still Ours, Paolo Genovese and Luca Miniero, 2008) as different from their antecedents, however, is the employment of a playful, self-directed irony at the metanarrative level. Two of these films are inflected by art-house influences mixed with comedy, while the third is a frankly commercial product aimed at teen audiences. Each of them adopts an ironic distance from the Italian characters' acceptance of orientalist stereotypes. Yet all of them have Italian protagonists, and the Chinese characters occupy either the position of love interest or that of the outsider who arrives on the scene simply to shake up the status quo.

Segre's *Io sono Li* takes a more focused approach to narrating the circumstances of Chinese immigration to Italy by constructing a story centered on a young woman from the People's Republic of China who has come to Italy to improve her economic circumstances. This is, in fact, the first Italian film with a Chinese immigrant as protagonist and the only one to draw on a melodramatic sensibility to invite sustained identification with a Chinese character. Although it self-reflexively reprises some of the tropes of the traditional maternal melodrama, this sensibility is balanced on the one hand by elements of social realism and, on the other, by intertextual references to Chinese art-house productions, particularly the early work of fifth-generation Chinese filmmaker Zhang Yimou.[34]

By the time he turned to writing and directing *Io sono Li*, Segre had already shown a sustained interest in contemporary global migrations, co-directing a small number of low-budget, collaboratively produced, and critically acclaimed documentary films on the topic, including *A sud di Lampedusa* (South of Lampedusa, 2007) and *Come un uomo sulla terra* (*Like a Man on Earth*, 2009).[35] In several online interviews he claims that the story for *Io sono Li* arose directly from a personal experience: making a return visit to Chioggia, his mother's hometown in the Venetian lagoon with which he was long familiar, he noticed that a Chinese woman had unexpectedly replaced the Italian barmaid in a traditional fisherman's wine bar, completely changing the atmosphere of this location.[36] The screenplay grew out of this moment as the director developed an imagined backstory for the woman so strangely out of place in the provincial tavern. On the realistic or sociological level of the film's development, the three labor sectors then dominant among Chinese immigrants become part of the protagonist's narrative: the textile industry, the restaurant business, and the wholesale sector. But the film also has a poetic, oneiric dimension, developed through images reminiscent of Chinese art cinema as well as poetic citations that are extraneous to the narrative development.

The protagonist, Shun Li (known as Li in the film), is played by Chinese actress Tao Zhao, who in 2012 won a Donatello Award for the role, the first Asian performer to achieve such a distinction.[37] As the film begins, Li is working as a seamstress for a Chinese garment producer in the Tor Pignattara district of Rome, a neighborhood that is home to several textile sweatshops. A bonded laborer, she is indebted to a Chinese agency that exerts control over every aspect of her life. This organization has paid for her travel from China and processed her travel documents. Once she has succeeded in liquidating all of her debt, the agency will arrange for her eight-year-old son to join her in Italy. Li is expected to work for an unspecified period of time and must carefully follow the rules imposed by the organization, which prohibit any kind of social interaction with the Italian population.

Li's status as a mother separated from her child brings a note of melancholy to the film. The pathos of melodrama is evoked in several scenes, the first of which captures the protagonist through a rain-swept window, the raindrops suggesting her tears, a familiar trope in classical Hollywood melodrama. Later she is seen sitting on the shore of the Venetian lagoon, composing a letter while intermittently gazing out toward the sea. The gray expanse of water conveys her sadness and sense of separation. On a realistic level, Li's situation reflects a prominent aspect of female migratory patterns; thousands of women entering Italy each year are obliged to leave their children in their place of origin while attempting to improve the family's financial circumstances. Having arrived in Italy, many of these women are obliged to make their livelihood taking care of other people's children, a scenario that is obliquely referenced in *Io sono Li*, where Li briefly takes care of an Italian boy of the same age as her own son after the child has been left behind by his father.

Following Li's dismissal from the sweatshop in Rome, she is transferred to Chioggia to work as a server at the Osteria Paradiso, a wine bar facing the old fishing harbor. The clients of this establishment, a group of aging fishermen, tease

Figure 6.2. Screen capture. Shun Li in Chioggia. *Io sono Li* (2011)

her a little, both for her inability to speak Italian fluently and her clumsiness as a waiter while she tries to learn the job. Among them is Bepi (Rade Šerbedžija), an immigrant from the former Yugoslavia who is more accommodating than the others. Although the older men quickly grow used to her presence, one of the bar's younger clients, Devis (Giuseppe Battiston), taunts her with comments that echo the racist sentiments of Lega Nord (in fact, he wears a tattoo of the so-called Alpine sun, symbol of the Lega). The balance among the various social actors in the wine bar shifts further when Bepi begins to develop a genuine friendship with Li. Though of different generations, the two immigrants are drawn together through similar memories of growing up in a fishing village under a socialist regime as well as the experience of emigrating to a different kind of society.

While the film constructs a realistic encounter between the non-Italian characters inhabiting a specific provincial environment that resonates with the economic tensions and racializing discourses characterizing Italy's social landscape more generally, it simultaneously develops a poetic dimension with recourse to symbolic flourishes. In the earliest scenes of the film, the viewer becomes aware that Li is fascinated by the celebrated poet of Chinese antiquity Qu Yuan, whose verses she quotes from memory. She also celebrates the poet's anniversary with the custom of floating paper lanterns on water. In the sequences shot in Chioggia, the lanterns acquire a more striking visual presence in two scenes featuring small red lanterns skimming the surface of the water. As Li engages Bepi in her love of poetry, she invites him to participate in this ritual, discovering that he is regarded as a poet by the other men who frequent the bar. Bepi, however, frankly admits that his verses are doggerel.

Bepi's friends soon misperceive his interest in the Chinese woman as a developing erotic attraction and cast her as predator. In their warnings to Bepi, a strain of paranoid anti-Chinese rhetoric finds explicit expression. The Chinese are taking over the world—the men insist—and Li will strip him of everything he has. As tensions mount, a fight breaks out with the most despicable of the clients, Devis, who strikes Bepi in fury, injuring him seriously and making it impossible for him to frequent the bar again. Bepi's relationship with the Chinese woman has effectively reinstated his alterity in the carefully mapped out spaces of the tavern and the town, despite his familiarity with the local dialect and his longtime residence in the area.

Bepi is a particularly interesting migrant figure insofar as he appears at first to be fully accepted and integrated into the local community. This acceptance may result from the fact that he is somatically indistinguishable from the other men who frequent the wine bar. Like them, he is a longtime fisherman, and his speech is inflected by the local dialect that they share. In other words, his difference has become invisible and almost inaudible. Yet his decision to cultivate a close friendship with the Chinese woman seems to violate a tacit agreement on a racial taboo—that certain social boundaries must not be crossed—and reverses his ability to be differentially included in Italian society as a white migrant from elsewhere in Europe. Fraternizing with a Chinese woman, perceived as irredeemably other, constitutes a kind of betrayal for the men who have previously allowed Bepi's own foreignness to pass uncommented.

The tensions that develop around the figure of the Chinese woman due to the disruptive effects of her presence in a homosocial community of local working-class men can perhaps be better understood by considering Segre's comments on the encounter that inspired him to create the story of Shun Li. Noting that he had witnessed a striking transformation in the atmosphere of the local wine bar in Chioggia following the arrival of the Chinese barmaid, he elaborates, "Sociologically, the barmaid plays a really important role in the traditional fishermen's wine bar. For many of the men drinking there, the wine bar is like a second home (or sometimes a first home). The person working at the bar is usually a woman, and all the people drinking there are men. She is very familiar with them, and this relationship is a strong one—it's not erotic, but it's a very important relationship."[38]

Segre's comments describe the mechanisms of certain types of affective labor performed in publicly accessible spaces and the gender dynamics that subtend them. As I have noted in chapter 2, the affective laborer, often a woman, provides the kind of comfort and reassuring support associated with "women's work." In a provincial osteria like the one constructed in the film, the female server is expected to create, for the male homosocial microcosm that constitutes her principal clientele, the illusion of a second home. The film powerfully demonstrates how, when the expectations associated with affective labor are complicated by the introduction of ethno-racial difference, the reproduction of "home" is no longer guaranteed. As noted above, affective labor is a component of the broader category of immaterial labor and spans a wide range of employment practices, including the hiring of foreign-born domestic workers or care providers who have become essential to the daily routines of many Italian families. Although domestic workers have the capacity to be absorbed in a circumscribed way into the space of the family home through a series of negotiations with family members, the unwritten rules that govern affective labor in publicly accessible locations aspiring to provide their clients with a second home are more complex. While Li manages to achieve some success in performing tasks that parallel those of the domestic employee—delivering food and drink orders without fuss, responding to cheerful banter, and humoring her moody clients as well as learning their names and circumstances—her unfamiliar appearance, imperfect command of the local language, and lack of training for her work perpetually threaten to rupture the desired illusion that the tavern is a second home.

Though long accepted in the local landscape, Bepi suddenly finds himself ostracized, even physically attacked, by his Italian colleagues for his stubborn affinity with the Chinese other. The racializing dynamics prevailing within the Chinese community are no less severe. Li's Chinese boss, hearing of her situation through an intermediary, tells her she must end the friendship with Bepi immediately or begin her obligatory period of service from the start. Fraternizing with the locals is considered bad for business. Although Li announces to Bepi that she must cut off communication with him as the result of these orders, she is still punished by her boss, who transfers her to another job in a different city, with no clear guarantee that her earlier months of work will be taken into account. At the same time, Bepi moves to Mestre to live with his adult son, only to die soon afterward. The film does not, however, end with hopelessness as Li is eventually rescued from bondage to her employers by the intervention of a former Chinese roommate, a woman who, before vanishing from the scene without explanation, quietly liquidates Li's debt, enabling Li's son to travel to Italy and join her there.

The presence of Lian, Li's mysterious Chinese benefactor, belongs to both the realistic register of the film and its oneiric dimension. Though her intervention turns out to be important at the film's end, this action is reported rather than visualized. Lian rarely appears on screen, and her motivations remain enigmatic. Sharing a bedroom with Li, she appears to work for the same Chinese agency. Yet the kind of labor she performs when she leaves for work each night remains unclear. Although she may be a sex worker, no specific information confirms this. She is sometimes visualized on the beach, a solitary, graceful figure slowly performing the motions of tai chi as she faces the water. Since her final disappearance is unexplained, she is ultimately a mystery. Lian's almost ghostly presence in the film recalls Cindy Wong's analysis of Chinese characters in contemporary European cinema, characters who tend to vanish or die as soon as their narrative function is fulfilled. As Wong observes, "They haunt these films rather than drive them. Their spectral quality includes death, mystery, disappearance, and the ethical transformation of the [European] protagonist although they themselves evaporate from the narrative."[39] This description applies to some extent to the "evaporating" Lian, but in Segre's film, it is the Chinese protagonist, Li, who benefits from the other Chinese woman's presence rather than a European character.

Segre's approach reveals a general sensitivity to issues of race and racism. Yet references to the ruthless ambition of Chinese immigrants, and particularly the harshness of the bosses, are not absent in the film. These references are usually delivered in the dialogue of characters that the film expects the viewers to distrust. The boss who controls the details of Li's everyday life is quiet but tyrannical, and he treats her without sensitivity or consideration. This configuration of a negatively connoted Chinese man juxtaposed with a positively connoted Chinese female character inadvertently plays into the conventional Western tendency to make abject Chinese masculinity while simultaneously fetishizing the figure of the attractive Chinese woman.

Despite overarching resonances of the maternal melodrama, the lingering mood of Segre's film is serene, as this is perhaps the only dramatic feature film about Italian immigration that offers what resembles a conventional happy ending. As mother and son are reunited, Li has fulfilled her greatest desire. In the film's final moments, Li is washing the boy in the bathtub, responding to his eagerness to learn Italian so that he can begin his new life in Italy, a scenario that implies at least the possibility of the child's eventual inclusion in Italian society. The scene is clearly in contrast with the tear-jerking conclusions of traditional maternal melodramas, but it is not without melancholy. The implicit sadness of this film's ending lies not in a scenario of thwarted maternal love but rather in the viewer's awareness of Bepi's demise, apparently precipitated by the brutal beating he sustained at the hands of an Italian thug, as well as the mysterious absence of Lian, the fleeting, unsmiling Chinese female figure, who seems to have exchanged her own possibility of presence for that of the little boy at the center of the shot.

(Post)colonial Desire

Claudio Noce's *Good Morning Aman* (2009) is one of a crop of recent Italian films that uses noir aesthetics to highlight the tensions and incommensurabilities of the transnational, postcolonial moment. In Noce's film, the noir sensibility is nonetheless heavily laced with melodramatic elements, including the tropes of "too-lateness," separation, and loss, as well as an emotionally charged music track that invites the viewers' empathy for the apparently irresolvable dilemmas of the two main characters. Furthermore, *Good Morning Aman* is one of the rare films featuring an immigrant from a former Italian colony. Set in contemporary

Rome, it offers a striking representation of the ambivalent matrix of attraction and repulsion that historically structured the encounter of the colonizer and the colonized other and points to the uncanny endurance of colonial desire in the postcolonial era.

Although Aman, the twenty-year-old Somali protagonist, was born in a country once occupied by Italy, neither he nor any of the other characters in the film refer to the historical project of Italian colonization. What the narrative exposes, however, is the difficulty, if not unlivability, of Aman's racialized, postcolonial status in a social environment that refuses to acknowledge or confront its racist legacy. Having grown up in the sprawling Corviale public housing project in the Roman periphery, he speaks Italian with a marked Roman accent. Yet all of his Italian interlocutors perceive him as an outsider and offer persistent reminders of his racial difference.

The film conveys Aman's mounting restlessness, frustration, and sense of exclusion through the abundant use of a handheld camera, elliptical editing, extreme close-ups, and the virtual absence of establishing shots. These stylistic choices allow the viewer limited access to the characters' motivations and create ontological confusion when counterfactual elements or diegetically unmarked fantasies are intercut with more reliably realistic elements in the course of the narrative's progression.

The affective relationship that dominates the film is the bond Aman establishes with a reclusive Italian ex-boxer named Teodoro. Though the nature of this relationship is not construed as sexual, a significant level of libidinal tension appears to invest the early scenes that the two men share, a tension that is linked to the asymmetrical power relations between them and the seemingly inexplicable pull of their need for each other. They clearly constitute an unlikely couple as Teodoro, who is twice Aman's age, persistently reveals an attitude of unabashed racism.

The young Somali's initial encounter with the Italian loner occurs by chance on the rooftop of Teodoro's building in Piazza Vittorio at a moment when the Italian is contemplating suicide by jumping over the parapet, although this detail is not revealed to the viewer or to Aman until much later in the film. Teodoro then invites Aman into his apartment and surreptitiously places a substantial bundle of money in his pocket. Far from a gesture of selfless generosity, this gift raises the possibility that Aman is expected to provide some form of service in exchange for cash. Yet the Italian reveals nothing of his expectations, and Aman, recently fired from his job by his explicitly racist Italian boss, returns regularly to the apartment, tacitly accepting additional wads of money. As the two begin to relax in each other's presence, the film's visual style points to the tensions that simmer under the surface of their puzzling alliance, which is explored exclusively through Aman's perceptual frame. Through the use of elliptical editing and the virtual absence of establishing shots, the narrative unfolds in a disorienting manner, denying the viewer a fuller awareness of Teodoro's unspoken agenda and of Aman's expectations.

The motive that impelled the Italian to invite the young Somali into his life is finally revealed in the course of an encounter between Aman and Teodoro's estranged wife, who suggests that her husband perceived the young Somali as a kind of compensatory replacement for a Senegalese youth he had run over and killed three years earlier in a moment of drunken folly. The absurdity of Teodoro's hope that his wife would allow him back into her life upon witnessing the bond he had created with a young black man is evident both to the wife and the film's viewers, and it does not fully explain the intensity of the relationship already established between the men.

Arguably, Teodoro's attachment to Aman is held in place not by any simple sense of remorse for the act of racially inflected violence that led to his estrangement from his own family but rather by the ambivalence of colonial desire broadly understood. The psychic stakes involved in the relationship begin to emerge in a crucial scene early in the film, which could be described as the staging of seduction. Here, Teodoro suddenly pulls Aman close to him and kisses him on the mouth. The young Somali recoils, suspecting a homosexual come-on, but Teodoro instantly mocks this reaction. He then turns around and raises his shirt, revealing an elaborate tattoo covering most of his back—a stylized image that depicts a nude woman from the rear. As she is leaning forward, her buttocks are raised in the direction of the viewer, apparently inviting penetration. "This is my woman," Teodoro tells Aman. "Someday I'll let you get to know her."

As Eve Kosofsky Sedgwick has argued in her important study on the representation of male friendships in English literature, the trope of two men involved in the sexual pursuit of the same woman is one of the defining elements of the male homosocial bond. Since the manifestation of intense male-to-male attachments on the part of heterosexual men risks raising the suspicion of homosexuality, disavowal of homoerotic desire becomes a compulsory component of such bonds. The disavowal is enacted through the introduction of a woman as the third term in an affectively charged triangle, a woman who becomes the ostensible object of desire for both men.[40] The introduction of a female figure as the third party in the relationship between Teodoro and Aman thus appears to instantiate the type of triangle that Sedgwick describes. In this case, however, the process of triangulation is particularly complex since the "woman" that Teodoro proposes to share with the disenfranchised black youth is introduced into the mise-en-scène as part of Teodoro's own (white) body. This uncanny displacement implicitly queers the ex-boxer's gender affiliation and heightens the erotic and racial ambiguities already present in the scene.

On the surface, however, the meaning of Teodoro's promise is quite conventional: he is offering Aman the possibility of participatory citizenship in the male, heterosexual, working-class social circles in which he himself used to move with ease but from which the younger man, by virtue of his racial difference, would generally be excluded. It seems that admission to this environment appears merely to require a specific set of shared values, behaviors, and prejudices, including an implicitly misogynist attitude. When Aman is eventually introduced to Teodoro's social world, however, it becomes evident that his racial identity constitutes an immediate barrier to the possibility of acceptance by the others. His repetition of a crude phrase in Roman slang already uttered by one of Teodoro's friends is enough to incite the hostility of the group, and in this way he is made to understand that the appropriation of such language assumes an equality that he has not been conceded.

Rey Chow's astute commentary on the stakes underpinning the central relationship in David Cronenberg's film *M. Butterfly* provides some useful insight toward an understanding of the seductive scenario, and its ultimate unraveling, in *Good Morning Aman*.[41] Drawing on both Edward Said's concept of Orientalism and Lacan's theory of the phallus, her analysis exposes the processes of projection and disavowal at work in *M. Butterfly*'s representation of the bond between its male French protagonist and a Chinese opera singer posing as a woman. Chow's formulation of the psychic structure of seduction is particularly compelling in this context: "What seduces . . . is not the truth of the other—what he or she really is—but the artifact, the mutual complicity in the weaving of a lure, which works as a snare over the field of encounter, ensuring that the parties meet at the same time that they miss each other, in a kind of rhythmic dance."[42] The dynamic of simultaneous "meeting and missing" at the heart of the seductive dance suggests a parallel quest for illusory wholeness by the parties complicit in the scenario. The configuration evoked by Chow enables an understanding of the libidinal dynamic at work between the two main characters in *Good Morning Aman* and, more generally, in scenes of (post)colonial desire.

In Noce's film the lure that sustains the relationship between the perpetually frustrated, immobilized black youth and the remorseful yet candidly racist Italian recluse is the fantasy that some form of wholeness or redemption can be achieved through the affiliation with the racialized other (a recurrent theme in narratives of orientalist awakening). In *Good Morning Aman*, the men's shared condition of need constitutes a kind of mutuality. At the same time, the asymmetrical power relations underlying any exchange between them, aggravated by Teodoro's apparent inability to relinquish his racism, forestall the possibility of reciprocity. Despite his relative wealth and apparent generosity, the unrepentantly racist Teodoro will never enable the racially marked Aman to attain full symbolic citizenship in the contemporary metropolis—the kind of citizenship that would allow him to move through and participate in Italy's social landscape with the ease and freedom that can be accessed by his white Italian counterparts. Nor can the mere presence of Aman at his friend's side serve to convince

Figure 6.3. Screen capture. The imaginary journey of Teodoro and Aman. *Good Morning Aman* (2009)

Teodoro's estranged wife to forgive him for killing the Senegalese youth three years earlier. As the former boxer's illusory hopes collapse and his behavior becomes increasingly destructive, the film adopts a forked narration, leading to an unresolved ending.

Scenes of the wounded Teodoro lying in a hospital bed and an image of what seems to be his eventual suicide—along with Aman's reactions to these events—are intercut in fragmentary fashion with a sequence that constructs a trip the two men take to the mountains. At first this journey, which begins with a shot of the two men traveling on a bus through the countryside, seems to belong to the film's realistic register, but it soon becomes apparent that it is instead a projection of Aman's imagination. The ultimate destination of the journey is a rugged landscape whose contours are inspired in Aman's fantasy by a painting hanging in Teodoro's apartment, a kitsch image of a solitary male figure standing on a mountain peak, overlooking the valley below. Accompanied on the soundtrack by the melancholy andante movement from Beethoven's third Razumovsky Quartet, the ascent of Teodoro and Aman toward the mountaintop evokes a strong sense of pathos. In this way, the seduction fantasy, or the dream of imagined wholeness, continues to unfold in tandem with hallucinatory scenes and images suggesting the men's eventual estrangement from each other, the ineluctability of Teodoro's suicide, and Aman's desire to act out his pent-up rage and frustration. If the mise-en-scène retains traces of noir conventions—low-key lighting, tight framing, and rapidly paced, elliptical editing that suggests rising tension—the construction of both men as victims of social isolation and unattainable desire, as well as an all-consuming melancholy and rage, draws increasingly on the melodramatic mode.

Much of the pathos generated by *Good Morning Aman* is associated with Aman's frustrated access to the expression of agency and desire, in other words, with the thwarted voice of the marginalized. This concern emerges interstitially through the disjunctive articulation of Aman's subjectivity. The desire he announces most frequently is his plan to abandon Italy and move to Canada—a clearly unachievable fantasy—where his purported brother, the real-life Somali-born rap star K'naan, has achieved fame and fortune and, perhaps more importantly, has asserted his voice. Although his association with Teodoro seems momentarily to offer Aman the possibility of social mobility and geographical movement, these hopes are dashed by the end of the film, even as the dying Teodoro promises to bequeath to him half of his house.

Early in the film, just after his best friend's departure for London, phone calls between Aman and his friend are heard at intervals on the soundtrack, which seem to be the product of his imagination. In the course of these calls, Aman offers Said cheerful updates on his life in Rome, conveying information that the viewer recognizes as false. Infusing the narrative with uncertainty, the contrast between the events shown on the image track and the information conveyed in these telephonic bulletins is the first clue to the film's investment in the register of the uncanny, or the "unhomely," as described by Homi Bhabha.[43]

Bhabha's analysis of the articulation of the liminal space of marginality in postcolonial cultural production revolves around the concept of unhomeliness, which draws not only on Freud's *unheimlich* (usually translated as the "uncanny") but also on Julia Kristeva's reformulation of that concept in her analysis of racism and nationalism.[44] In the context of postcolonial subjectivity, the unhomely relates to the impossibility of identifying the status of the self with conventional notions of habitation. While Noce's film registers this impossibility by unveiling the incommensurabilites that surround migrant subjectivity, it does not point to any discernible resolution. Its melodramatic sensibility is associated with the protagonist's liminality, homelessness, unfulfilled yearning, and loss.

Alì's Blue Eyes: The Unbearable Ambivalence of Diasporic Masculinity

So far, little cinematic attention has been paid to the experience of what is described in Italy as the *seconda generazione*—that is, the Italian-born offspring of Italy's initial wave of mass immigration at the end of the twentieth century.[45] Among feature films, Giovannesi's *Alì ha gli occhi azzurri* (Alì Has Blue Eyes, 2012) is one of the striking exceptions to this representational oversight as it focuses entirely on a sixteen-year-old Italian born to Egyptian parents whose loyalty is divided between the cultural codes modeled by his immigrant family and the behaviors taken for granted by his Italian peer group. Nader, the film's protagonist, sports blue contact lenses and favors the style of contemporary urban clothing worn by his Italian friends; at first glance he is barely distinguishable from his Italian classmates. Yet despite his efforts to embrace the signifiers of mainstream Italian masculinity, he sometimes reveals a keenly felt difference that is at odds with his outward appearance. With nervous, handheld camera movements, claustrophobic framing, and the near-absence of establishing shots, the film's visual register points to the character's internal conflict, not to invite identification with the pathos of an oppositional authenticity seeking to find expression but rather to suggest a sense of impasse or impossibility. The affect generated by this sense of impasse, which hinges on issues of gender, sexuality, and (un)belonging, is precisely where the film's melodramatic sensibility resides.

Alì ha gli occhi azzurri has its genesis in an earlier work by Claudio Giovannesi, the prize-winning documentary *Fratelli d'Italia* (Brothers of Italy, 2009), which investigates the lives of three teenagers of different ethnic origins attending a technical school in Ostia. The documentary's third and last segment is devoted to the sixteen-year-old Nader Sarhan, whose striking good looks and engaging if sometimes insufferable personality make him the most memorable presence in the film.[46] Sarhan's onscreen presence was so compelling that Giovannesi decided to build a feature film around him, convincing him, his friends, and his parents to perform in scripted roles that closely matched their real-life circumstances and using authentic locations as the setting for this production. Although the film was shot almost four years after the documentary segment, during which the family's circumstances had changed to some degree, its narrative is concerned with a conflict that erupted between Sarhan and his parents when he was a sixteen-year-old adolescent, expanding on the consequences that flowed from this event. Adopting a straightforward chronological progression that spans seven consecutive days in the teenager's life, the story ultimately withholds dramatic resolution.

Despite the key points of resemblance between *Fratelli d'Italia* and *Alì ha gli occhi azzurri*—such as the presence of some of the same characters performing a different version of themselves and the use of similar locations—the feature film cannot be considered simply as a development of the straightforward social inquiry underpinning the documentary. Nonetheless, the use of nonprofessional actors, authentic locations, and natural lighting—in addition to the almost complete absence of nondiegetic music—creates an aesthetic style evocative of documentary realism. Speaking of his technique in an interview, Giovannesi uses the word *pedinamento*, or stalking, to define his commitment to realistic representation.[47] This term was introduced by neorealist screenwriter and theorist Cesare Zavattini to describe what he considered a fundamental principle of neorealist filmmaking. From Zavattini's perspective, it was necessary for filmmakers "to know in order to provide," an epistemological necessity that could be fulfilled by painstakingly "stalking" places, people, and activities, and privileging techniques that might enable this process.⁴⁸ As Alessia Ricciardi observes, *pedinamento* differs from mimesis, insofar as it involves the simultaneous exploration and construction of reality.⁴⁹ To take Giovannesi's invocation of Zavattini at face value is to assume that his approach in *Alì ha gli occhi azzurri* is primarily an epistemological project. Yet the film itself suggests otherwise. As the narrative progresses, the intensity of the protagonist's internal struggle begins to interrupt the film's realist, investigative thrust as unresolved tensions and aporias emerge. The penultimate scene offers the film's most conventionally melodramatic set-up. Within a spatial configuration that blatantly evokes the balcony scene in *Romeo and Juliet*, Nader—no longer wearing his blue contact lenses—stands mutely in near-darkness several floors beneath the window of his girlfriend, Brigitte, weeping visibly as she returns his gaze, giving no hint of reconciliation. What infuses the film's realistic register with plausible affective power is precisely the pull of such compellingly irresolvable moments.

According to Marcantonio's theorization of global melodrama, the melodramatic mode can inform not only ostensibly dramatic films but also those committed to a more restrained or realistic expressive register. Among the examples she analyzes in detail are two films usually considered by critics and scholars as examples of contemporary realist approaches: *Juventude em Marcha* (*Colossal Youth*, Pedro Costa, Portugal, 2006), which is sometimes described as docufiction, and *The World* (Jia Zhangke, China, 2004). Marcantonio shows how, despite the apparent detachment of a style of narration that is influenced by the documentary approach, these films deploy a melodramatic sensibility in their construction of the ways in which globalized cities and the people obliged to live in them are "out of phase" with each other. For the characters in these films, their environment has become uninhabitable.

Marcantonio's concept of "uninhabitability" resonates with the atmosphere generated by Giovannesi's film, whose protagonist is driven to homelessness through his inability to come to terms with the implications of his identity as a second-generation Italian Egyptian youth. *Alì ha gli occhi azzurri* posits the difficulty, if not impossibility, of coming of age for diasporic subjects in a postcolonial society and suggests the complicated legibility of desire and identification in transcultural contexts. The persistence of these concerns in the film provides a melodramatic tonality that sharply contrasts with the stylistic sobriety of the cinematography and sound design. While *Alì ha gli occhi azzurri* has elements of global melodrama as defined by Marcantonio, its themes of impossibility and impasse, emphasized through tropes of liminality and circularity, also align it with what Jonathan Goldberg describes as the queer melodramatic aesthetics of Douglas Sirk, Todd Haynes, and Reiner Maria Fassbinder.⁵⁰ Significantly, Fassbinder's *Angst essen Seele auf* (*Ali: Fear Eats the Soul*, 1973) invokes a diasporic scenario that is not dissimilar to that of the protagonist of *Alì ha gli occhi azzurri*.

The title of Giovannesi's feature film already provides the clue to a more complex aesthetic endeavor than that achieved in his earlier documentary. Although Nader's blue-tinted contact lenses—already a noteworthy element of Sarhan's self-presentation in *Fratelli d'Italia*—are the ostensible point of reference for the title of the new film, Italian viewers are also likely to recognize in this title an almost exact echo of the title of a volume of essays published by Pier Paolo Pasolini in 1965, *Alì dagli occhi azzurri* (literally, "Blue-eyed Alì").[51] Among the texts contained within it is the prose poem "Profezia" (Prophesy), whose protagonist is a blue-eyed North African youth named Alì. Along with incalculable numbers of other young men from the global South, he is poised to sail toward Europe at an unspecified moment in the future to invade the cities of the old continent, shaking up the smug consumerism that has enveloped the West. As the poem develops, this prophesized invasion takes on a menacing yet simultaneously exultant tone: "Following blue-eyed/Alì— they will crawl up from below the ground to kill—/they will crawl up from the bottom of the sea to attack—they will plunge/down from the heavens to steal—and before they reach Paris/to teach us the joy of living . . ./they will destroy Rome."[52]

Like Gramsci, Pasolini believed in the revolutionary potential of the various souths of the world—including southern Italy—in whose impoverished inhabitants, purportedly untouched by modernization, he perceived the possibility of challenging the corruption of the contemporary West.[53] When read today, in the wake of neoliberalism's global triumph, the revolutionary dream fueling the journey of Alì and his legions seems naïve. Nonetheless, Pasolini's image of a great mass of young men sailing from the shores of North Africa to Italy can be read as an uncanny foreshadowing of the movement of tens of thousands of young men across the Mediterranean to the Italian coast in the decades following the writer's death. As a diasporic subject born and raised in Italy, however, Giovannesi's protagonist is not in any simple way a part of this cohort of the dispossessed.

With its self-consciously evocative title, *Alì ha gli occhi azzurri* obliquely invites its audiences to juxtapose Alì with the (seemingly) blue-eyed Nader. What such comparison inevitably highlights is not the resemblance between the two figures (despite their shared attributes of age, gender, and Arab ethnicity) but rather their incommensurability. Unlike Pasolini's Alì, Nader lives in a society irredeemably vanquished by neoliberalism, and the tinted contact lenses he wears to create the illusion of blue eyes are merely one of the many devices of self-fashioning available for sale in the Western marketplace. The desire for eyes of a color lighter than his own, however, hints at an unexpressed fear of being stereotyped as a nonwhite, immigrant subject.[54] His lenses can thus be read as a form of mimicry, an attempt to confound and overturn the stereotype, shot through with what Bhabha has described as colonial ambivalence.[55] As Bhabha has argued, just as the (post)colonial subject perpetually attempts to stabilize identities by imposing the fixity of the stereotype, the same process is simultaneously undone through the operations of mimicry, which expose the instability and hybrid underpinnings of all identity constructions.[56] In *Alì ha gli occhi azzurri*, although the protagonist's external appearance, clothing, and demeanor mirror those of his Italian peers, a fully convincing match is not always achieved.

Nader's Italian girlfriend, Brigitte, mocks him gently about his insistence on wearing his contact lenses. When he wears them, they provide an arresting contrast to his darker skin tone, drawing attention to his visible difference from those around him rather than deflecting it. Nader, in fact, never wholeheartedly attempts to "pass," betraying a lack of desire to fully embrace either his family's traditions or the world of his peers. Although he presumably hopes to look European, he perpetually draws attention to the ambivalence of being "not quite/not white," as Bhabha describes the outcome of racial mimicry.[57] In other words, his chosen masquerade, already marked as artifice, pointedly illustrates the dynamics at play in (post)colonial relations. Unlike Pasolini's Alì, Nader is not a leader or a revolutionary; rather, he is a restless, hybrid subject oscillating between the possibility of immersion in Italian society and a simultaneous resistance to abandoning some of the values of his resented diasporic family.

In Giovannesi's title, as in Pasolini's poem, the use of the proper name Alì signals a link to the "Orient" as it is perceived in European terms. It conjures up the Middle Eastern male as a construct that has circulated in European culture for centuries, a figure vacillating between exoticism and menace. Alì also happens to be the name attributed to the male protagonist of Rainer Maria Fassbinder's *Angst essen Seele auf* (*Ali: Fear Eats the Soul*, 1973) an embattled Moroccan immigrant living in Germany whose real name is judged too inconvenient for his German interlocutors to remember. Significantly, Fassbinder's work was the first widely circulated European feature film to register the cultural challenges of contemporary globalized migrations. The perhaps coincidental use of the name Alì in the titles of both Fassbinder's film—which is self-consciously styled as a melodrama—and *Alì ha gli occhi azzurri* seems relevant to the deeper melodramatic resonances of Giovannesi's predominantly realistic work.

The hybrid character of Nader's experience of the world is first signaled in the film by the use of Italian and Arabic titles that appear on screen to mark the beginning of each of the seven days over which his story unfolds, from Saturday morning to the following Friday evening. Almost all of the action is set in Ostia, which until recent years functioned primarily as Rome's seaside playground, particularly in the summers, but has by now become the site of multiple public housing projects and home to a larger percentage of immigrants than the city of Rome itself (as is immediately visible in the diversity of Nader's classmates). Ostia is part of a long coastal strip that has seen a high density of settlement by foreigners over the past twenty years—and it is no coincidence that the protagonist of *Saimir*, discussed in chapter 4, also lives in this general area. But Ostia is, of course, also associated with Pasolini, whose work inspired the film's title and who was murdered in a deserted public space on Via dell'Idroscalo on the night of November 2, 1975, allegedly by the seventeen-year-old Pino Pelosi, who had accompanied him there for sex.[58]

These extradiegetic references to Pasolini inevitably bring the question of non-heteronormative sexuality to bear on any approach to Giovannesi's film. Duncan's provocative analysis of several Italian films about male immigrants made during the 1990s and early years of the twenty-first century already prompts us to consider the queer implications of all film narratives foregrounding a heterosexual relationship between an Italian woman and a non-Italian man.[59] Drawing on the argument made by Harry Benshoff and Sean Griffin that the term "queer" can describe "any sexuality not defined as heterosexual procreative monogamy," Duncan observes the striking lack of reproductive capacity among the migrant male characters in contemporary Italian cinema.[60] In fact, the heterosexual romances in the films he examines inevitably end in rupture and mark the migrant's failure to assimilate into Italian society. Suggesting that these migrant characters link their assimilatory project to an imputed need to pass as Italians, he shows how their efforts to blend in or adapt to the host society are rendered "monstrous" by the films' signifying strategies, which highlight their incompatibility with the national landscape.[61] Their queerness coincides with this monstrosity—that is, with the failure to achieve the desired assimilation and to attain a foothold within the nation.

Nader is different on many levels from the characters in the Italian films described by Duncan: he was born in Italy rather than elsewhere; he speaks Italian without a foreign accent; he moves in a social circle largely composed of Italians; and he is accepted without question—at least in the early part of the film—in the locations frequented by his Italian peers. Yet he is also "monstrous" in the sense described by Duncan, a quality that accrues to him as he transitions from a state of near-assimilation to a state of homelessness, both literal and figurative. In the course of this unraveling, the unlivablity of his status as a diasporic male subject becomes evident to him and the viewer, and the queer connotations imbricated in his circumstances—which are much more explicit than those in the films described by Duncan—serve to accentuate his sense of unbelonging.

Framed on one side by the steely gray sheen of the sea in the dead of winter, the film's opening shot reveals a rocky stretch of shoreline. Onto this space the two friends, Nader and Stefano, emerge into view. In one of the concluding scenes, they will return to the same location, their close relationship violently altered by Nader's inability to reconcile the opposing forces that define him and his failure to find a home within himself. What emerges most powerfully throughout the film is Nader's desire to claim an assertive heteronormative masculinity based on models of masculinity he has observed in Italian society. In the film's opening sequence, he and Stefano hotwire a scooter, proceed to hold up the cashier at a grocery store, and split the spoils before showing up at school in time for class. Not only do they dress and move in a similar fashion, but they also share the distinctive speech patterns of their locality, generation, and social class. As soon as he enters the classroom, however, Nader begins to assert his difference. In this short scene, captured mostly in tight shots, he grabs the crucifix off the wall and informs his teacher that the cross represents her religion but not his. In an attempt at intercultural mediation, the teacher proposes that Nader explain his religious principles to the class so that everyone can learn something. In a defiant response he abruptly leaves the school, never to return except on a brief occasion some days later when expediency requires it.

The stakes of Nader's divided loyalties emerge in the course of lunch at his parents' home the following day. The family home is presented as a typical Italian working-class apartment. The only element that distinguishes it from thousands of similar homes in Italy is a tapestry marked with a Koranic inscription prominently displayed on the wall. Proceeding in a spontaneous mixture of Arabic and Italian, the conversation at lunch similarly reveals the hybrid influences underpinning this diasporic household.[62] After Nader's mother chides him for not attending prayers at the mosque and for staying out beyond his mandated curfew, he confronts the family with the explosive news that he has an Italian girlfriend—indeed, a *fidanzata*, a term that implies a committed relationship.

The ensuing disagreement pits the parents' insistence on the inadmissibility of premarital sex against Nader's defense of the liberal sexual practices of his Italian peers. The mother's opposition to Nader's relationship is clear: the sexual practices and moral values of Italians are at odds with those of the Muslim community and cannot be tolerated by the family. Mahmoud, an Egyptian friend or relative also present in the scene, agrees, citing the Islamic concept of haram, the forbidden. Nader appeals to his father, asking him to admit that he, too, had been sexually active at the age of sixteen. Shaking his head, the father responds, rather sheepishly, that this was not the case. Somewhat less firmly than his wife, he reiterates the prohibition against premarital sex.

In the course of the escalating argument, Nader provocatively frames his parents' resistance to his pursuit of an active sexual relationship with Brigitte as a putative rejection of his heterosexuality. If they refuse to allow him to behave like a heterosexual—he asks—is he supposed to be with men instead? Ignoring his provocation, the mother makes clear that she will never accept an Italian woman as Nader's companion or wife and warns him to end his relationship with Brigitte. She offers her explanation in Arabic: "We are not against them; we are different from them."

Despite Nader's intense defiance of his apparently weak father and of his mother's effort to impose Islamic law, the film subtly begins to raise doubts about the teenager's status as a heteronormative male, at least in the terms laid down by Italian society. The first time he tries to have sex with Brigitte following the heated argument with his family at lunch, he finds he cannot perform. He is distracted, he says, because her father is firing shots with his newly acquired rifle on the rooftop of the building along with a male friend. Nader succeeds in consummating the relationship, however, on a subsequent evening when he improvises an outdoor shelter at the edge of the woods in order to spend the night there with Brigitte. The mise-en-scène of their encounter is both touching and ridiculous: Nader has spray-painted the key words from a sentimental pop song on a sheet that he hangs nearby, and as the pair prepares to make love, he plays the same song on his cell phone. Whereas in a conventional love scene, extradiegetic music envelops the aural landscape, pulling the audience in to identify with the emotion of the moment, the inferior sound quality of the song emanating from Nader's phone serves to heighten a general sense of approximation and discomfort. The sex scene itself, shot in lighting conditions that approximate near-darkness, is accompanied only by sounds of breathing and grunting, underlining the awkwardness of the couple's circumstances. Brigitte's complaints about her discomfort upon waking up in the cold morning air suggest that this was scarcely a satisfying initiation.

Another element that raises uncertainty about Nader's heteronormative status is his relationship with his Egyptian friend or cousin Mahmoud. In the early scenes of the film, the older youth chides Nader like a self-appointed big brother, making clear that he disapproves of the teenager's relationship with Brigitte. In a subsequent scene, where the hungry Nader scrounges up enough money to buy a hot dog from a vendor near the beach, Mahmoud nags him about Islamic dietary prohibitions. But when Nader finds himself locked out of the family home, Mahmoud is the one to whom he turns, and he is allowed to stay for one night at the crowded men's hostel where Mahmoud lives. Two nights later, when Nader is obliged to sleep outdoors, Mahmoud helps him to improvise a sleeping space in a beachside shelter and lies down with him. Reaching toward Nader, he begins to caress his face and draws closer to him under the blanket. Although Nader harshly rejects Mahmoud's gesture, he remains beside him. Departing at dawn without a word, he has no further interaction with Mahmoud for the remainder of the film. The sequence in the beach shelter does not suggest in any easily legible way that Nader might be gay, and his sharp rebuke suggests at least that he does not wish to be perceived this way. Yet his presence alongside Mahmoud for the remainder of the night undercuts some of the certainty suggested by his initial rejection. It also gives context to the almost theatrical sentimentality he displays vis-à-vis Brigitte and his violent machismo on other occasions,

Figure 6.4. Screen capture. Stefano, Alì, and Brigitte. *Alì ha gli occhi azzurri* (2012)

getting into a fight in a disco, buying a gun to deal with the injured youth's angry relatives, and verbally attacking the cops when stopped in traffic.

These instances suggest that Nader is attempting at all costs to define the meaning of masculinity in his own diasporic context, a quest that is underpinned by a measure of tacit homophobia and a binary understanding of sexual identities and positionalities. His suggestion to his parents that by prohibiting him from engaging in such a relationship, they are prompting him to "be with men" is, of course, merely a provocation. Throughout the film he attempts with great resolve to be *like* men (specifically, like Italian heterosexual men) rather than to be *with* men in the sexual sense. Yet his relationship with Stefano ultimately unsettles this distinction between identification and desire.

Stefano has been Nader's closest companion since early childhood. Among the Italian characters in *Alì ha gli occhi azzurri*, only Stefano has blue eyes, suggesting the possibility that Nader's motivation for wearing blue lenses may lie at least in part in an attempt to resemble—or even mirror—his friend. Consistently throughout the film the two teenagers maintain a strong complicity, even when Stefano's father starts to worry about Nader's disruptive influence on his son. Together they progress toward increasingly violent behavior, and it is out of misguided loyalty to his friend that Nader gets involved in Stefano's fight with a Romanian youth, culminating with the stabbing of the Romanian, for which Nader is obliged to take responsibility. Later, out of fear of reprisal, he feels compelled to purchase a gun. But it is on Stefano that he will finally turn the weapon upon discovering a developing romantic interest between his friend and his own younger sister Laura.

When, toward the end of the film, Nader sees Stefano kissing Laura in a car, he bashes the car window and screams at his sister in Arabic, telling her to go home. The question arises, however, as to whether it is Stefano's betrayal of the relationship he shared with Nader or Laura's betrayal of her religious upbringing that most enrages him. The final exchange between the two friends reveals Stefano's unawareness of the complexity of Nader's distress. When Stefano asks his friend why he wants sexual freedom for himself but not for his sister, Nader cannot grasp the logic of the question. The incommensurability of their points of reference becomes even more evident when Stefano tries an argument more specifically tied to the homosocial ethos of Italian male friendships: Since Laura is going to have sexual relations with a man sooner or later, isn't it better that this man be Nader's close friend rather than some stranger? This question serves to drive Nader over the top, and Stefano, who knows that his friend is armed, takes flight. Nader then chases him onto the familiar rocky shore, firing several shots that miss their mark. Whether his failure to fire directly at Stefano is accidental or not, it offers a further symptom of Nader's ambivalent relationship with the model of aggressive Western masculinity that he had previously seemed to embrace.

The film's central hermeneutic question is how Nader's pursuit of adult masculinity can evolve in light of his conflicting cultural loyalties, his binary understanding of sexual behaviors and identities, and his fraught relationship to Western modernity. Confronted on the one hand with the quietly prohibitive yet ultimately passive behavior of his Muslim father and on the other with the hypermasculine swagger of the males he befriends outside his home, his initial impulse is to embrace the full-blooded heteronormativity exemplified by his Italian acquaintances. His choice results in homelessness, both literal and symbolic. Over the course of the week he spends in exile from his parents' home, he experiences hunger, cold, and sleep deprivation, hardships that are the consequences of a confused attempt to make sense of his fractured sense of belonging.

Despite the forward movement of the days of the week appearing on the screen, Nader's narrative trajectory is more circular than progressive. *Alì hagli occhi azzurri* begins on the rocky shore, and on the final day of the film's action, Nader ends up back in the same location, where he stages his failed attempt to shoot Stefano. This liminal space is, of course, his symbolic home. Belonging nowhere, his efforts at mobility are perpetually thwarted. Though constantly in motion, he is suspended or banned from various sites (his parents' home, Stefano's home, Brigitte's home, the disco, and Mahmoud's hostel), ending up with nowhere to go. It gradually becomes clear that the teenager's apparent desire to belong to mainstream Italian society is fruitless, and in his continued refusal to make peace with his family, he is ultimately deprived of any sense of belonging. This is Nader's conundrum, which the film refuses to wrap up in any definitive way, highlighting instead the aporia of his circumstances through the melodramatic excess of his tears.

The film's concluding scene, set in the Sarhan home at dinnertime, serves to reinforce the final impasse. A rapid establishing shot of the television screen indicates that the family has been watching an Al Jazeera news report of a massive protest in Cairo's Tahrir Square. Subsequent shots reveal Nader's parents and sister, Laura, seated on three sides of the dinner table. A fourth place has been set, located at the center of the shot, but it is unoccupied, revealing that Nader has not yet returned to the family. While eating, each member of the family intermittently glances at the events unfolding on television. By now, however, the television screen is no longer directly visible to the viewer. It is located instead in the offscreen space, in a spot close to the position of the camera lens. Thus, as the family members watch the news on television, they appear to be looking straight at the film viewer, rupturing the diegetic effect. Examining the composition of the shot more closely, the viewer can discern the scene that is absorbing the characters in a reflection flickering on a darkened windowpane behind them. It is with this poignant tableau that the image fades to black.

The film's final shot thus establishes a complex perceptual field, highlighting issues of presence and absence, of visibility and invisibility, of seeing and being seen. The doubling or mirroring performed by the mise-en-scène also evokes the condition of the diasporic subject, the troubled Nader, who, though excluded physically from the scene, is clearly on everyone's mind as his unoccupied place setting is located at the center of the shot. With the irruption of contemporary world politics into the domestic routine of the diasporic Egyptian family via the Arabic-language news broadcast, the narrative's temporal framework is pinpointed in January 2011, inviting the audience to consider Nader's story against a backdrop of broader geopolitical conflicts. For the Sarhan family the realities unfolding in Cairo are mediated by a single screen—the television set in their home—while the same images are remediated more faintly for the benefit of the viewers on the windowpane behind the characters. Yet, despite this process of imperfect remediation, the viewers' real, temporal distance from the images unfolding in January 2011 provide an enhanced register of legibility, thanks to historical hindsight. These, after all, are the events that precipitated the broadly based uprisings known as the Arab Spring and the subsequent upheavals across the Middle East. The consequences of these events are still playing out on the global stage, with large-scale uprooting, disruptions, and the constant flow of refugees and other migrants to the northern shore of the Mediterranean. The film thus invites its audience to consider what shifts will occur for its protagonist, in terms of identity, identification, and belonging, vis-à-vis the ongoing flow of Middle Eastern and Maghrebi refugees into the cities of Europe and beyond.

Conclusion

Apart from the comedies mentioned at the outset, the films I have examined in this chapter explore different expressive registers and combinations of genre elements to communicate the complexities of the transnational moment. As I have shown, *Gomorra* effectively mimics the ways in which migrant subjectivities are eclipsed both in Italian social life and audiovisual representation but accords little agency to the migrants themselves. The remaining three films, by contrast, foreground the presence of their migrant or second-generation subjects, allowing these characters to dominate the visual field. Insofar as their protagonists' hopes, dreams, and assumptions are repeatedly challenged or thwarted, misread or misunderstood, the viewer is actively called upon to identify with them, prompted by signifying conventions associated with the melodramatic mode. Both *Good Morning Aman* and *Alì ha gli occhi azzurri* poignantly deny their characters forward movement or resolution, leaving them at an impasse that reflects little change from their original positions. If *Io sono Li* visualizes a happy ending for its Chinese protagonist, it is at the cost of other migrant characters in the film's diegetic world. In this sense, the three films project a desolate if not entirely hopeless view of Italy's multiethnic present.

Although none of the films discussed here includes direct references to Italian colonialism, their narratives unfold against a backdrop that implies a lingering influence of the colonial legacy with its enduring but often disavowed racism. The films also refer with different levels of explicitness to the enmeshment of contemporary Italy in neocolonial capitalism, whose destructive economic effects on the most disenfranchised members of the population—including immigrants—are unlikely to abate. While it can scarcely be claimed that these Italian films contribute in a substantial way to the overcoming of embedded racist discourses, they nonetheless participate in the reformulation of the cinematic imaginary, deploying new combinations of noir and melodrama to convey the anxieties subtending the intersubjective encounters in which the ongoing effects of the colonial legacy might ultimately be interrogated and transformed.

Notes

1. ISTAT, http://www.istat.it/it/immigrati (accessed September 30, 2017).

2. According to data provided by ISTAT, between 2001 and 2011, the number of Italy's foreign residents grew from 1.3 million to 4 million, or an increase of 201.7 percent, contrasting with an increase of merely 4.3 percent in the national population as a whole. See ISTAT, http://www.istat.it/it/immigrati (accessed September 30, 2017).

3. Two offbeat comedies are exceptions from an earlier period: *Sud side stori* (South Side Story, Roberta Torre, 2000) and *Zora la vampira* (Zora the Vampire, Manetti Bros., 2000).

4. Revealing a range of comedic tonalities, comedies featuring immigrant characters produced in Italy in recent years include Claudio Cupellini's *Lezioni di cioccolato* (Chocolate Lessons, 2007); Paolo Genovese and Luca Miniero's *Questa notte è ancora nostra* (Tonight Is Still Ours, 2008); Cristina Comencini's *Bianco e nero* (Black and White, 2008); Carlo Verdone's *Io loro e Lara* (Me, Them and Lara 2009); Paola Randi's *Into Paradiso* (Into Paradise, 2010); Francesco Patierno's *Cose dell'altro mondo* (2011); Alessio Maria Federici's *Lezioni di cioccolato 2* (Chocolate Lessons 2, 2011); Fariborz Kamkari's *Pitza e Datteri* (Pizza and Dates, 2015); Luca

Miniero's *Non c'è più religione* (There's No Religion Anymore, 2016); and Salvatore Allocca's *Taranta On the Road* (2017) and Gennaro Nunziante's *Che bella giornata*. For an analysis of the deployment of genre hybridity and satire in three of these films, see Gaoheng Zhang, "Comedy Film and Immigration to Italy: Reading Masculinity, Hybridity, and Satire in *Lezioni di cioccolato* (2007), *Questa notte è ancora nostra* (2008), and *Into Paradiso* (Into Paradise 2010)," in Schrader and Winkler, *Cinemas of Italian Migration*, 263–79.

5. Although never distributed abroad, *Che bella giornata* earned a staggering total of 43,474,047 euro at the Italian box office, which surpassed the record previously set for Italian releases by Roberto Benigni's *La vita è bella* (*Life Is Beautiful*, 1997). See Vito Fatiguso, "La classifica delle pellicole che hanno realizzato più incassi: Zalone contro Cameron," *Corriere del Mezzogiorno. Spettacoli*, January 2, 2016. https://corrieredelmezzogiorno.corriere.it/bari/spettacoli/cards/italia-cinema-6-film-record/che-bella-giornata-43474047-euro.shtml?refresh_ce-cp (accessed July 21, 2018).

6. Andrea D'Addio, "Che bella giornata—La nostra recensione," Film.it, January 7, 2011, http://www.film.it/recensione/art/che-bella-giornata-la-nostra-recensione-7881/ (accessed July 21, 2018).

7. Derek Duncan, "Double Time: Facing the Future in Migration's Past," *California Italian Studies* 2, no. 1 (2011): 1–26, http://escholarship.org/uc/item/38q389mk.

8. Duncan, 6.

9. Paolo Russo, "Migration Told through Noir Conventions in *La sconosciuta* and *Gomorra*," in Bond, Bonsaver, and Falloppa, *Destination Italy*, 377–96.

10. See David Desser, "Global Noir: Genre Film in the Age of Transnationalism," in *Film Genre Reader III*, ed. Barry Keith Grant (Austin: University of Texas Press, 2003), 516–36; and Jennifer Fay and Justus Nieland, *Film Noir: Hard-Boiled Modernity and the Cultures of Globalization* (New York: Routledge, 2010).

11. *Gomorra*'s domestic takings were a mere $1,579,146, in comparison with earnings of $33,282,383 on foreign markets. See "Gomorrah," Box Office Mojo, http://www.boxofficemojo.com/movies/?id=gomorrah.htm (accessed August 20, 2017).

12. Roberto Saviano, *Gomorra: Viaggio nell'impero economico e nel sogno di dominio della camorra* (Milan: Mondadori, 2006); in English as Roberto Saviano, *Gomorrah: A Personal Journey into the Violent International Empire of Naples' Organized Crime System*, trans. Virginia Jewiss (New York: Farrar, Straus, Giroux, 2008).

13. See Rachel Donadio, "Living Where Crime Conquers All," *New York Times*, February 5, 2009, http://www.nytimes.com/2009/02/08/movies/08dona.html?pagewanted=all&_r=0 (accessed July 18, 2018).

14. See, for example, Silvia Carlorosi, "Neorealism, Cinema of Poetry, and Italian Contemporary Cinema," in *Global Neorealism: The Transnational History of a Film Style*, ed. Saverio Giovacchini and Robert Sklar (Oxford, MS: University Press of Mississippi, 2011), 240–56; and Roberta Di Carmine, "The Cinema of Matteo Garrone," *Wide Screen* 1, no. 2 (2010), http://widescreenjournal.org/index.php/journal/article/view/39/57.

15. See Russo, "Migration Told through Noir." See also Fabrizio Cilento, "Saviano, Garrone, *Gomorrah*: Neorealism and Noir in the Land of the Camorra," *Fast Capitalism* 8, no. 1 (2011), http://www.uta.edu/huma/agger/fastcapitalism/8_1/cilento8_1.html (February 2, 2017).

16. Russo, "Migration Told through Noir," 391.

17. According to Russo, "The aggregated data regarding these three stories reveal that twenty narrative units (of a total of forty-nine), corresponding to 27'30" out of around 71' in total—that is, more than one third—feature the related protagonists dealing with immigrants." Russo, 388.

18. For a discussion of Giorgio Agamben's formulation of this term, see chapter 1.

19. Russo, "Migration Told through Noir," 391.
20. Marcantonio, *Global Melodrama*.
21. See Marcia Landy, "The Italian Melodrama in the Italian Cinema 1929–1943," in *Imitations of Life: A Reader on Film and Television Melodrama*, ed. Marcia Landy (Wayne State University, 1991); and Maggie Günsberg, *Italian Cinema: Gender and Genre* (New York: Palgrave Macmillan, 2004).
22. Louis Bayman, "Melodrama as Realism in Italian Neorealism," in *Realism and the Audiovisual Media*, ed. Lucia Nagib and Cecilia Mello (New York: Palgrave Macmillan, 2009), 53.
23. Marcantonio, *Global Melodrama*.
24. Karl Schoonover, *Brutal Vision: The Neorealist Body in Postwar Italian Cinema* (Minneapolis: University of Minnesota Press, 2012); Marcantonio, *Global Melodrama*, 127.
25. Marcantonio, *Global Melodrama*, 127.
26. Peter Brooks, *The Melodramatic Imagination: Balzac, Henry James, Melodrama, and the Mode of Excess* (New York: Yale University Press, 1975). Gramsci, however, locates the birth of melodrama in the sixteenth century.
27. Brooks, *Melodramatic Imagination*, xiii.
28. Brooks, 4–5.
29. Marcantonio, *Global Melodrama*, 148.
30. Sandro Mezzadra and Federico Rahola, "The Postcolonial Condition: A Few Notes on the Quality of Historical Time in the Global Present," *Postcolonial Text* 2, no. 1 (2006), http://postcolonial.org/index.php/pct/article/viewArticle/393/819.
31. I use the term "differential inclusion" as formulated in Sandro Mezzadra and Brett Neilson's work on borderscapes, broadening its application to include the discriminatory practices governing migrant and second-generation subjects already residing within the borders of Italy. See Mezzadra and Neilson, "Borderscapes of Differential Inclusion."
32. For this and other relevant statistical information on migrations, see "Cestim on-line: Sito di documentazione sui fenomeni migratori," Centro Studi Immigrazione, http://www.cestim.it (accessed July 16, 2018).
33. These stereotypes include the notion that "the Chinese never die," a claim that encapsulates a widespread popular belief that the identity papers of deceased Chinese immigrants are routinely passed along to new arrivals while concealing the death of the individuals involved. In a more elaborate version of the same claim, it is said that the bodies of the dead are secretly shipped back to China in refrigerator containers for eventual burial, a scenario that is famously reiterated in the opening pages of Roberto Saviano's *Gomorra*.
34. The most obvious of these visual references is the recurring presence of red lanterns in the mise-en-scène, directly evoking Zhang Yimou's internationally successful *Raise the Red Lantern* (1991).
35. Segre's academic background is in sociology (he holds a doctorate in the sociology of communication), and his initial professional activities had brought him to Africa with a non-profit organization, where the circumstances surrounding contemporary migrations from the sub-Saharan region came vividly to his attention, later inspiring both *A sud di Lampedusa* (South of Lampedusa, 2007) and *Come un uomo sulla terra* (Like a Man on the Earth, 2009). He also co-directed an earlier film on migration to Italy from Albania, *A metà* (Half Way, produced by Andrea Segre, Francesco Cressati, Dritan Taulla, and Elidon Lamani, 2002). His most recent feature film, *L'ordine delle cose* (The Order of Things, 2017), explores the treatment of migrants from the sub-Saharan region in Libya in the post-Gaddafi era.
36. See Alison Frank and Andrea Segre, "Andrea Segre: Confronting Difference," The Free Library, *CineAction*, September 3, 2012, http://www.thefreelibrary.com/Andrea+Segre%3a+confronting+difference.-a0284222750 (accessed July 20, 2018).

37. Tao Zhao is best known for her work in films by the prominent sixth-generation Chinese director Jia Zhangke.
38. Frank and Segre, "Andrea Segre."
39. Cindy Hing-Yuk Wong, "'The Chinese Who Never Die': Spectral Chinese and Contemporary European Cinema," *Asian Cinema* 23, no. 1 (2012): 25.
40. Eve Kosofsky Sedgwick, *Between Men: English Literature and Male Homosocial Desire* (New York: Columbia University Press, 1985), 21–27.
41. Rey Chow, "The Dream of a Butterfly," in *Ethics after Idealism: Theory, Culture, Ethnicity, Reading* (Bloomington: Indiana University Press, 1998), 74–97.
42. Chow, 82.
43. See Homi K. Bhabha, "The World and the Home," in *Dangerous Liaisons: Gender, Nation and Postcolonial Perspectives*, ed. Anne McClintock, Aamir Mufti, and Ella Shohat (Minneapolis: Minnesota University Press, 1997), 445.
44. Julia Kristeva, *Strangers to Ourselves*, trans. Leon S. Roudiez (New York: Columbia University Press, 1991).
45. The use of "second generation" to translate *seconda generazione* may be misleading in English as this term is generally used in the United States to describe the grandchildren of immigrants rather than their sons and daughters. Since members of Italy's *seconda generazione* are often bereft of Italian citizenship there has been a long-standing political battle to make the acquisition of citizenship less complex and challenging for them. Fred Kuwornu's landmark documentary *18 Ius soli* (2012) offers a sharp critique of the difficulty of attaining citizenship status for those born in Italy to parents who are not Italians.
46. Despite his initial charm in *Fratelli d'Italia*, Sarhan is likely to alienate most audiences when, in the course of a conversation with his Italian friends, he becomes emboldened by the racist comments made by his interlocutors and launches into a diatribe calling for the extermination of Jews.
47. Giovanni Berardi, "Claudio Giovannesi: sui luoghi (e sui temi) di Pier Paolo Pasolini (e Sergio Citti)," TXDRVRS, December 17, 2014, https://www.taxidrivers.it/44467/rubriche/claudio-giovannesi-sui-luoghi-e-sui-temi-di-pier-paolo-pasolini-e-sergio-citti.html.
48. Cesare Zavattini, *Neorealismo* (Milan: Bompiani, 1979), 103.
49. Alessia Ricciardi, "The Italian Redemption of Cinema: Neorealism from Bazin to Godard," *Romanic Review* 97, nos. 3–4 (2006): 484.
50. Jonathan Goldberg, *Melodrama: An Aesthetics of Impossibility* (Durham, NC: Duke University Press, 2016).
51. Pier Paolo Pasolini, *Alì dagli occhi azzurri* (Rome: Garzanti, 1965).
52. The original text of "Profezia" is available on several internet sites as it has gained renewed attention in recent years due to its alleged prediction of the immigrant crisis.
53. For Pasolini in the 1960s even parts of Rome were aligned with what he called "Africa," since the shanty towns of the urban periphery were populated by migrants who had moved there from southern Italy and from other impoverished areas closer to the capital. In these communities he found the *ragazzi di vita*, the lawlessly exuberant boys and young men of the subproletariat who dominate his early writings and films. With the encroachment of consumer capitalism in subsequent years, Pasolini revised his optimistic perception of the Italian underclass.
54. Nader's quest for blue eyes is reminiscent of Pecola, protagonist of Toni Morrison's first novel, *The Bluest Eye*. Assuming that her blackness is equated with ugliness, Pecola dreams of possessing white skin and a pair of blue eyes. See Toni Morrison, *The Bluest Eye* (New York: Holt, Reinhart, Winston, 1970). In both cases the character perceives that it may be necessary to transcend the racial marker of dark skin and dark eyes to achieve greater self-acceptance.

This impulse suggests that the myth of white superiority has been internalized by the nonwhite subject.

55. See Bhabha, *The Location of Culture*, 66–84. Bhabha's understanding of the stereotype places an emphasis on the ambivalence of colonial authority and its orders of identification.

56. Bhabha, 66.

57. Bhabha, 92.

58. Although Pino Pelosi was tried and imprisoned for Pasolini's murder, controversy still surrounds the actual circumstances of the crime.

59. Derek Duncan, "Loving Geographies."

60. Harry Benshoff and Sean Griffin, "General Introduction," in *Queer Cinema: The Film Reader*, ed. Harry Benshoff and Sean Griffin (New York: Routledge, 2004), 17.

61. Duncan, "Loving Geographies," 171.

62. An astute analysis of the use of language in this film and in Giovannesi's earlier documentary, *Fratelli d'Italia*, is provided in Derek Duncan, "Translanguaging: Claudio Giovannesi's Postcolonial Practices," *Transnational Cinemas* 7, no. 2 (2016): 196–209.

Afterword
ACCENTED AND TRANSNATIONAL FILMMAKING IN ITALY

SINCE 1990 A substantial corpus of literary texts has been produced by Italian immigrant writers either fictionalizing or recounting in autobiographical mode the experiences of foreigners attempting to live and work in Italy.[1] Described as "migrant literature," "postcolonial literature," or categorized under other designations, this rich and varied archive has no direct equivalent in the world of cinema. Given the financial demands of film production and the institutional challenges of distribution and exhibition, the scarcity of feature films made by migrants is hardly surprising. As Mariagiulia Grassilli has pointed out, Italy does not offer the type of specific institutional support for minority filmmaking that exists in several other European countries, where the value of cultural diversity is publicly acknowledged.[2] In addition, Italy still lacks the type of large, long-established ethnic communities that have given rise to the production of distinctive clusters of diasporic films in France, Germany, and the United Kingdom. Since 1997, however, a handful of migrant, transnational, or second-generation filmmakers, working alone or in collaboration with Italian directors, have succeeded in making a number of short films, documentaries, and full-length features that creatively construct the migrants' experience of uprooting, dislocation, and nonbelonging from the perspective of the outsider.

The best-known migrant filmmaker active in Italy is unquestionably the Turkish-born Ferzan Özpetek, who has become a prominent figure in the Italian film industry and has, to date, directed eleven feature films. Although three of these, *Il bagno turco* (*Steam: Turkish Bath*, 1997), *Harem Suare* (1999), and *Rosso Istanbul* (Red Istanbul, 2017), are set in Turkey, his remaining eight films unfold in Italy and only occasionally feature non-Italian characters in important roles. Indeed, over the past fifteen years, the director's output has become progressively more similar to that of his mainstream Italian counterparts. With some minor exceptions, his Italian films remain largely unconcerned with the conflicts and dilemmas that often characterize the lives of immigrants and other diasporic subjects. Nonetheless, through the subtle deployment of specific musical references, the use of allusive "exotic" details in the mise-en-scène, and the frequent casting of Turkish actress Serra Yılmaz in minor roles, his work obliquely acknowledges the diversity and pluralism of contemporary Italian society. For this reason, Rada Bieberstein has astutely defined Özpetek as a *transcultural* rather than a *migrant* director.[3] Films by other migrant filmmakers such as Mohamed Zineddaine, Rachid Benhadj, and Edmond Budina, which highlight the interface of the local and the global, address in a more direct fashion the challenges facing migrants traveling to Italy or attempting to make their home there.[4]

In 2001, the publication of Hamid Naficy's influential study *Accented Cinema* drew critical attention to the rapidly growing body of transcultural films that had emerged in various parts of the world over the previous fifteen years. What Naficy describes as "accented" films do not fit within the traditional framework of national cinema since they occupy interstitial spaces that can be identified as *both* local and global.[5] Indeed, to some extent, this paradigm is an extension of auteur theory in the sense that, at the thematic level, accented films are influenced by the filmmakers' own experiences and worldviews.[6]

Although Naficy distinguishes three types of accented filmmakers based on the various kinds of geographical and cultural displacement that they have experienced, only one of these categories, that of exilic filmmakers, applies to Italy's immigrant directors, such as Benhadj, Budina, and Zineddaine, who have succeeded in making at least one feature film in Italy that focuses on migration, exile, or border crossing. According to Naficy, exilic filmmakers tend to maintain an ambivalent relation with both homeland and adopted country, and their films share similar themes, narrative structures, and visual forms as well as distinctive patterns of production, distribution, and reception. These characteristics can indeed be detected to varying degrees in Rachid Benhadj's *L'albero dei destini sospesi* (The Tree of Suspended Destinies, 1997), Edmond Budina's *Lettere al vento* (Letters in the Wind, 2004), and Mohamed Zineddaine's *Ti ricordi di Adil?* (Do You Remember Adil?, 2008), all of which highlight narratives of maritime crossing.[7] The topos of journeying or return is a major preoccupation of all three narratives, which are deeply invested in issues of territoriality, rootedness, and geography, issues identified by Naficy as prominent themes in exilic cinema. Moreover, each of these films has at least some connection with the biography of the filmmaker, bringing to the screen the geographical and cultural terrain best known to him.

Although *Io l'altro*, written and directed by Mohsen Melliti and discussed in chapter 5, might appear at first to belong to this category, it differs from the films mentioned above insofar that it features only Italian performers, is focalized mainly through the subjectivity of the Italian protagonist, and uses only the Italian language or a Sicilian variant. The film is, in fact, clearly addressed to Italian viewers, visibly foregrounding the star power of its leading actor, Raoul Bova. The films by Benhadj, Budina, and Zineddaine, by contrast, have a distinctive, transnational mode of address and feature actors who are unknown in Italy.[8] Unlike *Io, l'altro*, these films have not obtained commercial distribution in Italy and have been seen only on the festival circuit or on television.[9]

Although the "accented" feature films emerging in Italy in the first decade of the twenty-first century are unlikely to be screened again, the documentaries co-directed by Ethiopian refugee Dagmawi Yimer from 2008 onward continue to be screened in noncommercial settings in Italy and abroad. Yimer made his first feature-length documentary, *Come un uomo sulla terra* (Like a Man on Earth), in 2008 in collaboration with Andrea Segre and Riccardo Biadene under the auspices of the ZaLab collective.[10] Recounting his own year-long journey from Addis Ababa to Italy by way of various holding centers in Libya, where he and his fellow migrants endured extortion, brutality, and long periods of detention, Yimer engages in a series of riveting onscreen conversations with several other Ethiopian men and women who had arrived in Italy under similar circumstances.

The broader political context of *Come un uomo sulla terra* was the singing of the Treaty of Friendship, Partnership and Cooperation on August 30, 2008, by Silvio Berlusconi and Muammar Gaddafi, with which Italy and Libya officially put the memory of Italy's colonial-era abuses behind them and laid out profitable business arrangements for the future. These arrangements included Italy's continued support for detention centers like those where Yimer and his fellow travelers were imprisoned in order to stem northbound migration. At the time of its initial release, *Come un uomo sulla terra* thus functioned as a consciousness-raising experience for many Italians previously unaware of the abuses perpetuated in Libya under Italian sponsorship. Available on DVD, the documentary has been shown repeatedly in social centers, universities, schools, and similar settings in different parts of the world, even after the change of regime following Gaddafi's assassination in 2011. Since the circumstances experienced by sub-Saharan Africans traveling through Libya today have not changed substantially since the Gaddafi era, it retains an important testimonial dimension and a haunting affective impact.

Yimer has co-directed three additional documentaries on different aspects of migration since that time: *C.A.R.A. Italia* (2010), *Soltanto il mare* (Only the Sea, 2010), and *Va' pensiero* (*Walking Stories*, 2013), sharpening his artistic vision with each successive production.[11] Given their genesis within the framework of audiovisual activism and their specific modalities of distribution and exhibition, the "cinematic" status of these films is clearly anomalous. Nonetheless, given the consistency and distinctiveness of his contribution to contemporary documentary filmmaking, it is imperative to include Yimer in any formal acknowledgment of Italy's "accented" filmmakers.

In the second decade of the twenty-first century, a handful of young migrant or second-generation diasporic filmmakers began to obtain commercial distribution for their work, staking out new territory in the Italian film industry either by abandoning their "accents" (at least provisionally) or by embracing popular genres in an effort to reach as wide an audience as possible. An example of the former strategy is the case of Tunisian-born actor and filmmaker Hedy Krissane, who, after releasing a small number of stylistically accomplished shorts inspired by issues relating to migration, made his commercial debut with *Aspromonte* (2012). Funded largely by the Calabria Film Commission, this well-crafted, crowd-pleasing road movie starring veteran actor Franco Nero unfolds among the remote mountain locations and archaic traditions of the Italian peninsula's southernmost region. Unlike the mise-en-scène characteristic of other immigrant directors, the "exotic" elements in *Aspromonte*—including the Greek-inflected speech of the Calabrian highlands—are entirely home grown.

Laura Halilovic's *Io rom romantica* (Me, a Romantic Romani Girl, 2014) and Fariborz Kamkari's *Pitza e datteri* (Pizza and Dates, 2015) are among the first "accented" films made by diasporic or second-generation directors to achieve the designation of "films of cultural interest" from the Italian Ministry for Cultural Heritage and Tourism, accompanied by a subsidy of 200,000 euro each.[12] Receipt of this award marks a new phase in the institutional acceptance of second-generation directors creating films that acknowledge the distinctive perspectives of migrant communities. Addressed to national audiences, both films deploy a comedic register to narrate scenarios of conflicting values and traditions, foregrounding customs and experiences unfamiliar to many Italian citizens.

Halilovic, who identifies as Roma, was born in Turin to parents who had migrated from Bosnia decades earlier; Kamkari, by contrast, was born in Rome to Kurdish parents who had migrated from Iran. Their respective films derive their humor at least in part from the willfully "colorful" gaze cast by the directors on their own constituencies—an extended Romani family in the first instance and Italy's heterogeneous Muslim community in the second. Featuring popular Italian actor Giuseppe Battiston as an eccentric Muslim convert, *Pitza e datteri* deploys some of the exuberant conventions of mainstream comedy that render it immediately consumable as easy entertainment. *Io rom romantica*, by contrast, does not rely on strokes of broad humor, although comic situations are certainly present in the film. One of the principal challenges it presents is linguistic since almost all of the dialogue is delivered in Romani, requiring subtitles for Italian audiences—an extremely rare circumstance in Italian comedy films. Made on a restricted budget and funded mainly by the Torino Piemonte Film Commission, *Io rom romantica* does not feature well-known Italian actors in leading roles. Instead, the more substantial parts are played by actors of Romani origin, almost all of them nonprofessional performers. The linguistic challenge presented by this comedy film, along with the absence of well-known actors in the principal roles, may have been responsible at least in part for its modest box office returns and lukewarm reception by reviewers.

Halilovic's film is nonetheless a milestone achievement, not least because it calls into question commonplace ethnic stereotypes and prejudices vis-à-vis what is arguably Italy's most despised minority community, the Roma. The director, who grew up in a Romani encampment near Turin Airport and later in a public housing project in La Falchera, north of the city, made *Io rom romantica*—her first feature—at the age of twenty-five, drawing on material explored in her earlier autobiographical documentary *Io, la mia famiglia rom e Woody Allen* (*Me, My Gypsy Family, and Woody Allen,* 2009). Like the documentary, the feature film highlights, on the one hand, the challenges presented to Italy's Romani community by hostile elements in Italian society and, on the other, the filmmaker's own struggle to pursue a career in filmmaking in the face of her family's insistence that she adhere to Romani tradition, which requires early endogamous marriage for all girls. Both documentary and feature film end with a narrative triumph (however modest) for female agency and ambition, a thematic development that makes Halilovic's films unique among those directed by migrant or diasporic directors.

Per un figlio (For a Child, 2017), the debut feature film of another young diasporic filmmaker—Verona-based Suranga Deshapriya Katugampala—is to some extent comparable to *Io, rom romantica*, as this, too, is a story of intercultural tensions and conflicting generational positions in a diasporic setting. Yet the films are formally quite different. Made on a shoestring budget and set in a drab landscape of provincial Veneto, *Per un figlio* draws its principal strength from the compelling performance of Sinhalese actress Kaushalya Fernando, who plays Sunita, a harried, middle-aged single mother from Sri Lanka trying to raise her teenage son (Julian Wejesekarain) in a country that remains foreign to her. Bound by the obligations of her work as a *badante*, which keeps her away from home for many hours every day, she is dismayed by the boy's lack of loyalty to their shared cultural origins and by his contempt for her own foreignness. The son's rebelliousness is reminiscent of Giovannesi's *Alì ha gli occhi azzurri*, but the intersubjective focus in this film alternates between mother and son, allowing the viewer to understand the intimate tensions of both positions and combining moments of deeply affecting drama with comical elements.

Neither the paradigm of national cinema nor the category of accented cinema can adequately accommodate all of the films created in Italy by immigrant, diasporic, or second-generation filmmakers. Indeed Jonas Carpignano's *Mediterranea* (2015) provides an important example of the inadequacy of these categorizations. Shot for the most part in Italy with an international cast consisting mostly of nonprofessional performers playing versions of themselves, this critically acclaimed independent feature film, which narrates the journey of a migrant from Burkina Faso to the orchards of southern Italy, might best be described as a transnational film.[13] First screened at the Cannes Film Festival in 2015 and subsequently the recipient of important awards, it has been distributed in several countries across the world. Yet this French-German-US coproduction (which received postproduction support from Dubai), did not obtain regular commercial distribution in Italy.

The son of an Italian father and an African American mother of Caribbean origins, Carpignano was born in New York City, spent part of his childhood in Rome, and was educated in the United States. He has lived in Rosarno, Calabria, in the extreme south of Italy, since 2010. Here he shot two award-winning short films inspired by local circumstances before proceeding with his first feature, *Mediterranea* (2016), which was followed shortly thereafter by a second, *A Ciambra* (2017). Clearly, the definitions "Italian," "Italian American," and "accented" all seem too reductive to encompass the transnational, transcultural, bilingual, and mixed-race profile of this young filmmaker.

Mediterranea opens a new space for thinking about the representation of migration in film and media, not only in Italy but also across the world. Given its transnational production and postproduction history, the broad geographical span of its locations, the multiplicity of cultures represented by its actors and characters, as well as the complex profile of the director himself, this film is of special interest to my focus on the relationship between filmmaking in Italy on the one hand and transnational influences and mobilities on the other. It also differs from the films I have previously discussed in this volume. First, it opens the Africa-Italy borderscape in ways that other films unfolding in similar geographical territories fail to acknowledge. It does this not only by visualizing in greater detail than the earlier films the challenges involved in crossing desert and sea but also by referencing the function of digital technologies in the migrants' subjective experience of these landscapes as they communicate with their families and with others by phone, internet, and social media across daunting physical distances.

Second, *Mediterranea* is shot through with an acknowledgment of the ways in which immigrant labor is racialized by Italian society. Furthermore, the film offers a creative mix of documentary and fictional elements, drawing on the collective experiences of its nonprofessional African, Italian, and Romani actors, who contribute their specific local knowledge and familiarity with the situations depicted in the film to its dialogue and narrative development.

Finally, and perhaps most importantly, *Mediterranea* is so far the only feature film produced in Italy that gives decisive focus to an act of immigrant protest. By reconstructing the controversial Rosarno riot of 2010, it effectively shifts the conventional image of the immigrant as a victim to one of agency and active resistance. In other words, it presents its viewers with images of immigrants' "anger, revolt, and empowerment" that undercut the tropes of victimhood found in most films about Italian immigration more effectively than any countervailing effort to create "positive" representations.[14]

Organized immigrant protest has become more frequent and visible in various countries and border zones across the globe in the past decade as immigrant groups have mobilized to denounce injustice, discrimination, and violence of various kinds. Investigating instances of dissent, resistance, and revolt in light of the conditions faced by regular and irregular migrants, asylum seekers, refugees, and other unwanted "illegal" persons, a recent volume of essays edited by Katarzyna Marciniak and Imogen Tyler highlights the centrality of aesthetics to these resistance movements.[15] Drawing on the work of Jacques Rancière and other theorists, this project explores the connections among politics, aesthetics, and protest, showing how acts of immigrant resistance disrupt the social order by giving visibility and audibility to subjectivities and perspectives habitually occluded.

The social order is described by Rancière as a "police order," since its norms and conventions determine the distribution of roles in communities along with the forms of exclusion operating within them. It is founded on what he terms the "distribution of the sensible," indicating the ways in which the visible and invisible, the sayable and unsayable, the audible and inaudible are tacitly established and enforced.[16] As Marciniak and Tyler indicate, the visibility and audibility of counter-representational practices, such as immigrant protest, overturn conventionally accepted perceptions and generate uncertainty about commonsense understandings of belonging and nonbelonging. Following Rancière, they further argue "the political is located not within the official workings of government or the hegemonic aesthetics of mass media, nor in the 'event' of protests themselves, but rather in the 'dissensus'—or the 'third space'—such protests can open up in the public sphere." While individual acts or local forms of immigrant protest may appear to have limited public impact, "the restaging and repetition of these acts form part of a critical practice of countermapping, which creates a transnational fabric of political resistance."[17] As I will show, *Mediterranea* participates precisely in this critical practice of countermapping.

The product of years of research and gestation, Carpignano's feature film builds on an earlier short titled *A Chjàna*. Sometimes described as a docufilm, it straddles the divide between dramatic realism and documentary. In this respect, it recalls Vittorio De Seta's *Lettere dal Sahara* (Letters from the Sahara, 2006), there is none of the idealization of the immigrant figure found in that earlier film. Instead there is anger and drama as well as irony and humor. Set in 2009 and 2010, *Mediterranea* unfolds mainly within the community of irregular African migrants who come to southern Calabria every winter to harvest citrus fruit in the orchards around Rosarno and the adjoining town of Gioia Tauro. These men endure appalling living and working conditions. Obliged to labor outdoors at the coldest time of year, they receive a negligible wage, and without visas or contracts, they remain at the mercy of the proprietors and foremen. Since undocumented migrants cannot obtain regular rental contracts without a permit to stay, they are obliged to sleep in improvised shelters, principally in abandoned warehouses and silos, without running water, electricity, or heating. In an area where the presence of the Ndrangheta (the Calabrian mafia) permeates daily life, the Africans have frequently experienced aggression at the hands of local residents, whose mounting hostility prompted the confrontation generally referred to as the Rosarno riot.[18]

In January 2010, as news spread that three African laborers had been shot at by a local man armed with a pneumatic rifle and one had been badly injured, several dozen migrants assembled in the streets of Rosarno to stage a protest. Two years earlier, in response to a similarly violent incident committed by local thugs, a group of migrants had organized a peaceful demonstration to publicly denounce the circumstances to which they were being subjected, but their protest had failed to produce any change. In contrast to the peaceful march of 2008, the 2010 protest rapidly became violent as the protesting migrants began to break store windows and torch cars. They were then attacked by hostile local youths, and the violence escalated further. This confrontation lasted for two days, during which many Africans and local people were injured, though none seriously. Called in to quell the violence, the riot police took the side of the locals, ordering the African immigrants to leave town in what has since been described as a pogrom. Over a thousand of them were thus forced to relinquish their scant means of livelihood. Many were sent to processing and detention centers, where they faced the real possibility of deportation, while others escaped and dispersed rapidly throughout the country. Working in Italy on the set of Spike Lee's *Miracle at St. Anna* (2008) when an earlier riot erupted, Carpignano traveled south to Rosarno in an attempt to make sense of the incidents he had witnessed on the national news.

Not long after the filmmaker's arrival in Calabria, he befriended Koudous Seihon, a young worker from Burkina Faso who had experienced the riot firsthand. Intrigued by Seihon's story, he began to formulate the idea for a film based the young man's migratory trajectory, inviting him to play the lead. This project initially resulted in the seventeen-minute short *A Chjàna*, which competed at the Venice film festival in 2011 and won the Controcampo award. Following this success, Carpignano was in a position to raise money to transform his project into a feature film and wrote the screenplay with the support of the Sundance Institute.

The conditions experienced by the migrant agricultural workers in Rosarno are at the heart of the film's narrative and are recounted from the perspective of a single migrant named Ayiva (Seihon). Carpignano has claimed that 90 percent of the events constructed in the film are inspired by the stories recounted to him by Seihon, with whom he lived while developing the script. *Mediterranea* begins just as Ayiva sets out for Italy from Burkina Faso. In the company of his close friend Abas (Alassane Sy), he makes his way north, crossing the desert through Algeria and Libya, partly aboard crowded transport trucks and partly on foot. Along the way, Ayiva is obliged to earn money in whatever way he can to finance the next part of the journey. As the two friends pass through the desert with other migrants, they are accosted by armed brigands and robbed of their money. Finally, after Ayiva successfully arranges to have some additional funds sent to him by a relative, they arrive at the port of Tripoli.

To better understand the experience of the trans-Saharan crossing, Carpignano flew to Burkina Faso and traveled along the desert route taken by many migrants until it became too dangerous to continue. *Mediterranea*'s desert scenes were, in fact, shot in the Moroccan Sahara. The nervous movements of the handheld camera (with Super 16mm film stock), the use of tight framing as well as panoramic shots, and the alternation of scenes shot in bright sunlight with those shot in relative darkness give the construction of the migrants' desert crossing a sense of urgency and danger. Punctuated by narrative ellipses, the entire sequence unfolds with minimal dialogue.

Some of the difficulties involved in irregular maritime crossings are also visualized by the film. When the travelers arrive at the harbor in Tripoli, for example, they discover that the agency they have paid to transport them across the Mediterranean will not provide a captain to steer the boat. After a brief argument, Ayiva volunteers to steer the flimsy vessel, though he has never traveled by sea before. During the night, a violent storm dramatically disrupts the voyage. As it becomes clear that the fragile boat is in danger, the audio track signals the passengers' shouts and screams, and a single flare reveals their desperate effort to catch the attention of a passing ship. At dawn, the image cuts to a wide shot of dozens of men and women clinging to the frame of a giant tuna net, waiting for rescue, as corpses appear to float beneath the water's surface. This strangely tranquil scene has a hallucinatory effect, communicating both the beauty of the sea and sky and a deep sense of human frailty.

At the conclusion of the pair's dramatic journey by sea—which brings them through a reception and processing facility presumably located in Lampedusa—Ayiva and Abas are given a thirty-day permit to remain in Italy, and they head for Rosarno, where Ayiva's older relative already lives. The sequences in Rosarno, which constitute the remainder of the film, provide a realistic reconstruction of the conditions endured by seasonal workers like Seihon in the period leading up to the riot of 2010. Without excessive insistence, it shows, for example, the squalor and discomfort in which the laborers are obliged to live in the absence of furniture, running water, and electrical power. Desperate to survive the cold, Ayiva steals an Italian traveler's suitcase and wears the clothes he finds inside; he then sells an MP3 player found in the same suitcase to acquire some cash.

Quickly observing the injustice of the harvesting system, where men are paid no more than twenty-five euros a day for backbreaking labor conducted in the rain and cold, Ayiva does not rebel. Instead, he calculates ways to earn more through overtime or by selling gloves to other laborers to make their work easier. His friend Abas, by contrast, is unwilling to tolerate the injustice meted out to all the immigrants, and some tension arises between the two friends. Little by little, Ayiva manages to send money back to Burkina Faso, where he has left his seven-year-old daughter in the care of his sister.

Mediterranea sketches out a social world that is layered and complex. The migrants appearing in the film come from a range of African countries, and they are heard speaking in French, English, Arabic, Italian, and their native African languages. Although the fruit pickers share the same living and working conditions, they do not react in identical ways. Different personalities and levels of endurance quickly emerge. The sub-Saharan Africans are seen interacting with other non-Italian groups, who enjoy differential levels of self-determination and well-being. Ayiva buys necessities from the Moroccans, who seem slightly better off than the black Africans, and from a canny Romani boy, whose family trades in objects of dubious provenance.[19] The men spend their evenings drinking beer and listening to hip-hop music in the company of several cheerful Nigerian women who seem to make a living selling sex in the surrounding area. As Ayiva implies when rejecting the idea that his sister and small daughter should join him in Italy, sex work appears to be the only form of livelihood available to black women in this part of the world.

Just as the community of outsiders is composed of different layers, so, too, is the world of the locals. Italian youths openly express their hostility and aggression toward the Africans, swerving close to them in their cars as they pass on the road as though trying to run them over and hovering menacingly at the locations where migrants gather for harmless amusement in the evenings. The Italians who oversee the work in the orchards may appear less threatening than these shadowy young men, but they clearly abuse their power, withholding wages on trivial pretexts and often goading and insulting the African laborers.

The film also reveals some benevolent figures in the local community. An Italian charity organization offers Italian language classes, immigration advice, and other forms of support for migrants of all origins. In one of the most striking scenes, a local woman (the octogenarian Norina Ventre, playing herself) offers a communal dinner at her farmhouse for dozens of African men in the area. As her guests take their seats at the table, she welcomes them, introducing herself as "Mamma Africa" and insisting that they remove their caps before they eat ("because in Italy, we do it this way"). Her teacherly, somewhat patronizing demeanor is softened later in the scene when she sings a folk song a cappella for those assembled at the meal.

The scenes that chart the evolving relationship between Ayiva and the owner of the orchard where he works are among the most significant in the film. As the young African begins to distinguish himself from the other workers because of his speed and efficiency, he attracts the attention of Rocco, the proprietor, who offers him additional work at his home. Ayiva is invited to have dinner with Rocco's family and develops a spontaneous complicity with Marta, the man's fifteen-year-old daughter, who is both teasingly defiant and fascinated by his appearance and background. In a remarkable conversation around the family dinner table, the Italian hosts perform a disconcerting mixture of hospitality and racialized condescension.

Taking his cue from Rocco's apparent openness, Ayiva subsequently asks for the man's assistance in obtaining a work permit so that he will not have to return to Africa and will be able instead to bring his daughter to Italy. Rocco refuses immediately with the excuse that, when his Italian relatives emigrated to the United States in the past, they turned to their own emigrant countrymen, not to outsiders, for a solution. With this pronouncement, which effectively instructs Ayiva to seek help from those who clearly cannot provide it, Rocco reveals the hollowness of his hospitality and his ongoing collusion with a system of profit making based on the subjugation and exploitation of the weakest, most precarious members of the labor force.

As the film suggests, underpaid irregular labor is more advantageous to the orchard owners, such as Rocco, than regulated labor. It is clear to the viewer that if Ayiva returns to Africa, he will soon be replaced by another undocumented migrant forced, because of his irregular status, to labor for the same pathetic wages. Despite the demonization of the figure of the irregular migrant in the global North, it is in the interest of the economy that the flow of migration from the global South be manipulated, accelerated, or slowed down rather than genuinely impeded. Writing on labor and migration in the first decade of the twenty-first century, Sandro Mezzadra and Brett Neilson argue that the border should not be understood as a fortress but rather as a kind of diaphragm or dam that serves global capitalism, shaping in violent ways the subjectivity of those laborers who traverse it: "As labor power travels, ducks and covers, traverses and remakes borders in various parts of the world, so its mobility is also shaped by real and violent processes of subjectification, which increasingly take place through the temporality of blocking, decelerating and accelerating as well as the correlate processes of differential inclusion."[20]

Mediterranea does not offer clear narrative closure as it remains uncertain to the viewers if the young African laborer, who has shown himself capable of remarkable resourcefulness and ingenuity throughout the narrative, will be able to surmount the problem of his imminently expiring permit. In the narrative economy of the film, Rocco's blunt rejection of Aviya's request for assistance is followed by a phone call informing him that two Africans have been shot by locals, and a protest is taking shape. It is at this moment that he assumes the position of active resistance.

Shot at night with limited illumination, the sequence that follows recreates the protest of January 2010 with striking visual economy and dramatic force. Alternating between tight framing and wide shots, the scenes are noisy and chaotic, showing the escalation of violence as protesting immigrants are challenged by local thugs. Ayiva, though thoughtful and measured in all of his actions up to this moment, joins in the process of torching cars and breaking windows. These events, shot from the perspective of the Africans and contextualized within the narrative as a response to abuses of which the viewer is already aware, are not presented as a random outbreak of violence on the part of angry migrants. On the contrary they emerge as a dramatic, collective appropriation of visibility and agency.

Retaining an important, historically documented detail, the film shows the protesting Africans carrying a white sheet inscribed with the words "Stop shooting blacks" and chanting these words in unison. A variation of this slogan was shown in television reports during the Rosarno uprising, pointing to the centrality of race in the migrants' perception of their own victimization at the hands of local forces. In Carpignano's references to the Rosarno protest, he persistently uses the term "race riots," although this term, or its Italian equivalent, was not used in public discourse at the time. Describing the events in this way is an important gesture as it acknowledges that the discourse of race is inextricably interwoven into the processes of subordination, dehumanization, and exploitation against which the Africans articulated their protest.

Ayiva's last conversation with his seven-year-old daughter, via Skype, constitutes the concluding scene of the film and is perhaps the most moving. Listening to the recording by Rihanna that he has sent her along with the gift of an MP3 player, the little girl dances joyfully to the music as she faces her father through the computer camera without realizing that he is on the verge of tears. When he cannot contain himself any longer and begins to weep, he cuts the connection. Clearly, he does not wish to reveal to his sister or child that he has been tempted to give up his migratory project. Although it seemed at the outset of this conversation that he was likely to announce his homecoming, the final shot puts this decision in doubt as he heads toward a location where his friends are beckoning him to join them.

There is much in *Mediterranea* that differs from conventional representations of Italian immigration. The binary oppositions that typify many narratives of migration are not dominant here. The Africans are far from idealized; though likable and even charismatic. For the most part Ayiva is remarkably considerate of the needs of others, but he steals a suitcase without hesitation when needs to do so. More importantly, this film is remarkably less interested in the Italian characters than almost all Italian films of this kind. There is therefore no hint of redemption or healing achieved by Italians through their interaction with the migrants.

Many of the environments and activities seen in this film are part of real migrants' everyday world but are curiously missing from other films—the money-transfer office, the call center, and the use of social media. Communication technology is by now crucial to all migrants' experience, enabling them to remain in contact with their families far away. Skype, Facebook, and cell phones feature in significant ways in *Mediterranea*, linking the characters and their homelands across the vast, globalized landscape. The characters in Africa listen to the same music as those in Italy (and presumably elsewhere across the globe). Ayiva's daughter dances joyfully to popular songs, just like Rocco's daughter, Marta, at her home in Rosarno. Music technology thus provides a sound bridge across social worlds and continents. Far from attached to outdated practices or ideas, the migrants of *Mediterranea* are technologically savvy and fully wired participants in the digital age.

For Marciniak and Tyler, immigrant protest takes multiple forms, from artistic production to organized public protest.[21] This form of protest also includes the creative remediation of immigrant resistance by the allies of immigrants, and it is precisely in this category that *Mediterranea* falls. All of these forms have an aesthetic aspect insofar as they function to make migrants visible in ways that transcend the dominant logic of negativity, superfluity, deficiency, or waste. Immigrants are, of course, already visible in hegemonic representations. Indeed, they are hypervisible as figures of abjection in mainstream news reports, as imputed terrorists in the sensational press, or as victims in humanitarian discourses. Against these configurations, many well-intentioned Italian films about migration promote a more benign form of immigrant visibility by suggesting the possible benefits that Italian-born citizens can derive from their presence. The same narratives, however, often dispense with the presence of the immigrant on Italian soil once the necessary effect on the Italian citizen has been achieved. *Mediterranea* interrupts these representational habits by striving to make visible the endurance, strength, and subjective experience of the immigrants who participated in the Rosarno riot. The complexity of their world, as constructed by the film, offers depth and meaning to the spectacle of their fiery protest.

Conclusion: National Cinema in a Transnational Frame

With their focus on migrant or diasporic subjectivities, the feature films discussed in this afterword provide very different perspectives on the Italian migratory landscape from those offered by most of the Italian films previously discussed, in which the agency of the migrant or diasporic subject is rarely articulated with convincing force. Most of these "accented" films, however, share a consistent characteristic with Italian representations of the migrant experience insofar as their narrative trajectory is most often focused on the figure of the male migrant. Only Halilovic's contribution offers a striking exception to this pattern by foregrounding a young female protagonist endowed with the strength of will to shape her life according to her talents and desires.

Since all of the films discussed in this afterword are, in different ways and to different degrees, accented, transnational, or transcultural, one might well ask: can they also be described as Italian? Put another way: can these films be included in the currently disputed category of Italian cinema? The simple answer is perhaps yes since Italian characters, landscapes, and language (or local dialects) are featured, at least to some extent, in all of them. Yet at least half of these films have never been commercially distributed in Italy and are mostly unknown to Italian audiences, challenging the possibility of their recognition as "Italian," at least within Italy.

It is necessary to renew discussion of the fraught issue of national cinema in a way that moves beyond the question of language and landscape. Chris Berry has offered a productive way to proceed with these questions by identifying the need to place both the national-cinema approach and transnational cinema within a larger framework of issues around cinema and the national. The key awareness offered by such a critical perspective is that "the national is no longer confined to the form of the territorial nation-state" but includes "multiple, proliferating, contested, and overlapping" projects with multiple cinematic approaches and solutions.[22] Italian cinema has for a long time been traversed by international resonances and influences; it has by now become imperative to recognize the impact of transnational elements originating within Italy itself via the contribution of migrant, transmigrant, or diasporic filmmakers to the country's evolving cinematic imaginary.

Notes

1. In the early 1990s several immigrants living in Italy began to publish accounts of their migratory experiences in collaboration with Italians who assisted them with the writing process. In the years that followed, immigrant and second-generation writers began to publish literary works written directly in Italian, without the assistance of intermediaries. Some of these authors, including Amara Lakhous, Mohsen Melliti, Younis Tawfik, Igiaba Scego, Gabriella

Ghermandi, and Ubax Cristina Ali Farah, have by now attained international recognition as many of their works have been translated into English.

2. Mariagiulia Grassilli, "Migrant Cinema: Transnational and Guerrilla Practices of Film Production and Representation," *Journal of Ethnic and Migration Studies* 34, no. 8 (2008): 1250.

3. Rada Bieberstein, "'Mine Vaganti': Film Theoretical Considerations on Transculturality and the Cinema of Ferzan Özpetek," in Shrader and Winkler, *Cinemas of Italian Migration*, 201–30.

4. Hamid Naficy, *An Accented Cinema: Exilic and Diasporic Filmmaking* (Princeton: Princeton University Press, 2001).

5. Naficy, 4.

6. Naficy, 12.

7. Naficy, 222.

8. For an analysis of these three films, see Áine O'Healy, "An Accented Gaze: Migrant and Transmigrant Filmmaking," in *A Companion to Italian Cinema*, ed. Frank Burke (Hoboken: Wiley Blackwell, 2017), 484–99.

9. *L'albero dei destini sospesi*, for example, was originally created as part of a miniseries produced by Pergiorgio Bellocchio for Rai2 in 1997, which was entirely devoted to the topic of Italian immigration. Titled "Another Country for Your Eyes," the series proved to be one of the rare initiatives undertaken by the public television service to acknowledge the shift in Italy's demographic profile in the wake of mass immigration. Among the four feature-length films that constituted "Another Country for Your Eyes," only *L'albero dei destini sospesi* was made by a non-Italian director.

10. For an account of the aims and activities of ZaLab, see Ardizzoni, "Narratives of Change, Images for Change: Contemporary Social Documentaries in Italy," 311–26.

11. The title of Yimer's documentary *C.A.R.A. Italia* is impossible to translate adequately. *Cara* translates to the English word "dear," so the title can be quickly understood as "Dear Italy." The acronym CARA, however, stands for "centri di accoglienza per richiedenti asilo," or "reception centers for asylum seekers," and the film provides a sharp critique of these structures.

12. Fariborz Kamkari's earlier film, *I fiori di Kirkuk* (Flowers of Kirkuk, 2010), an Italian, Swiss, and Iraqi coproduction set entirely in Iraq, also received this designation.

13. While initial attempts to theorize transnational cinema tended to focus on the movement of films and filmmakers in relation to production, distribution, and exhibition, subsequent treatments of this category concentrated on films foregrounding narratives of migration, exile, and displacement. Indeed, many of these productions emerge from within specific diasporic configurations and show an awareness of the interconnectedness between the local and the global in diasporic communities. See Higbee and Lin, "Concepts of Transnational Cinema," 7–21.

14. Ella Shohat and Robert Stam, *Unthinking Eurocentrism: Multiculturalism and the Media* (London: Routledge, 1994), 203.

15. Katarzyna Marcinak and Imogen Tyler, eds., *Immigrant Protest: Politics, Aesthetics, and Everyday Dissent* (New York: State University of New York Press, 2014).

16. See Jacques Rancière, *The Politics of Aesthetics: The Distribution of the Sensible*, trans. Gabriel Rockhill (New York: Continuum, 2004).

17. Katarzyna Marcinak and Imogen Tyler, "Introduction: Immigrant Protest: Noborder Scholarship," in Marcinak and Tyler, *Immigrant Protest*, 18.

18. At the time of the Rosarno riots, Roberto Saviano (author of *Gomorra*) wrote an op-ed noting that the African workers at Rosarno had "already handed over all they owned, risked all they had, just to get to Italy. But they came to make a better life for themselves—and they're not

about to let anyone take the possibility of that life away . . . It's a mistake to view the Rosarno rioters as criminals. The Rosarno riots were not about attacking the law, but about gaining access to the law." Robert Saviano, "Italy's African Heroes," *New York Times*, January 25, 2010, http://www.nytimes.com/2010/01/25/opinion/25saviano.html.

19. In Carpignano's latest film, *A Ciambra* (2017), the same Romani boy, Pio Amato, is cast in a similar role that combines both fictional and documentary elements.

20. Sandro Mezzadra and Brett Neilson, "Border as Method, or, the Multiplication of Labor," *Transversal* (European Institute for Progressive Cultural Policies, March 2008), http://eipcp.net/transversal/0608/mezzadraneilson/en.

21. Marciniak and Tyler, "Introduction: Immigrant Protest."

22. Chris Berry, "From National Cinema to Cinema and the National," in *Theorising National Cinema*, ed. Valentina Vitali and Paul Willemen (London: British Film Institute, 2006), 149.

Filmography

For foreign-language titles that were never translated, I offer a literal translation in roman (not italic) type in parentheses immediately following the foreign-language title. For foreign language films that have also circulated with English titles, I supply the English titles in italics in parentheses.

18 Ius soli. 2012. Fred Kudjo Kuwornu. Italy.
Abre los ojos (*Open Your Eyes*). 1997. Alejandro Amenábar. Spain.
Accattone. 1961. Pier Paolo Pasolini. Italy.
A Chjàna (The Plain). 2011. Jonas Carpignano. United States, Italy.
A Ciambra. 2017. Jonas Carpignano. Italy, Brazil, Germany, France, United States, Sweden.
Adua e le sue compagne (*Adua and Her Friends*). 1956. Antonio Pietrangeli.
Alì ha gli occhi azzurri (*Alì Blue Eyes*). 2012. Claudio Giovannesi. Italy.
Amore e Anarchia (*Love and Anarchy*). 1973. Lina Wertmüller. Italy.
Anche libero va bene (*Along the Ridge*). 2006. Kim Rossi Stuart. Italy.
Angst essen Seele auf (*Ali: Fear Eats the Soul*). 1973. Reiner Maria Fassbinder. Germany.
Aprile (April). 1997. Nanni Moretti. Italy.
Aspromonte. 2012. Hedy Krissane. Italy.
A sud di Lampedusa (South of Lampedusa). 2007. Andrea Segre and Stefano Liberti. Italy.
Bell'amico (Fine Friend). 2001. Luca D'Ascanio. Italy.
Bianco e nero (Black and White). 2008. Cristina Comencini. Italy.
Billo il Gran Dakhaar (Billo the Big Guy). 2007. Laura Muscardin. Italy.
Biutiful. 2010. Alejandro González Iñárritu. Mexico, Spain.
Broken Blossoms. 1919. D. W. Griffith. United States.
Captains Courageous. 1939. Victor Fleming. United States.
C.A.R.A. Italia. 2010. Dagmawi Yimer. Italy.
Che bella giornata (What a Beautiful Day!). 2011. Gennaro Nunziante. Italy.
Code Inconnu (*Code Unknown*). 2000. Michael Haneke. France, Austria, Romania.
Come un uomo sulla terra (Like a Man on the Earth). 2009. Andrea Segre, Dagmawi Yimer, and Riccardo Biadene. Italy.

Cose dell'altro mondo (Things from Another World). 2011. Francesco Patierno. Italy.
Cover boy: L'ultima rivoluzione (Cover Boy: The Last Revolution). 2006. Carmine Amoroso. Italy.
Dirty Pretty Things. 2002. Stephen Frears. United Kingdom.
Eastern Promises. 2007. David Cronenburg. United Kingdom, Canada, United States.
Elvjs & Merilijn (*Elvis and Marilyn*). 1998. Armando Manni. Italy.
The English Patient. 1996. Anthony Minghella. United States.
Eyes Wide Shut. 1997. Stanley Kubrick. United Kingdom, United States.
Figli di Annibale (Sons of Hannibal). 1998. Davide Ferrario. Italy.
Fratelli d'Italia (Brothers of Italy). 2009. Claudio Giovannesi. Italy.
Fuocoammare (*Fire at Sea*). 2016. Gianfranco Rosi. Italy.
Gegen die Wand (*Head-On*). 2004. Fatih Akın. Germany.
Germania anno zero (*Germany Year Zero*). 1948. Roberto Rossellini. Italy.
Gianni e le donne (Gianni and the Women). 2011. Gianni Di Gregorio. Italy.
Giorni (*Days*). 2001. Laura Muscardin. Italy.
Gomorra (*Gomorrah*). 2008. Matteo Garrone. Italy.
Good Morning Aman. 2009. Claudio Noce. Italy.
Gorbaciof (Gorbachev). 2010. Stefano Incerti. Italy.
Harem Suare. 1999. Ferzan Özpetek. Turkey, Italy, France.
I cento passi (*The Hundred Steps*). 2000. Marco Tullio Giordana, Italy.
I fiori di Kirkuk (Flowers of Kirkuk). 2010. Fariborz Kamkari. Iraq, Italy, Switzerland.
Il bagno turco (*Steam: The Turkish Bath*). 1997. Ferzan Özpetek. Italy, Turkey, Spain.
Il carniere (The Game Bag). 1997. Maurizio Zaccaro. Italy.
Il fiore delle mille e una notte (*Arabian Nights*). 1974. Pier Paolo Pasolini. Italy, France.
Il ladro di bambini (*Stolen Children*). 1992. Gianni Amelio. Italy.
Il signor Robinson (Mr. Robinson). 1976. Sergio Corbucci. Italy.
Il toro (The Bull). 1994. Carlo Mazzacurati. Italy.
Il villaggio di cartone (The Cardboard Village). 2011. Ermanno Olmi. Italy.
Imitation of Life. 1934. John Stahl. United States.
Intervista (*Interview*). 1988. Federico Fellini. Italy.
Into Paradiso. 2010. Paola Randi. Italy.
Io, l'altro (I, the Other). Mohsen Melliti. 2006. Italy.
Io, la mia famiglia rom e Woody Allen (Me, My Gypsy Family, and Woody Allen). 2009. Laura Halilovic. Italy.
Io, loro e Lara (Me, Them, and Lara). 2009. Carlo Verdone. Italy.
Io, rom romantica (Me, a Romantic Romani Girl). 2014. Laura Halilovic. Italy.
Io sono Li (*Shun Li and the Poet*). 2011. Andrea Segre. Italy.
Juventude em Marcha (*Colossal Youth*). 2006. Pedro Costa. Portugal.
La bella gente (Good People). 2009. Ivano De Matteo. Italy.
Là-bas: educazione criminale (Down There: A Criminal Education). 2011. Guido Lombardi. Italy.
La corsa dell'innocente (*The Flight of the Innocent*).1992. Carlo Carlei. Italy.
La doppia ora (*The Double Hour*). 2009. Giuseppe Capotondi. Italy.
La giusta distanza (*The Right Distance*). 2007. Carlo Mazzacurati. Italy.
La grande bellezza (*The Great Beauty*). 2013. Paolo Sorrentino. Italy. .
L'albero dei destini sospesi (The Tree of Suspended Destinies). 1997. Rachid Benhadj. Italy.

La meglio gioventù (*The Best of Youth*). 2003. Marco Tullio Giordana. Italy.
Lamerica. 1994. Gianni Amelio. Italy.
Lampedusa, Europa. 2014. Alfredo di Giovampaolo, Paolo Poggio, and Serena Scorzoni. Italy.
La notte. 1961. Michelangelo Antonioni. Italy.
La Promesse (The Promise). 1996. Jean-Pierre and Luc Dardenne. Belgium.
La romana (*Woman of Rome*). 1954. Luigi Zampa. Italy.
L'articolo 2 (Article 2). 1993. Maurizio Zaccaro. Italy.
La sconosciuta (*The Unknown Woman*). 2006. Giuseppe Tornatore. Italy.
L'assedio (Besieged). 1997. Bernardo Bertolucci. Italy.
Last Tango in Paris. 1972. Bernardo Bertolucci. Italy, France.
La terra trema (*The Earth Trembles*). 1948. Luchino Visconti. Italy.
La vita è bella (*Life Is Beautiful*). 1997. Roberto Benigni. Italy.
Le notti di Cabiria (*Nights of Cabiria*). 1957. Federico Fellini. Italy.
Lettere al vento (Letters to the Wind). 2004. Edmond Budina. Italy.
Lettere dal Sahara (Letters from the Sahara). 2006. Vittorio De Seta. Italy.
Lezioni di cioccolato (Chocolate Lessons). 2007. Claudio Cupellini. Italy.
Lezioni di cioccolato 2 (Chocolate Lessons 2). 2011. Alessio Maria Federici. Italy.
Lilya 4-Ever. 2002. Lukas Moodysson. Sweden, Denmark.
L'italiano (The Italian). 2002. Ennio De Dominicis. Italy.
L'ordine delle cose (The Order of Things). 2017. Andrea Segre. Italy.
L'ultimo imperatore (*The Last Emperor*). 1987. Bernardo Bertolucci. Italy, United Kingdom.
Mamma Roma. 1962. Pier Paolo Pasolini. Italy.
Mare chiuso (Closed Sea). 2012. Stefano Liberti and Andrea Segre. Italy.
Mare largo (Open Sea). 1997. Ferdinando Vicentini Orgnani. Italy.
Mare Magnum (The Great Sea). 2014. Letizia Gullo and Ester Sparatore. Italy.
Mar Nero (Black Sea). 2008. Federico Bondi. Italy, Romania, France.
M. Butterfly. 1993. David Cronenberg. United States.
Mediterranea. 2015. Jonas Carpignano. Dubai, France, Germany, United States.
Mio fratello è figlio unico (*My Brother Is an Only Child*). 2007. Daniele Luchetti. Italy.
Miracle at St. Anna. 2008. Spike Lee. United States.
The Mysterious Dr. Fu Manchu. 1923. A. E. Coleby. United Kingdom.
Mozzarella Stories. 2012. Edoardo De Angelis. Italy.
Nema problema (No Problem). 2002. Giancarlo Bocchi. Italy.
Non c'è più religione (There's No Religion Anymore). 2016. Luca Miniero. Italy.
Non ho paura (*I'm Not Scared*). 2002. Gabriele Salvatores. Italy.
Non ti muovere (*Don't Move*). 2004. Sergio Castellitto. Italy.
Nuovomondo (*Golden Door*). 2006. Emanuele Crialese. Italy.
Occidente (West). 1998. Corso Salani. Italy.
Oltre il confine (Beyond the Border). 2002. Rolando Colla. Italy, Switzerland.
The Others. 2001. Alejandro Amenábar. Spain, United States.
Paisà (*Paisan*). 1946. Roberto Rossellini. Italy.
Per un figlio (For a Son). 2017. Suranga Deshapriya Katugampala. Italy.
The Piano. Jane Campion. 1997. New Zealand.
Pitza e datteri (Pizza and Dates). 2015. Fariborz Kamkari. Italy.
Portami via (Take Me Away).1994. Gianluca Maria Tavarelli. Italy.

Pummarò (Tomato). 1990. Michele Placido. Italy.
Quando sei nato non puoi più nasconderti (Once You're Born You Can No Longer Hide). 2005. Marco Tullio Giordana. Italy.
Questa notte è ancora nostra (Tonight Is Still Ours). 2007. Paolo Genovese and Luca Miniero. Italy.
Radio West. 2002. Alessandro Valori. Italy.
Raise the Red Lantern. 1991. Zhang Yimou. China.
Rocco e i suoi fratelli (Rocco and His Brothers). 1960. Luchino Visconti. Italy, France.
Rosso Istanbul (Red Istanbul). 2017. Ferzan Özpetek. Italy.
Saimir. 2004. Francesco Munzi. Italy.
Salò o le 120 giornate di Sodoma (Salò, or the 120 Days of Sodom). 1975. Pier Paolo Pasolini. Italy. *The Sheltering Sky*. 1990. Bernardo Bertolucci. Italy, United Kingdom.
Soltanto il mare (Only the Sea). 2011. Dagmawi Yimer, Fabrizio Barraco, and Giulio Cederna. Italy.
Sophie's Choice. 1982. Alan J. Pakula. United States.
Stella Dallas. 1937. King Vidor. United States.
Sudeuropa 2005–2007 (South Europe 2005–2007). 2007. Raphael Cuomo and Maria Ionio. Switzerland.
Sud side stori (South Side Story). 2000. Roberta Torre. Italy.
Svetlana's Journey. 2004. Michael Cory Davis. Bulgaria.
Taken. 2009. Pierre Morel. France.
Tano da morire (To Die for Tano). 1988. Roberta Torre. Italy.
Taranta on the Road. 2017. Salvatore Allocca. Italy.
Teatro di guerra (Rehearsals for War). 1998. Mario Martone. Italy.
Terra di mezzo (Land in Between). 1996. Matteo Garrone. 1996. Italy.
Terraferma (Terra Firma). 2011. Emanuele Crialese. Italy.
Tesoromio (Sweetheart). 1979. Giulio Paradisi. Italy.
Teste rasate (Skinheads). 1993. Claudio Fragasso. Italy.
Ti ricordi di Adil? (Do You Remember Adil?). 2008. Mohamed Zineddaine. Italy, Morocco.
Tornando a casa (Going Home). 2001. Vincenzo Marra. Italy.
Una bella governante di colore (A Beautiful Black Housekeeper). 1976. Luigi Russo. Italy.
Un'altra vita (Another Life). 1992. Carlo Mazzacurati. Italy.
Va' pensiero (Walking Stories). 2013. Dagmawi Yimer. Italy.
Venuto al mondo (Twice Born). 2012. Sergio Castellitto. Italy.
Vesna va veloce (Vesna Runs Fast). 1996. Carlo Mazzacurati. Italy.
Viaggio a Lampedusa (Voyage to Lampedusa). 2010. Giuseppe di Bernardo. Italy.
West Side Story. 1961. Robert Wise. United States.
The World. 2004. Jia Zhangke. China.
Zora la vampira (Zora the Vampire). 2000. Manetti Brothers. Italy.

Bibliography

Abulafia, David. *The Great Sea: A Human History of the Mediterranean*. New York: Oxford University Press, 2011.
Achebe, Nwando. "The Road to Italy: Nigerian Sex Workers at Home and Abroad." *Journal of Women's History* 15, no. 4 (2004): 178–85.
Agamben, Giorgio. *The Coming Community*. Translated by Michael Hardt. Minneapolis: University of Minnesota Press, 2000.
———. *Homo Sacer: Sovereign Power and Bare Life*. Translated by Daniel Heller-Roazen. Palo Alto: Stanford University Press, 1998.
———. *Means without End: Notes on Politics*. Translated by Vincenzo Binetti and Cesare Casarino. Minneapolis: University of Minnesota Press, 2000.
Amelio, Gianni, and Goffredo Fofi. *Amelio secondo il cinema. Conversazione con Goffredo Fofi*. Rome: Donizelli, 1994.
Amelio, Gianni, and Jean A. Gili. "Entretien avec Gianni Amelio: un film non sur l'Albanie d'aujourdhui, mais sur l'Italie d'après-guerre." *Positif* 406 (1994): 25–31.
Andall, Jacqueline. *Migration and Domestic Service: The Politics of Black Women in Italy*. Aldershot, UK: Ashgate, 2000.
Anderson, Benedict. *Imagined Communities: Reflections on the Origin and Spread of Nationalism*. London: Verso, 1984.
Anderson, Bridget. *Doing the Dirty Work? The Global Politics of Domestic Labour*. London: Zed Books, 2000.
Andrijasevic, Rutvica. "The Difference Borders Make: (Il)legality, Migration and Trafficking in Italy among Eastern European Women in Prostitution." In *Uprootings/Regroundings: Questions of Home and Migration*, edited by Sara Ahmed, Claudia Castada, Anne-Marie Fortier, and Mimi Sheller, 251–72. New York: Berg, 2003.
Appadurai, Arjun. *Modernity at Large: Cultural Dimensions of Globalization*. Minneapolis: University of Minnesota Press, 1997.
Ardizzoni, Michela. "Narratives of Change, Images for Change: Contemporary Social Documentaries in Italy." *Journal of Italian Cinema and Media Studies* 1, no. 3 (2013): 311–26.

———. "*Posse*'s Music of Occupation and Practices of Social Justice." In *Matrix Activism: Global Practices of Resistance*, 113–36. New York: Routledge, 2017.
Ba, Saidou Mousa, and Allessandro Micheletti. *La promessa di Hamadi*. Novara: De Agostini Scuola, 2008. Originally published 1991.
Balibar, Étienne. "'Es gibt keinen Staat in Europa': Racism and Politics in Europe Today." *New Left Review* 186 (March–April 1991): 5–19.
———. *We, the People of Europe? Reflections on Transnational Citizenship*. Princeton: Princeton University Press, 2004.
Balibar, Étienne, Sandro Mezzadra, and Ranabir Samaddar, eds. *The Borders of Justice*. Philadelphia: Temple University Press, 2011.
Ballestreros, Isolina. *Immigration Cinema in the New Europe*. Bristol: Intellect, 2015.
Bardan, Alice. "The New European Cinema of Precarity: A Transnational Perspective." In *Work in Cinema: Labor and the Human Condition*, edited by Ewa Mazierska, 69–90. New York: Palgrave Macmillan, 2013.
Bardan, Alice, and Áine O'Healy. "Transnational Mobility and Precarious Labor in Post–Cold War Europe: The Spectral Disruptions of Carmine Amoroso's *Cover Boy*." In *The Cinemas of Italian Migration: European and Transatlantic Narratives*, edited by Sabine Schrader and Daniel Winkler, 69–90. Newcastle: Cambridge Scholars Publishing, 2013.
Bauböck, Rainer. *Transnational Citizenship Membership and Rights in International Migration*. Florence: Edward Elgar, 1994.
Bayman, Louis. "Melodrama as Realism in Italian Neorealism." In *Realism and the Audiovisual Media*, edited by Lucia Nagib and Cecilia Mello, 47–62. New York: Palgrave Macmillan, 2009.
Bayraktar, Nilgun. *Mobility and Migration in Film and Moving Image Art*. New York: Routledge, 2016.
Behan, Tom. "Putting Spanners in the Works: The Politics of the 99 Posse." *Popular Music* 26, no. 3 (2002): 497–504.
Ben-Ghiat, Ruth. *Italian Fascism's Empire Cinema*. Bloomington: Indiana University Press, 2015.
Berardi, Giovanni. "Claudio Giovannesi: sui luoghi (e sui temi) di Pier Paolo Pasolini (e Sergio Citti)." TXDRVRS. December 17, 2014. https://www.taxidrivers.it/44467/rubriche/claudio-giovannesi-sui-luoghi-e-sui-temi-di-pier-paolo-pasolini-e-sergio-citti.html.
Berghahn, Daniela, and Claudia Sternberg, eds. *European Cinema in Motion: Migrant and Diasporic Film in Contemporary Europe*. New York: Palgrave Macmillan, 2010.
Berry, Chris. "From National Cinema to Cinema and the National." In *Theorising National Cinema*, edited by Valentina Vitali and Paul Willemen, 148–57. London: British Film Institute, 2006.
Bettio, Francesca, Annamaria Simonazzi, and Paola Villa. "Change in Care Regimes and Female Migration: The 'Care Drain' in the Mediterranean." *Journal of European Social Policy* 16, no. 3 (2006): 271–85.
Bhabha, Homi K. *The Location of Culture*. New York: Taylor and Francis, 1994.
———. "The World and the Home." In *Dangerous Liaisons: Gender, Nation and Postcolonial Perspectives*, edited by Anne McClintock, Aamir Mufti, and Ella Shohat, 445–55. Minneapolis: Minnesota University Press, 1997.

Bieberstein, Rada. "'Mine Vaganti': Film Theoretical Considerations on Transculturality and the Cinema of Ferzan Özpetek." In *The Cinemas of Italian Migration: European and Transatlantic Narratives*, edited by Sabine Schrader and Daniel Winkler, 201–30. Newcastle: Cambridge Scholars Publishing, 2013.

Bond, Emma. "Towards a Trans-national Turn in Italian Studies?" *Italian Studies* 69, no. 3 (2014): 415–24.

Bonsaver, Guido. "Accented Voices in Contemporary Italian Cinema." In *Destination Italy: Representing Migration in Contemporary Media and Narrative*, edited by Emma Bond, Guido Bonsaver, and Federico Falloppa, 345–64. Oxford: Peter Lang, 2015.

Borriello, Massimo. "Raoul Bova in barca contro il pregiudizi." Movie Player. May 14, 2007. http://movieplayer.it/articoli/raoul-bova-in-barca-contro-il-pregiudizio_3515/ (accessed January 10, 2017).

Bouchard, Norma, and Valerio Ferme. *Italy and the Mediterranean: Words, Sounds, and Images of the Post–Cold War Era*. New York: Palgrave Macmillan, 2013.

Brambilla, Chiara. "Exploring the Critical Potential of the Borderscapes Concept." *Geopolitics* 20, no. 1 (2014): 14–34.

Brooks, Peter. *The Melodramatic Imagination: Balzac, Henry James, Melodrama, and the Mode of Excess*. New York: Yale University Press, 1975.

Brown, William, Dina Iordanova, and Leshu Torshin. *Moving People, Moving Images: Cinema and Trafficking in the New Europe*. St. Andrews, UK: St. Andrews Film Studies, 2010.

Bruno, Marco. "The Journalistic Construction of 'Emergenza Lampedusa': The 'Arab Spring' and the 'Landings' Issue in Media Representations of Migration." In *Destination Italy: Representing Migration in Contemporary Media and Narrative*, edited by Emma Bond, Guido Bonsaver, and Federico Faloppa, 59–83. Oxford: Peter Lang, 2015.

Bullaro, Grace, ed. *From Terrone to Extra-Comunitario: The New Manifestations of Racism in Contemporary Italian Cinema*. Leicester: Troubador, 2010.

Caminati, Luca. "Gianni Amelio's *Lamerica* and the National Body Politics." In *Italian Political Cinema: Public Life, Imaginary, and Identity in Contemporary Italian Film*, edited by Giancarlo Lombardi and Christian Uva, 319–28. Oxford, UK: Peter Lang, 2016.

Campassi, Gabriella, and Maria Teresa Sega. "Uomo bianco, donna nera: L'immagine della donna nella fotografia coloniale." *Rivista di storia e teoria della fotografia* 4, no. 5 (1983): 54–62.

Campesi, Giuseppe. "The Arab Spring and the Crisis of the European Border Regime: Manufacturing Emergency in the Lampedusa Crisis." Working paper 59. European University Institute, Robert Schuman Centre of Advanced Studies Working Papers. 2011. 1, http://cadmus.eui.eu/handle/1814/19375.

Caponetto, Rosetta Giuliani. "Blaxploitation Italian Style: Exhuming and Consuming the Colonial Black Venus in 1970s Cinema inItaly." In *Postcolonial Italy: Challenging National Homogeneity*, edited by Cristina Lombardi-Diop and Caterina Romeo, 191–203. New York: Palgrave Macmillan, 2012.

Carlorosi, Silvia. "Neorealism, Cinema of Poetry, and Italian Contemporary Cinema." In *Global Neorealism: The Transnational History of a Film Style*, edited by Saverio Giovacchini and Robert Sklar, 240–56. Oxford, MS: University Press of Mississippi, 2013.

Cassano, Franco, Norma Bouchard, and Valerio Ferme. *Southern Thought and Other Essays on the Mediterranean*. Translated by Norma Bouchard and Valerio Ferme. New York: Fordham University Press, 2012.
Celik, Ipek A. *In Permanent Crisis: Ethnicity in Contemporary European Media and Cinema*. Ann Arbor: University of Michigan Press, 2015.
Cento Bull, Anna. "Ethnicity, Racism and the Northern League." In *Italian Regionalism: History, Identity, and Politics*, edited by Carl Levy, 171–87. Oxford: Berg, 1996.
"Central Mediterranean: Death Toll Soars as EU Turns Its Back on Refugees and Migrants." Amnesty.org, July 6, 2017. https://www.amnesty.org/en/latest/news/2017/07/central-mediterranean-death-toll-soars-as-eu-turns-its-back-on-refugees-and-migrants/ (accessed July 28, 2018).
Cestim on-line: Sito di documentazione sui fenomeni migratori, Centro Studi Immigrazione, http://www.cestim.it (accessed July 16, 2018).
Chambers, Iain. *Mediterranean Crossings: The Politics of an Interrupted Mobility*. Durham, NC: Duke University Press, 2008.
Champagne, John. *Italian Queer Masculinity as Melodrama: Caravaggio, Puccini, Contemporary Cinema*. New York: Palgrave Macmillan, 2015.
Chen, Nancy N., and Trinh Minh-ha. "'Speaking Nearby': A Conversation with Trinh T. Minh-ha," *Visual Anthropology Review* 8, no. 1 (1992): 82–91.
Choate, Mark I. "Tunisia Contested: Italian Nationalism, French Imperial Rule, and Migration in the Mediterranean Basin." *California Italian Studies Journal* 1, no. 1 (2010): 1–20. http://escholarship.org/uc/item/8k97g1nc#page-1.
Chow, Rey. "The Dream of a Butterfly." In *Ethics After Idealism: Theory, Culture, Ethnicity, Reading*, 74–97. Bloomington: Indiana University Press, 1998.
Cicinelli, Sonia. *Senza frontiere: L'immigrazione nel cinema italiano*. Rome: Editore Kappa, 2011.
Cilento, Fabrizio. "Saviano, Garrone, *Gomorrah*: Neorealism and Noir in the Land of the Camorra." *Fast Capitalism* 8, no.1 (2011). http://www.uta.edu/huma/agger/fastcapitalism/8_1/cilento8_1.html (accessed February 2, 2017).
"Constitution of the Italian Republic." 1947. Senato della Repubblica. https://www.senato.it/documenti/repository/istituzione/costituzione_inglese.pdf (accessed July 15, 2018).
Conti, Davide. *L'occupazione italiana dei Balcani. Crimini di guerra e mito della "brava gente" (1940–1943)*. Rome: Odradek, 2008.
Coppola, Manuela, and Sonia Sabelli. "Not a Country for Women, nor for Blacks." In *Teaching "Race" with a Gendered Edge*, edited by Brigitte Hipfl and Kristín Loftsdóttir, 143–59. Utrecht: Atgender, 2012.
Curcio, Anna, and Miguel Mellino. "La razza al lavoro. Rileggere il razzismo, ripensare l'antirazzismo in Italia." In *La razza al lavoro*, edited by Anna Curcio and Miguel Mellino, 7–36. Rome: Manifestolibri, 2012.
Cuttitta, Paolo. "'Borderizing' the Island: Setting and Narratives of the Lampedusa 'Border Play.'" *ACME: An International E-Journal for Critical Geographies* 13, no. 2 (2014): 202.
D'Addio, Andrea. "Che bella giornata—La nostra recensione," Film.it. January 7, 2011. http://www.film.it/recensione/art/che-bella-giornata-la-nostra-recensione-7881/ (accessed July 21, 2018).

Dal Lago, Alessandro. *Non-persone: L'esclusione dei migranti in una società globale*. Rome: Feltrinelli, 2004.
D'Arcangeli, Luciana. "Migration and Identity in *L'albero dei destini sospesi*." *Studi d'italianistica nell'Africa australe/Italian Studies in Southern Africa* 23, no. 1 (2010): 36–62.
D'Arma, Antonella. "Lo stereotipo della donna nera nel cinema italiano." *Studi emigrazione* 169 (2008): 59–71.
Dasgupta, Partha, Karl-Göran Mäler, and Alessandro Vercelli, eds. *The Economics of Transnational Commons*. Oxford: Oxford University Press, 1997.
Dawson, Ashley, and Patrizia Palumbo. "Hannibal's Children: Immigration and Antiracist Youth Subcultures in Contemporary Italy." *Cultural Critique Journal* 59, no. 1 (2005): 165–86.
De Franceschi, Leonardo. *Lo schermo e lo spettro. Sguardi postcoloniali su Africa e afrodiscendenti*. Sesto San Giovanni: Mimesis, 2017
De Genova, Nicholas. "Migrant 'Illegality' and Deportability in Everyday Life." *Annual Review of Anthropology* 31 (2002): 419–47.
———. "Spectacles of Migrant 'Illegality': The Scene of Exclusion, the Obscene of Inclusion." *Ethnic and Racial Studies* 36, no. 7 (2013): 1180–98.
de Lauretis, Teresa. "Desire in Narrative." In *Alice Doesn't: Feminism, Semiotics, Cinema*, 103–57 Bloomington: Indiana University Press, 1982.
Dell'Agnese, Elena, and Anne-Laure Amilhat Szary. "Borderscapes: From Border Landscapes to Border Aesthetics." *Geopolitics* 20, no. 1 (January 2, 2015): 4–13.
Derrida, Jacques. "Hospitality, Justice, and Responsibility: A Dialogue with Jacques Derrida." In *Questioning Ethics: Contemporary Debates in Philosophy*, edited by Richard Kearney and Mark Dooley, 65–83. New York: Routledge, 1999.
———. *Of Hospitality: Anne Dufourmantelle Invites Jacques Derrida to Respond*. Translated by Rachel Bowlby. Stanford: Stanford University Press, 2000.
———. *Specters of Marx: The State of the Debt, the Work of Mourning and the New International*. Translated by Peggy Kamuf. New York: Routledge, 2006.
Desser, David. "Global Noir: Genre Film in the Age of Transnationalism." In *Film Genre Reader III*, edited by Barry Keith Grant, 516–36. Austin: University of Texas Press, 2003.
Detassis, Piera. *Gianni Amelio. Lamerica, film e storia del film*. Turin, IT: Einaudi, 1994.
Diaconescu-Blumenfeld, Rodica. "*Lamerica*: History in Diaspora." *Romance Languages Annual* 11 (2000): 167–73.
Diamanti, Ilvo. "Quei film sugli immigrati nel Paese di Terraferma." *La Repubblica*, September 12, 2011. www.repubblica.it/politica/2011/09/12/news/mappe_12_settembre-21534651/.
Di Carmine, Roberta. "The Cinema of Matteo Garrone." *Wide Screen* 1, no. 2 (2010). http://widescreenjournal.org/index.php/journal/article/view/39/57.
Dines, Nick, Nicola Montagna, and Vincenzo Ruggiero. "Thinking Lampedusa: Border Construction, the Spectacle of Bare Life and the Productivity of Migrants." *Ethnic and Racial Studies Review* 38, no. 3 (2015): 430–45.
Donadio, Rachel. "Living Where Crime Conquers All." *New York Times*, February 5, 2009, http://www.nytimes.com/2009/02/08/movies/08dona.html?pagewanted=all&_r=0 (accessed July 18, 2018).

Douglas, James. "Configuring Alterity: Towards a Third Cinema Approach in Gianni Amelio's *Lamerica*." *Italian Studies* 67, no. 2 (2012): 188–200.

Duncan, Derek. "Double Time: Facing the Future in Migration's Past." *California Italian Studies Journal* 2, no. 1 (2011): 1–26. http://escholarship.org/uc/item/38q389mk.

———. "'Il clandestino è l'ebreo di oggi': Imprints of the Shoah on Migration to Italy." *Quest: Issues in Contemporary Jewish History* 10 (December 2016): 60–88. http://www.quest-cdecjournal.it/focus.php?id=384.

———. "Italy's Postcolonial Cinema and its Histories of Representation." *Italian Studies* 63, no. 2 (2008): 195–211.

———. "Loving Geographies: Queering Straight Migration to Italy." *New Cinemas: Journal of Contemporary Film* 6, no. 3 (February 1, 2009): 167–82.

———. "Shooting the Colonial Past in Contemporary Italian Cinema." In *Postcolonial Italy*, edited by Cristina Lombardi-Diop and Caterina Romeo, 115–24. New York: Palgrave Macmillan, 2012.

———. "The Sight and Sound of Albanian Migration in Contemporary Italian Cinema," *New Readings* 8 (2007): 1–15. http://ojs.cf.ac.uk/index.php/newreadings/article/view/21/16.

———. "Translanguaging: Claudio Giovannesi's Postcolonial Practices," *Transnational Cinemas* 7, no. 2 (2016): 196–209.

Dyer, Richard. *The Matter of Images: Essays on Representations*. New York: Routledge, 1993.

Ebner, Michael R. *Ordinary Violence in Mussolini's Italy*. New York: Cambridge University Press, 2010.

Eco, Umberto, and Richard Kearney. "Chaosmos: The Return of the Middle Ages." In *Debates in Continental Philosophy: Conversations with Contemporary Thinkers*, edited by Richard Kearney, 223–28. New York: Fordham University Press, 2004.

Ehrenreich, Barbara, and Arlie Russell Hochschild, eds. *Global Woman: Nannies, Maids, and Sex Workers in the New Economy*. New York: Holt, 2004.

Elsaesser, Thomas. "Real Location, Fantasy Space, Performative Place: Double Occupancy and Mutual Interference in European Cinema." In *European Film Theory*, edited by Temenuga Trifanova, 47–64. New York: Routledge, 2009.

Ezra, Elizabeth, and Terry Rowden, eds. *Transnational Cinema: The Film Reader*. New York: Routledge, 2006.

Fallaci, Oriana. *The Rage and the Pride*. New York: Rizzoli, 2002.

Fatiguso, Vito. "La classifica delle pellicole che hanno realizzato più incassi: Zalone contro Cameron." *Corriere del Mezzogiorno. Spettacoli*. January 2, 2016. https://corrieredelmezzogiorno.corriere.it/bari/spettacoli/cards/italia-cinema-6-film-record/che-bella-giornata-43474047-euro.shtml?refresh_ce-cp (accessed July 21, 2018).

Favretto, Ilaria. "Italy, EU Enlargement and the 'Reinvention' of Europe between Historical Memories and Present Representations." *Journal of Southern Europe and the Balkans* 6, no. 2 (2004): 161–81.

Fay, Jennifer, and Justus Nieland. *Film Noir: Hard-Boiled Modernity and the Cultures of Globalization*. New York: Routledge, 2010.

Ferrario, Davide. "Figli di Annibale." *La Repubblica*. January 29, 1998. Cited in *Enciclopedia del Cinema in Piemonte*. http://www.torinocittadelcinema.it/schedafilm.php?film_id=1386&stile=large.

Fielding, Anthony. "Migrations, Institutions and Politics: The Evolution of European Migration Policies." In *Mass Migration in Europe: The Legacy and the Future*, edited by Russell King, 40–64. London: Bellhaven, 1993; New York: Halsted Press, 1993.
Fiore, Teresa. *Pre-Occupied Spaces: Remapping Italy's Transnational Migrations and Colonial Legacies*. New York: Fordham University Press, 2017.
Forgacs, David. "African Immigration on Film: *Pummarò* and the Limits of Vicarious Representation." In *Media and Migration: Constructions of Mobility and Difference*, edited by Russell King and Nancy Wood, 83–94. New York: Routledge, 2001.
Foucault, Michel. "Of Other Spaces." *Diacritics* 16, no. 1 (1986): 22–27.
Frank, Alison, and Andrea Segre. "Andrea Segre: Confronting Difference." The Free Library. *CineAction*. September 3, 2012. http://www.thefreelibrary.com/Andrea+Segre%3a+confronting+difference.-a0284222750 (accessed July 20, 2018).
Friese, Heidrun. "Border Economies: Lampedusa and the Nascent Migration Industry." *Shima: The International Journal of Research into Island Cultures* 6, no. 2 (2012): 66–84.
———. "Representations of Gendered Mobility and the Tragic Border Regime in the Mediterranean." *Journal of Balkan and Near Eastern Studies* 19, no. 5 (2017): 541–56.
"*Fuocoammare*: Considerazioni del collettivo Askavusa." *Askavusa*. February 24, 2016. https://askavusa.wordpress.com/2016/02/24/1428/ (accessed May 2, 2017).
Gallo, Ester, and Francesca Scrinzi. *Migration, Masculinities and Reproductive Labour: Men of the Home*. New York: Palgrave Macmillan, 2016.
Galt, Rosalind. "The Prettiness of Italian Cinema." In *Popular Italian Cinema*, edited by Louis Bayman and Sergio Rigoletto, 52–68. New York: Palgrave Macmillan, 2013.
Gates, Henry Louis, Jr. *The Signifying Monkey: A Theory of Afro-American Literary Criticism*. New York: Oxford University Press, 1988.
Gatti, Fabrizio. "Io clandestino a Lampedusa." *L'espresso*, October 7, 2005. http://espresso.repubblica.it/palazzo/2005/10/07/news/io-clandestino-a-lampedusa-1.594 (accessed July 15, 2018).
Giordana, Marco Tullio, Sandro Petraglia, and Stefano Rulli. *Quando sei nato non puoi più nasconderti*. Venice: Marsilio, 2005.
Giordano, Benito. "Italian Regionalism or 'Padanian' Nationalism: The Political Project of the Lega Nord in Italian Politics." *Political Geography* 19, no. 4 (2000): 445–71.
Giuliani, Gaia. "Mediterraneità e bianchezza. Il razzismo italiano fra fascismo e articolazioni comtemporaneo (1861–2015)." *Iperstoria—Testi Letterature Linguaggi* 6 (Fall 2015). http://www.iperstoria.it/joomla/images/PDF/Numero_6/monografica_6/Giuliani_mediterraneita_e_bianchezza.pdf.
Giuliani, Gaia, and Cristina Lombardi-Diop. *Bianco e nero: Storia dell'identità razziale degli italiani*. Milan: LeMonnier Università, 2013.
Goldberg, Jonathan. *Melodrama: An Aesthetics of Impossibility*. Durham, NC: Duke University Press, 2016.
"Gomorrah," Box Office Mojo, http://www.boxofficemojo.com/movies/?id=gomorrah.htm (accessed August 20, 2017).
Gramsci, Antonio. *The Southern Question*. Translated by Pasquale Verdicchio. Toronto: Guernica Editions, 2006.

Grassilli, Mariagiulia. "Migrant Cinema: Transnational and Guerrilla Practices of Film Production and Representation." *Journal of Ethnic and Migration Studies* 34, no. 8 (2008): 1237–55.

Greene, Shelleen. *Equivocal Subjects: Between Italy and Africa—Constructions of Racial and National Identity in the Italian Cinema.* New York: Continuum, 2012.

Grewal, Inderpal, and Caren Kaplan, eds. *Scattered Hegemonies: Postmodernity and Transnational Feminist Practices.* Minneapolis: University of Minnesota Press, 1994.

Guadagnucci, Lorenzo. *Parole sporche. Clandestini, nomadi, vu cumprà: il razzismo nei media e dentro di noi,* Milan: Altreconomia: Milan 2010.

Guglielmo, Jennifer, and Salvatore Salerno, eds. *Are Italians White? How Race Is Made in America.* New York: Routledge, 2003.

Günsberg, Maggie. *Italian Cinema: Gender and Genre.* New York: Palgrave Macmillan, 2004.

Gutiérrez-Rodríguez, Encarnación. "The 'Hidden Side' of the New Economy: On Transnational Migration, Domestic Work, and Unprecedented Intimacy." *Frontiers* 28, no. 3 (2007): 60–83.

Hall, Stuart. "The Question of Cultural Identity." In *Modernity: An Introduction to Modern Societies,* edited by Stuart Hall, David Held, Don Hubert, and Kenneth Thompson, 594–634. Hoboken: Wiley-Blackwell, 1996.

Hannerz, Ulf. *Transnational Connections: Culture, People, Places.* New York: Routledge, 1996.

Hardt, Michael, and Antonio Negri. *Empire.* Cambridge, MA: Harvard University Press, 2000.

Higbee, Will, and Song Hwee Lin. "Concepts of Transnational Cinema: Towards a Critical Transnationalism in Film Studies." *Transnational Cinemas* 1, no. 1 (2010): 7–21.

Higson, Andrew. "The Limiting Imagination of National Cinema." In *Cinema and Nation,* edited by Mette Hjort and Scott MacKenzie, 63–74. New York: Routledge, 2000.

Hipkins, Danielle. *Italy's Other Women: Gender and Prostitution in Italian Cinema, 1940–1965.* Oxford: Peter Lang, 2016.

Hipkins, Danielle, and Dana Renga. "A New Canon? Contemporary Italian Cinema and Television and the Role of Quality." *Communicazioni sociali* no. 3 (2016): 375–97.

Hjort, Mette. "Plurality of Cinematic Transnationalism." In *World Cinemas, Transnational Perspectives,* edited by Natasa Durovicová and Kathleen Newman, 12–33. New York: Routledge, 2009.

Hoberman, J. "Artists in Love." *Village Voice* 44, no. 21 (June 1, 1999): 119.

Hochschild, Arlie. *The Managed Heart: Commercialization of Human Feeling.* Berkeley: California University Press, 1983.

hooks, bell. *Black Looks.* Boston: South End, 1992.

Horden, Peregrine, and Nicholas Purcell. "Mobility of Goods and People." In *The Corrupting Sea: A Study of Mediterranean History,* 342–400. Oxford: Blackwell, 2000.

Hou, Jeffrey. "Your Place and/or My Place?" In *Transcultural Cities: Border-Crossing and Placemaking,* edited by Jeffrey Hou, 1–16. New York: Routledge, 2013.

ISTAT (Istituto Statistico di Italia). http://www.istat.it/it/immigrati.

Jay, Paul. *Global Matters: The Transnational Turn in Literary Studies*. New York: Cornell University Press, 2010.
Kaplan, E. Ann. *Looking for the Other: Feminism, Film and the Imperial* Gaze. New York: Routledge, 1997.
Kaplan, Robert. *Balkan Ghosts: A Journey through History*. New York: St. Martin's Press, 1993.
King, Russell, and Nicola Mai. "Italophilia Meets Albanophobia: Paradoxes of Asymmetric Assimilation and Identity Processes among Albanian Immigrants in Italy." *Ethnic and Racial Studies* 32, no. 1 (2008): 117–38.
Kotef, Hagar. *Movement and the Ordering of Freedom: On Liberal Governances of Mobility*. Durham, NC: Duke University Press, 2015.
Kristeva, Julia. *Powers of Horror: An Essay on Abjection*. New York: Columbia University Press, 1980.
———. *Strangers to Ourselves*. Translated by Leon S. Roudiez. New York: Columbia University Press, 1991.
Lan, Pei-Chia. *Global Cinderellas: Migrant Domestics and Newly Rich Employers in Taiwan*: Duke University Press, 2006.
Landy, Marcia. "The Italian Melodrama in the Italian Cinema 1929–1943." In *Imitations of Life: A Reader on Film & Television Melodrama*, edited by Marcia Landy, 569–77. Detroit: Wayne State University, 1991.
———. "On the Road with *Lamerica*: Immigrants, Refugees and the Poor." In *Metaphoricity and the Politics of Mobility*, edited by Maria Margaroni and Effie Yiannopoulou, 141–58. Amsterdam: Rodopi, 2006.
Lerner, Giovanna Falaschini. "From the Other Side of the Mediterranean: Hospitality in Italian Migration Cinema." *California Italian Studies Journal* 1, no. 1 (2010): 1–19. http://escholarship.org/uc/item/45h010h5.
Levinas, Emmanuel. *Entre Nous: On Thinking of the Other*. Translated by Michael B. Smith and Barbara Harshav. New York: Columbia University Press, 2000.
———. *Otherwise Than Being, or, Beyond Essence*. Translated by Alphonso Lingis. Pittsburgh: Duquesne University Press, 1981.
———. *Totality and Infinity: An Essay on Exteriority*. Pittsburgh: Duquesne University Press, 1969.
"Libia. Al Parlamento europeo proiezione de 'L'ordine delle cose.'" *Articolo 21*. January 30, 2018. https://www.articolo21.org/2018/01/libia-al-parlamento-europeo-proiezione-de-lordine-delle-cose/ (accessed July 18, 2018).
Lombardi, Giancarlo. "Can the Price Ever Be Right? Television and Cultural Imperialism in *Lamerica*," *Romance Languages Annual* 12 (2001): 191–95.
Lombardi-Diop, Cristina. "Postracial, Postcolonial Italy." In *Postcolonial Italy: Challenging National Homogeneity*, edited by Cristina Lombardi-Diop and Caterina Romeo, 175–90. New York: Palgrave Macmillan, 2012.
Lombardi-Diop, Cristina, and Caterina Romeo. "Paradigms of Postcoloniality in Contemporary Italy." In *Postcolonial Italy: Challenging National Homogeneity*, edited by Cristina Lombardi-Diop and Caterina Romeo, 1–29. New York: Palgrave Macmillan, 2012.
Loshitzky, Yosefa. *Screening Strangers: Migration and Diaspora in Contemporary European Cinema*. Bloomington: Indiana University Press, 2010.

Lu, Sheldon Hsiao-peng. *Transnational Chinese Cinemas: Identity, Nationhood, Gender*. Honolulu: University of Hawaii Press, 1997.
Lyon, Dawn, "The Organization of Care Work in Italy: Gender and Migrant Labor in the New Economy," *Indiana Journal of Global Legal Studies* 13, no. 1 (2006): 207–24.
Mai, Nicola. "'Italy Is Beautiful': The Role of Italian Television in Albanian Migration to Italy." In *Media and Migration: Constructions of Mobility and Difference*, edited by Russell King and Nancy Wood, 95–109. New York: Routledge, 2001.
Marcantonio, Carla. *Global Melodrama: Nation, Body and History in Contemporary Film*. New York: Palgrave Macmillan, 2015.
Marciniak, Katarzyna. "Palatable Foreignness." In *Transnational Feminism in Film and Media*, edited by Katarzyna Marciniak, Anikó Imre, and Áine O'Healy, 187–205. New York: Palgrave Macmillan, 2007.
Marcinak, Katarzyna, and Imogen Tyler, eds. *Immigrant Protest: Politics, Aesthetics, and Everyday Dissent*. New York: State University of New York Press, 2014.
———. "Introduction: Immigrant Protest: Noborder Scholarship." In *Immigrant Protest: Politics, Aesthetics, and Everyday Dissent*, edited by Katarzyna Marciniak and Imogen Tyler, 1–23. New York: State University of New York Press, 2014.
Marks, Laura. *The Skin of Film: Intercultural Cinema, Embodiment, and the Senses*. Durham, NC: Duke University Press, 2000.
Martin, Michael T. "'Fortress Europe' and Third World Immigration in the Post–Cold War Global Context," *Third World Quarterly* 20, no. 4 (1999): 821–38.
Martini, Emanuela. *Gianni Amelio*. Turin: Il Castoro, 2006.
Martone, Mario. *Teatro di Guerra: un diario*. Milan: Bompiani, 1998.
Mellino, Miguel. "Deprovincializing Italy: Notes on Race, Racialization, and Italy's Coloniality." In *Postcolonial Italy: Challenging National Homogeneity*, edited by Cristina Lombardi-Diop and Caterina Romeo. New York: Palgrave Macmillan, 2012.
Menarini, Roy. *Il cinema dopo il cinema: Dieci idee sul cinema italiano, 2001–2010*. Genoa: Le Mani, 2010.
Mezzadra, Sandro. "Citizen and Subject: A Postcolonial Constitution for the European Union?" *Situations: Project of the Radical Imagination* 1, no. 2 (2006).
———. "The New European Migratory Regime and the Shifting Patterns of Contemporary Racism." In *Postcolonial Itay: Challenging National Homogeneity*, edited by Cristina Lombardi-Diop and Caterina Romeo, 37–50. New York: Palgrave Macmillan, 2012.
———. "Taking Care: Migration and the Political Economy of Affective Labor." Caring Labor: An Archive. July 29, 2010. Originally published March 16, 2006. https://caringlabor.files.wordpress.com/2010/12/mezzadra_taking_care.pdf (accessed July 19, 2018).
Mezzadra, Sandro, and Brett Neilson. "Border as Method, or, the Multiplication of Labor." *Transversal*. European Institute fo Progressive Cultural Policies. March 2008. http://eipcp.net/transversal/0608/mezzadraneilson/en.
———. *Border as Method, or, the Multiplication of Labor*. Durham, NC: Duke University Press, 2013.
———. "Borderscapes of Differential Inclusion: Subjectivity and Struggles on the Threshold of Justice's Excess." In *The Borders of Justice*, edited by Étienne Balibar, Sandro Mezzadra, and Ranabir Samaddar, 181–203. Philadelphia: Temple University Press, 2011.

Mezzadra, Sandro, and Federico Rahola. "The Postcolonial Condition. A Few Notes on the Quality of Historical Time in the Global Present." *Postcolonial Text* 2, no. 1 (2006). http://postcolonial.org/index.php/pct/article/viewArticle/393/819.

Morgoglione, Claudia, "Il mistero della Sconosciuta. Tornatore fra cronaca e noir. *La Repubblica*, October 18, 2006. http://www.repubblica.it/2006/10/sezioni/spettacoli_e_cultura/cinema/roma/sconosciuta-tornatore/sconosciuta-tornatore/sconosciuta-tornatore.html (accessed July 20, 2018).

Morrison, Toni. *The Bluest Eye*. New York: Holt, Reinhart, Winston, 1970.

Mulvey, Laura. "Visual Pleasure and Narrative Cinema," *Screen* 16, no. 3 (1975): 6–18.

Muraro, Luisa. *L'ordine simbolico della madre*. Rome: Riuniti, 1991.

Naficy, Hamid. *An Accented Cinema: Exilic and Diasporic Filmmaking*. Princeton: Princeton University Press, 2011.

Nathan, Vetri. *Marvelous Bodies: Italy's New Migrant Cinema*. West Lafayette, IN: Purdue University Press, 2017.

Nestingen, Andrew, and Trevor G. Elkington, eds. *Transnational Cinema in a Global North: Nordic Cinema in Transition*. Detroit: Wayne University Press, 2005.

Niceforo, Alfredo. *Italiani del nord e italiani del sud*. Turin: Fratelli Bocca, 1901.

Nicolini, Giusi, and Marta Bellingreri. *Lampedusa: Conversazioni su isole, politica, migranti*. Turin: Edizione Gruppo Abele, 2013.

O'Healy, Áine. "An Accented Gaze: Migrant and Transmigrant Filmmaking." In *A Companion to Italian Cinema*, edited by Frank Burke, 484–99. Hoboken: Wiley Blackwell, 2017.

———. "Border Traffic: Reimagining the Voyage to Italy." In *Transnational Feminism in Film and Media*, edited by Katarzyna Marciniak, Anikó Imre, and Áine O'Healy, 59–72. New York: Palgrave Macmillan, 2007.

———. "Bound to Care: Gender, Affect, and Immigrant Labor." In *Italian Political Cinema: Public Life, Imaginary, and Identity in Contemporary Italian Film*, edited by Giancarlo Lombardi and Christian Uva, 56–67. Oxford: Peter Lang, 2016.

———. "Hospitality, Humanity and the Detention Camp: Envisioning Migration in Contemporary Italian Cinema." *International Journal of the Humanities* 4, no. 3 (2006): 68–77.

———. "Imagining Lampedusa." In *Italian Mobilities*, edited by Ruth Ben-Ghiat and Stephanie Malia Hom, 152–74. New York: Routledge, 2015.

———. "*Lamerica*." In *The Cinema of Italy*, edited by Giorgio Bertellini, 244–53. London: Wallflower, 2004.

———. "Mediterranean Passages: Belonging and Abjection in Contemporary Italian Cinema." *California Italian Studies Journal* 1, no. 1 (2011). http://escholarship.org/uc/item/2qh5d59c.

———. "'[Non] è una somala': Deconstructing African Femininity in Italian Film." *The Italianist* 29, no. 2 (2009): 175–98.

———. "Postcolonial Theory and Italy's 'Multicultural' Cinema." In *The Italian Cinema Book*, edited by Peter Bondanella, 295–302. New York: Palgrave Macmillan, 2014.

———. "Screening Intimacy and Racial Difference in Postcolonial Italy." In *Postcolonial Italy: Challenging National Homogeneity*, edited by Cristina Lombardi and Caterina Romeo, 205–20. New York: Palgrave Macmillan, 2012.

———. "Towards a Transnational Approach to the Study of Contemporary Italian Film." *The Italianist* 34, no. 2 (2014): 269–72.

O'Leary, Alan. "What Is Italian Cinema?" *California Italian Studies Journal* 7, no. 1 (2017). https://escholarship.org/uc/item/7z9275bz.

O'Rawe, Catherine. "'I padri e i maestri': Genre, Auteurs, and Absences in Italian Film Studies." *Italian Studies* 63, no. 2 (2008): 173–94.

———. *Stars and Masculinity in Contemporary Italian Cinema*. New York: Palgrave Macmillan, 2015.

O'Riley, Michael F. "Postcolonial Haunting: Anxiety, Affect, and the Situated Encounter." *Postcolonial Text* 3, no. 4 (2007).

Orsini, Giacomo. "Lampedusa: From a Fishing Island in the Middle of the Mediterranean to a Tourist Destination in the Middle of Europe's External Border." *Italian Studies* 70, no. 4 (2015): 521–36.

Ottieri, Maria Pace. *Quando sei nato non puoi più nasconderti: viaggio nel popolo sommerso*. Rome: Nottetempo, 2003.

Parreñas, Rhacel Salazar. *Servants of Globalization*. Palo Alto: Stanford University Press, 2001.

Parvulescu, Anca. *The Traffic in Women's Work: East European Migration and the Making of Europe*. Chicago: University of Chicago Press, 2014.

Parvulescu, Constantin. "Inside the Beast's Cage: Gianni Amelio's *Lamerica* and the Dilemma of Post-1989 Leftist Cinema." *Italian Culture* 28, no.1 (2010): 50–67.

Pasetti, Anna Maria. "Terrafirma di Emanuale Crialese: Odissea Liquida." *Vivilcinema* 4 (2011): 20–21.

Pasolini, Pier Paolo. *Ali dagli occhi azzurri*. Rome: Garzanti, 1965.

Pastore, Ferruccio, Paola Monzini, and Giuseppe Sciortino. "Schengen's Soft Underbelly? Irregular Migration and Human Smuggling across Land and Sea Borders to Italy." *International Migration* 44, no. 4 (2006): 95–119.

Peano, Irene. "Excesses and Double Standards: Migrant Prostitutes, Sovereignty and Exceptions in Contemporary Italy." *Modern Italy* 17, no. 4 (2012): 419–32.

"Per Cambiare l'Ordine delle Cose—Forum Nazionale Roma," Cronache di ordinario razzismo, November 9, 2017, http://www.cronachediordinariorazzismo.org/cambiare-lordine-delle-cose-forum-nazionale-roma/ (accessed July 18, 2018).

"Per Cambiare l'ordine delle cose: le proposte per i candidati alle prossime elezioni." Cronache di ordinario razzismo. 21 February, 2018. http://www.cronachediordinariorazzismo.org/cambiare-lordine-delle-cose-le-proposte-candidati-alle-prossime-elezioni/ (accessed July 18, 2018).

Perera, Suvendrini. "A Pacific Zone? (In)Security, Sovereignty, and Stories of the Pacific Borderscape." In *Borderscapes: Hidden Geographies and Politics at Territory's Edge*, edited by Prem Kumar Rajaram and Carl Grundy-Warr, 201–27. Minneapolis: University of Minnesota Press, 2007.

Pinkus, Karen. *Bodily Regimes: Italian Advertising under Fascism*. Minneapolis: University of Minnesota Press, 1995.

Ponzanesi, Sandra. "Beyond the Black Venus: Colonial Sexual Politics and Contemporary Visual Practices." In *Italian Colonialism: Legacy and Memory*, edited by Jacqueline Andall and Derek Duncan, 166–89. Oxford: Peter Lang, 2005.

Pontiggia, Federico. "Mostra del Cinema di Venezia 2017, Segre scuote 'L'ordine delle cose' sui Migranti." *Il fatto quotidiano*, September 1, 2017. http://www.ilfattoquotidiano.it/premium/articoli/segre-scuote-lordine-delle-cose-sui-migranti/.

Pravadelli, Veronica. "Identity, Masculinity, and Postcolonial Scenarios in Gianni Amelio's Lamerica (1994)." In *The Cinemas of Italian Migration: European and Transatlantic Narratives*, edited by Sabine Schrader and Daniel Winkler, 31–40. Newcastle: Cambridge Scholars Publishing, 2013.

Pugliese, Joseph. "Crisis Heterotopias and Border Zones of the Dead." *Continuum: Journal of Media and Cultural Studies* 23, no. 5 (2009): 663–79.

Purpura, Marco. "Racial Masquerade Italian Style? Whiteface and Blackface in Zeudi Araya's 1970s Comedies," *Italian Studies* 69, no. 3 (2014): 394–414.

Rancière, Jacques. *The Politics of Aesthetics: The Distribution of the Sensible*. Translated by Gabriel Rockhill. New York: Continuum, 2004.

Rapold, Nicolas. "On a Sicilian Island, Boat People Who Can't Be Ignored: Emanuele Crialese Tackles Migration in 'Terraferma,'" *New York Times*, July 23, 2013, http://www.nytimes.com/2013/07/24/movies/emanuele-crialese-tackles-migration-in-terraferma.html.

Re, Lucia. "Italians and the Invention of Race: The Poetics and Politics of Difference in the Struggle over Libya, 1890–1913." *Italian Studies Journal* 1, no. 1 (2010): 1–58. http://escholarship.org/uc/item/96k3w5kn.

Rhodes, John David. *Stupendous Miserable City: Pasolini's Rome*. Minneapolis: University of Minnesota Press, 2007.

Ricciardi, Alessia. "The Italian Redemption of Cinema: Neorealism from Bazin to Godard." *The Romanic Review* 97, nos. 3–4 (2006): 483–500.

Rodogno, Davide. *Fascism's European Empire: Italian Occupation during the Second World War*. Translated by Adrian Belton. Cambridge: Cambridge University Press, 2006.

Romeo, Caterina. "Italian Postcolonial Literature," *California Italian Studies Journal* 7 (2017). https://escholarship.org/uc/item/55d0f4j7.

———. "Racial Evaporations." In *Postcolonial Italy*, edited by Cristina Lombardi-Diop and Caterina Romeo, 221–36. New York: Palgrave Macmillan, 2012.

Rosi, Gianfranco, and Alberto Barbera. "A Conversation with Gianfranco Rosi." American Film Institute Fest, Egyptian Theater, Los Angeles, November 17, 2016.

Rovelli, Marco. *I lager italiani*. Rome: Biblioteca Università Rizzoli, 2006.

Rugolotto, Silvana, Alice Larotonda, and Sjaak van der Geest. "How Migrants Keep Italian Families Italian: Badanti and the Private Care of Older People." *International Journal of Migration, Health and Social Care* 13, no. 2 (2017): 185–97. https://doi.org/10.1108/IJMHSC-08-2015-0027.

Russo, Paolo. "Migration Told through Noir Conventions in *La sconosciuta* and *Gomorra*." In *Destination Italy: Representing Migration in Contemporary Media and Narrative*, edited by Emma Bond, Guido Bonsaver, and Federico Falloppa, 377–96. Oxford: Peter Lang, 2015.

Said, Edward W. *Orientalism*. New York: Pantheon Books, 1978.

Sassi, Federica. *Autobiografie negate: Immigrati nei lager del presente*. Rome: Manifestolibri, 2002.

Saviano, Roberto. *Gomorra: Viaggio nell'impero economico e nel sogno di dominio della camorra*. Milan: Mondadori, 2006.

———. *Gomorrah: A Personal Journey into the Violent International Empire of Naples' Organized Crime System*. Translated by Virginia Jewiss. New York: Farrar, Strauss, Giroux, 2008.

———. "Italy's African Heroes," *New York Times*, January 25, 2010, http://www.nytimes.com/2010/01/25/opinion/25saviano.html.

Scalzo, Domenico. *Gianni Amelio: Un posto al cinema*. Turin: Lindau, 2001.

Schoonover, Karl. *Brutal Vision: The Neorealist Body in Postwar Italian Cinema*. Minneapolis: University of Minnesota Press, 2012.

Sciorra, Joseph. "Hip Hop from Italy and the Diaspora: A Report from the 41st Parallel," *Altreitalie* 24 (January–June 2002), http://www.altreitalie.it/.

Sedgwick, Eve Kosofsky. *Between Men: English Literature and Male Homosocial Desire*. New York: Columbia University Press, 1985.

Shiel, Mark. *Italian Neorealism: Rebuilding the Cinematic City*. London: Wallflower, 2006.

Shohat, Ella, and Robert Stam, eds. *Unthinking Eurocentrism: Multiculturalism and the Media*. New York: Routledge, 1994.

Sklarew, Bruce H. "Musical Blending and Altruistic Surrender in Bertolucci's *Besieged* (1999)." *Psychoanalytic Inquiry* 27, no. 4 (2009): 409–18.

Sklarew, Bruce H., and Bernardo Bertolucci. "Returning to My Low-Budget Roots." *Cineaste* 24, no. 4 (1999): 16–20.

Sòrgoni, Barbara. "'Defending the Race': The Italian Reinvention of the Hottentot Venus during Fascism." *Journal of Modern Italian Studies* 8, no. 3 (2003): 411–24.

Spivak, Gayatri Chakravorty. "Can the Subaltern Speak?" In *Marxism and the Interpretation of Culture*, edited by Cary Nelson and Lawrence Grossberg, 271–313. Urbana: University of Illinois Press, 1988.

Stacul, Jaro. "Claiming a European Ethos at the Margins of the Italian Nation State." In *Crossing European Boundaries: Beyond Conventional Geographical Categories*, edited by Jaro Stacul, Christina Moutsou, and Helen Kopnina, 210–28. Oxford: Berghahn, 2006.

Stefanutto Rosa, Stefano. "La sacra Lampedusa di Rosi." *Luce Cinecittà*, June 5, 2014. http://www.cinecitta.com/IT/it-it/news/45/5014/la-sacra-lampedusa-di-rosi.aspx.

Stella, Gian Antonio. *L'orda: Quando gli albanesi eravamo noi*. Milan: BUR, 2003.

Tazzioli, Martina. "Border Displacements: Challenging the Politics of Rescue between Mare Nostrum and Triton." *Migration Studies* 4, no. 1 (2016): 1–19.

———. "The Politics of Counting and the Scene of Rescue: Border Deaths in the Mediterranean," *Radical Philosophy* 192 (July/August 2015), https://www.radicalphilosophy.com/commentary/the-politics-of-counting-and-the-scene-of-rescue.

Tedesco, Lucia. "'L'ordine delle cose.' Libia, Europa e migranti nel film di Segre." *Officina dei Saperi*. September 18, 2017. http://www.officinadeisaperi.it/eventi/lordine-delle-cose-libia-europa-e-migranti-nel-film-di-segre/ (accessed September 30, 2018).

Tintori, Giorgio. "Italian Mobilities and the *Demos*." In *Italian Mobilities*, edited by Ruth Ben-Ghiat and Stephanie Malia Hom, 111–25. New York: Routledge, 2015.

Todorova, Maria. *Imagining the Balkans*. New York: Oxford University Press, 1997.

"Tornando a casa," Cinema Italiano, http://cinemaitaliano.info/tornandoacasa (accessed July 15, 2018).

Trappolin, Luca. "Gender Victims and Cultural Borders: The Globalization of Prostitution in Italy." *Dialectical Anthropology* 29, nos. 3–4 (2005): 335–48.

Trento, Giovanna. "Pier Paolo Pasolini in Eritrea: Subalternity, Grace, and the 'Rediscovery' of Italian Colonization in the Horn of Africa." In *Postcolonial Italy*, edited by Cristina Lombardi-Diop and Caterina Romeo, 139–55. New York: Palgrave Macmillan, 2012.
Trifanova, Temenuga. "*Code Unknown*: European Identity in Cinema." *Scope* 8 (2007): 1–20. http://www.nottingham.ac.uk/scope/documents/2007/may-2007/trifonova.pdf (accessed June 15, 2017).
Tyler, Imogen, *Revolting Subjects: Social Abjection and Resistance in Neoliberal Britain*. London: Zed Books, 2013.
———. "'Welcome to Britain': The Cultural Politics of Asylum." *European Journal of Cultural Studies* 9, no. 2 (2006): 185–202.
Tyler, Imogen, and Katarzyna Marciniak. "Afterword: The Human Waste Disposal Industry or Immigrant Protest in Neoliberal Times." In *Immigrant Protest: Politics, Aesthetics, and Everyday Dissent*, edited by Katarzyna Marciniak and Imogen Tyler, 277–90. New York: State University of New York Press, 2014.
United Nations General Assembly. "Universal Declaration of Human Rights." 1948. http://www.un.org/en/universal-declaration-human-rights/ (accessed July 15, 2018).
van Hooren, Franca. "When Families Need Immigrants: The Exceptional Position of Migrant Domestic Workers and Care Assistants in Italian Immigration." *Bulletin of Italian Politics* 2, no. 2 (2010): 21–38.
Vehbiu, Adrian, and Rando Devole. *La scoperta dell'Albania. Gli albanesi secondo i mass-media*. Milan: Paoline, 1996.
Verdicchio, Pasquale. *Bound by Distance: Rethinking Italian Nationalism through the Italian Diaspora*. Cranbury: Fairleigh Dickinson University Press, 1997.
———. "The Preclusion of Postcolonial Discourse in Southern Italy." In *Revisioning Italy: National Identity and Global Culture*, edited by Beverly Allen and Mary Russo, 91–212. Minneapolis: Minnesota University Press, 1997.
Viano, Maurizio. *A Certain Realism: Making Use of Pasolini's Film Theory and Practice*. Berkeley: University of California Press, 1993.
Vitali, Valentina, and Paul Willemen, eds. *Theorizing National Cinema*. London: British Film Institute, 2006.
Webb, Clive. "The Lynching of Sicilian Immigrants in the American South, 1886 to 1910." *American Nineteenth Century History* 3, no. 1 (2002): 45–76.
Welch, Rhiannon Noel. "Contact, Contagion, Immunization: Gianni Amelio's *Lamerica* (1994)." In *Italian Mobilities*, edited by Ruth Ben-Ghiat and Stephanie Malia Hom, 68–87. London: Routledge, 2015.
———. *Vital Subjects: Race and Biopolitics in Italy, 1860–1920*. Liverpool: Liverpool University Press, 2016.
White, Jerry. "National Belonging: Renewing the Concept of National Cinema for a Global Culture." *New Review of Film and Television Studies* 2, no. 2 (2004): 211–32.
Wigon, Zachary. "*Twice Born* Irresponsibly Appropriates the Siege of Sarajevo for a Romantic Drama." *Village Voice*. December 4, 2013. http://www.villagevoice.com/film/twice-born-irresponsibly-appropriates-the-siege-of-sarajevo-for-a-romantic-drama-6440264.
Williams, Linda. "Mirrors without Memories: Truth, History, and the New Documentary," *Film Quarterly* 46, no. 3 (Spring, 1993): 9–21.

———. "'Something Else besides a Mother': *Stella Dallas* and the Maternal Melodrama." *Cinema Journal* 24, no. 1 (1984): 2–27.
Wong, Cindy Hing-Yuk. "'The Chinese Who Never Die': Spectral Chinese and Contemporary European Cinema." *Asian Cinema* 23, no. 1 (2012): 5–29.
Young, Robert. *Colonial Desire: Hybridity in Theory, Culture and Race*. New York: Routledge, 1995.
Zagarrio, Vito, ed. "In & Out: Migrazioni nel/del cinema italiano." Special issue, *Quaderni del CSCI: Rivista annuale di cinema italiano* 8 (2012).
Zavattini, Cesare. *Neorealismo, ecc*. Milan: Bompiani, 1979.
Zhang, Gaoheng. "Comedy Film and Immigration to Italy: Reading Masculinity, Hybridity, and Satire in *Lezioni di cioccolato* (2007), *Questa notte è ancora nostra* (2008), and *Into Paradiso* (2010)." In *The Cinemas of Italian Migration: European and Transatlantic Narratives*, edited by Sabine Schrader and Daniel Winkler, 243–79. Newcastle: Cambridge Scholars Publishing, 2013.
Zhang, Yingjin. *Cinema, Space, and Polylocality in a Globalizing China*. Honolulu: University of Hawaii Press, 2010.
Žižek, Slavoj. "Caught in Another's Dream in Bosnia" In *Why Bosnia? Writings on the Balkan War*, edited by Rabia Ali and Lawrence Lifschultz, 233–40. Stony Creek CT: Pamphleteers Press, 1993.
———. "Ethnic Dance Macabre." *Guardian*, August 28, 1992. http://zizek.uk/ethnic-dance-macabre/.
———. *The Metastases of Enjoyment: Six Essays on Women and Causality*. London: Verso, 1998.

Index

abjection, 53, 66, 97, 112, 118; of Albanians, 29, 30; of Eastern European female migrants, 29, 56, 57, 59, 76n24
Abre los ojos, 135n17
Abulafia, David, 172n7
Accattone, 122
accented filmmaking, 10, 214–17, 226
A Ciambra, 228n19
Adriatic migration, 146
Adua e le sue campagne, 75n21
affective labor, 8, 42, 53, 54, 67, 73, 74, 190–91
Africa and Africans: 97–98, 136–37, 146–47, 153, 158, 160, 168, 220–25; designator for southern Italy 15, 82; Horn of Africa, 18, 78, 81; images of, 68, 81–82, 86, 91, 93–94; migration from, 16, 78–79, 144; sex workers, 100–101, 222; sub-Saharan, 8, 82, 83, 90, 137, 159, 168, 215, 222. *See also* Eritrea and Eritreans; Libya; Maghreb; Morocco and Moroccans; North Africa; Senegal; Somalia; Tunisia
Agamben, Giorgio, 8, 34–35, 42; bare life, 42, 154
Akın, Fatih, 135n17
Albania and Albanians, 8, 16–17, 34–35, 45, 49n33, 130, 186, 210n35; migration to Italy, 16–17, 20, 23–24, 28–32, 34, 122–23, 125; in Italian films, 20–45, 114, 119–25; target of Italian xenophobia, 186
Ali Farah, Ubax Cristina, 227n1
Alì ha gli occhi azzurri, 10, 183, 197–208, 217
Allocca, Salvatore, 209n4
Amato, Pio, 228n19
Amelio, Gianni, 8, 19–22, 28, 30, 32, 34, 45, 60, 114, 123. See also *Lamerica*

Amenábar, Alejandro, 135n17
Amoroso, Carmine, 9, 125, 127
Andall, Jacqueline, 68
Anderson, Benedict, 3, 12n5
Anderson, Bridget, 68
Angst essen Seele auf (*Ali: Fear Eats the Soul*), 201
Antonioni, Michelangelo, 106n26
Appadurai, Arjun, 172n4
Aprile, 8, 30–32
Arabs, 9; racialized figure, 83; representation of, 79
Arab Spring, 153, 161, 207
Araya, Zeudi 92
Aristarco, Guido, 22
Aspromonte, 216
A sud di Lampedusa, 187

Baartman, Sara, 106n24
badante, 54, 68, 69, 72, 217
Balibar, Étienne, 79, 127
Balkans, 7, 8, 17, 19, 38, 61, 119; Balkanist discourse, 36, 38, 40; in Italian films, 19, 35–37, 41, 59; Italian occupation of, 19, 38, 46; symbolic abjection of, 59; war in, 1, 16, 35, 36, 38, 41; whiteness, 35, 45. *See also* southeastern Europe
Ballestreros, Isolina, 14n18
Bardan, Alice, 135n13
Barraco, Fabrizio, 75n46
Bartolo, Pietro, 162, 163, 166
Bayman, Louis, 184
Bell'amico, 14n20

249

Ben-Ghiat, Ruth, 104n2
Benhadj, Rachid, 10, 214, 15
Benshoff, Harry, 202
Berghahn, Daniela, 14n18
Bergoglio, Jorge (Pope Francis), 153
Berlusconi, Silvio, 15, 25, 108, 116, 129, 137, 144, 215
Berry, Chris, 226
Bertolucci, Bernardo, 9, 90, 94-98
Bertorelli, Toni, 61
Bhabha, Homi, 144, 197, 200-201; colonial mimicry 85, 201
Biadene, Ricardo, 215
Bianco e nero, 208n4
Bieberstein, Rada, 214
Billo il Gran Dakhaar, 9, 145, 150-52, 168
biopolitics, 8, 41, 46
Biutiful, 7
Black Venus, 90-92, 94, 106n33
Bocchi, Giancarlo, 35
Bond, Emma, 12n10, 13n14
Bondi, Federico, 8, 69, 72
Bonini, Marco, 150
Bonsaver, Guido, 13n14, 173n11; 209n22
borderscapes, 136-38, 137, 143, 165, 210n31; 164; Italy-Africa, 138; Mediterranean, 9, 164; of differential inclusion, 210n31; North-South, 145
Bosnia-Herzegovina, 35, 36-39, 216; conflict, 40
Bossi-Fini Law, 108, 175n36
Bossi, Umberto, 19
Bouchard, Norma, 159
Bova, Raoul, 140, 143, 215
Broken Blossoms, 187
Brooks, Peter, 185
Brugnolo, Serena, 123
Bruno, Marco, 152
Budina, Edmond, 10, 214, 215
Bullaro, Grace, 13n14

Caminati, Luca, 48n17
Camorra, 14, 40, 181, 182
Campassi, Gabriella, 105n21
Capotondi, Giuseppe, 135n17
Captains Courageous, 110, 134n2
C.A.R.A. Italia (2010), 215
care work, 70; care worker, 8, 54-55, 68-70, 73. See also *badante*
Carlei, Carlo, 134n4
Carpignano, Jonas, 10, 218-21, 224, 228n19
Cassano, Franco, 172n7
Castañeda, Claudia, 75n20

Castellitto, Sergio, 8, 35, 40, 45
Ceaușescu, Nicolae, 125
Che bella giornata, 179
China and Chinese, 19, 181-89, 191-92, 210n33
Choate, Mark, 144
Chow, Rey, 195
Cianchetti, Fabio, 155
Cicinelli, Sonia, 14n15
Citi, Ugo, 69
Code Inconnu, 7
Colla, Rolando, 35, 37
colonial desire, 85, 90-91, 193, 194, 195
Colossal Youth, 199
comedy, 179
Come un uomo sulla terra, 176n48
Comencini, Cristina, 208n8
Corbucci, Sergio, 92
Cose dell'altro mondo, 208n8
Cover boy: L'ultima rivoluzione, 9, 125-34
Crialese, Emmanuele, 2, 9, 153, 155, 159
Curcio, Anna, 18

Dal Lago, Alessandro, 29-30
Dardenne, Jean-Pierre and Luc, 7, 122
D'Ascanio, Luca, 14n20
De Dominicis, Ennio, 8, 32, 45
De Franceschi, Leonardo, 13n15
De Genova, Nicholas, 54
de Lauretis, Teresa, 57, 125
Derrida, Jacques, 9, 111, 116, 132, 144, 173n15; hospitality, 111, hauntology, 133
De Santis, Giuseppe, 184
De Seta, Vittorio, 9, 145, 146, 147-50, 219
Desser, David, 180
Diaconescu-Blumenfeld, Rodica, 48n17
differential inclusion, 10, 54, 186, 210n31, 224
Dirty Pretty Things, 7
La doppia ora, 135n17
Duncan, Derek, 13n14, 30, 34, 48n17, 179, 183, 202
Durovicová, Natasa, 13n11

Eastern Europe, 10, 15, 45, 51, 63, 69, 71, 73, 128, 181; images of Eastern European women, 8, 42, 53, 54, 59; migration from, 16: traffic in Eastern European women, 55
Eastern Promises, 74
Ebner, Michael R., 154
Eco, Umberto, 79-80, 103-1
Elsaesser, Thomas, 131, 132
Elvjs & Merilijn, 8, 56, 59-62, 76n22
English Patient, The, 41

Eritrea and Eritreans, 55, 81, 155
Europe, 1, 4, 7, 10, 16, 21, 36, 54–55, 74, 79–81, 103–4, 135n14, 153, 155, 161–62, 166–67, 178, 213; Border and Coast Guard Agency (Frontex), 137, 161; border regime, 153, 162; European Union, 1, 16–17, 52, 54, 69, 118, 126, 132, 137, 161, 178; external border of EU, 175n46; Parliament, 172; postcolonial, 20
Eyes Wide Shut, 62
Ezra, Elizabeth, 13n11

Falaschini Lerner, Giovanna, 13n14, 149
Falloppa, Federico, 13n14
Fascism, 16–17, 32, 46, 90–91, 93; cinema, 22, 104n22; propaganda, 22, 82, 91, 106n24
Fassbinder, Rainer Maria, 199, 201
Fay, Jennifer, 179
Federici, Alessio Maria, 208n4
Fellini, Federico, 76n21, 83
Ferme, Valerio, 159
Ferrario, Davide, 102, 103
Figli di Annibale, 102–3
Film Commissions, 5, 12n3; Calabria, 216; Torino Piemonte, 217
Fini, Gianfranco, 16
Fiore, Teresa, 173n9
Fiorentini, Sergio, 72
Five Star Movement, 174n29
Forgacs, David, 85
Foucault, Michel, 34, 42
Fragasso, Claudio, 9, 90, 93
Fratelli d'Italia, 198, 200, 211n46
Friese, Heidrun, 154, 160, 164
Frontex, 137, 161
Fuocoammare (Fire at Sea), 5, 9, 153, 162–68, 176n48

Gaddafi, Muammar, 137, 144, 153, 169, 170, 215
Gallo, Ester, 52
Galt, Rosalind, 41
Garrone, Matteo, 5, 10, 180
Gatti, Fabrizio, 174n31
Gegen die Wand (Head-On), 135n17
Genovese, Paolo, 187
Germania anno zero (Germany Year Zero), 116
Ghermandi, Gabriella, 226n1
Gianni e le donne, 69
Giordana, Marco Tullio, 9, 53, 87, 109–11, 116, 118, 141
Giorni, 150
Giovannesi, Claudio, 10, 183, 197–202

Giuliani, Gaia, 47n13, 105n12
global South, 1, 9, 20, 79, 129, 136, 145, 160, 200, 223
Goldberg, Jonathan, 199
Gómez-Peña, Guillermo, 138
Gomorra, 5, 10, 180–83, 187, 208, 210n33, 227n18
González Iñárritu, Alejandro, 7
Good Morning Aman, 10, 183, 192–97, 208
Gorbaciof, 187
Gramsci, Antonio, 18, 47n4, 80, 184, 200
Grassilli, Mariagiulia, 213
Greene, Shelleen, 104n2
Griffin, Sean, 202
Günsberg, Maggie, 184
Günsür, Mehmet, 32, 49n33
Gutiérrez-Rodríguez, Encarnación, 54, 68

Halilovic, Laura, 10, 216, 217
Hannerz, Ulf, 12n8
Harem Suare, 213
Haynes, Todd, 199
Herman, Bernard, 65
Higbee, Will, 13n11
Higson, Andrew, 13n12
Hipkins, Danielle, 12n3, 76n21
Hirsch, Emile, 40
Hjort, Mette, 13n11, 13n12
Hoberman, J., 106n33
Hochschild, Arlie Russell, 53, 67
Horden, Peregrine, 172n7
Hou, Jeffrey, 7

I cento passi, 109
Il bagno turco (Steam: Turkish Bath), 213
Il carniere, 35
Il fiore delle mille e una notte (Arabian Nights), 92, 106n27
Il ladro di bambini (Stolen Children), 20
Il signor Robinson, 92
Il toro, 71
Il villaggio di cartone, 2
Imitation of Life, 65
immigrant protest, 219, 225
immigrants in Italy, 18, 71, 178; African, 14n20, 59, 105n15, 152–53, 220; Albanian, 45, 123; Arab, 83, 173n12; Chinese, 186, 187–88, 192; Eastern European, 16, 118; Egyptian, 78; Ethiopian, 176n48, 215; Horn of Africa, 78; Moroccan, 78, 186; Muslim, 89, 168, 203; Nigerian, 78; Romanian, 186; second-generation, 198; Senegalese, 78; Tunisian, 141

Imre, Anikó, 13n11
Intervista, 83
Into Paradiso, 208n4
Io, l'altro, 9, 138, 140–45, 158, 215
Io loro e Lara, 69, 72–73
Io rom romantica, 216–17
Io sono Li (*Shun Li and the Poet*), 2, 10, 183, 186–90, 208
Italian East Africa, 91
Italy: birthrates, 26; borders, 56, 87, 137, 169; citizenship, 211n45; Coast Guard, 137, 142, 155, 165; colonial history, 2, 18, 46, 80, 82, 90–93, 104, 143–44, 186, 192, 215; emigration, 2, 3, 4, 20, 21; immigration, 1, 2, 6, 7, 13n14, 18, 20, 48n17, 71, 99, 129, 133, 138, 145–46, 178, 192, 219, 213, 225, 227n9; invasion of Albania, 28; film industry, 5–6, 10, 213, 216; media, 2, 5, 20, 25, 26, 36, 51, 90, 170, 152, 168; migration policy, 171, 172; military, 19, 32, 38, 46, 137, 165–66, 176; nation-state, 17, 80; occupation of Albania, 26; ratification of Schengen Agreement, 52; television, 5, 20, 22, 25–26, 29, 48n18, 60; unification, 17, 18, 154. *See also* northern Italy, southern Italy
Italians: constructions of race and subalternity, 80; identity, 17; lynching, 18; populism, 8; postcolonial status, 13n15, 81, 82, 89, 91, 104; racial status, 17, 18; in Tunisia, 144; in United States, 18; whiteness, 3, 17, 18, 19, 45–46, 47n13, 74, 82, 103, 105n13

Jay, Paul, 4, 12n9
Jim Crow segregation, 18

Kadaré, Ismail, 28
Kamkari, Fariborz, 227n12
Kaplan, E. Ann, 135n10
Krissane, Hedy, 216
Kristeva, Julia, 29, 59, 76n24, 197
Kuwornu, Fred Kudjo, 211n45

Là-bas: Educazione criminale, 2
Lacan, Jacques: theory of the phallus, 195
La giusta distanza, 14n20
La grande bellezza (*The Great Beauty*), 5
Lakhous, Amara, 226n1
L'albero dei destini incrociati, 214
La meglio gioventù (*The Best of Youth*), 141
Lamerica, 8, 19–29, 30, 32, 45, 46, 71, 123, 160; critique of Italian television in, 20, 25, 60; images of bare life in, 34; intertextual resonance with *Quando sei nato non puoi più nasconderti*, 114, music in, 26, 155; ongoing critical discussion of, 48n17
Lampedusa, 147, 153–56, 161–65, 167, 172n1, 174n31, 175n46, 176n50, 187, 221; border zone, 168, 175n46
Lan, Pei-Chia, 73
Landy, Marcia, 48n17, 184
La Promesse, 7, 122
La romana (*Woman of Rome*), 75n21
L'Articolo 2, 9, 83, 87–89, 148
La sconosciuta, 8, 56, 62–68, 180
L'assedio (*Besieged*), 9, 90, 94–98
Last Emperor, The, 98
La terra trema, 139, 155
Lega Nord, 8, 15, 18–19, 47n11, 51, 75n5, 80, 108, 189; coalition with Five Star Movement, 174n29
Le notti di Cabiria (*Nights of Cabiria*), 76n21, 106n26
Lettere al vento, 214
Lettere dal Sahara, 9, 145–50, 152, 168
Levinas, Emmanuel, 9, 111–12, 116, 134n5
Lezioni di cioccolato, 208–9n4
Lezioni di cioccolato 2, 208
Liberti, Stefano, 176n60
Libya, 20, 137, 144, 153, 161, 164, 169–72, 174n28, 176n48, 210n35, 215, 221; detention in, 138, 169, 171; Italian colonial history in, 18, 144; militia leaders, 169. *See also* Gaddafi, Muammar
Lilya 4-Ever, 74
Lin, Song Hwee, 13n11
Linosa, 153–56, 165, 174n28
L'italiano, 8, 30, 32–34
Lombardi-Diop, Cristina, 81, 105n12
Lombardi, Giancarlo, 48n18
Lombardi, Guido, 2, 14n20
LUCE, 22, 162
Luchetti, Daniele, 87
Lyon, Dawn, 73

Maastricht Treaty, 79
Maghreb, 8, 83, 102. *See also* North Africa
Mai, Nicola, 46n2
male homosocial desire, 143, 194, 206
Mamma Roma, 122
Manni, Armando, 8, 56, 59
Marcantonio, Carla, 44, 183, 184–85, 199
Marciniak, Katarzyna, 13n11, 219, 225
Mare largo, 35
Margaroni, Maria, 48n17

Mar Nero, 8, 69–72
Marra, Vincenzo, 35, 138, 139
Martelli Law, 16, 78
Martone, Mario, 8, 39–40, 49n45
Martorana, Giovanni, 140–41, 143, 173n11
masculinity, 108–9, 203, 205; abject Chinese, 192; adult, 206; heteronormative, 20; Italian, 23, 74, 198; Western, 206
Masslo, Jerry, 78, 83, 84
Mazzacurati, Carlo, 8, 56, 58, 71
Mazzantini, Margaret, 40, 50n46
McKenzie, Scott, 13n12
Medici, Luca. *See* Zalone, Checco
Mediterranea, 10, 218–25
Mediterranean, 19, 79, 136, 139, 140, 145, 153, 159, 167; affinities, 102; border, 137, 164, 168–69; central Mediterranean, 1; crossings, 138, 169, 172n7; migrations, 138, 161; populations, 141; southern Mediterranean, 141; surveillance, 137
Mediterraneo, 19
Mellino, Miguel, 18
Melliti, Mohsen, 9, 138, 140, 143, 145, 158, 215, 226n1
melodrama, 32, 34, 37, 41, 44, 63, 178, 183, 184, 201; with noir; 208; classical Hollywood, 188; global, 44, 183, 185, 192, 199; in neorealist cinema, 184, 185; Italian, 184; male, 143; maternal, 41, 65, 66, 187, 192; origins, 185; signifying conventions, 208; queer, 199
Merlin Law, 75n18
Mezzadra, Sandro, 8, 47n6, 53–54, 67–68, 70, 223
Miniero, Luca, 187, 208n8
Minniti, Marco, 170
Mio fratello è figlio unico, 87
Moretti, Nanni, 8, 30–31, 45
Morgoglione, Claudia, 76n27
Morocco and Moroccans, 82, 89, 141, 186, 222
Morricone, Ennio, 64
Mozzarella Stories, 187
Mulvey, Laura, 57
Munzi, Francesco, 9, 118–20, 122–23, 135n10
Muscardin, Laura, 9, 145, 150, 173n19
Mussolini, Benito, 23, 175n43

Naficy, Hamid, 214
Nathan, Vetri, 6–7
national cinema, 4, 13n12, 214, 226
Nederveen Pieterse, Jan, 79
Neilson, Brett, 8, 54, 75n8, 210n31, 223
Nema problema, 35
neorealism, 22, 111, 139, 146, 184–85, 198

Newman, Kathleen, 13n11
Newton, Thandie, 97
N'Dour, Youssou, 150
Niceforo, Alfredo, 18
Nicolini, Giusi, 165
Nieland, Justus, 179
Nigeria and Nigerians, 78, 99, 100–101, 164, 222
Noce, Claudio, 10, 183, 192, 195, 197
Non ti muovere, 135n17
North Africa, 16, 19, 140, 153, 161, 168, 200; coast, 136; migration from, 15, 168; proximity to Italy, 82, 139
northern Italy, 19, 82, 109, 111–12
North-South axis, 137
Nunziante, Gennaro, 179, 209n4
Nyman, Michael, 113

Occidente, 56
O'Healy, Áine, 13n11
O'Leary, Alan, 13n13
Olmi, Ermanno, 2
Operation Mare Nostrum, 161, 166
Operation Triton, 161
Orientalism, 36, 49n39, 195
Others, The, 135n17
Ottieri, Maria Pace, 110, 111, 116
Özpetek, Ferzan, 49n33, 213–14

Paisà (Paisan), 180
Palombella rossa, 31
Palumbo, Patrizia, 107n39
Paradisi, Giulio, 92
Parreñas, Rhacel Salazar, 68
Parvulescu, Anca, 42, 54–55
Parvulescu, Constantin, 27–28
Pasolini, Pier Paolo, 62, 91, 122, 127, 200, 201, 202
Pellegrini, Ines, 91–92
Peploe, Clare, 94; 106n3
Perera, Suvendrini, 138
Petraglia, Sandro, 84, 87, 110
Petri, Elio, 109
Piano, The, 113
Piersanti, Franco, 26, 155
Pietrangeli, Antonio, 75n21
Pinkus, Karen, 93
Pitza e datteri, 216
Placido, Michele, 9, 23, 64, 83, 105n14, 147
Pontecorvo, Gillo, 109
Ponzanesi, Sandra, 90
Portami via, 59

postcolonial: discourse, 80–81; haunting, 132, 144
"post-mortem" cinema, 131, 132
Pravadelli, Veronica, 48n17
Prodi, Romano, 30, 52
Pugliese, Joseph, 154
Pummarò, 9, 83–87, 89, 103, 110, 147
Purcell, Nicholas, 172n7
Purpura, Marco, 92

Quando sei nato non puoi più nasconderti, 9, 109–18, 119, 124, 133, 169
Questa notte è ancora nostra, 187, 208n4

racial masquerade, 92
racism, 8, 10, 68, 93, 102, 115, 126, 145, 192, 197; anti-Southern, 81; Italian, 2, 7, 17, 18, 20, 67, 80, 101, 186; depiction of, 70, 193-195; differential, 186, disavowed, 208
Radio West, 35
Raise the Red Lantern, 210n35
Rancière, Jacques, 219
Randi, Paola, 208n4
Re, Lucia, 46n3
realism, 3, 184
Renga, Dana, 12n3
reproductive labor, 8, 42, 55
Ricciardi, Alessia, 199
Rocco e i suoi fratelli (*Rocco and his Brothers*), 76n21
Rodogno, Davide, 38
Roma, 51, 69, 120, 123, 216–17, Romani language, 121
Romania: accession to EU, 126
Romanzo criminale, 5
Romeo, Caterina, 81
Rosarno, 218, 219, 220–22, 224, 225, 227n18
Rosi, Gianfranco, 153, 160, 162–70
Rosi, Francesco, 109
Rossellini, Roberto, 116, 180
Rossi Stuart, Kim, 134n4
Rosso Istanbul, 213
Rovelli, Marco, 75n6
Rowden, Terry, 13n11
Rubin, Gayle, 55
Rulli, Stefano, 84, 87, 110
Russo, Luigi, 92
Russo, Paolo, 180–83

Sacro GRA, 162
Sahara, 9, 145–48, 150, 152, 164, 168, 219; Moroccan Sahara, 221

Said, Edward, 36, 49n39, 195
Saimir, 9, 118–25, 133, 135n10, 202
Salani, Corso, 56, 59
Salvatores, Gabriele, 19, 134n4
Salvini, Matteo, 172
Sarajevo, 38–43; siege of, 38, 40–41
Sarhan, Nader, 198, 200; family, 207
Saviano, Roberto, 180, 210n33; 227n18
Scego, Igiaba, 226n1
Schengen Agreement, 52; conventions, 16–17, 52; directives, 52; zone, 52, 137
Schoonover, Karl, 184
Scrinzi, Francesca, 52
Sega, Maria Teresa, 105n21
Sedgwick, Eve Kosofsky, 194
Segre, Andrea, 2, 8, 9, 10, 169–72, 183, 186, 187, 190–92, 215
Seihon, Koudous, 220–22
Senegal, 78; in Italian films, 145–52
Seven against Thebes (Aeschylus), 38–39
sex workers, 54; indentured, 100; Italian, 56; African 146; Eastern European, 59, 112; Nigerian, 99–101
Sheltering Sky, The, 98
Shohat, Ella, 3
Sicilian immigrants in the United States, 47n7
Soltanto il mare, 215
Somalia, 143, 192; Somali women, 93
Sophie's Choice, 41
Sorrentino, Paolo, 5
southern Italy, 18, 24–25, 28, 45, 78, 102, 147, 200, 218; annexation of, 80; Italy's "Africa," 18, 101; racialization of Southern Italians, 82
southeastern Europe, 3, 8, 17, 19, 35–36, 38, 46, 53, 60, 62, 125
southern Italy, 18, 24–25, 28, 45, 78, 80–82, 101, 102, 147, 159–60, 200, 218; racialization of Southern Italians, 82
Spivak, Gayatri Chakravorty, 101
Stacul, Jaro, 19
Stam, Robert, 3
Stella Dallas, 65
Stella, Gian Antonio, 74n1
stereotypes, 159, 160; African women, 90–91; Chinese, 189, 210n33; colonial-era, 80; Homi Bhabha on, 200; Islam, 179; male migrants, 51; orientalist, 187; racialized, 85, 86; Romani people; 217; southeastern Europeans, 36; women migrants, 52
Sternberg, Claudia, 14n18

Strait of Sicily, 79, 136, 143, 153, 161, 162, 167, 168, 170; border control in, 137, 154, 167, 168, 180; in Italian films 137–38; 139–40
Sudeuropa, 175n46
Sud side stori, 90, 92, 94, 99–102, 103.
Svetlana's Journey, 74

Taken, 74
Tangentopoli (bribery scandal), 15, 24, 46n1
Tano da morire, 99
Tavarelli, Gianluca Maria, 59
Taviani, Vittorio and Paolo, 109
Tawfik, Younis, 226n1
Tazzioli, Martina, 166–67, 175n44
Teatro di guerra, 8, 39–40, 49n45
Tedesco, Lucia, 176n61
Terraferma, 2, 9, 153, 155–62, 165, 168–69, 174n35
Tesoromio, 92
Teste rasate, 9, 90, 92–94, 103
Thiam, Thierno, 150
Tito, Marshal Josip Broz, 39
Todorova, Maria, 7, 36
Tornando a casa, 9, 138–41
Tornatore, Giuseppe, 8, 53, 56, 62–63, 180
Torre, Roberta, 9, 90, 99–101
Toscani, Oliviero, 130
transnational film, 4, 13n11, 218, 226, 227n13
Trappolin, Luca, 106n37
Treaty of Friendship, Partnership and Cooperation (Italy-Libya, 2008), 215
Treaty of London (1951), 11n2
Treaty of Rome (1957), 16
Trento, Giovanna, 92, 106n27
Trinh, Minh-ha T., 135n11
Tunisia, 20, 78, 140–42, 161, 174n28; French protectorate, 144
Turco-Napolitano Law, 52
Tyler, Imogen, 29, 76n24, 219, 225

Una bella governante di colore, 92
Un'altra vita, 8, 56, 57

Valori, Alessandro, 35
Va' pensiero, 215
Venuto al mondo (Twice Born), 8, 35, 40–45, 54
Vercelli, Alessandro, 12n8
Verdicchio, Pasquale, 46–47n3, 80, 105n13
Verdone, Carlo, 69, 72
Vesna va veloce, 8, 56, 58–59
Vicentini Orgnani, Ferdinando, 35
Vento di terra, 35
Visconti, Luchino, 139, 155
Vlora, 21, 26, 32, 51, 130

Welch, Rhiannon, 47n3, 48n17
West Side Story, 99, 101
White, Jerry, 13n12
Wigon, Zachary, 41
Williams, Linda, 65
women's work, 190; traffic in, 42
Wong, Cindy Hing-Yuk, 191
World, The, 199

xenophobia, 11, 18, 67, 79, 102, 126, 140; in Europe and United States, 2, 10; depiction in films, 7, 59, 69; 83; in Italy, 18, 102

Yiannopoulou, Effie, 48n17
Yılmaz, Serra, 214
Yimer, Dagmawi, 176n48; 215–16
Young, Robert, 90

Zaccaro, Maurizio, 9, 35, 37
Zalone, Checco, 179
Zampa, Luigi, 75n21
Zavattini, Cesare, 198–99
Zhang, Ronghua, 181
Zhang, Yimou, 187
Zhao, Tao, 188
Zineddaine, Mohamed, 10, 214, 215
Žižek, Slavoj, 36, 62
Zora la Vampira, 208n8

ÁINE O'HEALY
is Professor of Modern Languages and Literatures at Loyola Marymount University. She is editor with Anikó Imre and Katarzyna Marciniak of *Transnational Feminism in Film and Media.*

www.ingramcontent.com/pod-product-compliance
Lightning Source LLC
Chambersburg PA
CBHW052056230426
43662CB00037B/1926